THE LETTERS OF
THOMAS BABINGTON MACAULAY

VOLUME II

Detail from the engraving published in June 1836, by S. W. Reynolds, Jr,
and William Walker of S. W. Reynolds,
'The Reform Bill Receiving the King's Assent by Royal Commission,
Thursday June 7, 1832' (British Museum).
The scene (ideal not actual) shows TBM third from the right among the MPs gathered at the bar of
the House of Lords. The others are, from the left, Edward Stanley, Sir James Graham,
Lord Jeffrey, James Abercromby, Sir James Mackintosh, Charles Grant,
Thomas William Coke, and George Byng.

THE LETTERS OF
THOMAS BABINGTON
MACAULAY

EDITED BY

THOMAS PINNEY

PROFESSOR OF ENGLISH
POMONA COLLEGE, THE CLAREMONT COLLEGES
CLAREMONT, CALIFORNIA

VOLUME II

MARCH 1831–DECEMBER 1833

CAMBRIDGE UNIVERSITY PRESS

1974

Published by the Syndics of the Cambridge University Press
Bentley House, 200 Euston Road, London NW1 2DB
American Branch: 32 East 57th Street, New York, N.Y. 10022

© Cambridge University Press 1974

Library of Congress Catalogue Card Number: 73–75860

ISBN: 0 521 20202 7

First published 1974

Printed in Great Britain
at the University Printing House, Cambridge
(Brooke Crutchley, University Printer)

The title-page device is
the Macaulay coat of arms, taken from Macaulay's seal
on a letter of 17 December 1833;
it was later the basis of Macaulay's arms as Baron Macaulay.
Acknowledgement is made to the Master and Fellows of
Trinity College, Cambridge.

CONTENTS

BIOGRAPHICAL CHRONOLOGY

1831 March 1
Reform Bill introduced
- March 2
Makes first speech on Reform Bill
- April
Offers to resign his seat over the
slavery question
- May 2
Re-elected for Calne, following
dissolution of Parliament
- May 3
TBM's mother dies
- May 29
First visit to Holland House
- June 11
Finishes 'Moore's *Life of Lord
Byron*' (*ER*, June)
- July 5
Speech on Reform Bill
- August 16–26?
At Rothley Temple to recuperate
after 'cholera simplex'
- September 7
Completes first part of 'Croker's
Edition of Boswell's *Johnson*'
(*ER*, September)
- September 20
Speech on Reform Bill
- October 5
Accepts invitation to stand
for Leeds should Reform Bill
pass
- October 10
Speech on Reform Bill
- December 16
Speech on Reform Bill

1832 January 2
Corrects proofs of 'Southey's
Edition of *Pilgrim's Progress*'
(*ER*, December 1831)
- January 11
Commissionership of Bankrupts
abolished
- January 12
Finishes 'Lord Nugent's *Hampden*'
(*ER*, December 1831)
- February 28
Speech on Reform Bill
- March 19
Speech on Reform Bill
- April 12
Finishes 'Nares' *Memoirs of
Lord Burghley*' (*ER*, April)
- Early June
Appointed member of the Board
of Control
- June 13
Re-elected for Calne in conse-
quence of accepting office. Reform
Bill dinner speech at Leeds
- June 22
Appointed to committee of
inquiry into East India Company
charter
- July 12
Finishes 'Dumont's *Recollections
of Mirabeau*' (*ER*, July)
- September 3–8
Campaigning in Leeds
- October 6–7
Visits Cambridge with Hannah
and Margaret

— November 28–December 15
In Leeds for election
— December 8
Appointed Secretary to the Board
of Control
— December 11
Margaret Macaulay married
— December 14
Elected at Leeds
1833 January 9
Finishes 'Lord Mahon's
War of the Succession'
(*ER*, January)
— February 6
Speech on Irish union
— February 28
Speech on Irish Coercion Bill
— April 17
Second speech on Jewish dis-
abilities
— Early May
Offers to resign his office over
Anti-Slavery Bill

— Early July
Again offers resignation
— July 10
Speech on India Bill
— July 24
Speech on Anti-Slavery Bill
— August
Offered appointment to Supreme
Council of India
— August 29–September 20
Tour in Scotland with Hannah
— October 14
Finishes 'Walpole's *Letters to
Horace Mann*' (*ER*, October)
— November 7
Speech at Leeds Mechanics'
Institution
— December 4
Appointed to Supreme Council
of India
— December 26
Resigns Secretaryship of Board
of Control

THE LETTERS

THE REFORM BILL
7 MARCH 1831 – 8 JUNE 1832

1831 March 1
Reform Bill introduced

— March 2
Makes first speech on Reform Bill

— April
Offers to resign his seat over the slavery question

— May 2
Re-elected for Calne, following dissolution of Parliament

— May 3
TBM's mother dies

— May 29
First visit to Holland House

— June 11
Finishes 'Moore's *Life of Lord Byron*' (*ER*, June)

— July 5
Speech on Reform Bill

— August 16–26?
At Rothley Temple to recuperate after 'cholera simplex'

— September 7
Completes first part of 'Croker's Edition of Boswell's *Johnson*' (*ER*, September)

— September 20
Speech on Reform Bill

— October 5
Accepts invitation to stand for Leeds should Reform Bill pass

— October 10
Speech on Reform Bill

— December 16
Speech on Reform Bill

1832 January 2
   Corrects proofs of 'Southey's Edition of *Pilgrim's Progress*' (*ER*, December 1831)

— February 28
   Speech on Reform Bill

— March 19
   Speech on Reform Bill

- April 12
   Finishes 'Nares' *Memoirs of Lord Burghley*' (*ER*, April)

TO THOMAS FLOWER ELLIS, 7 MARCH 1831

MS: Trinity College. *Address:* T F Ellis Esq / Northern Circuit / Lancaster. *Frank:* London March seven 1831 / T B Macaulay. *Published:* John Clive and Thomas Pinney, eds., *Selected Writings of Macaulay*, Chicago, 1972, pp. 425–7.

London March 7 – 1831

Dear Ellis,

I have been so busy during the last few days that I have not been able to spare a moment.[1] The H[ouse] of Commons lasts from 3 in the afternoon to 2 in the morning – and the rest of my time has been spent in preparing for the press the speech[2] which I made on Wednesday night and which has had a great success. I will send a copy to you under franked covers when it is published.

London is thoroughly well disposed towards us; and the country will, I hope, follow the lead of London. Give me news from Lancashire. What say the manufacturers? What say the Squires? What say the lawyers? And of the lawyers what say, in especial, Milner, Holinshed,[3] – (or how does the brute spell his name?) – Adolphus, Henderson,[4] – and the Devil?[5] – By the bye is not Holt's nickname an excellent illustration of the title of Ben Jonson's play – The Devil is an Ass.

How things will go seems a little doubtful. But I have a good hope.–

[1] The debate on the introduction of the Reform Bill ran for seven days between 1 and 9 March.

[2] TBM's speech on the second night of the debate on the Reform Bill, 2 March, put him at once in the first rank of parliamentary orators. He spoke having 'a bad cold, which very much injured his voice' (Margaret Macaulay, *Recollections*, p. 204), and so rapidly that 'it was impossible for the reporters to do justice to it' (Selina Macaulay, Diary, 24 March 1831). TBM corrected the speech for *Hansard* and for separate publication; it was issued as 'A Speech Delivered in the House of Commons, in the Debate of Wednesday, March 2, 1831, on Lord John Russell's Motion for Leave to Bring in a Bill to Amend the Representation of the People in England and Wales,' London, James Ridgway, 1831. It is perhaps to this speech that J. L. Adolphus refers in a letter describing TBM's effect as an orator: 'one great speech of his on the Reform question I heard....The House was entranced, almost breathless: and I recollect that, when I overtook him the same night walking home, I could hardly believe that the little, draggled, ordinary-looking man plodding by himself up the Strand was the same creature whom I had seen holding the House of Commons absorbed as the Opera house is by a first-rate singer' (to Henry Hart Milman, 14 December 1861: MS, Dr A. N. L. Munby).

[3] Bryan Blundell Hollinshead ([1788?]–1837), on the Northern Circuit since 1815; a Commissioner of Bankrupts, though not on the same list with TBM. His name is spelled both 'Hollingshed' and 'Hollinshed' in the *Law List*, 1831: I have followed Venn, *Alumni Cantabrigienses*.

[4] Gilbert Henderson (1797–1861: *Boase*), Fellow of Brasenose College, 1819–27; on the Northern Circuit from 1824; Q.C. and leader on circuit; Recorder of Liverpool, 1843–61.

[5] Francis Ludlow Holt (1780–1844: *DNB*), joined the Northern Circuit in 1809; K.C. and Bencher of the Inner Temple, 1831; author of several legal treatises and 'for many years principal editor of *Bell's Weekly Messenger*' (*Gentleman's Magazine*, 1844, Part II, 650). The *Gentleman's Magazine* describes him as 'warmly and sincerely pious,' which may have something to do with his nickname.

Lord Duncannon,[1] who knows the House of Commons better than any other man in it – Billy Holmes[2] excepted who maketh a lie and loveth it[3] – is quite confident of success. He is sure, he says, of a majority. Peel is evidently trimming. Croker would trim, if his infernal impudence and spite were not beyond even his own controul. By the bye, you never saw such a scene as Croker's oration on Friday night.[4] He abused Lord J Russell.[5] He abused Lord Althorpe.[6] He abused the Lord Advocate – and we took no notice – never once groaned or cried – no! – But he began to praise Lord Fitzwilliam[7] – "a venerable nobleman, – an excellent and amiable nobleman, –" and so forth: – and we all broke out together – " Question – no – no – this is too bad – don't – don't –" and such other exclamations. He then called Canning his right honourable friend. "Your friend! damn your impudent face!" said the member who sate next me.

Croker is now beyond all comparison the most impudent man in the house.[8] I always thought him so. But some of us gave the palm to O'Gorman Mahon.[9] O'Gorman fell greatly. Cæsar in the senate did not die with more attention to the proprieties of character. He came to hear, what few people care to hear, his own sentence read at the bar by the chairman of the Committee. To make the matter better he was expelled for bribery by his agents. The fellow sate on the Treasury bench – heard the report, – and never stirred. "Sir" – said the Speaker[10]– "you must

---

[1] John William Ponsonby (1781–1847: *DNB*), styled Lord Duncannon, afterwards fourth Earl of Bessborough, sat in the House of Commons, 1805–34; he was chief whip for the Whigs, and was one of the committee who drew up the first Reform Bill.

[2] William Holmes (1779–1851), M.P. almost continuously for various constituencies, 1808–41, 'whipper-in to the Tory party 30 years' (*Boase*). 'In the high and palmy days of Toryism the peculiar talents of Mr. Holmes were in great request, for in the private management of the members of an unreformed House of Commons he was without a rival' (*Annual Register*, 1851, p. 257).

[3] Cf. Revelation 22: 15.   [4] 4 March: *Hansard*, 3rd Series, III, 81–107.

[5] Lord John Russell (1792–1878: *DNB*), later first Earl Russell; Whig M.P. since 1813; introduced the Reform Bill; leader of the Whigs in the House of Commons and Home Secretary in Melbourne's administration; Prime Minister, 1846–52; 1865–6.

[6] John Charles Spencer (1782–1845: *DNB*), styled Lord Althorp; afterwards third Earl Spencer. In Parliament from 1804, he was leader of the House of Commons under Grey.

[7] Croker said that 'I consider Lord Fitzwilliam as one of the most amiable men alive' (*ibid.* 96). William Wentworth Fitzwilliam (1748–1833: *DNB*), second Earl Fitzwilliam, was a survivor from the previous generation of Whigs. His son and heir Lord Milton was an active Reformer.

[8] The impudence of the speech for TBM may have consisted in Croker's sarcasms on the fact that Calne, among other Whig close boroughs, had escaped from the provisions of the Reform Bill; at the same time Croker praised TBM's 'able and eloquent speech' (*ibid.* 98).

[9] Charles James Patrick Mahon (1800–91: *DNB*), called The O'Gorman Mahon, one of O'Connell's lieutenants in the Catholic Association; M.P. for Clare, 1830, but unseated, 2 March 1831. After this he spent more time in foreign travel and adventure than in politics. For an example of his style in the House of Commons see *Hansard*, 3rd Series, II, 311–23.

[10] Charles Manners-Sutton (1780–1845: *DNB*), afterwards first Viscount Canterbury, Speaker of the House of Commons, 1817–35.

withdraw." Up he got and swaggered off as fast as he could with his acre of ruff and his three bushels of dirty hair. Sorrow such another we will be having any how plaze God – or be wishing to have; and no great blame to us for that same – the craturs.

I will not tell you the compliments that I have received on my speech, lest you should think that I am telling lies –.

Ever yours truly
T B Macaulay

TO MACVEY NAPIER, 8 MARCH 1831

MS: British Museum. *Address:* Macvey Napier Esq / Castle Street / Edinburgh. *Frank:* London March eight / 1831 / T B Macaulay. *Published:* Napier, *Correspondence*, p. 110.

London March 8 – 1831

My dear Napier,

I have a moment, and but a moment, to write. I cannot however delay thanking you for your kind expressions. I succeeded certainly far beyond my expectations. I am about to publish the speech. I will send you a copy under franked covers. But say nothing about it in the Review. I speak thus plainly because Brougham's published speeches are generally puffed in the number which follows their appearance. My taste on these subjects differs from his, and, as my connection with the Review is known, I wish my name to be never mentioned in it.

The Lord Advocate did wonders.[1] His manner is not as yet suited to the House. But he fully sustained his character for talent; and that he should do so was very extraordinary – Macintosh says, miraculous. There were some beautiful passages in his speech.

I shall, I fear, have nothing for you this number. What arrangement have you made about Byron? If you have not yet engaged any body, I will try my hand. I will certainly review Croker's Boswell[2] when it comes out.

Ever yours
T B M

[1] Jeffrey's speech in the debate on the Reform Bill, 4 March, 'was published immediately afterwards, at the special request of Government, and made a strong impression on those who really wished to understand the question.... Still, as a debating speech, it fell below the expectations both of his friends and of himself' (Cockburn, *Life of Lord Jeffrey*, I, 314).

[2] John Wilson Croker, ed., *The Life of Samuel Johnson, LL.D., Including a Journal of a Tour to the Hebrides, by James Boswell, Esq.*, 5 vols., 1831; the subject of TBM's 'Croker's Edition of Boswell's Life of Johnson,' *ER*, LIV (September 1831), 1–38, it was published in mid-June. The edition, on which Croker had been at work since early 1829, is a valuable source of original information.

TO MACVEY NAPIER, 14 MARCH 1831

MS: British Museum. *Address:* Macvey Napier Esq / Castle Street / Edinburgh. *Frank:*
London March fourteen 1831 / T B Macaulay.

London March 14. 1831

Dear Napier,

I am extremely sorry to say that [I][1] cannot by any possibility do any
thing for [this][1] Number. I have been very busy; and I have [con][1]se-
quently put off the History of [Fr][1]ance to the last moment. Every minute
that I can spare from the House of Commons must be for some weeks
given to completing the first volume for Lardner.

I enclose my speech. Jeffrey succeeded decidedly. The fellows who
assert the contrary are low envious liars.

Ever yours
T B Macaulay

TO THE BURGESSES AND INHABITANTS OF CALNE,
19 MARCH 1831

Text: Devizes and Wiltshire Gazette, 24 March 1831.

House of Commons, London, March 19, 1831.

Gentlemen,

A rumour having reached us that, while we are necessarily detained
here by the important measures brought under the consideration of the
legislature for the improvement of the representation of the people, your
town is about to be canvassed on the faith of the probable prospective
operation of those measures.[2] We take the liberty of expressing to you our
confidence that no advantage will be taken of our absence, and that you
will not commit yourselves until you have seen what the legislature will
do, and how we shall have discharged our duty towards you.

We must however add that not even the certainty of in any way
injuring our personal interests by promoting those measures could turn

---

[1] Paper torn away with seal.
[2] The number of the *Devizes and Wiltshire Gazette* in which this letter appears explains that,
in anticipation of the passage of the Reform Bill, one of TBM's opponents in August 1830,
Edmund Hopkinson, and a Mr Heneage had already begun canvassing at Calne. Heneage
was probably George Heneage Walker-Heneage (1799–1875: *Boase*), High Sheriff of
Wiltshire in 1829; M.P., Devizes, 1838–57. Calne, though a pocket borough, was untouched
by the first Reform Bill, no doubt through Lord Lansdowne's influence; the bill finally
passed reduced its two members to one. In the event, Lord Kerry, Lansdowne's heir, was
the first member for Calne returned to the reformed Parliament.

us from the course which we deem most beneficial to you and to the people of England at large.

We have the honour to remain, Gentlemen,

Your faithful humble Servants,

J. Macdonald

T. B. Macaulay

TO THOMAS FLOWER ELLIS, 30 MARCH 1831

MS: Trinity College. *Address:* T F Ellis Esq / Northern Circuit / York. *Frank:* London March thirty 1831 / T B Macaulay. *Published:* Clive and Pinney, *Selected Writings of Macaulay*, pp. 427–30.

London March 30. 1831

Dear Ellis,

I have little news for you, except what you will learn from the papers as well as from me. It is clear that the Reform Bill must pass, either in this or in another Parliament. The majority of one[1] does not appear to me, as it does to you, by any means inauspicious. We should perhaps have had a better plea for a dissolution if the majority had been the other way. But surely a dissolution under such circumstances would have been a most alarming thing. If there should be a dissolution now there will not be that ferocity in the public mind which there would have been if the House of Commons had refused to entertain the Bill at all. – I confess that, till we had a majority, I was half inclined to tremble at the storm which we had raised. At present I think that we are absolutely certain of victory, and of victory without commotion.

Such a scene as the division of last Tuesday I never saw, and never expect to see again. If I should live fifty years the impression of it will be as fresh and sharp in my mind as if it had just taken place. It was like seeing Cæsar stabbed in the Senate House, or seeing Oliver taking the mace from the table, a sight to be seen only once and never to be forgotten. The crowd overflowed the House in every part. When the strangers were cleared out and the doors locked we had six hundred and eight members present, more by fifty five than ever were at a division before. The Ayes and Noes were like two vollies of cannon from opposite sides of a field of battle. When the opposition went out into the lobby, – an operation by the bye which took up twenty minutes or more, – we spread ourselves over the benches on both sides of the House. For there were many of us who had not been able to find a seat during the evening. When the doors were shut we began to speculate on our numbers. Every body was desponding. "We have lost it. We are only two hundred and eighty at most.

---

[1] The Reform Bill passed its second reading, 22 March, by a vote of 302 to 301.

9

I do not think we are two hundred and fifty. They are three hundred. Alderman Thompson[1] has counted them. He says they are two hundred and ninety nine." This was the talk on our benches. I wonder that men who have been long in parliament do not acquire a better coup d'œil for numbers. The House when only the Ayes were in it looked to me a very fair house, – much fuller than it generally is even on debates of considerable interest. I had no hope however of three hundred. As the tellers passed along our lowest row on the left hand side the interest was insupportable, – two hundred and ninety one: – two hundred and ninety two: – we were all standing up and stretching forward, telling with the tellers. At three hundred there was a short cry of joy, at three hundred and two another – suppressed however in a moment. For we did not yet know what the hostile force might be. We knew however that we could not be severely beaten. The doors were thrown open and in they came. Each of them as he entered brought some different report of their numbers. It must have been impossible, as you may conceive, in the lobby, crowded as they must have been, to form any exact estimate. First we heard that they were three hundred and three – then the number rose to three hundred and ten, then went down to three hundred and seven. Alexander Baring[2] told me that he had counted and that they were three hundred and four. We were all breathless with anxiety, when Charles Wood[3] who stood near the door jumped on a bench and cried out, "They are only three hundred and one." We set up a shout that you might have heard to Charing Cross – waving our hats – stamping against the floor and clapping our hands. The tellers scarcely got through the crowd: – for the house was thronged up to the table, and all the floor was fluctuating with heads like the pit of a theatre. But you might have heard a pin drop as Duncannon read the numbers. Then again the shouts broke out – and many of us shed tears – I could scarcely refrain. And the jaw of Peel fell; and the face of Twiss[4]

[1] William Thomson (1792?–1854), a wealthy iron-master, alderman of London, Lord Mayor, 1828–9. A Reformer, he sat for London, 1826–32, and for other constituencies until his death.

[2] Alexander Baring (1774–1848: *DNB*), afterwards first Baron Ashburton, banker and politician. M.P. for various constituencies, 1806–35; opposed the Reform Bill. He held office in Peel's first administration, after which he was raised to the peerage. Baring is said to have offered TBM a place in his bank, which TBM declined, 'preferring literature to a business career' (Alston, 'Recollections of Macaulay,' p. 61).

[3] Wood (1800–85: *DNB*), afterwards first Viscount Halifax, Whig M.P. since 1826. Between 1832 and 1866 Wood held office under Grey, Melbourne, Russell, Aberdeen, and Palmerston, notably as Chancellor of the Exchequer, 1846–52; First Lord of the Admiralty, 1855–8; and Secretary of State for India, 1859–66. Wood was one of the many members of Lord Grey's family to enjoy a place under his administration, having married Grey's daughter Mary in 1829.

[4] Horace Twiss (1787–1849: *DNB*), barrister, Tory M.P. since 1820. He spoke against the Reform Bill on the first night of the debate and was not returned to Parliament after the dissolution in April.

was as the face of a damned soul; and Herries looked like Judas taking his neck-cloth off for the last operation. We shook hands and clapped each other on the back, and went out laughing, crying, and huzzaing into the lobby. And no sooner were the outer doors opened than another shout answered that within the house. All the passages and the stairs into the waiting rooms were thronged by people who had waited till four in the morning to know the issue. We passed through a narrow lane between two thick masses of them; and all the way down they were shouting and waving their hats; till we got into the open air. I called a cabriolet – and the first thing the driver asked was, "Is the Bill carried?" – "Yes, by one." "Thank God for it, Sir." And away I rode to Grey's Inn – and so ended a scene which will probably never be equalled till the reformed Parliament wants reforming; and that I hope will not be till the days of our grand-children – till that truly orthodox and apostolical person Dr. Francis Ellis[1] is an archbishop of eighty.

What are your movements? Mine are not absolutely determined. Have you had many briefs? At any rate you have, I suppose, been employed against the coiners.[2] However the weightier matters of the law may fare, the tithe of mint, I hope, goes on.

As for me, I am for the present a sort of lion. My speech has set me in the front rank, if I can keep there; and it has not been my luck hitherto to lose ground when I have once got it. Shiel[3] and I are on very civil terms. He talks largely concerning Demosthenes and Burke. He made, I must say, an excellent speech[4] – too florid and queer; but decidedly successful.

Why did not the great Samuel Grove Price[5] speak? He often came to the

---

[1] Francis Ellis (1824?–72), Ellis's second son, called Frank; B.A., Trinity College, 1846; called to the bar, 1849. He collaborated for a time with his father on the series of Queen's Bench reports, but after his father's death accepted appointment as a County Judge for Northamptonshire, when Sir John Le Couteur called him 'the youngest looking and handsomest judge I have ever seen' (Diaries, 23 May 1861: MS, La Société Jersiaise; information from Mrs Joan Stevens). Frank, after his marriage, took his mother's maiden name, McTaggart. The distinguished Cambridge philosopher J. M. E. McTaggart was his son.

[2] Several cases of uttering base coin were tried at the Lancaster assizes (Lancaster *Gazette*, 12 March); a counterfeiter was sentenced to transportation at the York assizes (York *Courant*, 29 March); but TBM may mean any or none of these cases.

[3] Richard Lalor Sheil (1791–1851: *DNB*), Irish barrister, playwright, and journalist, active in the Catholic Association, had entered Parliament only three weeks before (8 March) and made his maiden speech in the debate on the second reading of the Reform Bill. Sheil remained in the House until 1850.

[4] *Hansard*, 3rd Series, III, 646–56.

[5] Price (1793–1839), M.P. for Sandwich, 1830–1; 1835–7. B.A., Trinity, 1815; Fellow of Downing; called to the bar, 1818, but did not practise. He is said to have 'distinguished himself by an uncompromising opposition to the Reform Bill' (*Gentleman's Magazine*, 1839, Part II, 200), but he spoke only once on the question, immediately before the dissolution, and was not returned to the next Parliament. Lord Teignmouth calls Price the principal Tory speaker at the Cambridge Union in his day (*Reminiscences*, I, 48–9).

front rows, and sate making notes. Every body expected him to rise, and prepared night-caps accordingly. But he always sneaked away. On my soul, I believe that he is a craven with all his bluster. Indeed if he is afraid, it is the best thing that I ever knew of him. For a more terrible audience there is not in the world. I wish that Praed[1] had known to whom he was speaking. But with all his talent, he has no tact, no perception of the character of his audience; and he has fared accordingly. Tierney[2] used to say that he never rose in the House without feeling his knees tremble under him: and I am sure that no man who has not some of that feeling will ever succeed there.

Ever yours
T B Macaulay

TO THOMAS FLOWER ELLIS, [30 APRIL 1831]

MS: Trinity College.

Gray's Inn Saturday

My dear Ellis,

I shall not be able to see you before I leave town;[3] and I therefore write to tell you how I am circumstanced with respect to the Cambridge election.[4]

I have received this morning a letter from Lord Lansdowne's Steward at Calne in which he tells me that Hopkinson, – the same person who stood against Macdonald and me last year, and who subsequently petitioned against our return, intends to make his appearance and to go through the forms of a contest again. This intelligence makes me very uneasy, – not on account of my own election; for after the last decision of the House of Commons, it is impossible that the opponents of Lord Lansdowne's interest can have any hope of opening the borough; – but on account of the effect which Hopkinson's proceedings may have on the Lansdowne interest after a reform in Parliament. The man's object evidently is to keep himself before the eyes of the Calne householders, in the hope that they may consider him as their champion, and return him to parliament when the suffrage shall be extended to them. Lord

---

1 Praed spoke on 8 March, the sixth day of the Reform Bill debate, the last speech of the evening: see *Hansard*, 3rd Series, III, 240–7; the report (246) notes that towards the end of the speech Praed was 'frequently interrupted by calls of " Question".'

2 George Tierney (1761–1830: *DNB*), among the leaders of the Whigs in the House of Commons during the long years of the Tory domination.

3 Parliament was dissolved on 23 April, following the defeat of the Reform Bill on 19 April. TBM was re-elected at Calne on 2 May, and must have left London on the day this letter was written.

4 At Cambridge, where the poll was taken from 3 to 6 May, Henry Goulburn and William Yates Peel defeated the incumbents Palmerston and William Cavendish (p. 13, n. 4).

Lansdowne has sent Lord Kerry down for the purpose of counteracting the effect which these manœuvres of Hopkinson's may produce. I have no expectation of being returned for Calne by the new constituency which the reform bill will create; but it is my duty and my inclination to do every thing which may secure Lord Lansdowne's interest there.

Now I had meant to make an apology to my constituents for leaving them immediately after the election, to say something about the importance of the contest at Cambridge and to prevail on them to excuse me from the necessity of paying them visits of thanks and of presiding at the election-dinner. But, under these circumstances, no point of courtesy must be omitted. Fox[1] is a stranger, and his coming has given great dissatisfaction even to our own people. Lord Kerry cannot sit late after dinner on account of his health. It will be necessary that I should do all the honours.[2] I fear that it will be utterly impossible for me to be at Cambridge before Thursday,[3] and it will be with great difficulty and probably only by sacrificing the rest of two successive nights that I shall be able to be there even on Thursday. If, under these circumstances, you could find me a good pair I should be very much relieved. If your Committee cannot find a good pair perhaps Cavendish's[4] may be able to procure one. At this time I should think that really good pairs might easily be procured.

Ever yours

T B Macaulay

[1] Charles Richard Fox (1796–1873: *DNB*), illegitimate eldest son of Lord Holland, was elected for Calne in 1831 in the place of Macdonald, who was returned for Hampshire in the general election. Fox held a commission in the Grenadier Guards and was ultimately promoted to general. The dissatisfaction felt at his introduction as a candidate appears in the fact that, though only fifteen burgesses voted, Fox was not unanimously elected (*Salisbury and Winchester Journal*, 9 May 1831; *Devizes and Wiltshire Gazette*, 5 May 1831). Oscar Browning, who knew Fox in his later years, tells an anecdote that may have Fox's authority: Fox and TBM travelled together to Calne for the election, and TBM provided diversion on the journey by repeating 'large portions of Napier's *Peninsular War*, then just published. Being asked if he had read the book, he replied that he had not seen it, but that he had read reviews of it' (*Memories of Sixty Years*, 1910, p. 77).

[2] TBM spoke at the election and presumably attended the dinner afterwards at the Lansdowne Arms, where Lord Kerry was present and announced his intention to stand at the next election (*Devizes and Wiltshire Gazette*, 5 May 1831).

[3] 5 May, the day before the poll closed.

[4] William Cavendish (1808–91: *DNB*), afterwards second Earl of Burlington and the seventh Duke of Devonshire, had been elected M.P. for the University of Cambridge in 1829, two months after attaining his majority.

TO MACVEY NAPIER, 6 MAY 1831

MS: British Museum.

London May 6. 1831

My dear Napier,

Your letter reached me just after I had learned that a cruel blow had fallen on me. While I was at Calne, canvassing, speaking, and presiding at public dinners, my dear mother was unexpectedly taken from me by a complaint which, when I left London, had excited no apprehensions.[1] On my return I found my father's house darkened, and all the family in tears. The first shock is over;[2] – and I mean to betake myself vigorously to some employment which may occupy my mind. I shall begin almost immediately an article on Moore's Byron. I think of saying something about Hunt's[3] and Galt's[4] Books on the same subject. What is your latest day? The sooner the next Number is out the better. The elections are proceeding wonderfully.

Ever yours
T B Macaulay

TO MACVEY NAPIER, 11 MAY 1831

MS: British Museum. *Address:* Macvey Napier Esq / Castle Street / Edinburgh. *Frank:* London May eleven 1831 / T B Macaulay.

London May 11. 1831

My dear Napier,

To morrow I fall to work. If the article on Byron should be shorter than two sheets, I will eke it out with a few pages on the late debate about slavery.[5] I think that I could produce a sharp, concise pamphlet on that

---

[1] Selina Mills Macaulay died on 3 May. Zachary Macaulay had been severely ill early in 1831, and the family afterwards thought that the strain of nursing him during this time had worn out his wife.

[2] Writing to her Aunt Virtue Mills, 5 May, Fanny Macaulay says that 'Tom is in the deepest affliction, he heard of his loss in a very painful mode. Returning late on Tuesday night from his election at Calne, he did not of course call here, and the next morning on taking up the newspaper he was thunderstruck at reading the distressing tidings. He came here instantly, in a state of distraction – so little was he prepared for such an event that he was instantly setting off for Cambridge to vote for Lord Palmerston – when he was thus prevented' (MS, University of London).

[3] Leigh Hunt, *Lord Byron and Some of his Contemporaries*, 1828.

[4] John Galt, *The Life of Lord Byron*, 1830.

[5] TBM did not write on the subject. On 15 April Buxton had moved a resolution calling for an abolition measure in view of the failure of the colonial legislatures to act; Peel replied that the time was not ready for such interference (*Hansard*, 3rd Series, III, 1407–69). This was the first of at least three occasions on which TBM prepared to make a sacrifice of his political fortunes to the anti-slavery cause; fearing that the government was going to oppose Buxton's motion, TBM told Lord Lansdowne that he must then vote and speak

subject which would put Sir R Peel in particular, to shame. At all events, something, well or ill done, you shall have from me, very early in June.

It might be right to have the Review out before the deliberations in Parliament recommence.[1] But this will not be much before the 20th, as some time must be spent in chusing the Speaker and swearing the Members. I am glad to hear of Jeffrey's success at Perth. All here goes on well.

Many and sincere thanks to you for your kind expressions of sympathy. My father has suffered much. But he has on the whole borne up wonderfully.

Ever yours
T B M.

TO HANNAH MACAULAY, 27 MAY 1831

MS: Mrs Humphry Trevelyan. *Partly published:* Trevelyan, I, 204–5.

London May 27. 1831

My dear Hannah,

Let me see if I can write a letter à la Richardson – a little less prolix it must be or it will exceed my ounce. By the bye I wonder that Uncle Selby never grudged the postage of Miss Byron's letters. By the nearest calculation that I can make her correspondence must have enriched the post-office of Ashby Canons by something more than the whole annual interest of her fifteen thousand pounds.[2]

I dined with George Babington – was bored by George Marriott,[3] and

against government and that his seat was therefore at Lansdowne's disposal. Lansdowne assured TBM that he was free to act according to his conscience. See TBM's speech at Leeds, 3 December 1832, in Leeds *Mercury*, 8 December 1832. As Margaret Macaulay makes clear (*Recollections*, p. 209) TBM acted not out of zeal for the cause but only in duty to his father.

[1] The June number of the *ER* was published on 21 June (*Literary Gazette*, 18 June, p. 400). Parliament met on 14 June; the second Reform Bill was introduced on 24 June. The topical articles in the June *ER* are Brougham's 'The Dissolution and General Election, with Suggestions to the Peers,' and Empson's 'Political and Vested Rights.'

[2] From this and other references to *Sir Charles Grandison* in the letters of this period it seems likely that TBM was re-reading the novel. He told Greville in 1833 that he had read it fifteen times (*Memoirs*, II, 419), and Mrs Conybeare recalled that 'Sir C. Grandison he could repeat almost by heart, and used to say that if it went out of print he thought he could republish it' (Recollections of TBM).

[3] George Wharton Marriott (1778?–1833), barrister, magistrate at Queen Square Police Court and Chairman of Middlesex County Sessions, lived at 32 Queen Street and was thus a neighbor of the Macaulays in Ormond Street. He was a High Churchman and served as Chancellor of the Diocese of St David's from 1824. Marriott is the subject of TBM's comic verses on a button-puller in Trevelyan, I, 133–4, where he is identified as an acquaintance 'who had a habit of detaining people by the button, and who was especially addicted to the society of the higher order of clergy.' Trevelyan prints only fourteen lines

forced to go back to chambers and have two of the front buttons of my waistcoat repaired before I could go to Lansdowne house. I reached Berkeley Square at a quarter to eleven – and passed through the large suite of rooms to the great Sculpture Gallery. There were seated and standing perhaps three hundred people, listening to the performers or talking to each other. The room is the handsomest and largest, I am told, in any private house in London. It is certainly large and handsome – seventy five feet by twenty five, I should guess by the eye, and extremely lofty. I enclose our musical bill of fare. Fanny, I suppose, will be able to expound it better than I. The singers were more showily dressed than the auditors, and seemed quite at home. They were loudly clapped.

As to the company there was just everybody – everybody in London – except that little million and a half that you wot of – The Chancellor, and the first Lord of the Admiralty,[1] and Sydney Smith, and Lord Mansfield,[2] and Mr. Harford of Blaise Castle, and Protheroe,[3] and all the Barings[4] and the Fitzclarences,[5] and a hideous Russian spy whose face I see everywhere, with a star on his coat. During the interval between the delights of "I tuoi frequenti," and the ecstasies of "Se tu m'ami,"[6] I contrived to squeeze up to Lord Lansdown. I was shaking hands with Sir James Macdonald, when I heard a command behind us – "Sir James, introduce me to Mr. Macaulay" – and we turned; and there sate a large, bold-looking woman, with the remains of a fine person, and the air of Queen Elizabeth. "Macaulay," said Sir James, "let me present you to Lady Holland."[7] Then was her ladyship gracious beyond decription, and

of these extemporized verses; forty-six are given in Margaret Macaulay, *Recollections*, pp. 197–8. Margaret says of Marriott that he is 'exceedingly fond of bishops. He never hardly talks of any other people, and his dining-room is hung round with them in all the dignity of wig and lawn sleeves' (*Recollections*, p. 197).

[1] Sir James Graham (1792–1861: *DNB*), entered Parliament in 1818; regarded as an advanced Reformer, he was one of the cabinet committee who drew up the Reform Bill. Graham left the Whigs in 1834 over the question of the Irish Church; Home Secretary, 1841–6, under Peel, and First Lord of the Admiralty, 1852–5, under Aberdeen.

[2] David William Murray (1777–1840), third Earl of Mansfield, a Tory who voted against the Reform Bill to the last.

[3] Edward Davis-Protheroe (1798?–1852: *Boase*), M.P. for Evesham, Bristol, and Halifax, 1826–47. A Reformer, he had just been returned for Bristol.

[4] The Barings, sons and grandsons of Sir Francis Baring, formed an extensive cousinhood; in addition to Alexander, Sir Thomas (1772–1848), William Bingham (1799–1864: *DNB*), Francis (1796–1866: *DNB*), and Thomas (1799–1873: *DNB*) were all active in public life. Between 1835 and 1901 the Baring family acquired seven peerages.

[5] The illegitimate children of William IV by Mrs Jordan; there were ten, one of whom was married to Charles Fox.   [6] From Pergolesi's *Arie da Camera*.

[7] Elizabeth Vassall Fox (1770–1845: *DNB*), Lady Holland, the autocratic but highly successful hostess of Holland House, the center of Whig society, where she had presided since 1797. Lady Holland's wish to meet TBM no doubt testifies to the celebrity created by his Reform Bill speech; but she would have a more immediate interest in him as the colleague of her son, just elected M.P. for Calne. She had written on Lansdowne's bringing TBM

asked me to dine and take a bed at Holland house next Tuesday. I accepted the dinner, but declined the bed, and I have since repented that I so declined it. But I probably shall have an opportunity of retracting on Tuesday.

I chatted with Sydney Smith about the company, and with Cavendish about politics, shook hands with the Chancellor who charged me to say all kind things for him to my father, and retired at, I suppose, about the time that you were bestirring yourself to set out for Leamington.[1]

To night I go to another musical party at Marshall's[2] the late M P for Yorkshire.

Write soon, my darling. Give my love to my father and the two dear girls who are with you. I shall be so busy all day that I scarcely know whether I shall see Margaret.

Ever yours, my love, –

T B Macaulay

TO HANNAH MACAULAY, 28 MAY 1831

MS: Trinity College. *Address:* Miss H M Macaulay. *Partly published:* Trevelyan, I, 206–7.

London May 28. 1831

My dear Hannah,

More gaieties and music-parties – not so fertile of adventures as that memorable masquerade whence Harriet Byron was carried away.[3] But still I hope that the narrative of what passed there will gratify the "venerable circle."[4]

into Parliament that she had heard he 'was not pleasant nor good to look at' (the Earl of Ilchester, ed., *Elizabeth Lady Holland to Her Son, 1821–1845,* 1946, p. 108n.) and now wished to see for herself. The moment of TBM's admission through Holland House into the select inner circle of Whig society has been half-seriously interpreted by G. K. Chesterton as the 'chief turn of nineteenth-century England' (*The Victorian Age in Literature,* 1913, p. 28).

[1] Zachary Macaulay sold the house in Great Ormond Street soon after the death of his wife (Knutsford, *Zachary Macaulay,* p. 465) and took Selina, Fanny, and Hannah to Leamington for the sake of his own and Selina's health. Margaret remained in London at the home of her cousin George Babington in Golden Square. In the fall the family stayed at Buxton's house while Zachary went house-hunting: in November they moved into 44 Bernard Street.

[2] John Marshall (1765–1845), M.P. for Yorkshire, 1826–30. The owner of a flax-spinning mill in Leeds from which he had made a large fortune, Marshall maintained a London house at 34 Hill Street, Berkeley Square. A Benthamite, a promoter of popular education, a member of the council of the London University, he was the first mill-owner to represent the West Riding in Parliament; his career in the House of Commons was undistinguished, and he retired at the dissolution of 1830. See W. G. Rimmer, *Marshalls of Leeds: Flax-Spinners, 1788–1886,* Cambridge, 1960, pp. 110–13. His son was elected with TBM for Leeds, 1832.   [3] *Sir Charles Grandison,* 3rd edn, I, 160–4.

[4] *Ibid.* p. 294, etc.: a term of convenience for Miss Byron's grandmother, aunt, uncle, and two cousins.

Yesterday I dressed, early in the evening, and went to Brunswick Square[1] –. There I sate with Margaret and Jane Babington till ten o'clock – Mary was out. Then I called a cab and was whisked away to Hill Street. I found old Marshall's House a very fine one. He ought indeed to have a fine one; for he has, I believe, at least thirty thousand a year.[2] I had not thought that the houses in Hill-Street were so good. So I was ushered through the front drawing room into a large back-drawing room. The carpet was taken up, and chairs were set out in rows, as if we had been at a religious meeting. Then we had flute-playing by the first flute-player in England; – and piano-forte-strumming by the first piano-forte-strummer in England; and singing by all the first singers in England. And Signor Rubini's[3] incomparable tenor, and Signor Curioni's[4] incomparable contra tenor. And Pasta's[5] incomparable expression. You who know how airs much inferior to these take my soul and lap it in Elysium will form some faint conception of my transports.

Sharp beckoned me to sit by him in the back row. – These old fellows are so selfish. "Always," said he, "establish yourself in the middle of the row next to the wall: for if you sit in the front or next the edges, you will be forced to give up your seat to the ladies who are standing." I had the gallantry to surrender mine to a damsel who had stood for a quarter of an hour; and I lounged into the anti-rooms which were all crowded by midnight. There was Rice and his wife and daughter,[6] and Rumbold[7] the member for Yarmouth, and the Lowthers,[8] and a crowd of Northern Circuit Barristers, and Lady Parke,[9] one of Empson's fifty loves, and,

1 James and Mary Babington Parker lived at 4 Brunswick Square. 'You must not confound us with London in general, my dear sir. The neighbourhood of Brunswick Square is very different from almost all the rest' (Mrs John Knightley to Mr Woodhouse, *Emma*, ch. 12).

2 'On his death in 1845, the press guessed his wealth to have been between £1 1/2 and £2 1/2 million' (Rimmer, *Marshalls of Leeds*, p. 97).

3 Giovanni Battista Rubini (1795–1854), tenor, made his first appearance in England on 26 April.

4 Alberico Curioni (1785–1875), tenor, had been in London since 1821.

5 Giuditta Pasta (1798–1865), soprano, had just returned, after a three years' absence, to London, where she appeared with Rubini and Curioni in Meyer's *Medea*, 12 May, and with Rubini in Rossini's *Tancredi*, 24 May.

6 Spring-Rice married Lady Theodosia Pery, second daughter of the first Earl of Limerick. Their eldest daughter, Mary, married in 1841 James Marshall, the son of their host on this evening; shortly after, Spring-Rice himself married Marshall's eldest daughter, Lady Theodosia having died in 1839.

7 Charles Edmund Rumbold (1788–1857: *Boase*), Whig M.P. for Great Yarmouth almost continuously, 1818–57.

8 William Lowther (1787–1872: *DNB*) and Henry Cecil Lowther (1790–1867), sons of the first Earl of Lonsdale of the second creation, and their cousin John Henry Lowther (1793–1868), were all Tory M.P.s. The Lowthers were the most famous of borough-mongering families.

9 Sir James Parke married Cecilia Arabella Frances Barlow (1794?–1879).

though last, not least, Samuel Rogers.[1] Rogers and I sate together on a bench in one of the passages and had a good deal of very pleasant conversation. He was, – as indeed he has always been to me, – extremely kind, and told me that, if it were in his power, he would contrive to be at Holland House with me, to give me an insight into its ways. He is the great oracle of that circle.

He has seen the King's letter to Lord Grey, respecting the Garter;[2] – or at least has authentic information about it. It is a happy stroke of policy, and will, they say, decide many wavering votes in the House of Lords. The King it seems requests Lord Grey to take the order, as a mark of Royal confidence in him "at so critical a time" – significant words I think.

Between the acts of the performance, all the company adjourned to the dining room to obtain refreshments. I had the honour of escorting a very musical and pretty young lady[3]– Sharp's ward, and of obtaining for her, at great risk of being crushed to death, a mouthful of lemon-ice. But to wait for the second act was beyond my fortitude so I walked home, drank two large tumblers of milk and water, and at half past one, went to bed.

Good bye, dearest. Remember that I expect letters as long and as full as mine. Love to Selina and Fanny. I wished for Fanny's company yesterday on two accounts – because of the music, and because of the refreshments.

Ever yours, my darling,

T B Macaulay

---

[1] Samuel Rogers (1763–1855: *DNB*), banker, poet, and connoisseur. Rogers lived in society, had long been an intimate of Holland House, and was famous for his breakfasts at his house in St James's Place.

[2] William wrote to Lord Grey, 23 May, that he would confer the first vacancy in the Order of the Garter on Grey, the King being 'sensible...of the importance of doing so at this crisis' (*Correspondence of Earl Grey with King William IV*, 1867, 1, 271). Grey was made a Knight of the Garter on 27 May.

[3] Maria Kinnaird (1810–91), Sharp's ward and adopted child; 'her singing was famed' ([C. Kegan Paul], *Maria Drummond, A Sketch*, 1891, p. 26). Such attentions as TBM here pays to Miss Kinnaird soon produced widely accepted rumors that he was engaged to her, rumors all the more plausible because she was known to possess a fortune and he was known to be in want of one. 'A report is very much about now, that Tom is going to be married to Conversation Sharpe's niece... who has seventy thousand pounds. Tom is very much annoyed by it, which I do not wonder; as it will make visiting at the house, which is really very pleasant, rather awkward. He says that he should not know the lady if he met her in the streets, and that he has not spoken to her ten times. He says she is rather pretty, but wears spectacles. He once gave her tea in the Ventilator of the House of Commons, but says his conscience is clear from all flirting imputation' (Margaret Macaulay, *Recollections*, p. 219: 22 November [1831]). A friend's version of the rumor is in the remarks of the younger James Stephen, reported in a letter of Marianne Thornton's: '" I think from what I have seen that Tom Macaulay will soon have achieved the Kinnaird, and as far as I understand the concerns of Sharp and Boddington he will through her be possessed of

TO HANNAH MACAULAY, 30 MAY 1831

MS: Trinity College. *Address:* Miss H M Macaulay. *Mostly published:* Trevelyan, I, 207–9.

London May 30. 1831

My dearest girl, –

Thank you for your letter. But I must begin with criticism. You say that Fanny is quite *épris* of Miss Mortlock. Now Fanny is surely a feminine noun – and can only be *éprise* of Miss Mortlock. If Miss Mortlock were the loveliest creature on earth, I defy Fanny to be *épris* of her. I remark this because it is a bad habit to use foreign words even in the most familiar chat or writing with inaccuracy.

Well, I have been to Holland House.[1] They sent to ask me for an earlier day, I believe because Charles,[2] my Colleague, is just on the point of going to Paris. He starts this afternoon. I took a glass coach[3] and arrived, through a fine avenue of elms at the great entrance, towards seven o'clock. The house is delightful, – the very perfection of the old Elizabethan style, – a considerable number of very large and very comfortable rooms, rich with antique carving and gilding, but carpeted and furnished with all the skill of the best modern upholsterers. The library is a very long room, as long, I should think, as the gallery at the Temple, with little cabinets for study branching out of it, warmly and snugly fitted up, and looking out on very beautiful grounds. The collection of books is not, like Lord Spenser's,[4] curious; but it contains almost every thing that one ever wished to read. Round the library hang some very interesting portraits, Addison – who, you know, lived at Holland house after his marriage with Lady Warwick, Crabbe the poet, Moore the poet, and many other distinguished men. The famous bust of Mr. Fox by Nollekens[5] stands on a table. I found nobody there when I arrived but

---

some hundreds of niggers, a fact which the John Bull will make the most of, but he must, as his next move, marry a woman of fortune somehow or other, and if he does he is prime minister – no not prime minister – after all he has not sound sense enough to take the confidence of the country, but he may be anything else – "'' ([November? 1831?]: MS, Cambridge University Library).

1 Holland House, in Kensington, a seventeenth-century mansion, was largely destroyed by bombing in 1940; its grounds are now a public park.
2 Charles Fox.
3 A coach with glass windows (*OED*).
4 The collection formed by the second Earl Spencer (1758–1834: *DNB*), then the largest private library in England and now the basis of the John Rylands Library, Manchester.
5 Joseph Nollekens (1737–1823: *DNB*), sculptor. There are many versions, variously dated, of Nollekens's busts of Fox, which were part of the sculptor's stock in trade. TBM probably refers to that of 1793 ([Lord Stavordale], *Catalogue of Pictures belonging to the Earl of Ilchester at Holland House*, [London], privately printed, 1904, p. 138).

Lord Russell[1] – the son of the Marquess of Tavistock. We are old House of Commons friends: so we had some very pleasant talk, and, in a little while in came Allen,[2] who is warden of Dulwich College, and who lives almost entirely at Holland House. There are several stories against him. He is certainly a man of vast information and great conversational powers. Some other gentlemen dropped in, and we chatted till Lady Holland made her appearance. Lord Holland[3] dined by himself on account of his gout.

We sate down to dinner in a fine long room the wainscot of which is rich with gilded coronets, roses, and portcullises. There were Lord Albemarle,[4] Lord Alvanley,[5] Lord Russell, Lord Mahon,[6] – a violent Tory, but a very agreable companion, and a very good scholar. There was Cradock,[7] a fine fellow who was the Duke of Wellington's Aide de Camp in 1815, and some other people whose names I did not catch. Oh! I cry you mercy. There was my friend Boddington,[8] Sharp's relation and quondam partner.

What however is more to the purpose, there was a most excellent dinner. I have always heard that Holland House is famous for its good cheer, and certainly the reputation is not unmerited.

During dinner I had some chat with Allen and Lord Mahon about the great European libraries, and particularly that at the Escurial, about the Jesuits, about Macintosh's new volume,[9] and about the Collection of old

[1] William Russell (1809–72), afterwards eighth Duke of Bedford, only son of Francis Russell, Lord Tavistock, afterwards seventh Duke of Bedford. William entered the House of Commons in 1830.

[2] John Allen (1771–1843: *DNB*), a Scotsman, had originally joined the Hollands as a doctor to accompany them on a foreign tour in 1801; he remained with them as friend, adviser, and factotum until his death. Allen was Warden of Dulwich College, 1811–20, and Master from 1820, but he resided at Holland House and seems to have had no significant life apart from it.

[3] Henry Vassall Fox (1773–1840: *DNB*), third Baron Holland, the nephew of Charles James Fox, had since taking his seat in the House of Lords in 1796 been a steadfast opponent of government repression and a supporter of Whig causes. He was Chancellor of the Duchy of Lancaster in Grey's ministry and held the same place under Melbourne.

[4] William Charles Keppel (1772–1849), fourth Earl of Albemarle; an old-school Whig and friend of Charles James Fox; Master of the Horse to William IV and to Victoria.

[5] William Arden (1789–1849), second Baron Alvanley; wit and profligate: see Greville, *Memoirs*, 23 January 1850.

[6] Philip Henry Stanhope (1805–75: *DNB*), afterwards fifth Earl Stanhope, M.P., 1830–52. Mahon was a copious writer of history, including a *History of England*, 1870, designed as a continuation of TBM's. He had an honorable record in promoting the official support of arts and letters.

[7] John Hobart Caradoc (1799–1873: *DNB*), afterwards second Baron Howden, called 'le beau Caradoc' (GEC, *Complete Peerage*); aide-de-camp to Wellington, 1817–18; entered the diplomatic service, 1824, and held various posts.

[8] Samuel Sidney Boddington (1767?–1843), Sharp's business partner.

[9] Volume 2 of Mackintosh's unfinished *History of England*, 3 vols., 1830–[32], in Lardner's 'Cabinet Cyclopaedia,' was published at the end of April.

State Papers which has lately been published by the Government.[1] After dinner Lord Holland was wheeled in; and placed very near me. He was extremely amusing and good-natured.

In the drawing-room I had a long talk with Lady Holland about the antiquities of the House and about the purity of the English language – wherein she thinks herself a most exquisite critic. I happened in speaking about the Reform bill to say, that I wished that it had been possible to form a few commercial constituencies, if the word constituency were admissible.[2] "I am glad you put that in," said her Ladyship, "I was just going to give it you. It is an odious word. Then there is *talented*, and *influential*, and *gentlemanly*. I never could break Sheridan of *gentlemanly*, though he allowed it to be wrong." I joined in abusing *talented* and *influential*; but *gentlemanly*, I said, had analogy in its favour, as we say *manly* and *womanly*. But her ladyship was perverse. She said truly enough that analogy was not a safe guide. "As to the word *womanly*," said she, "I hate it. You men never use it but as a term of reproach." – It is a reproach, thought I, which I shall scarcely bring against your ladyship. We talked about the word *talents* and its history. I said that it had first appeared in theological writing – that it was a metaphor taken from the parable in the new testament, and that it had gradually passed from the vocabulary of divinity into common use. I challenged her to find it in any classical writer in general subjects before the restoration or even before the year 1700. I believe that I might safely have gone down later.[3] She seemed surprised and amused by this theory, never having, as far as I could judge, heard of the parable of the talents, or at all events having no distinct remembrance of it. I did not tell her, though I might have done so, that a person who professed to be a critic in the delicacies of the English language ought to have the Bible at his finger's ends.[4]

She is certainly a woman of considerable talents and great literary acquirements. To me she was excessively gracious; yet there is a haughtiness in her courtesy which, even after all that I had heard of her, surprised me. The Centurion did not keep his soldiers in better order than she keeps her guests. It is to one "Go," and he goeth, and to another "Do this" and it is done.[5] "Ring the bell, Mr. Macaulay." "Lay down that

---

[1] The first of eleven volumes of *State Papers, Published Under Authority of His Majesty's Commission: King Henry the Eighth* was published in late April.

[2] This passage is quoted in the *OED* as the earliest instance of the word; TBM uses it in his letter of [30 April 1831].

[3] The *OED* gives an instance from 1633, but in the fully non-metaphorical sense its first example is from Bulwer's *Falkland*, 1827.

[4] E. E. Kellett, a good judge, has said that, with the possible exception of Ruskin, TBM is the Victorian writer 'whose pages show the closest acquaintance with our Bible' (*London Quarterly Review*, 148 [1927], 203).

[5] Matthew 8: 9; Luke 7: 8.

screen, Lord Russell; – you will spoil it." "Mr. Allen, take a candle and shew Mr. Cradock the picture of Buonaparte."

Lord Holland is, on the other hand, all kindness, simplicity, and vivacity. He talked very well both on politics and on literature. He asked me in a very friendly manner about my father's health and begged to be remembered to him.

When my coach came Lady Holland made me promise that I would, on the first fine morning, walk out to breakfast with them, and see the grounds; – and, after drinking a glass of very good iced lemonade, I took my leave, much amused and pleased. The house certainly deserves its reputation for pleasantness and her Ladyship used me, I believe, as well as it is her way to use any body.

Love to Selina and Fanny. I see Margaret every day. She seems to be very comfortable.

Ever, my darling, yours
T B M.

TO HANNAH MACAULAY, 31 MAY 1831

MS: Mrs Humphry Trevelyan. *Address:* Miss H M Macaulay. *Mostly published:* Trevelyan, I, 209–11.

Court of Commissioners – /Basinghall Street May 31 / 1831

My darling sister,

How delighted I am that you like my letters – and how obliged by yours! But I have little more than my thanks to give for your last sweet prattle. – I have nothing to tell about great people to-day – I heard no fine music yesterday, – saw nobody above the rank of a baronet, – was shut up in my own room reading and writing all the morning – walked with Margaret in the afternoon, and sate for an hour with Ellis at his chambers in the evening. This day seems likely to pass in much the same way, except that I have some bankruptcy business to do and a couple of Sovereigns to receive. So here I am, with three of the ugliest Attorneys that ever deserved to be transported sitting opposite to me, a disconsolate-looking bankrupt – his hand in his empty pockets – standing behind, a lady scolding for her money and refusing to be comforted because it is not,[1] and a surly butcher-like looking creditor, growling like a house-dog, and saying, as plain as looks can say, "If I sign your certificate, blow me, that's all." – Among these fair and interesting forms – on a piece of official paper, with a pen and with ink found at the expence of the public -- I am writing to my darling.

[1] Cf. Jeremiah 31: 15.

These dirty courts, filled with Jewish-looking money-lenders, sheriff's officers, attorneys' runners, and a crowd of people who live by giving sham bail and taking false oaths – fellows as deep in perjury as Mary Elliott[1] – are not by any means such good subjects for a lady's correspondent as the sculpture gallery at Lansdowne House, or the Conservatory at Holland House, or the notes of Pasta, or the talk of Rogers. But we cannot be always fine. When my Richardsonian epistles are published there must be dull as well as amusing letters among them – and this letter is, I think, as good as those sermons of Sir Charles to Geronymo which Miss Byron hypocritically asked for[2] – or as the greater part of that stupid last volume.

We shall soon have finer subjects than bankrupts and attorneys. I shall soon walk out to breakfast at Holland House, and I am to dine with Sir George Philips, and with his son[3] the Member for Steyning, who have the best company, and I am going to the fancy-ball of Goldsmidt the Jew. He met me in the street and implored me to come. "You need not dress more than for an evening party. You had better come. You will be delighted. It will be so very pretty." I thought of Dr. Johnson and the herdsman with his "See such pretty goats."[4] However I told my honest Hebrew that I would come. I may perhaps, like the Benjamites, steal away some Israelite damsel in the middle of her dancing.[5]

But the noise all round me is becoming louder and a baker in a white coat is bellowing for the Book to prove a debt of nine pounds fourteen shillings and four pence. So I must finish my letter and fall to business. Farewell, my dearest. Give my love to my father, Selina and Fanny.

Ever yours, my love
T B M

TO HANNAH MACAULAY, 1 JUNE 1831

MS: Trinity College. *Address:* Miss H M Macaulay / Post Office / Leamington / Warwick. *Frank:* London June one 1831 / T B Macaulay. *Mostly published:* Trevelyan, 1, 211–14.

London June 1 1831

My dearest Sister,

My last letter was a dull one. I mean this to be very amusing. My last was about Basinghall Street, attorneys and bankrupts. But for this – take it dramatically in the German style.

---

[1] Identification uncertain, but perhaps Mary Sophia Elliott (1790–1843), one of the Elliott family of Grove House, Clapham. Her 'perjury' is, I suppose, one of TBM's jokes with his sister.
[2] *Sir Charles Grandison*, 3rd edn, III, 198; 200.
[3] George Richard Philips (1789–1874), M.P. for various constituencies, 1818–32; 1835–52. He succeeded his father as second Baronet, 1847.
[4] Boswell, *Tour to the Hebrides*, 1 September 1773.   [5] Cf. Judges 21: 20–3.

Time morning. Scene the great entrance of Holland House. Enter
Macaulay and two Footmen in livery.

First Footman.

  Sir may I venture to demand your name?

Macaulay.

  Macaulay, and thereto I add M.P.
  And that addition even in these proud halls
  May well insure the bearer some respect.

Second Footman.

  And art thou come to breakfast with our Lord?

Macaulay.

  I am: for so his hospitable will
  And hers – the peerless dame ye serve – hath bade.

First Footman.

  Ascend the stair, and thou above shalt find,
  On snow-white linen spread, the luscious meal.
  (Exit Macaulay up stairs.)

In plain English prose – I went this morning to breakfast at Holland
House. The day was fine, and I arrived at twenty minutes after ten. After
I had lounged a short time in the dining-room, I heard a gruff good-
natured voice asking, "Where is Mr. Macaulay. Where have you put
him;" and in his arm-chair Lord Holland was wheeled in. He took me
round the apartments, he riding and I walking. He gave me the history
of the most remarkable portraits in the library – where there is by the
bye, one of the few bad pieces of Lawrence[1] that I have seen – a head of
Charles James Fox, – an ignominious failure: Lord Holland said that it
was the worst ever painted of so eminent a man by so eminent an artist.
There is a very fine head of Machiavelli[2] – another of Earl Grey,[3] a very
different sort of man. I observed a portrait of Lady Holland[4] painted some
thirty years ago. I could have cried to see the change. She must have been
a most beautiful woman. She is now, I suppose, very near sixty, very
large, and with a double chin. She still looks however as if she had been
handsome; – and shews in one respect great taste and sense. She does not
rouge at all; or at least not in any manner which I could detect; and her
costume is not youthful, so that she looks as well in the morning as in
the evening.

---

[1] Sir Thomas Lawrence (1769–1830: *DNB*), President of the Royal Academy; his portrait
of Fox, 1800.
[2] After Bronzino (Thomas Faulkner, *History and Antiquities of Kensington*, 1820, p. 111).
[3] By Thomas Phillips, 1811.
[4] Probably that by Robert Fagan, 1793, though another, by Louis Gauffier, 1795, also hung
in Holland House.

We came back to the dining room. Our breakfast party consisted of My Lord and Lady – myself – Lord Russell, – Luttrell[1] – and another person whose name I could not catch. You must have heard of Luttrell. I met him once at Rogers's; and I have seen him, I think, in other places. He is a famous wit – the most popular, I think, of all the professed wits, – a man who has lived in the highest circles, – a scholar, and no contemptible poet. He wrote a little volume of verse entitled "Advice to Julia,"[2] – not first-rate, but neat, lively, piquant, and shewing the most consummate knowledge of fashionable life.

Well, we breakfasted on very good coffee and very good tea and very good eggs, – butter kept in the midst of ice and hot rolls. Lady Holland told us her dreams; how she had dreamed that a mad dog bit her foot, and how she set off to Brodie,[3] and lost her way in St Martin's lane and could not find him; – she hoped, she said, the dream would not come true. I said that I had had a dream which admitted of no such hope. For I had dreamed that I heard Pollock[4] speak in the House of Commons, that the speech was very long, and that he was coughed down. This dream of mine diverted them much, and we talked of Pollock, of law and lawyers, of the art of decyphering, and of the art of acoustics. Lord Holland told us that there was formerly something in the structure of his library which conveyed the voice from one recess to another at a great distance. He had opened a bow window between them and this had removed the evil. An evil it was indeed by his account. "Why, Sir," said he, "a friend of mine asked another friend of mine in one of those recesses whether he should propose to a girl – and the adviser dissuaded him most strongly. The lady was in the other recess, and heard every word." – A pretty business indeed!

After breakfast Lady Holland offered to conduct me to her own drawing-room; – or rather commanded my attendance. A very beautiful room it is, opening on a terrace, and wainscotted with miniature paintings interesting from their merit, and interesting from their history. Among them I remarked a great many, thirty I should think, which even I, who am no great connoisseur, saw at once could come from no hand but Stothard's.[5] They were all on subjects from Lord Byron's poems. "Yes," said she; "poor Lord Byron sent them to me a short time before the

---

[1] Henry Luttrell (1765?–1851: *DNB*), natural son of the second Earl of Carhampton, lived entirely as a diner-out and figures in all of the memoirs of the first half of the century.

[2] 1820.

[3] (Sir) Benjamin Brodie (1783–1862: *DNB*), surgeon to St George's Hospital; attended George IV and William IV; Baronet, 1834, President of the Royal College of Surgeons, 1844, and of the Royal Society, 1858–61.

[4] Pollock, a Tory, had just been returned for the close borough of Huntingdon and had not yet been heard in the House.

[5] Thomas Stothard (1755–1834: *DNB*), painter and book illustrator. There were only twelve of these watercolors, which were engraved for Byron's *Works*, 8 vols., 1818–20.

separation. I sent them back, and told him that if he gave them away, he ought to give them to Lady Byron. But he said that he would not – and that, if I did not take them, the bailiffs would, and that they would be lost in the wreck." Her ladyship then honoured me so far as to conduct me through her dressing room into the great family-bedchamber to shew me a very fine picture by Reynolds of Fox[1] when a boy bird's-nesting. I had seen it at the British Gallery.[2] She then consigned me to Luttrell, asking him to shew me the grounds.

Through the grounds we went and very pretty I thought them. Much more, however, might be done at little cost. But Lady Holland, has not, I find, paid much attention to gardening. In the Dutch garden – a very appropriate and pretty appendage to such an antique building as the house, – there is an interesting object – a very fine bronze bust of Napoleon,[3] which Lord Holland put up in 1817, while Napoleon was a prisoner at St Helena. The inscription was selected by his Lordship, and is remarkably happy. It is from Homer's Odyssey. I will translate it as well as I can extempore into a measure which gives a better idea of Homer's manner than Pope's sing-song couplet.

> "For not, be sure, within the grave
> Is hid that prince, the wise, the brave, –
> But in an islet's narrow bound,
> With the great Ocean roaring round,
> The captive of a foeman base,
> He pineth for his native place." –[4]

There is a seat near the spot which is called Rogers's seat. The poet loves, it seems, to sit there. A very elegant inscription by Lord Holland is placed over it.

> "Here Rogers sate; and here forever dwell
> With me those pleasures which he sang so well."[5]

[1] Not certainly identified. No such painting is listed in Greaves and Cronin's catalogue of Reynolds, nor in either of the inventories of Holland House, Faulkner, *History of Kensington*, and [Stavordale], *Catalogue of Pictures...at Holland House*. Lord Holland owned Sir Joshua's portrait of Fox, Lady Sarah Lennox and Lady Susan Fox-Strangways, 1761, exhibited at the British Institution, 1820; in this Fox is a boy of twelve, and Lady Susan holds a dove, but it is difficult to imagine how TBM, if he means this picture, could have described Fox as 'bird's-nesting.'

[2] The gallery of the British Institution in Pall Mall, founded in 1805 for promoting the fine arts in the United Kingdom, held two exhibitions annually until 1866.   [3] By Canova.

[4] *Odyssey*, I, 196–9. Lord Holland's own translation runs thus:

> 'He is not dead, he breathes the air
> In lands beyond the deep,
> Some distant sea-girt island where
> Harsh men the hero keep'
> (Derek Hudson, *Holland House in Kensington*, 1967, p. 68).

[5] The seat is still in place; the phrase in the second line should read 'that he sings.'

Very neat and condensed, I think. Another inscription by Luttrell hangs there. Luttrell adjured me with mock pathos to spare his blushes; but I am author enough to know what the blushes of authors mean. So I read the lines; and very pretty and polished they were – but too many to be remembered from one reading.[1]

Having gone round the grounds I took my leave, very much pleased with the place. Lord Holland is extremely kind. But that is of course; for he is kindness itself. Her Ladyship too, which is by no means of course, is all graciousness and civility. But, for all this, I would much rather be quietly walking with you, my darling. And the great use of going to these fine places is to learn how happy it is possible to be without them. Indeed I care so little for them that I certainly should not have gone to day, but that I thought that I should be able to find materials for a letter which you might like. Farewell – my sweet sister. Give my love to Selina and Fanny. I am delighted to hear that Selina has placed herself under Dr. Jephson[2] with good hopes. I believe that the hope, in her case, is half the cure. Love to my father.

Ever yours, dearest,
T B M

TO HANNAH MACAULAY, 3 JUNE 1831

MS: Trinity College. *Address:* Miss H M Macaulay. *Mostly published:* Trevelyan, I, 215–16.

London June 3. 1831

My dearest sister,

I cannot tell you how delighted I am to find that my letters amuse you. But sometimes I must be dull like my neighbours. I paid no visits yesterday and have no news to relate to day. I am sitting again in Basinghall Street; and a bore compared with whom Marriott is an agreable companion, a bore of the bores, even Basil Montague[3] is haranguing about Lord Verulam and the way of inoculating one's mind with truth; and all this àpropos of a lying bankrupt's balance sheet.

I dine at Parker's to day. I generally have a very pleasant walk of an

---

1 They are printed in P. W. Clayden, *Rogers and His Contemporaries*, 1889, I, 264.
2 Henry Jephson (1798–1878), established the popularity of Leamington as a spa. He 'made his patients eat moderately and abstain from stimulants and prescribed the Leamington waters internally and externally' (*Boase*). Zachary Macaulay had visited Leamington for reasons of health as early as July 1823 (Knutsford, *Zachary Macaulay*, p. 387).
3 Basil Montagu (1770–1851: *DNB*), the friend of Wordsworth and Coleridge and editor of Bacon; a barrister, he had 'an extensive practice in chancery and bankruptcy' (*DNB*). The *Life of Bacon* which completed Montagu's edition was used by TBM for the subject of his essay on Bacon in 1837.

hour or two with Margaret every afternoon.[1] But to day I am detained by business, and shall not see her till dinner time. There will be no great men at Parker's I will answer for it – nothing better than some prosing conveyancer – so that probably I shall have no more materials for a letter to morrow than I have to day.

Send me some gossip, my love. Tell me how you go on with German. Can you yet read about the wretched man who had no shadow,[2] – or about the crazy half-farthing man, – or the crowd of witches and elemental spirits and secret tribunals of the Saxon romancers. I must fall to that language or you will be wiser than your teacher, and I do not know how I shall bear being put to shame by your superiority. What novel have you commenced – ? or rather how many dozen have you finished? – Recommend me one. What say you to Destiny?[3] Is the Young Duke[4] worth reading? and what do you think of Lawrie Todd?[5]

I am writing about Lord Byron so pathetically that I make Margaret cry – but so slowly that I am afraid I shall make Napier wait. Rogers, like a civil gentleman, told me last week to write no more reviews, and to publish separate works – adding what for him is a very rare thing, a compliment. "You may do any thing, Mr. Macaulay." See how vain and insincere human nature is. I have been put into so good a temper with Rogers that I have paid him what is as rare with me as with him, a very handsome compliment in my review.[6] I cannot understand the popularity of his poetry. It is pleasant and flowing enough, less monotonous than most of the imitations of Pope and Goldsmith and calls up many agreable images and recollections. But that such men as Lord Grenville,[7] Lord Holland, Hobhouse,[8] Lord Byron, and others of high rank in intellect should place Rogers, as they do, above Southey, Moore, and even Scott himself, is what I cannot conceive. But this comes of being in the highest

---

[1] Margaret writes of this summer in her *Recollections*, p. 214, that 'for above two months I was quite alone with him in London, that is, without any of my own family, and during that time was with him during the full flow of London business, and visiting at least three hours every day. During this time we generally walked a good deal, and never did I find him more agreable.'

[2] Adelbert von Chamisso, *Peter Schlemihl*, 1814.

[3] Susan Ferrier, *Destiny, or, the Chief's Daughter*, 3 vols., published 30 March 1831.

[4] Disraeli, *The Young Duke*, 3 vols., published in mid-April 1831.

[5] John Galt, *Lawrie Todd, or the Settlers in the Woods*, 3 vols., 1830.

[6] In 'Byron,' *ER*, LII, 556, TBM quotes three lines from Rogers's *Human Life*, 1819, p. 40, calling them 'sweet and graceful'; in the 1843 edition of the *Essays* the passage quoted is extended to twelve lines.

[7] William Wyndham Grenville (1759–1834: *DNB*), first Baron Grenville; Whiggish statesman; Prime Minister, 1806–7.

[8] John Cam Hobhouse (1786–1869: *DNB*), afterwards first Baron Broughton, Byron's friend, minor writer, a Radical turned Whig, M.P., 1820–51. He was President of the Board of Control during TBM's residence in India and while TBM was Secretary at War; again, in the cabinet in which TBM was Paymaster-General.

society of London. What Lady Jane Granville called the Patronage of Fashion can do as much for a middling poet as for a plain girl – a Miss Arabella Falconer.[1]

I am glad to hear that Selina finds her head relieved. Margaret tells me strange things about Mr. Jephson's theology. How do he and Fanny agree?

But I must stop. This rambling talk has been scrawled in the middle of haranguing, squabbling, swearing and crying. Since I began it I have taxed four bills, taken forty depositions, and rated several Mary-Elliotish witnesses. Farewell, my own darling. I long to see you again. But a trip to Leamington is, I fear, quite out of the question. Yet if I thought that you would leave Leamington without seeing Warwick Castle, I think I should come down to avert such a misfortune. Love to my father and the girls.

Ever yours, my dearest,

T B M.

TO HANNAH MACAULAY, 6 JUNE 1831

MS: Trinity College. *Address:* Miss H M Macaulay.

London June 6. 1831

My darling,

It is but a minute that I can steal from my Review which must be sent off in two or three days. Yet I cannot refrain from writing to you though I have next to nothing to say. I dine at Mr. Marshall's to night. At Sir George Philips's to morrow. Our parliamentary business – though nominally it begins on the 14th – will not really begin for a week later. I have a letter from Lord Althorpe desiring my attendance on the 21st.

I saw Sheil yesterday and congratulated him on his election for Louth.[2] He gives but a bad account of the state of Ireland, which seems indeed to be quite heart breaking. What fools by the bye those Irish patriots and heroes in the County of Clare have been making of themselves[3] – challenging each other, – challenging each other's seconds, – challenging each other's brothers, first cousins, and second cousins, – and yet never fighting – never able to agree on a proper place, or a proper day, or

---

[1] Maria Edgeworth, *Patronage*, 1814, ch. 10.

[2] Sheil was returned for both Milborne Port and Louth at the general election and chose to sit for the latter.

[3] The contest in Clare between Maurice O'Connell and The O'Gorman Mahon led to a challenge from Mahon's brother to O'Connell. Mahon's second, however, changed the ground of meeting four times and was finally challenged by O'Connell's second. In the event, neither duel took place, though O'Connell's brother Charles challenged and actually fought a Mr Cummins. See *The Times*, 24 and 26 May.

a proper man to carry the message. I hope that these wretched pol-
trooneries and follies will bring the swaggering tone which the Irish
politicians have of late been adopting into discredit.

Hawkins[1] is to be brought into parliament for Tavistock. Hyde Villiers[2]
for some place – I do not know what; – Lord Sandon[3] seems to be certain
of Liverpool; so that I hope no reformer will have lost his seat on account
of his vote. –

But you will be tired to death of this political chit-chat. Yet I have
nothing else to tell you – unless you would like to hear how I dined at
Parker's on Friday, and how baby[4] imitated cows, doves, horses, asses,
and all other sorts of creatures – how I walked in Brunswick Square with
Margaret and Jane Babington in the evening, and how copious and minute
an analysis Jane gave us of the character of Henry Drummond. –

But I must stop. Write to me, my love. It vexes me to open letter after
letter from Leamington and not to see your handwriting. Prattle away –
never mind what. I shall love to read it, and to read it over and over again.
I did not know how much I loved you, my dearest, till I missed you.
Kindest love to my father, Selina and Fanny.

Ever yours, my love,
T B M.

TO HANNAH MACAULAY, 7 JUNE 1831

MS: Trinity College. *Mostly published:* Trevelyan, 1, 205; 216–19.

London June 7. 1831

My dearest girl,

Yesterday I dined at Marshall's; and was almost consoled for [not]
meeting Ramohun Roy,[5] by a very pleasant party. There were Protheroe

---

[1] John Heywood Hawkins (1802–77: *Boase*), B.A., Trinity College, Cambridge, 1825; Whig
M.P., St Michael, 1830–1; Tavistock, 1831–2; Newport, 1832–41.

[2] Thomas Hyde Villiers (1801–32: *DNB*), after sitting for Hedon and Wootton Bassett,
1826–31, was brought in for Bletchingley, 1831–2. Villiers, brother of Lord Clarendon, was
at St John's College, Cambridge, where he was one of TBM's group. At the time of his
early death he was Secretary of the Board of Control and was succeeded by TBM.

[3] Dudley Ryder (1798–1882: *DNB*), afterwards second Earl of Harrowby; M.P., Tiverton,
1819–31; Liverpool, 1831–47. A moderate Tory, he had accepted the secretaryship of the
Board of Control under Grey but had just resigned it, to be succeeded by Hyde Villiers.
'He advocated the principle of the Reform Act, but opposed Ministers in the greater part of
its details' (*Dod's Parliamentary Pocket Companion*, 1833).

[4] Perhaps Margaret Parker, of whom it is said that TBM was very fond: 'She was a very
clever intelligent child, and delighted from 2 years old to listen to his stories and nursery
rhymes' (Eliza Conybeare's Recollections: MS, Trinity).

[5] Raja Ram Mohan Roy (1774–1833), Indian religious reformer, founder of an eclectic sect,
the Brahma Samaj; worked for the improvement of education in India and supported the
British government's effort to abolish suttee. He had just arrived in England, and had
attracted great attention as virtually the first Westernized Indian to appear there.

the member for Bristol, and Colonel Davies[1] the member for Worcester, and Lady Henry Howard,[2] and many other unknown gentlemen and ladies. But the great sight was the two great wits, Rogers and Sydney Smith. Singly I have often seen them. But to see them both together was a novelty – and a novelty not the less curious because their mutual hostility is well known, and the hard hits which they have given to each other are in every body's mouth. They were very civil however. But I was struck by the truth of what Matthew Bramble, – a person of whom you probably never heard, – says in Smollett's Humphrey Clinker. One wit in a company, like a knuckle of ham in soup, gives a flavour. But two are too many.[3] Rogers and Sydney Smith would not come into conflict. If one had possession of the company the other was silent, and, as you may conceive, the one who had possession of the company was always Sydney Smith, and the one who was silent was always Rogers. Sometimes however the company divided, and each of them had a small congregation. I had a good deal of talk with both of them; for, in whatever they may disagree, they agree in always treating me with very marked kindness.

I had a good deal of pleasant conversation with Rogers. He was telling me of the curiosity and interest which attached to the persons of Sir W Scott and Lord Byron. When Sir Walter Scott dined at a gentleman's in London some time ago, all the servant-maids in the House asked leave to stand in the passage and see him pass. He was, as you may conceive, greatly flattered.

About Lord Byron whom he knew well, he told me some curious anecdotes. When Lord Byron passed through Florence Rogers was there. They had a good deal of conversation, and Rogers accompanied him to his carriage. The inn had fifty windows in front. All the windows were crowded with women, mostly English women, to catch a glance at their favourite poet. Among them were some at whose houses he had often been in England, and with whom he had been on friendly terms. He would not notice them or return their salutations. Rogers was the only person that he spoke to.[4]

The worst thing that I know about Lord Byron is the very unfavourable impression which he made on men, who certainly were not inclined to judge him harshly, and who, as far as I know, were never personally

[1] Thomas Henry Hastings Davies (1789–1846), Whig M.P. for Worcester, 1818–34; 1837–41. He was a Peninsular veteran.

[2] Henrietta Elizabeth (d. 1892), daughter of Ichabod Wright, married the Very Rev. Henry Howard, youngest child of the fifth Earl of Carlisle, 1824.

[3] J. Melford to Sir Watkin Phillips, 5 June, *Humphry Clinker*, New York, 1908, 1, 178.

[4] An expansion of the episode mentioned by Rogers in a letter of 11 November 1821 (Clayden, *Rogers and His Contemporaries*, 1, 321).

ill used by him. Sharp and Rogers both speak of him as an unpleasant, affected, splenetic, person. I have heard hundreds and thousands of people who never saw him rant about him. But I never heard a single expression of fondness for him fall from the lips of any of those who knew him well. Yet, even now, after the lapse of five and twenty years there are those who cannot talk for a quarter of an hour about Charles Fox without tears. What strongly attached friends Canning made every body knows.

Sydney Smith leaves London on the 20th – the day before parliament meets for business. I advised him to stay and see something of his friends who would be crowding to London. " My flock," said this good shepherd. " My dear Sir, remember my flock.

'The hungry sheep look up and are not fed.'"[1]

I could say nothing to such an argument – but I could not help thinking that if Mr. Daniel Wilson[2] had said such a thing it would infallibly have appeared in his funeral sermon and in his Life by Baptist Noel. But in poor Sydney's mouth it sounded like a joke. He begged me to come and see him at Combe Flory.[3] " There I am, Sir, – the priest of the Flowery Valley – a delightful parsonage about which I care a good deal – and a delightful country, about which I do not care a straw." I told him that my meeting with him was some compensation for missing Ramohun Roy. Sydney broke forth. "Compensation! Do you mean to insult me – a beneficed clergyman – an orthodox clergyman – a nobleman's chaplain – to be no more than compensation for a Brahmin – and a heretic Brahmin too – a fellow who has lost his own religion and can't find another – a vile heterodox dog who, as I am credibly informed, eats beef-steaks in private – a man who has lost his caste – who ought to have melted lead poured down his nostrils, if the good old Vedas were in force as they ought to be." He then told me that he had dined with Scarlet. "Oh, Macaulay! – A fallen angel![4] – And a complete Pandæmonium of his brethren he had assembled to dinner – all the powers and dominations who are out of place. There was Mammon Herries, and there was Beelzebub Twiss." These are some Boswelleana of Sydney – not very clerical, you will say, –

---

[1] 'Lycidas,' line 125.

[2] Wilson (1778–1858: *DNB*), Evangelical minister of St John's Chapel, Bedford Row, 1812–24, where Baptist Noel later assisted. Wilson was Vicar of St Mary's, Islington, until 1832, when, through the influence of the Grants, Robert and Charles, he was appointed Bishop of Calcutta.

[3] Smith had exchanged his Yorkshire living for that of Combe Florey, near Taunton, in 1829.

[4] Scarlett, though he had always been regarded as a Whig, had accepted appointment as Attorney-General under Wellington, and on the introduction of the Reform Bill confirmed his alteration by opposing it. In the general election of May he was returned as a Tory for Cockermouth.

but indescribably amusing to the hearers whatever the readers may think of them. Nothing can present a more striking contrast to his rapid, loud, laughing utterance, and his rector-like amplitude and rubicundity than the low, slow, emphatic tone and the corpse-like face of Rogers. There is as great a difference in what they say as in the voice and look with which they say it. The conversation of Rogers is remarkably polished and artificial. What he says seems to have been long meditated, and might be published with little correction. Sydney talks from the impulse of the moment, and his fun is quite inexhaustible.

The Miss Marshalls were full of Paganini[1] and his violin. The man seems to be a miracle. The newspapers say that long streamy flakes of music fall from his string interspersed with luminous points of sound which ascend the air and appear like stars.[2] Fanny probably understands this eloquence. But it is quite beyond me. Love to her, to Selina, and to my father. Write to me, my sweet darling.

Ever yours, dearest,
T B M.

to Hannah Macaulay, 8 June 1831

MS: Trinity College. *Address:* Miss H M Macaulay / Post-Office / Leamington / Warwick. *Frank:* London June eight 1831 / T B Macaulay. *Partly published:* Trevelyan, I, 219–21.

London June 8. 1831

My dearest sister,

Yesterday night I went to the Jew's. I had indeed no excuse for forgetting the invitation. For about a week after I had received the green varnished billet of Mrs. Goldsmid and answered it, came another in the self-same words and addressed to Mr. Macaulay Junr. I thought that my answer had miscarried. So down I sate and composed a second Epistle to the Hebrews. I afterwards found that the second invitation was meant for Charles.

Having attired myself simply, as for a dinner-party, I went to Ellis's and drank tea with him and his wife, – read them some of Mrs. Thrale's anecdotes[3] which I had lent Mrs. Ellis, and had a good laugh over them. At a little after ten I went to number 1 Bryanstone Square. The house is a very fine one – more fine, I think, than comfortable. The door was guarded by peace-officers and besieged by starers. The coaches were

---

[1] Paganini's first London concert was given at the King's Theatre on 3 June.
[2] '...he commenced with a soft streamy note of celestial quality; and with three or four whips of his bow elicited points of sound that mounted to the third heaven, and as bright as the stars' (*The Times*, 6 June).
[3] *Anecdotes of the Late Samuel Johnson*, 1786.

numerous. In I walked, left my hat with the porter, received a ticket for it, and marched up stairs. The passages and the back-court of the house were filled with laurels and blazing with lamps.

The party assembled in three large drawing rooms on the first floor. The carpets were taken up – the chairs and tables moved away, the floors chalked in wreaths, flower-pots and stars. Old Goldsmid met me in a superb court-dress, with his sword at his side. Then up came his son[1] in the dress of a gallant forester, with a pair of spectacles on his nose. There was a most sumptuous looking Persian, covered with gold lace. Then there was an Italian bravo with a long beard. Two old gentlemen who ought to have been wiser were fools enough to come in splendid Turkish costumes at which every body laughed. The fancy-dresses were worn almost exclusively by the young people. There was a very fine looking Robin Hood, a splendid Richard the Third, a well-dressed Spanish peasant with a guitar – a good many military and naval uniforms, and some court-dresses.

The ladies for the most part contented themselves with a few flowers and ribbands oddly disposed. There was however a beautiful Mary Queen of Scots – who looked as well as dressed the character perfectly – an angel of a Jewess in a Highland plaid, – an old woman – or rather a woman – for through her disguise it was impossible to ascertain her age – in the absurdest costume of the last century – with flounces, powder, and green spectacles. These good people soon began their quadrilles and galopades, and were enlivened by all the noise that twelve fiddlers could make for their lives.

You must not suppose that all the company was made up of these mummers. There was Dr. Lardner, – and Long the Greek Professor in the London University, – and Shiel, and Strutt,[2] and Romilly, and Owen[3] the philanthropist. Owen laid hold on Shiel and gave him a lecture on co-operation which lasted for half-an-hour. At last Shiel made his escape; – then Owen seized Mrs. Shiel – a good catholic, and a very agreable woman, and began to prove to her that there could be no such a thing as moral responsibility. I had fled at the first sound of his discourse – and was talking with Strutt and Romilly – when behold! I saw Owen leave Mrs. Shiel and come towards us. So I cried out "Sauve qui peut." And we ran off. But before we had got five feet from where we were standing who should meet us face to face but old Basil Montague. "Nay then," said I, "the game is up. The Prussians are on our rear. If we are to be

---

[1] (Sir) Francis Henry Goldsmid (1808–78: *DNB*), admitted to the bar, 1833, the first Jewish barrister; M.P. for Reading, 1860–78.
[2] Edward Strutt (1801–80: *DNB*), afterwards first Baron Belper, was at Trinity with TBM and had been president of the Cambridge Union; M.P. for Derby, 1830–47.
[3] Robert Owen (1771–1858: *DNB*), mill-owner, philanthropist, and socialist.

bored to death there is no help for it." Basil siezed Romilly; – Owen took possession of Strutt. I was blessing myself on my escape when behold! the only human being worthy to make a third with such a pair, William Smith, caught me by the arm, and begged to have a quarter of an hour's conversation with me.

While I was suffering under Mr. William Smith, a smart impudent looking young dog, dressed like a sailor in a blue jacket and check shirt, marched up, and asked a Jewish-looking damsel near me to dance with him. I thought that I had seen the fellow before; and after a little looking, I perceived that it was Charles; and most knowingly, I assure you, did he perform a quadrille with Miss Hilpah Manasses, or whatever her name is.

If I were to tell you all that I saw I should exceed my ounce. There was Martin[1] the painter, and Procter[2] – *alias* Barry Cornwall – the poet or poetaster, – Sir Robert Wilson[3] Knight and Rat, and Protheroe whom I meet wherever I go. But, to say the truth, the company was not such as we exclusives think quite the thing. There was a little too much of St Mary Axe about it, – Jewesses by dozens, and Jews by scores. There was Braham[4] the singer and his wife for example, and four or five Kezias and Kerrenhappuchs[5] with them. I did not see one Peer – or one star, except a foreign order or two, – which I generally consider as an intimation to look to my pockets. A German Knight is a dangerous neighbour in a crowd.

After seeing a galopade very prettily danced by the Israelitish women, I went down stairs, reclaimed my hat, and walked into the dining-room. There with some difficulty I squeezed myself between a Turk and a Bernese peasant and obtained an ice, a macaroon and a glass of wine. Charles was there, very active in his attendance on his fair Hilpah. I bade him good night. "What," said young Hopeful, "are you going yet?" It was near one o'clock; but this joyous tar seemed to think it impossible that any body could dream of leaving such delightful enjoyments till day-break. I left him staying Hilpah with flagons,[6] and walked quietly home. But it was some time before I could get to sleep. The sound of fiddles was in mine ears, and gaudy dresses, and black hair, and Jewish noses were fluctuating up and down before mine eyes.

[1] John Martin (1789–1854: *DNB*), painter of grandiose historical and biblical subjects.
[2] Bryan Waller Procter (1787–1874: *DNB*), lawyer and miscellaneous writer, published much poety under his pseudonym of Barry Cornwall.
[3] General Sir Robert Thomas Wilson (1777–1849: *DNB*), veteran of the Napoleonic wars. As Whig M.P. for Southwark, Wilson refused to support the Reform Bill and resigned his seat.
[4] John Braham (1774?–1856: *DNB*), the most popular tenor of the time and composer of light opera; Braham was a Jew.
[5] Job 42: 14.   [6] Song of Solomon 2: 5.

There is a fancy-ball for you. If Charles writes a history of it, tell me which of us does it best. Thank you, my darling, for your sweet letter. Thanks to Fanny for hers. I am much pleased to hear that she likes Rogers.[1] As to Doddridge[2] I believe that he was a very good, honest, man. The letters are foolish enough. But I do not know that they make out any very heinous charge against him. They shew him to have been a frivolous young fellow – a freer kind of Mr. Elton[3] – freer because the manners of the age were freer. I do not wonder at his keeping copies of them when he was more advanced in life. Every man likes to preserve the memorials of his youth, even when there is much in them to be sorry for and ashamed of. Would you have had Pepys, when he became an eminent statesman, burn the journal of his early life, because it contains much that is ridiculous and some things that are blameable?

Read the novel called the Young Duke by the author of Vivian Grey. I have not read it. But I hear that I am praised in it.[4] On this the rascal may rely, that, when I take him and his tribe of slanderers in hand, as I shall do one of these days, I will not bate him one lash for all his panegyric. My article on Byron is nearly finished. It is, without exception, the worst thing I ever wrote in my life. Love to my father and girls.

Ever yours, darling,

T B M

TO HANNAH MACAULAY, 10 JUNE 1831

MS: Mrs Humphry Trevelyan. *Address:* Miss H M Macaulay / Post Office / Leamington / Warwick. *Frank:* London June ten 1831 / T B Macaulay. *Partly published:* Trevelyan, 1, 221–3.

London June 10. 1831

My darling,

I am at Basinghall Street, and I snatch this quarter of an hour, the only quarter of an hour which I am likely to have for that purpose during the day, to write to you. I will not omit writing two days running, because, if my letters give you half the pleasure which your letters give me, you will, I am sure, miss them. I have not however very much to tell you. I have been busy with my article on Lord Byron which I shall send off to Napier to morrow. It will, I fear, be printed without my being able to revise the proofs. But I shall do my best to prevent this. I never wrote anything with less heart. I do not like the book. I do not like the hero;

---

[1] Probably the 1830 edition of his *Italy.*

[2] The last volume of *The Correspondence and Diary of Philip Doddridge*, 5 vols., 1829–31 was published in April.

[3] In Jane Austen's *Emma.*   [4] See 22 June.

and yet knowing Moore I must speak civilly of him and of his friend.
I shall be abused, I have no doubt, for speaking so coldly of Lord Byron
as I have done.

I dined the day before yesterday at Sir George Philips's with Sotheby,
Morier[1] the author of Hadgi Baba, and Sir James Mackintosh. Morier
I think a great bore. He began to quote Latin before the ladies had left
the room, and quoted it by no means to the purpose. After their departure
he began to repeat Virgil – passages that every body else knows by heart
and does not repeat. – He, though he tried to repeat them, did not know
them and could not get one without my prompting. Sotheby I thought
a greater bore than Morier. He is full of his translation of Homer's Iliad,[2]
some specimens of which he has already published. I think it a complete
failure – more literal than that of Pope, but still tainted with the deep
radical vice of Pope's, a thoroughly modern and artificial manner. It bears
the same kind of relation to the Iliad that Robertson's narrative bears to
the story of Joseph in the Book of Genesis.

There is a pretty allegory in Homer – I think in the last book but
I forget precisely where – about two vessels – the one filled with blessings
and the other with sorrow which stand, says the poet, on the right and
left hand of Jupiter's throne, and from which he dispenses good and evil
according to his pleasure among men. What word to use for these vessels
has long posed the translators of Homer. Pope who loves to be fine calls
them *urns*. Cowper who loves to be coarse calls them *casks* – a translation
more improper than Pope's; for a cask is, in our general understanding,
a wooden vessel; and the Greek word means an earthen vessel. There is
a curious letter of Cowper's to one of his female correspondents about this
unfortunate word. She begged that Jupiter might be allowed a more
elegant piece of furniture for his throne than a cask. But Cowper was
peremptory.[3] I mentioned this incidentally when we were talking about
translations. This set Sotheby off. "I," said he, "have translated it *vase*.[4]
I hope that meets your ideas. Don't you think vase will do. Does it
satisfy you." I told him sincerely enough that it satisfied me. For I must
be most unreasonable to be dissatisfied at a[ny][5] thing that he chuses to
put in a book w[hi]ch[5] I never shall read. Sotheby is a male blue-stocking –
a thing which I detest more than a female blue-stocking; and that is
saying a good deal.

[1] James Justinian Morier (1780?–1849: *DNB*), diplomat, Eastern traveller, and writer; his *Hajji Baba of Ispahan* was published in 1824.
[2] Sotheby's *The Iliad of Homer*, 2 vols., a complete translation in heroic couplets, was published in March; it had been preceded by his *The First Book of the Iliad*, 1830.
[3] To Lady Hesketh, 9 February 1786: Thomas Wright, ed., *The Correspondence of William Cowper*, 4 vols., 1904, II, 462.
[4] 'Two urns stand ever at the throne of Jove' is in fact Sotheby's version (II, 411).
[5] Obscured by seal.

Mackintosh was very agreable; and, as usually happens when I meet him, I learned something from him. Mrs. Marcet[1] was there, and Poulett Thompson[2] — between whom, as political œconomists, there is a ludicrous sort of flirtation. I like Mrs. Marcet. She is a clever and not obtrusively a learned woman.

We talked of Mrs. Siddons's death.[3] The news came while I was in the drawing-room. What a queer coincidence. The only time that I ever saw Mrs. Siddons was in that very room four years ago, on the first night on which I visited Sir George Philips.[4] She was a great friend of the Philips's, and Sir George means to send his carriage to the funeral.

Charles lost his heart, Margaret tells me, at Goldsmidt's ball to a Miss Levi — and I give him credit for his taste. She is the most beautiful young women that I have almost ever seen, a splendid specimen of the Jewish breed.

I enclose a check from Stokes[5] for my father, and a note which I opened unawares. The servant who brought it told me that it was for me.

Henry's ship-franks will ruin me. I had to pay 10s yesterday and five shillings a day or two ago for them. Love to my father, Fanny, and Selina. I hear good accounts of Jephson's success. Sir G Philips told me that he was a sad quack. "Why," said I, "I am no believer in any people who pretend to be much better physicians than others of equal experience and opportunities." "No," said Sir George. "My friend Prout[6] is indeed a prodigy. But I do not believe in Jephson." I said nothing. But I thought my friend's hatred of quacks rather partial. He and Selina would hold a dialogue together resembling that of Mr. Woodhouse and Mrs. J. Knightley about their doctors.[7]

Farewell, my sweet love,

T B M

---

1 Mrs Jane Marcet (1769–1858: *DNB*), writer of textbooks for children; her most successful work was *Conversations on Political Economy*, 1816, of which TBM wrote: 'Every girl who has read Mrs Marcet's little Dialogues on Political Economy, could teach Montague or Walpole many lessons in finance' ('Milton,' *ER*, XLII, 307).

2 Charles Edward Poulett Thomson (1799–1841: *DNB*), afterwards first Baron Sydenham, a merchant and Benthamite, in Parliament since 1826; Vice-President of the Board of Trade in Grey's administration; Governor-General of Canada, 1839–41.

3 June 8.

4 TBM perhaps means 16 May 1826, when, according to Selina Macaulay's Diary, he dined with Philips; it was on this occasion that he first met Sydney Smith.

5 Robert Stokes (1783–1859: *Boase*), for many years clerk both to Zachary Macaulay and to the African Institution.

6 William Prout (1785–1850: *DNB*), physician and pioneer physiological chemist.

7 *Emma*, ch. 12.

TO MACVEY NAPIER, 11 JUNE 1831

MS: British Museum. *Address:* Macvey Napier Esq / Castle Street / Edinburgh. *Frank:* London June eleven 1831 / T B Macaulay. *Published:* Napier, *Correspondence*, p. 112.

London June 11. 1831

My dear Napier,

I send off my article to day by the mail; and if you should send it back to me I shall not be offended; for it is wretchedly bad. I never wrote any thing so much against the grain in my life.

I do not wish the faults of the printer's devil to be added to mine, which are alone quite enough for one review. If you can let me have the sheets without real inconvenience, I should like to have them. If not, I commend the article to your particular and most careful revision. There are some Italian quotations which will require attention.[1]

Ever yours most truly

T B Macaulay

TO HANNAH MACAULAY, 13 JUNE 1831

MS: Trinity College. *Address:* Miss H M Macaulay.

London June 13. 1831

My dearest Girl,

I have nothing to tell you – nothing at all. For I suppose that you are not curious to hear about Poles and Russians, about the line to be taken by the opposition in the House of Peers, about the revolution in Brazil, or about Casimir Périer's circular to the French Prefects.[2] Brunswick Square news you will have from Margaret; and George will carry you in person full intelligence about Golden Square. Gray's Inn is as quiet as possible. – But I write, though I have nothing to say, that I may set you an example of writing to me when you have nothing to say. Indeed I altogether deny the validity of the excuse of "nothing to say" when pleaded by a lady. From a man it has a meaning. But the very boast, the very peculiarity of female correspondence, consists in the art of saying nothing prettily. Say it to me, dearest – and let me at least see "Dearest Tom" at the top of your letter – and "your affectionate Sister" at the end of it.

So you are very intimate with Miss Palmer[3] – and Fanny with

---

[1] TBM quotes Alfieri in 'Byron,' *ER*, LIII, 561–2.

[2] TBM is perhaps running his eye over the first two pages of *The Times*, 11 June, where all of these topics appear, including the text of Périer's circular.

[3] One of the sisters of Sir George Joseph Palmer, Bt, of Wanlip Hall, Leicestershire, near Rothley Temple; perhaps Louisa Catherine (b. 1803), the eldest.

Miss Elliott. I hope that your political principles will not be infected by Wanlip Toryism; and I hope above all that Fanny's morals will not receive any taint from the perjured family with which she is now on such good terms. – It would be a dreadful thing to have her in the pillory. Tell her that, though the punishment of the pillory is abolished in all other cases, it is still inflicted on people who forswear themselves. I saw an attorney mount last year. It was very disagreable; and would have been more so, if he had been pelted, as people in that situation generally are, with dead cats, rotten eggs, and trampled cabbage-stalks. Impress this on Fanny. Point out to her, from time to time, the pain which such an event befalling her would give to us all. Let your conversation with her turn much on this subject. I have requested Margaret to address her on it in writing.

My article on Lord Byron went off on Saturday. If Napier has the least sense, he will send it back to me, and refuse to take it. I dine at Philips's to day – at his father's on Thursday, at Rice's on Friday. To night Sarah Anne and Jane Babington are going to hear Paganini. The eloquence of the amateurs in the newspapers about the vagabond charms me beyond measure. "Sometimes he hugs his violin to his bosom, and seems to be lulling it there like a baby, – sometimes he lashes it like a man scourging a furious wild beast."[1] For my part I stick to the sentiment contained in an impromptu into which a judicious poet[2] of my acquaintance broke out at Goldsmidt's the other night.

> "The dull crowd that flocks
>   To an opera-box
> Had much better come to the Jewess's ball
>   For it costs a good guinea
>   To hear Paganini,
> And here are twelve fiddlers for nothing at all."

Sweet lines! – are they not. Farewell, dearest, dearest, girl.

Ever yours, my love,

T B M.

---

[1] 'You would take the violin to be a wild animal which he is endeavouring to quiet in his bosom, and which he occasionally, fiend-like, lashes with his bow' (*The Times*, 6 June). Paganini gave his second London recital on 10 June.

[2] TBM's own verses were 'invariably attributed to an anonymous author whom he styled "the Judicious Poet"' (Trevelyan, I, 133).

TO UNIDENTIFIED RECIPIENT, 13 JUNE 1831

MS: John Rylands Library.

Calne[1] June 13. 1831

Sir,

It was in February 1830 that I first took my seat in the House of Commons. / I have the honor to be, / Sir,

Your most obedient Servant

T B Macaulay

TO HANNAH MACAULAY, 14 JUNE 1831

MS: Trinity College. *Address:* Miss H M Macaulay / Post Office / Leamington / Warwick. *Frank:* London June fourteen 1831 / T B Macaulay.

London June 14. 1831 —

My dearest girl,

I have looked at the Morning Chronicle.[2] But I have not been able to procure a copy for you. The thing is set right; — and indeed it was never worth caring about. They spoke civilly of my father even while they considered him as responsible for the passage which they were reprobating. My father is in high favour with the liberals on account of his conduct at the London University. All the members of the Council whom I see tell me that they can do nothing without him, and that he was the most valuable of their members.[3]

I dined yesterday evening at Philips's — the son of Sir George, and member of Parliament for Steyning. Philips lives in Hill Street. Sir George must be a very rich man to keep up two such handsome town establishments. I should judge that he can hardly allow his son less than five thousand a year. The house is large, handsomely furnished, and fashionably situated, and the display of plate and of every other

---

[1] Thus in MS, but clearly an error: either TBM has misdated the letter, or, more likely, in thinking of Calne, has inadvertently written that for London.

[2] The *Morning Chronicle*, 10 June, printed a letter quoting an attack in the *Christian Observer* on the elevation to the peerage of William IV's illegitimate son Col. Fitzclarence; the letter states that '*The Christian Observer* is well known to be under the controul of Mr. M———, the father of the junior member for Calne.' To this the *Chronicle* adds, 'we are sure that the respected individual, under whose controul this publication is said to be, must have read this illiberal passage with the greatest regret.' On 11 June the *Chronicle* printed a notice stating that Zachary Macaulay has no control over the *Christian Observer*, that he has been ill in bed for several weeks, and has just lost his wife.

[3] Zachary Macaulay, one of the original members of the Council of the London University, remained in service until 1834, when he resigned on grounds of ill health (Zachary Macaulay to Thomas Coates, 6 January [1834]: MS, University College).

ornament quite equal to what I have seen at Sir George's own house in Mount Street.

Philips married a Miss Cavendish[1] – a sister of Lord Waterpark. The company consisted of Sir George and Lady P[hilips], Rice and Rice's wife and daughter, – Sydney Smith, – George Lamb,[2] – Tom Moore, – Whishaw or Wishaw,[3] – I forget how he spells his name, – and myself. Rice came looking as fine as if he had been going to a Jew's fancy ball. There was a great party and dancing at the Palace yesterday night – and all the official men were invited with their families. Rice had on his official dress – a superb brown coat covered with rich gold embroidery, looking something between an uniform and a livery. He told me that it cost at least a hundred pounds, and that some of his friends threatened that he would not have less than a hundred and twenty to pay for the coat alone. He had also a sword and a gorgeous cocked hat. George Lamb had to leave us early in order to attire himself in a similar fool's coat.

We had a pleasant evening. Moore was very silent, – Sydney very loud and George Lamb very diverting. I heard one good story. Lord Dudley[4] – I do not know whether you ever heard of his habit – has an inveterate trick of talking to himself. He cannot help doing it, – and it sometimes brings him into scrapes. Many people think that it is all affectation. But his friends say that he struggles against it and laments it. He was in a carriage with the late Chancellor[5] – when only Sir John Copley; and began to murmur in an audible tone. "Shall I ask Sir John to dinner? Hum – Ha – Hum. Shall I ask Sir John to dinner? Hey. Shall I ask Sir John to dinner? – No. I won't. Not to day." Sir John who was excessively diverted began to mutter in the other corner of the chariot. "Shall I dine with Dudley if he asks me? Hey. Shall I? No. I'll see him hanged first. No. Not to day." This recalled Lord Dudley to his recollection and half killed him with laughing.

We talked about prosecutions for blasphemy, – and about Taylor,[6] and

---

[1] Sarah Georgiana, eldest daughter of the second Baron Waterpark, married the younger Philips in 1819.

[2] George Lamb (1784–1834: *DNB*), Lord Melbourne's youngest brother, an early Edinburgh Reviewer; Whig M.P. and Under-Secretary of State for the Home Department in Grey's administration.

[3] John Whishaw (1764–1841), a barrister, Commissioner of Public Audit, 1806–35. Whishaw, called the 'Pope of Holland House,' was a friend of many of the high Whigs of his generation and active in such enterprises as the African Institution, the London University, and the SDUK.

[4] John William Ward (1781–1833: *DNB*), fourth Viscount and first Earl Dudley; M.P., 1802–23; Foreign Secretary under Canning; opposed the Reform Bill. He died insane.

[5] Lyndhurst.

[6] Robert Taylor (1784–1844: *DNB*), once a protégé of Simeon at Cambridge, deistic and anti-clerical writer. He had been imprisoned for blasphemy in 1828; in July he was brought to trial again and sentenced to two years' imprisonment.

Carlisle,[1] and the Rotunda. I was surprised at the way in which we divided on the matter. Sydney, Tom Moore, and Lamb, were for prosecution, – at least in extreme cases, – Rice and I against prosecuting in any case. I somewhat doubtingly – Rice quite warmly and decidedly.

We talked of statesmen and great parliamentary orators. They all agreed that Tierney was the clearest speaker that ever they heard. Fox, they said, was sometimes too refined in his arguments. "I have never heard," said Sir G[eorge], "any thing that reminded me of Fox in the House of Commons except now and then a burst of Whitbread's."[2] But none of the company would allow this. "I know," said George Lamb, "that people who dined at Whitbread's brew house used to butter him by telling him that he spoke like Fox. I dare say, Rice, when you eat beef-steaks at Buxton's brewery,[3] you tell him that he speaks like Fox." We talked about Percival.[4] Sydney described him with great cleverness and bitterness. "The most mischievous little man that ever lived, – just every thing that John Bull likes, – moral, and religious, with a wife and ten children, quiet and meek, with the heart of a lion, – and always in the wrong, – always flattering some rascally prejudice, always oppressing and humbugging and, – hang the fellow! – making oppression and humbug respectable by his decent character and his admirable demeanour, and his skill in debating." I believe this to be very near the truth. Sir Robert Inglis, I remember, once told me that England never had but one government quite after his own heart and that government was Mr. Percival's. My notion of Perceval is that he was Inglis with great talents for debate, – the same opinions both religious and political, – the same rectitude of principle, the same sweetness of temper, and the same bigotry and narrowness.

The day after to-morrow I dine at Sir G Philips's – on Friday at Rice's, and on Sunday *en famille* at Mackintosh's, to meet nobody but Empson and Malthus.

[1] Richard Carlile (1790–1843: *DNB*), publisher and journalist, the leading source of free-thinking and Radical literature in England. He and Taylor were associated, Taylor preaching at the Rotunda in Blackfriars Road which Carlile had leased as the place of meeting for his followers. Carlile, who had been imprisoned from 1819 to 1825, was sentenced in January 1831 to two years' imprisonment and heavy fines for seditious libel.

[2] Samuel Whitbread (1758–1815: *DNB*), son of the founder of Whitbread's brewery, was one of the leaders of the Whig opposition and an abolitionist. He was a frequent speaker in Parliament.

[3] Dining at a brewery seems to have been a fashion of the time. Zachary Macaulay speaks of going to eat at Buxton's brewery in 1822, and Lady Knutsford explains that 'the dinners given at the Brewery in Spitalfields consisted professedly of beef-steaks cooked in one of the furnaces' (Knutsford, *Zachary Macaulay*, p. 379). For Buxton, see 15 July 1831.

[4] Spencer Perceval (1762–1812: *DNB*), Prime Minister, 1809–12; assassinated by a man with an imaginary grievance against him. Perceval was an Evangelical, and had been attacked by Sydney Smith in the *Letters of Peter Plymley:* 'I fear he will ruin Ireland, and pursue a line of policy destructive to the true interest of his country: and then you tell me, he is faithful to Mrs. Perceval, and kind to the Master Percevals!' (Letter II).

Write to me, my love. I had a short note from you yesterday enclosed in a letter to Margaret the length of which made me quite envious. I shall be angry, not with you, but with my self, if I think that you cannot write to me with as much ease and freedom as to her. You never need want a subject. A book, a walk, a friend, a bore, – any th[ing or]¹ any body will do. Remember that [I have]¹ never been at Leamington. Write a Leamington guide for me with a fine description of scenery. Tell me what sort of Pump room there is, how the town is built – whether of brick or stone, to how many circulating libraries you subscribe, whether you ride on donkies – whether you have yet been to Warwick castle and how you liked it. I am more and more pleased by what I hear of Selina. Kindest love to her and Fanny. I enclose a paper for my father, which has just been sent to me by Margaret. George, I suppose, is in London again by this time.

Ever, my darling, yours
T B M

TO HANNAH MACAULAY, 17 JUNE 1831

MS: Trinity College. *Address:* Miss H M Macaulay / Post Office / Leamington / Warwick. *Frank:* London June seventeen 1831 / T B Macaulay.

London June 17. 1831

My love,

Ten thousand thanks for your letter. Write me many such. A few such sweet words in the morning as those which I have just been reading will be most acceptable after the bitter words which I shall soon have to hear for hours every night. The fury of the minority surpasses all description. And as to us – our blood is up, and we know our strength.

The day before yesterday I was sworn in – first by Bernal² who sate for the Lord Steward in the Long Gallery, and then at the table of the House. – Bernal is to be Chairman of the ways and means.

Yesterday I dined at Sir G Philips's. We had a very small party – Empson – Malthus – Smythe the Professor of Modern History at Cambridge – and myself. Whishaw was poorly and could not come. I do not know whether you are aware that Whishaw, Malthus, and Smythe form an inseparable trio. They are very old friends; and it is a sort of fashion to ask them together. Malthus is a very superior person to the other two. Smythe has been nicknamed Mrs. Whishaw; and I think the nickname

---

¹ Paper torn away with seal.
² Ralph Bernal (1785?–1854: *DNB*), Whig M.P. for various constituencies, 1818–52, and Chairman of Committees, 1830–50; a noted art collector. In politics he was a Reformer, but as a West India proprietor he opposed the abolition of slavery.

one of the happiest that ever was given. There is a most curious un-
likeness and likeness between the two friends. Both are Whigs. Yet both
are narrow-minded, timid, and servile in their submission to authority
beyond almost any Tories. Whishaw lives in London and sees much of
the world; Smythe at Cambridge and reads much. Whishaw is accordingly
governed by the last speaker and Smythe by the last book. A man so
blown about as Whishaw by every wind of doctrine I never knew. It is
a favourite diversion of Ellis and Malkin to put absurd opinions about
books into his mouth, and then to hear him deliver them as his own.
I sometimes hear him say one thing in the morning, and the direct reverse
in the afternoon. Then I know that he has been with some person who
disagreed with him in the interval. Smythe is not so much governed by
what he hears in company. His life is monastic, and his habits studious.
But he is under the tyranny of printed nonsense as Whishaw is under the
tyranny of spoken nonsense.

In manners they are both thorough old bachelors – Whishaw a bearish
old bachelor, Smythe a finical old bachelor. Malthus is a more agreable
as well as an abler man than either of them. Marriage has done him good.
You must take care that I do not become such a twaddle as Whishaw or
Smythe. Empson admires Whishaw – though I sometimes make him
laugh in spite of himself at his friend's oddities.

Well, – after dinner and coffee Empson and I walked to the Lord
Advocate's, and found him and Mrs. Jeffrey surrounded by a large circle –
all Malthus's family, and some other friends. There we staid gossiping
till twelve at night; and then I came away. Empson seemed still quite
fresh, and was so actively engaged in flirting with a golden-haired damsel
whose name I did not catch that I came off without him.

To night I dine at Rice's. I believe it is to be a parliamentary dinner.
Lord Althorpe is prevented, by Lady Spencer's death,[1] from entertaining
his colleagues. Lord Palmerston I suppose will take his place for a day
or two in the House of Commons.

I send you two more sheets of my History.[2] I do not know whether
any more will be printed at present. Kindest love to my father – to Selina
and to Fanny.

Ever yours dearest,
T B M

---

[1] Althorp's mother died on 8 June.
[2] *A View of the History of France*: on 16 April it had been advertised as 'forthcoming' in two
volumes (*Literary Gazette*, p. 256).

TO HANNAH MACAULAY, 20 JUNE 1831

MS: Trinity College. *Address:* Miss H M Macaulay / Post Office / Leamington / Warwick. *Frank:* London June twenty 1831 / T B Macaulay. *Extracts published:* Trevelyan, I, 223.

London June 20. 1831

My love,

I am very busy this morning. But I cannot let another day pass by without sending you a few lines. I received your last letter on Saturday. I was very glad to find that you and my father were pleased with the History. The passage to which you refer is incorrectly printed. It stood as you supposed, and I have corrected it in the proof-sheets.

I dined at Rice's on Friday evening, and at Mackintosh's yesterday. Ramohun Roy had promised Mackintosh to come in the evening. But after waiting for him till twelve o'clock I went away in despair. He seems by all that I can learn of him to be a very remarkable man. He is, it appears, less struck by our streets, our roads, our manufactories, our bridges, and our shops, – and more struck by our political and moral state, – than almost any foreigner that I have ever heard of. His religious notions are peculiar. He believes the Hindu and Christian religions to be at bottom the same – both pure Theism – in the Hindu religion disguised by a mythology which was at first only figurative, but which, being now literally understood by the multitude, is the source of all sorts of absurdities and crimes, – and in the Xtn religion also disguised, though not so completely, by the glosses of early fathers and councils. He says explicitly, Mackintosh tells me, that Christianity is a divine revelation, and that the mission of Christ was from God. But Mackintosh, who is well acquainted with the modes of thinking and expression in use among the Oriental philosophers, has some doubt about the sense in which Ramohun uses the words, and whether he means that Christ was instructed in divine truth by a direct communication of a supernatural kind from the Deity, – or merely that, like Socrates or Ramohun himself, Christ by the natural powers which God had bestowed on him, discovered those great truths which the Jews neglected for mere ceremonies. Ramohun says that he agrees more nearly with the Socinians than with any other sect – that he thinks Christianity as held by that sect, the most perfect development of the one great primitive religion. The morality of the New Testament he acknowledges to be superior to any that the most studious search can discover in the most ancient and purest records of the Hindu theology.

He says one singular thing. He says that he is firmly convinced that in twenty five years the *caste* will be no more – that there will not be a Brahmin in Hindustan who will not eat beef. He does not however eat

47

beef himself – solely from a sort of disgust like that which we feel to a food to which we are not used – snails or frogs for example.

The great topic now in London is not, as you may perhaps fancy, reform or the King's Speech – but cholera.[1] There is a great panic – as great a panic as I remember, – particularly in the city. Rice shakes his head and says that this is the most serious thing that has happened in his time; and assuredly if the disease were to rage in London as it has lately raged at Riga, it would be difficult to imagine any thing more horrible. I, however, feel no uneasiness. In the first place I have a strong leaning towards the doctrines of the anti-contagionists. In the next place I repose a great confidence in the excellent food and the cleanliness of the English. And Dr. Chambers,[2] I am glad to say, is quite of my mind. He says that the disease has hitherto been found only, out of the tropics at least, in countries where the people live wretchedly, and on the track of great armies which is the constant seat of pestilence. We know that in 1822 when a typhus of the most malignant kind and generally believed to be contagious was mowing down the starving Irish by thousands, and when, as Rice told me, one third of the whole population of Dublin passed in the course of one summer through the hospitals, we in England were perfectly secure, and that without any quarantine.

I enclose a letter for my father from my Uncle Colin. He seems by a few lines which I have received from him to be on the point of returning to London. I have this instant received [you]r[3] letter of yesterday with the enclosed [she]ets.[3] Your criticism is to a certain [extent?][3] just. – But you have not considered the whole sentence together. *Depressed* is in itself better than *weighed down*. But "the *oppressive* privileges which had *depressed* industry"[4] would be a horrible cacophony. I hope that hard word convinces you. I have often observed that a fine Greek compound is an excellent substitute for a reason.

I expect Napier and his new Number together by the Edinburgh Steam boat of this day.[5] I hope for his sake that there are under his blue and yellow cover some better articles than mine.

Kindest love to my father, Selina and Fanny. You say nothing in your letter of yesterday about Selina's health. Never forget to mention it.

Ever yours my love

T B M.

1 The disease had not yet reached England, but quarantine measures had already been taken against traffic from Russia and the Baltic ports.
2 William Frederick Chambers (1786–1855: *DNB*), the Macaulay family doctor, with George Babington on the staff of St George's Hospital. He was Physician in Ordinary to Queen Adelaide, William IV, and Victoria.
3 Paper torn away with seal.
4 This rejected line is apparently all that remains of TBM's *A View of the History of France*.
5 The June number of the *ER* was published on 21 June (*Literary Gazette*, 18 June, p. 400).

TO HANNAH MACAULAY, 22 JUNE 1831

MS: Trinity College. *Address:* Miss H M Macaulay / Post Office / Leamington / Warwick. *Frank:* London June twenty two: 1831 / T B Macaulay. *Extracts published:* Trevelyan, I, 224.

London June 22. 1831

My dearest Girl,

I thank you over and over again for your kind letter. You write longer letters, you say, because Margaret has left me. She is not going. But do not write shorter letters on that account. Much as I love her, do not think that she or any thing in the world, is dearer to me than you, my darling.

I took her yesterday to see the procession.[1] Jane Babington went with us. I could have done without your friend Jane. I have the highest opinion of her character – and I rate her understanding very high. But her prosing is insupportable. It is really a hard trial to me to be civil to her now and then. She comes out with Margaret and me – begins on some matter which neither of us care a straw about, – the way in which Mr. Danvers[2] uses his wife – or some strange peculiarity in the character of Mr. Thomas Pares,[3] and holds forth on it without a moment's intermission for a good hour. However I took her and Margaret yesterday to the balcony of the Athenæum, where a crowd of ladies had assembled. We saw the King return through St James's park in the midst of an innumerable multitude. The view was not very distinct, but was, I think, finer on that very account. A cloud of dust was raised by the trampling; and the trees in some degree obscured the procession. The whole had something of that hazy gorgeousness which characterises Turner's pictures. The long succession of State carriages, white horses, red liveries, heralds in coats of Cloth of Gold, life-guards with helmets and cuirasses, passed through a roaring ocean of heads and waving hats with a kind of dim magnificence which was quite delightful. When you come back to London I will take you and Selina and Fanny. For it is really a sight worth seeing.

We had in the evening a full house, and – as you will see by the papers – a warm debate[4] – but no amendment and no division. I thought it foolish to throw away my fire on an occasion on which we were all of one mind as to the question before us. When the reform bill comes on I shall speak – but probably not on Friday night.

[1] William IV opened the session of Parliament in person on 21 June.
[2] George John Danvers-Butler (b. 1794), of Swithland Hall, Leicestershire, near Rothley Temple. He was High Sheriff of Leicestershire in this year.
[3] A Leicestershire neighbor: see 1 June 1826.
[4] On the address in answer to the King's speech.

Napier and his Review are here at last. Napier looking very well – the Review looking very indifferent. Empson sticks to the theological line. There is an article of his on the miracles and prophecies of the Irvingites[1] written with great decency – but too prolix and languid – less figurative however than most of his compositions. He and Napier will not allow me to abuse my article on Byron. I suppose that you will have the Review on the table of the reading-rooms at Leamington. But, to make assurance sure, I will send it you to morrow by a government frank, if I can procure one to-night at the House.

To night I dine – en famille – with Ellis. On Friday morning I break-fast with Sam Rogers. 1 hope he will be pleased by the compliment – not an undeserved one – which I have paid to a passage in his Human Life. I met him yesterday at the Athenæum. He begged me to breakfast with him and to name my day, and promised that he would procure as agreable a party as he could find in London. Very kind of the old man – is it not? And if you knew how Rogers is thought of in the highest circles, you would think it as great a compliment as if it had been paid by a Duke. Have you seen what the author of the Young Duke says about me? – how rabid I am – and how certain I am to rat.[2] My dear Uncle stands up most (Come – you shall have another page though I meant to bring my letter within a single sheet) – My dear Uncle – as I was saying – stands up most stoutly against the imputation. "Rabid! dear me! dear me! – Tom is not rabid – I wonder what he means! He must be a very silly man. I am sure you are not rabid, my dear Tom." What an excellent old man he is. I cannot tell you how kind he has been in his expressions and demeanour towards me.

Love to my father, Selina, and Fanny. I am glad to hear that Selina places so much confidence in her Doctor. James Stephen all but worships him, and read me a lecture at the Athenæum yesterday of half an hour long – with folded hands, – head hung down – and eyes turned up – for being so wicked as to call the great man a QU*CK. I really do think it probable from what I hear both from you and from others that he may do Selina great good. –

[no signature]

---

[1] 'Pretended Miracles — Irving, Scott, and Erskine,' *ER*, LIII (June 1831), 261–305.

[2] 'I hear that Mr. Macaulay is to be returned. If he speaks half as well as he writes, the House will be in fashion again. I fear that he is one of those who, like the individual whom he has most studied, will "give up to party what was meant for mankind." At any rate he must get rid of his rabidity. He writes now on all subjects, as if he certainly intended to be a renegade, and was determined to make the contrast complete' (Book 5, ch. 6).

TO HANNAH MACAULAY, 24 JUNE 1831

MS: Trinity College. *Address:* Miss H M Macaulay / Post Office / Leamington / Warwick. *Frank:* London June twenty four 1831 / T B Macaulay. *Mostly published:* Gordon S. Haight, ed., *The Portable Victorian Reader*, New York, 1972, pp. 3–6.

London June 24. 1831

My love,

I am to breakfast with Rogers this morning; and here I am in my dressing gown writing to you at seven o'clock – which we Members of Parliament call the Middle of the night – because I shall be so busy all the day that, if I do not write now, you have no chance of a letter. And I have such a subject! – such a noble subject! – If Margaret gave you a hint of it yesterday evening, I never will forgive her. It would be like telling the catastrophe of a novel, just at the moment when the Hero and Heroine have been parted – never – as it should seem – to meet again. Suppose that I had told you that Lord St Orville was Lady Stora-mont[1] – or that Frank Yates was Lord Caerleon[2] – before the proper time – would you ever have forgiven me? –

This morning,[3] as I was sitting at breakfast in my dressing-gown – the Times before me – sipping a full bason of tea and eating between whiles of a well-baked loaf, the accompanying note was delivered at my door. Read here enclosure marked A, as the Diplomatists say. I send it, because I love accuracy; and because I wish to teach you to love it. File this note – (it is from Lord Althorp) with your papers. A hundred years hence people will give ten pounds for it. It will then be a relique of famous times.

Well, – having received this note, I was not disobedient to the summons. I attired myself in my drawing-room dress; – and at half after twelve was in the house of Commons. We mustered, gradually, about a hundred and eighty members – all of us ministerial. There were a few court-dresses – many official uniforms; – and some members in the uniforms of the regular army or of the local militia. There were many in boots. But the majority were dressed, like me, as for an evening party. Admire, I pray you, for a moment the tact which I showed, in dressing myself quite comme-il-faut, without the least instruction. Burdett,[4] who

---

[1] In Catherine Cuthbertson, *Santo Sebastiano, or the Young Protector*, 5 vols., 1806. Another of TBM's favorite bad books, a copy of the third edn, 1814, is in the collection at Walling-ton; it contains the list of fainting fits occurring in the novel printed (not quite accurately) in Trevelyan, 1, 132.

[2] From one of Mrs Meeke's novels?

[3] Clearly a slip for yesterday morning.

[4] Sir Francis Burdett (1770–1844: *DNB*), M.P. since 1796 and for Westminster since 1807; a champion of Reform, though he became a Tory in his last years.

never went up with an address before in his life, was in full court dress. So was Sir Richard Price[1] and Bernal. Admire, again, I beseech you, these little touches of narrative. Lord Althorpe came in court mourning – Rice – Stanley[2] – Graham – Tennyson[3] – Howick,[4] Baring and Macdonald – were blazing with gold lace and white satin. We nicknamed my late colleague Marshal Macdonald.[5]

In came Mr. Speaker with a gown flowered with gold and a long lace ruff. We had prayers; and then Lord Althorpe moved that we should adjourn till four, and go to the King with our address. The motion was, of course, carried, and we set forth in a train of carriages which reached from Westminster Hall to the Horse Guards, if you know – which I much doubt – where those two places are. Shiel gave me a place in his carriage together with Mr. Perrin[6] and Sir Robert Harty[7] the successful candidates for Dublin at the late election. We went on at a foot's pace, – the Speaker preceding us in a huge old-fashioned, painted, gilded, coach, drawn by two immense black horses. The Serjeant, with the mace, and the Chaplain, went in the Speaker's coach.

At half after one we reached St James's Palace. The coaches set down their inmates, one by one, and we were among the last. In we went – and I was in the inside of a real King's Palace for the first time in my life.

I have seen finer houses. We passed first through a long matted passage with wooden benches, bearing the royal arms, set on both sides. Beef-eaters with their red coats and gold lace stood here and there; and now and then we met a magnificent looking person in a blue suit loaded with dazzling embroidery. At the end of this matted passage was a staircase of stone – not by any means very fine – I have seen finer at several country-seats, and those at the London Club houses beat it all to nothing. Up this staircase we went and were ushered by two tall yeomen of the guard into a large antiroom. – A few fine pictures hung round the walls. I caught

---

[1] TBM probably means Sir Robert Price (1786–1857: *Boase*), Whig M.P. for Herefordshire, 1818–41; 1845–57.

[2] Edward George Stanley (1799–1869: *DNB*), afterwards fourteenth Earl of Derby, was Whig M.P. for Windsor and Irish Secretary in 1831; joined the Tories, 1835; Prime Minister, 1852; 1858–9; 1866–8.

[3] Charles Tennyson, later Tennyson-d'Eyncourt (1784–1861: *Boase*), Whig M.P., 1818–52; uncle of Lord Tennyson.

[4] Henry George Grey (1802–94: *DNB*), Viscount Howick and afterwards third Earl Grey, was at Trinity with TBM and in the London Debating Society with him in 1826; entered Parliament in 1826, where he was an active reformer and abolitionist; Under-Secretary for the Colonies in his father's administration; Secretary-at-War, 1835–9, when TBM succeeded him; Colonial Secretary, 1846–52, under Palmerston.

[5] After the Marshal of France, Jacques Alexandre Macdonald (1765–1840).

[6] Louis Perrin (1782–1864: *DNB*), barrister; Whig M.P., 1831–5.

[7] Sir Robert Harty (1779–1832), first Baronet; Lord Mayor of Dublin, 1830–1.

a glimpse of one of Vandyke's Henrietta-Marias as we passed through. The room was however comfortless. The only furniture consisted of two or three large scarlet benches. The floor was covered with red cloth which looked as if his Majesty was in the habit of riding over it with the whole Royal Hunt. From this Anti-room we passed into a reception room – smaller than the Anti-room – but still of noble size – with pictures round the walls and a general air of great magnificence in the furniture. We had scarcely assembled here when a large pair of folding-doors at the further end was thrown open, and we advanced, pushing as hard as we could without making a disturbance; – and thus we squeezed ourselves into the presence-chamber. – The room is handsome – the walls and cieling covered with gilding and scarlet hangings. – On the walls is a picture of the battle of Vittoria – another of the battle of Waterloo – a full-length of George IV by Lawrence – and two or three older pictures which I could not examine on account of the crowd. Fronting us was the throne under a gorgeous canopy. We marched up to it between two rows of officers, in scarlet and gold, bearing halberts. His Majesty was seated in all his glory – wearing an admiral's uniform. Lord Wellesley[1] – in a state of fine preservation looking as if he had just been taken out of a band box – held the white staff at the King's elbow. What a sublime dandy that Marquess Wellesley is! I could see little of the other attendants of the King – by reason of the crowd. The Speaker read our address. The King bowed at the end of every sentence and at all the peculiarly emphatic words. When the Speaker had done the King turned to one of the Lords in waiting who handed him a paper containing what he was to say in answer to us. Another presented a pair of spectacles. His majesty placed them on his royal nose – read a short answer which you will see in the paper – and bowed us out. The Speaker stept forward and kissed the Sacred hand of our Gracious Sovereign. Then came the worst part of the show. For we had to walk out backwards – bowing all the way down the presence chamber. You may conceive how two hundred people cooped pretty close in a room performed this ceremony. We came out with broken shins and broken toes in abundance – vowing – many of us – that we would never do Ko-tou[2] more.

I went only because I wanted to find something to tell you – and if you like to hear about these fine doings, I am satisfied. Kindest love to my father – Selina – and Fanny. Fanny sends me some very kind lines

---

[1] Richard Colley Wellesley (1760–1842: *DNB*), Marquess Wellesley, the Duke of Wellington's older brother; Governor-General of India, 1797–1805; Foreign Secretary, 1809–12; Lord Lieutenant of Ireland, 1821–8; 1833–4. He was Lord Steward of the Household at this time. 'In late life he used to wear his garter, star and ribbon over his dressing gown' (GEC, *Complete Peerage*).

[2] The *OED* cites an example of the word in this spelling from 1817.

now and then. I do not answer them particularly only because I know that she sees all that I write to you. Selina will, I hope, soon be brought by Dr. Jephson into condition to be an equally good correspondent.

Ever yours, dearest,

T B M.

TO HANNAH MACAULAY, 25 JUNE 1831

MS: Trinity College. *Address:* Miss H M Macaulay / Post Office / Leamington / Warwick. *Frank:* London June twenty five 1831 / T B Macaulay. *Mostly published:* Trevelyan, 1, 224–6.

London June 25. 1831

My love,

There was, as you will see, no debate in the House of Commons on Lord J Russell's motion.[1] The bill is to be brought in, read once, and printed, without discussion. The contest will be on the second reading, and will be protracted, I should think, through the whole of the week after next. Next week it will be when you read this letter.

I breakfasted with Rogers yesterday. There was nobody there but Moore. We were all on the most friendly and familiar terms possible; and Moore, who is, Rogers tells me, excessively pleased with my review of his book, shewed me very marked attention. I was forced to go away early on account of bankrupt business. But Rogers said that we must have the talk out. So we are to meet at his house again to breakfast. What a delightful house it is. It looks out on the Green Park just at the most pleasant point. The furniture has been selected with a delicacy of taste quite unique. Its value does not depend on fashion; but must be the same while the fine arts are held in any esteem. In the drawing room for example the chimney pieces are carved by Flaxman[2] into the most beautiful Grecian forms. The book case is painted by Stothard in his very best manner with groups from Chaucer, Shakespear and Boccacio. The pictures are not numerous; but every one is excellent. In the dining-room there are also some beautiful paintings. But the three most remarkable objects in that room are, I think, a cast of Pope taken after death by Roubiliac[3] – quite unique, I believe, – a noble model in terra-cotta by Michael Angelo from which he afterwards made one of his finest statues – that of Lorenzo dei Medici – and lastly a mahogany table on which stands an antique vase. I may

[1] For leave to bring in the second Reform Bill, 24 June.

[2] John Flaxman (1755–1826: *DNB*), sculptor; Rogers was a particular admirer of his work and that of Stothard among English artists.

[3] A terra-cotta bust (1738?) by Louis François Roubiliac (1705?–62: *DNB*); TBM is mistaken in thinking it a cast taken after death. See W. K. Wimsatt, *The Portraits of Alexander Pope*, New Haven, 1965, p. 232, and pp. 230–1, where the bust is reproduced.

possibly have told you the story of this mahogany table – as I heard it when I first visited Rogers. But, as Margaret had never heard it or had forgotten it, you may perhaps be in the same case.

When Chantrey[1] dined with Rogers some time ago he took particular notice of the vase and the table on which it stands; and asked Rogers who made the table. "A common carpenter," said Rogers. "Do you remember the making of it?" said Chantrey. "Certainly" said Rogers, in some surprise. "I was in the room while it was finished with the chisel and gave the workman directions about placing it." "Yes," said Chantrey, "I was the carpenter. I remember the room well and all the circumstances." A curious story, I think, and hono[urable][2] both to the talent which raised Chantrey from so low a situation and to the magnanimity which kept him from being ashamed of what he had been.[3]

Rogers gave us a very good breakfast and a dessert of strawberries and cream. We talked about politics, poetry, and great men – the Duke of Wellington and the late King. At twelve I went off to bankruptcy business. In the afternoon, expecting a debate of twelve hours, I dined early at the Athenæum with Lord Nugent,[4] who is full of a life of Hampden which he is bringing out and promises me a copy. We went down to the House and heard what you will read in the papers. – I am shocked to find that I have sent a letter exceeding my ounce. I will take more care in future. Kindest love to my father, Selina and Fanny. / Ever yours affectionately

My darling

T B M

I cannot I am afraid procure an office frank to day or I would send the Edinburgh Review.

---

[1] Sir Francis Chantrey (1781–1842: *DNB*), sculptor.

[2] Paper torn away with seal.

[3] According to Daniel Weeks, 'Samuel Rogers: Man of Taste,' *PMLA*, 62 (1947), 474, this story about Chantrey, 'if its frequent appearance in print is any indication...must have been one of the most repeated anecdotes of the nineteenth century.' Weeks's article is a useful summary description of Rogers's house and collection.

[4] George Nugent Grenville (1788–1850: *DNB*), Baron Nugent, Whig M.P. since 1812 and an active abolitionist. For his book on Hampden, see 1 November 1831.

TO HANNAH MACAULAY, 29 JUNE 1831

MS: Trinity College. *Address:* Miss H M Macaulay / Post Office / Leamington / Warwick. *Frank:* London June twenty nine 1831 / T B Macaulay. *Mostly published:* Trevelyan, I, 226–8.

London June 29. 1831

My love,

It will be a week to morrow since I have received a line from Leamington, except letters for other people, of which I have had abundance. This is my fourth letter since I heard from you. I am afraid that I make my correspondence cheap by its plenty.

We are not yet in the full tide of parliamentary business. Next week the debates will be warm and long. I should not wonder if we had a discussion of five nights. I shall probably take a part in it.

I have dined at Rolfe's[1] since I wrote to you, – at least since I wrote a long letter. The Lord Advocate was there, and very agreable he was. I never heard him talk so well. His conversation is not so witty as Sydney's – but has more eloquence and sentiment, without effort, than that of any person that I know. He once or twice shocked Evans[2] by strong expressions. On the whole however all the company was delighted with him. His daughter, who is out, looked very pretty, and Empson flirted with her most assiduously.[3] –

I have also breakfasted again with Rogers. The party was a remarkable one – Lord John Russell – Tom Moore – Tom Campbell[4] – and Luttrell. We were all very lively, and I thought all the party – Campbell excepted – very agreable. I never saw manners so offensive as that man's. He and Tom Moore, it seems, have made up their quarrel about Lord and Lady Byron.[5]

An odd incident took place after breakfast, while we were standing at the window and looking into the Green Park. Somebody was talking about diners-out. "Aye" said Campbell –

"Ye diners-out from whom we guard our spoons."

Tom Moore asked where the line was. "Don't you know?" said Campbell. "Not I," said Moore. "Surely" said Campbell, "it is your own." "I never saw it in my life," said Moore. "It is in one of your best things in the Times," said Campbell. Moore denied it. Hereupon I put in my claim

---

[1] Robert Rolfe (1790–1868: *DNB*), a graduate of Trinity and a barrister; Baron of the Exchequer, 1839; created Baron Cranworth, 1850; Lord Chancellor, 1852–8; 1865–6.
[2] Probably William Evans: see 4 August 1824.
[3] Empson married Charlotte Jeffrey, 1838.
[4] Thomas Campbell (1777–1844: *DNB*), the poet.
[5] Campbell had taken Lady Byron's side in her objections to Moore's *Life*: see *New Monthly Magazine*, XXVIII (1830), 377–82.

and told them that it was mine. Do you remember it? It is in some lines
called the Political Georgics which I sent to the Times about three years
ago.[1] – They made me repeat the lines, and were vociferous in praise of
them. Tom Moore then said, oddly enough – " There is another poem in
the Times that I should like to know the author of – a Parson's account
of his journey to the Cambridge election." I laid claim to that also.[2] " That
is curious," said Moore. "1 begged Barnes[3] to tell me who wrote it. He
said that he had received it from Cambridge and touched it up himself,
and pretended that all the best strokes were his. I believed that he was
lying – because I never knew him make a good joke in his life. And now
the murder is out." See how a lye is discovered after a long lapse of time.
It is more than four years since the Journey to Cambridge was written.
They asked me whether I had put any thing else in the Times. I told them
nothing except the Sortes Virgilianæ,[4] which Lord John remembered well.
I never mentioned the Cambridge Journey or the Georgics to any but my
own family. And I was therefore as you may conceive not a little flattered
to hear in one day Moore praising one of them and Campbell praising the
other.[5]

I find that my article on Byron is very popular – one among a thousand
proofs of the bad taste of the public. I am to review Croker's edition of
Bozzy. It is wretchedly ill done. The notes are poorly written and shamefully inaccurate. There is however much curious information in it. The
whole of the Tour to the Hebrides is incorporated with the Life. So are
most of Mrs. Thrale's anecdotes, and much of Sir John Hawkins's
lumbering book. The whole makes five large volumes.[6] There is a most
laughable sketch of Bozzy taken by Sir T Lawrence when young.[7] I never
saw a character so thoroughly hit off. I intend the book for you when I have
finished my criticism on it. You are, – next to myself – the best read
Boswellite that I know.

The lady whom Johnson abused for flattering him was certainly,
according to Croker, Hannah More.[8] Another ill-natured sentence about

---

[1] *The Times*, 18 March 1828, signed 'Malcolm Macgregor, jun.' in allusion to the satirical
poems of William Mason.
[2] 'The Country Clergyman': see 3 August 1827.
[3] Thomas Barnes (1785–1841 : *DNB*), editor of *The Times*, 1817–41.
[4] *The Times*, 17 April 1827; this was attributed to Moore at the time (*The Times*, 18 April
1827).
[5] Moore reports substantially the same conversation in his diary and adds that 'Macaulay
gave us an account of the state of the *Monothelite* controversy, as revived at present among
some of the fanatics of the day' (*Memoirs, Journal, and Correspondence of Thomas Moore*,
ed. Lord John Russell, Boston, Mass., VI [1853], 213).
[6] In the first edition, but not afterwards, the accounts of Mrs Thrale, Hawkins, and others
were interpolated in Boswell's narrative, making a pastiche.
[7] The frontispiece to vol. 4.
[8] Croker, IV, 152, and V, 255, is able to identify Hannah More as the flatterer from the
Malone MS.

a Bath lady whom Johnson called "empty-headed" is also applied to your godmother.[1]

Kindest love to my father, Selina, and Fanny.

Ever yours my darling

T B M.

TO HANNAH MACAULAY, 30 JUNE 1831

MS: Trinity College. *Address:* Miss H M Macaulay / Post Office / Leamington / Warwick. *Frank:* London June thirty 1831 / T B Macaulay.

London June 30. 1831

My love,

I am delighted to learn that you and my father like my article on the whole. There are several misprints – but none, I think, which an intelligent reader will find much difficulty in rectifying. I enclose a letter for your maid servant. It is from a brother of hers, I believe.

Lady Holland has written to ask me to dinner on Saturday. I was forced to excuse myself, as I am to dine on that day with the Attorne[y][2] General.[3] I called on Napier the day bef[ore][2] yesterday. While we were talking Professor Leslie[4] came in – a man whom I had long wished to see. I saw enough of him to last me my life. A second shewed him to have the coarsest, ugliest, and most corpulent of human bodies – and ten minutes shewed him to have one of the most ill-natured of human minds. He abused every eminent name in science; Babbage,[5] Herschel, in short all his rivals. The Lord Advocate had told me something of this: but I did not believe that it had been half so bad.

Lieutenant Gordon[6] has begun to harangue us; and promises to be a bore of the first order. The influenza which prevails at present in London is severely aggravated among members of the house by his oratory.

I must stop. I have little to say, and little time to say that little. Write to me many such sweet letters as your last – my love. Kindest love to my father, Selina, and Fanny.

Ever yours, dearest,

T B M

[1] Croker says only that 'this has been supposed to be Miss Hannah More; yet it seems hard to conceive in what wayward fancy he could call her "*empty-headed*"' (III, 413). According to Boswell's Journal the lady was in fact a Miss Owen (Boswell, *Life of Johnson*, ed. Hill and Powell, III, 48).   [2] Paper torn away with seal.   [3] Denman.

[4] (Sir) John Leslie (1766–1832: *DNB*), Professor of Mathematics, and then of Natural Philosophy, Edinburgh, 1805–32; contributed to the *ER* and to the *Encyclopaedia Britannica*. Scott called him 'as abominable an animal as ever I saw' (Edgar Johnson, *Sir Walter Scott*, New York, 1970, I, 309).

[5] Charles Babbage (1792–1871: *DNB*), scientist and mathematician, now remembered especially for his pioneering work on calculating machines.

[6] Captain William Gordon (1784–1858), the second son of the third Earl of Aberdeen; eventually promoted Vice-Admiral; Tory M.P., Aberdeenshire, 1820–54.

TO HANNAH MACAULAY, 1 JULY 1831

MS: Trinity College. *Address:* Miss H M Macaulay / Post Office / Leamington / Warwick. *Frank:* London July one 1831 / T B Macaulay.

London July 1 1831

My darling,

I am quite angry with myself for having written any thing that could vex you – and the more so because I never receive from you a line which does not give me pleasure. I have little to tell you. I am at the House every evening, and reading and writing in Chambers every morning. The political business in which everybody is engaged has interrupted the succession of parties – and Saturday and Sunday are the only days on which anybody dines out. I am engaged at Lansdown House on Sunday.

Sharp has asked me to go down on Saturdays with him to the country[1] and to come back on Mondays. I shall probably take some opportunity of accepting his invitation.

Croker's book is more and more offensive to me the more and more I read of it. It contains however one or two good stories – one excellent about Goldsmith. Burke was going to the Club with Langton and saw Goldsmith standing in the midst of a crowd in Leicester Square. The crowd was staring at some French ladies who, dressed in the fullest splendour of the Parisian fashion of that time, were seated in the window of a Hotel. Burke told Langton to say nothing, and on they went to the club. – When Goldy arrived Burke looked very coldly on him and declined to shake hands with him. Poor Goldy was in great agitation, and begged to know how he had been so unfortunate as to offend one whom he respected so highly. "Really, Dr. Goldsmith" said Burke, "it is impossible for me to keep company with a person so indiscreet – with a person who exposes himself so strangely as you do." "Why, bless me" cried Goldy, – "what have I done." "Why" said Burke, "you were standing in Leicester square as Langton and I came by, and we heard you say 'How can the people be such fools as to stare at those painted Jezebels in the window, instead of looking at a great author like me?'" – "Did I say so" – cried poor Goldy. "If you had not said so," answered Burke, "how could I have known any thing about it?" – "Well" said Goldsmith, "I am shocked. I did not know that I had said it aloud. It was in my mind to be sure. I will take more care another time."[2]

My literary vanity is not so sensitive as Goldsmith's: for I most readily subscribe to the justice of your criticisms on my article about Byron. The

[1] Sharp had a cottage near Dorking.

[2] In Croker's version of the anecdote, which he had from a Colonel O'Moore, Burke and O'Moore (not Langton) are on their way to dine with Reynolds; the ladies are merely 'some foreign women' (Croker's *Boswell*, ch. 15: 1, 423).

remarks on his poetry are feeble and imperfect; and the conclusion is huddled up. I never wrote any thing so much against the grain. The Political Georgics about which you enquire owe two thirds of their wit to the imitation of Virgil. I will transcribe the lines for you, as nearly as I can remember them.[1] They were written soon after the Duke of Wellington became prime minister.

> "How cabinets are formed and how destroyed,
> How Tories are confirmed and Whigs decoyed,
> How in nice times a prudent man should vote,
> At what conjuncture he should turn his coat,
> The truths fallacious, and the candid lies,
> And all the lore of sleek majorities,
> I sing, great Premier. Oh mysterious two,
> Lords of our fate, the *Doctor and the *Jew,
> If by your care preferred th'aspiring †clerk
> Quits the close alley for the breezy park,
> And mutton-chops and Reid's Entire resigns
> For odorous fricassees and costly wines,
> And you, great pair, through Windsor's shades who rove,
> The Faun and Dryad of the conscious grove,
> All, all, inspire me; – for of all I sing
> Doctor and Jew and Marchioness[2] and King.
>   Thou to the maudlin Muse of Rydal[3] dear,
> Thou more than Neptune, Lowther,[4] lend thine ear.
> When Neptune spake, the horse with flowing mane
> And pawing hoof, sprang from th'obedient plain.
> But at thy voice the yawning earth in fright
> Ingulphed the victor steed from mortal sight.

* Knighton[5] Rothschild[6] [TBM's note].
† Herries [TBM's note].

[1] There are many variations in detail between this text and that printed in *The Times*.
[2] The Marchioness Conygham (1769?–1861: *DNB*), George IV's mistress.
[3] Wordsworth lived at Rydal Mount from 1813.
[4] TBM appears to have confused two Lowthers: William Lowther (1757–1844: *DNB*), first Earl of Lonsdale of the second creation, was Wordsworth's patron, to whom *The Excursion* was dedicated. His son William, afterwards the second Earl, was Tory M.P. from 1808 and Chief Commissioner of Woods and Forests in Wellington's ministry. The Lowthers owned extensive coal mines, and the allusion to the 'yawning earth' may be to some accident in one of them.
[5] Sir William Knighton (1776–1836: *DNB*) had been one of George IV's physicians, and, from 1822, was Keeper of the Privy Purse. He was an object of special hostility to the enemies of the King.
[6] Nathan Meyer Rothschild (1777–1836: *DNB*), the founder of the English house of Rothschild. Wellington consulted him on financial affairs.

Haste from thy woods, mine *Arbuthnot,[1] with speed,
Rich woods, where lean Scotch cattle love to feed,[2]
Ye veteran Swiss of senatorial wars,
Who glory in your well-earned sticks and stars,
Ye diners-out from whom we guard our spoons,
Ye smug defaulters – ye obscene buffoons,
Come all of every shape and size and form,
Corruption's children, – brethren of the worm –
From those gigantic monsters who devour
The pay of half a squadron in an hour
To those foul reptiles doomed to want and scorn
Of filth and stench equivocally born –
From royal tigers down to toads and lice,
From Clintons,[3] Bathursts,[4] Fanes,[5] to Hook and Price.[6]
Thou last, by nature and by habit blest
With every art that suits a Courtier best,
The lapdog spittle, – the hyæna bile, –
The maw of shark, – the tear of Crocodile –
Whate'er high station, undetermined yet,
Awaits thee in the longing cabinet,
Whether thou seat thee in the room of Peel,
Or from Lord Prig[7] extort the privy seal,
Or our field-marshal treasurer fix on thee,
A legal admiral, to rule the sea,
Or Chancery suits beneath thy well known reign
Turn to their nap of fifty years again, –
(Already Lyndhurst, prescient of his fate,
Yields half his woolsack to thy mightier weight)

---

* Commissioner of Woods and forests at that time. [TBM's note].

[1] Charles Arbuthnot (1767–1850: *DNB*), Commissioner of Woods and Forests, 1823–7, and for a short time in 1828. Arbuthnot and his wife lived with the Duke of Wellington.
[2] Six lines appearing in *The Times* text are omitted here:

> Let Gaffer Gooch and Boodle's patriot band,
> Fat from the leanness of a plundered land,
> True Cincinnati, quit their patent ploughs,
> Their new steam-harrows, and their premium sows;
> Let all in bulky majesty appear,
> Roll the dull eye, and yawn th'unmeaning cheer.

[3] Sir William Henry Clinton (1769–1846: *DNB*), general and Tory M.P.; Lieutenant General of the Ordnance in Wellington's ministry.
[4] Henry Bathurst (1762–1834: *DNB*), third Earl Bathurst, Lord President of the Council under Wellington.   [5] Lieutenant General Sir Henry Fane: see 8 September 1835.
[6] Perhaps Richard Price (1773?–1861), Tory M.P. for Radnor continuously from 1796; he was 'father' of the House of Commons by the time of his retirement in 1847.
[7] Lord Ellenborough was Lord Privy Seal, January 1828 – June 1829.

Oh Eldon,[1] in whatever sphere thou shine,
For opposition sure will ne'er be thine,
Though scowls apart the lonely pride of Grey,
Though Devonshire[2] flings his gilded staff away,
Though Lansdowne trampling on the broken chain
Shines forth the Lansdowne of our hearts again,
Assist me thou; – for, well I deem, I see
An abstract of mine ample theme in thee.
Thou, as thy glorious self has justly said,
From earliest youth wast pettifogger bred,
And raised to power by fortune's fickle will
Art, head and heart, a pettifogger still.
So where once Fleet-Ditch ran confessed, we view
A crowded mart and stately avenue; –
But the black stream beneath runs on the same
Still brawls in Wetherell's key, still stinks like Herries name."

If you will look at the beginning of Dryden's Georgics or of any other translation you will see something of the parody. Kindest love to my father, Selina, and Fanny. I write in the midst of noise from Basinghall Street.

Yours ever, darling,

T B M

TO HANNAH MACAULAY, 6 JULY 1831

MS: Trinity College. *Address:* Miss H M Macaulay / Post Office / Leamington / Warwick. *Frank:* London July six 1831 / T B Macaulay. *Published:* Clive and Pinney, *Selected Writings of Macaulay*, pp. 430–1.

London July 6. 1831

My love,

I have been so busy during the last two or three days that I have found no time to write to you. I have now good news for you. I spoke yesterday night[3] with a success beyond my utmost expectations. I am half ashamed to tell you the compliments which I have received. But you well know that it is not from vanity, but to give you pleasure, that I tell you what is said about me. Lord Althorpe told me twice that it was the best speech he had ever heard. Graham and Stanley and Lord John Russell spoke of it

---

[1] Eldon was excluded from Wellington's ministry.

[2] The sixth Duke (1790–1858: *DNB*), Lord Chamberlain of the Household, 1827–8.

[3] The second of TBM's speeches on the Reform Bill: *Hansard*, 3rd Series, IV, 773–83. Margaret Macaulay says of this speech that TBM 'is going to correct it for the Mirror of Parliament' (to Frances Macaulay, 6 July 1831: MS, Huntington). See, however, to Selina Macaulay, 13 July.

in the same way. Grahame told me that I had surpassed myself out and out. Robert Grant said that he liked this speech far better than my speech of last Parliament. O'Connell[1] followed me out of the house to pay me the most enthusiastic compliments, and old John Smith[2] cried as he talked to me. But what flattered me most was to come on a knot of old members whom I did not know, and who did not see me, who were disputing whether Plunket[3] or I were the better speaker. I delivered my speech much more slowly than any that I had before made – and it is in consequence better reported than its predecessors – though not well. I send you several papers. You will see some civil things in the leading articles of some of them.[4] My greatest pleasure in the midst of all this praise is to think of the pleasure which my success will give to my father and my sisters. It is happy for me that ambition – the fiercest and most devouring of all passions – has in my mind been softened into a kind of domestic feeling – and that affection has at least as much to do as vanity with my wish to distinguish myself. This I owe to my dear mother and to the interest which she always took in my childish successes. From my earliest years the gratification of those whom I love has been associated with the gratification of my own thirst of fame, until the two have become inseparably joined in my mind.

Do not, – my love, – but of course you will not – shew this letter to anybody but my father and sisters, or talk to any body else about the compliments which I repeat to you. I should appear ridiculously conceited to people who do not understand the feeling which induces me to repeat them. Kindest love to my father, Selina, and Fanny.

Ever yours my darling
T B M

---

[1] Daniel O'Connell (1775–1847: *DNB*), 'the Liberator,' the leader of the Catholic interest in Ireland and in Parliament.

[2] John Smith (1767–1842), M.P. for Buckinghamshire; father of John Smith, M.P. for Chichester, and therefore 'old John Smith.' Smith, a banker, after offering £20,000 to Zachary Macaulay when Macaulay and Babington were in peril during the panic of 1825, then gave £22,000 (Zachary Macaulay to James Stephen, 7 May 1831: MS, Huntington).

[3] William Conygham Plunket (1764–1854: *DNB*), first Baron Plunket, for many years the champion in Parliament of Catholic relief; Lord Chancellor of Ireland, 1830–41. Margaret Macaulay's letter to Fanny, 6 July, says that she and TBM met Plunket that day.

[4] E.g., 'Mr Macauley delivered last night the best speech which has yet been made on the question of Reform, and the effect it produced on the House was very great' (*Morning Chronicle*, 6 July).

TO HANNAH MACAULAY, 8 JULY 1831

MS: Trinity College. *Address:* Miss H M Macaulay / Rothley Temple / Mountsorrel / Leicestershire. *Frank:* London July eight 1831 / T B Macaulay. *Published:* Clive and Pinney, *Selected Writings of Macaulay*, pp. 431–3.

London July 8 1831

My love,

I have not been for some days so active a correspondent as usual, owing to the pressure of parliamentary business. I ought scarcely, you will say, to make this an excuse. For I am now writing at Basinghall Street, in the middle of attorneys, bankrupts, and false witnesses.

So you want to hear all the compliments that are paid to me. I shall never end, if I stuff my letters with them. For I meet nobody who does not give me joy. Baring tells me that I ought never to speak again. The newspapers are still filled with compliments. The Herald of yesterday, in particular, contained a very flattering article.[1] Howick sent a note to me yesterday to say that his father wished very much to be introduced to me, and asked me to dine with them yesterday – as, by great good luck, there was nothing to do in the house of Commons. At seven I went to Downing Street where Earl Grey's official residence stands. It is a noble house. There are two splendid drawing-rooms which overlook St James's Park. Into these I was shewn. The servant told me that Lord Grey was still at the House of Lords; and that her Ladyship[2] had just gone to dress. Howick had not mentioned the hour in his note. I sate down, and turned over two large portfolios of political caricatures. Earl Grey's own face was in every print. I was very much diverted. I had seen some of them before. But many were new to me, and their merit is extraordinary. They were the caricatures of that remarkably able artist who calls him-self H B.[3]

1 'We call the attention of our readers to the speech of Mr. Macaulay on Tuesday night, as being an effort worthy of the very best days of the House of Commons' (*Morning Herald*, 7 July).
2 Mary Elizabeth Ponsonby (1776–1861), married Lord Grey in 1794.
3 John Doyle (1797–1868: *DNB*), political cartoonist; by signing himself 'H.B.' kept his identity generally unknown. In numbers 296 (1834), 602 (1839), 636 (1840), and 691 (1841) of Doyle's 'Political Sketches' there are very lightly-indicated figures identified as TBM; they are in no sense portraits. A genuine caricature portrait of TBM does appear in number 891 of the 'Sketches,' showing him among the 'Unhappy Ghosts Wandering on the Banks of the Styx' following his defeat at Edinburgh, 1847. Two of the original pencil sketches for this are in the British Museum Print Room. According to the *DNB* Doyle did the 'original drawing' of 'The Reform Bill Receiving the King's Assent by Royal Commission,' a group portrait including TBM of which an engraving by William Walker and S. W. Reynolds, Jr, was published in 1836 (frontispiece). The caption of the print, however, attributes the original to S. W. Reynolds, Sr; an oil sketch of a version of the same subject now in the House of Lords is also attributed to the elder Reynolds (R. J. B. Walker, *Catalogue of Paintings, Drawings, Sculpture and Engravings in the Palace of Westminster*, Part II, 1960, p. 135). The caption of the 1836 engraving refers to 'original and authentic sketches' from which the portraits were taken; the *DNB* statement may refer to these.

In about half an hour Lady Georgiana Grey[1] – the only daughter of Earl Grey who is still unmarried, and the Countess, made their appearances. We had some pleasant talk – and they made many apologies for Howick's carelessness and their absence. The Earl, they said, was unexpectedly delayed by a question which had arisen in the Lords. Lady Holland arrived soon after, and gave me a most gracious reception – shook my hand very warmly, and told me in her imperial decisive manner that she had talked with all the principal men on our side about my speech – that they all agreed that it was the best that had been made since the death of Fox, and that it was more like Fox's speaking than any body's else. Then she told me that I was too much worked – that I must go out of town, and absolutely insisted on my going to Holland House to dine and take a bed on the next day on which there is no parliamentary business. At eight we went to dinner. Lord Howick took his father's place; and we feasted very luxuriously. At nine Lord Grey came from the House with Lord Durham,[2] Lord Holland, and the Duke of Richmond.[3] They dined on the remains of our dinner with great expedition, as they had to go to a cabinet council at ten. Of course I had scarcely any talk with Lord Grey. He was however extremely polite to me, and so were his colleagues. I liked extremely the ways of the family. Lady Grey and her daughter seemed to be on the easiest and kindest terms with each other. Lord Howick shewed more domestic feeling than, from what I knew of his habits, I had expected – and Lord Grey, whom I had rather believed to be a domestic tyrant, seemed to be very comfortable and very much beloved.

I picked up some news from these Cabinet ministers. There is to be a Coronation on quite a new plan – no banquet in Westminster Hall – no feudal services – no champion, – no procession from the Abbey to the Hall and back again. But there is to be a service in the Abbey. All the Peers are to come in state and in their robes, and the King is to take the oaths and be crowned and anointed in their presence. The spectacle will be finer than usual to the multitude out of doors. The few hundreds who could obtain admittance to the Hall will be the only losers.

In the evening our cabinet Ministers went, and the Duke of Bedford[4] and Sam Rogers dropped in – the Duke in his blue ribband – Sam Rogers looking, as usual, like a dead man. I came away at twelve.

---

[1] Lady Georgiana Grey (1801–1900), died unmarried.

[2] John George Lambton (1792–1840: *DNB*), then first Baron Durham and afterwards first Earl, married Grey's eldest daughter. Called 'Radical Jack,' he was Lord Privy Seal in Grey's cabinet and was one of the framers of the Reform Bill; Governor-General of Canada, 1838.

[3] Charles Gordon-Lennox (1791–1860: *DNB*), fifth Duke, Postmaster-General in Grey's cabinet.

[4] John Russell (1766–1839: *DNB*), sixth Duke.

I have had a very kind note from Lord Lansdowne. I dined at his house on Sunday – but not with him; for he had an attack of this influenza which kept him confined to his room and, I believe, to his bed. I called on him yesterday, and found him recovering. I am to dine with him to morrow week.

I must stop. Give my thanks to my father for his kind note – and take my thanks yourself – my darling – for your letter. I only wish that I could find words to tell you [h]¹ow much I love you. Kindest love [and]¹ thanks to Selina and Fanny.

Ever yours, dearest,
T B M.

Sarah Anne and Meg have an order for the Ventilator to night. But I do not know that they will hear much that is worth hearing.

TO HANNAH MACAULAY, 11 JULY 1831

MS: Trinity College. *Address:* Miss H M Macaulay / Rothley Temple / Mountsorrel / Leicestershire. *Frank:* London July eleven 1831 / T B Macaulay. *Mostly published:* Trevelyan, I, 230–2.

London July 11. 1831

My darling,

Since I wrote to you I have been out to dine and sleep at Holland House. We had a very agreable and splendid party – the Duke and Duchess of Richmond,² – the Marquess and Marchioness of Clanricarde,³ – Lord Duncannon, Denison⁴ the Member for Nottinghamshire, – and Allen the common goer on errands and fetcher and carrier of trifles. Lady Holland sent him, five or six times, out of the room on footman's messages, and called him once from the other end of the drawing-room where he was talking to pick up her fan. The Duchess of Richmond is not so handsome as her charming portrait by Lawrence⁵ would have led me to expect. But Lady Clanricarde is very beautiful, and very like her father, with eyes full of fire and great expression in all her features. She and I had a great deal of talk. She shewed great cleverness and information – but, I thought, a little more of political virulence than is quite beseeming in a pretty

---

¹ Paper torn away with seal.
² Lady Caroline Paget (1796–1874), eldest daughter of the first Marquess of Anglesey, married the Duke of Richmond in 1817.
³ Ulick John De Burgh (1802–74), first Marquess; he married, in 1825, Harriet (1804–76), Canning's daughter.
⁴ John Evelyn Denison (1800–73: *DNB*), afterwards first Viscount Ossington; in Parliament since 1823 as a moderate Whig; Speaker of the House of Commons, 1857–72.
⁵ Exhibited at the Royal Academy, 1829; at the British Institution, 1830.

woman. However she has been placed in peculiar circumstances. The daughter of a statesman who was a martyr to the rage of faction may be pardoned for speaking sharply of the enemies of her parent – and she did speak sharply. With knitted brows, and flashing eyes, and a look of feminine vengeance about her beautiful mouth, she gave me such a character of Peel as he would certainly have had no pleasure in hearing. Her husband is a poor creature, – a great gawky schoolboy who grins at every thing that is said in such a way as to shew an enormous row of tusks and the whole cavity of a most capacious mouth. The Marchioness should have said to him, as Lady G said to her poor Lord, who was not, I believe, more henpecked than Lord Clanricarde, – "And why must thou show all thy teeth man."[1]

In the evening Lord John Russell came; and soon after old Talleyrand.[2] I had seen Talleyrand in very large parties, but had never been near enough to him to hear a word that he said. I now had the pleasure of listening for an hour and a half to his conversation. He is certainly the greatest curiosity that I ever fell in with. His head is sunk down between two high shoulders. One of his feet is hideously distorted. His face is as pale as that of a corpse, and wrinkled to a frightful degree. His eyes have an odd glassy stare quite peculiar to them. His hair thickly powdered and pomatumed hangs down his shoulders on each side as straight as a pound of tallow-candles. His conversation however soon makes you forget his ugliness and infirmities. There is a poignancy without effort in all that he says, which reminded me a little of the character which the wits of Johnson's circle give of Beauclerk.[3] For example – we talked about Metternich – Talleyrand said – "L'on a voulu faire un parallèle de M. de Metternich au Cardinal Mazarin. J'y trouve beaucoup à redire. Le Cardinal trompoit; mais il ne mentoit pas. Or M. de Metternich ment toujours, et ne trompe jamais." He mentioned M. de St Aulaire,[4] – now one of the most distinguished public men of France. I said – "M. de St Aulaire est beau-père de M. le Duc de Cazes;[5] – n'est-ce pas?" "Non, Monsieur,"

---

[1] *Sir Charles Grandison*, 3rd edn, IV, 100–1.

[2] Charles Maurice de Talleyrand-Périgord, Prince de Talleyrand (1754–1838), after his many political roles, was French ambassador to Great Britain, 1830–5. TBM saw him at Lord Lansdowne's in November 1830 (Selina Macaulay, Diary, 26 November 1830) when he wondered 'who is this old Chelsea pensioner?' (Margaret Macaulay, *Recollections*, p. 192). Greville describes a later meeting at Holland House: '[TBM] was introduced to Tally, who told him that he meant to go to the H. of Commons on Tuesday, and that he hoped he would speak, "qu'il avait entendu tous les grands orateurs, et il désirait à présent entendre Monsieur Macaulay"' (6 February 1832: *Memoirs*, II, 249).

[3] Topham Beauclerk (1739–80: *DNB*); see, e.g., Johnson to Boswell, 8 April 1780, Boswell, *Life of Johnson*.

[4] Louis-Clair de Beaupoil, Comte de Saint-Aulaire (1778–1854), French diplomat.

[5] Elie, Duc Decazes (1780–1860), leading statesman under Louis XVIII; driven from power in 1819.

said Talleyrand, "l'on disoit, il y a douze ans, que M. de St Aulaire étoit beau-père de M. de Cazes. L'on dit maintenant que M. Decazes est gendre de M. de St Aulaire." It was not easy to describe the change in the relative positions of two men more tersely and sharply; – and these remarks were made in the lowest tone, and without the slightest change of muscle, – just as if he had been remarking that the day was fine. He added – "M. de St Aulaire a beaucoup d'esprit. Mais il est devot, – et, ce qui pis est, devot honteux. – Il va se cacher dans quelque hameau pour faire ses Pâques." This was a curious remark from a Bishop. He told several stories about the political men of France – not of any great value in themselves. But his way of telling the[m is][1] beyond all praise, concise, pointed, and delica[tely][1] satirical. When he had departed, I could not help breaking out into praise of his talent for relating anecdotes. Lady Holland said that he had been considered for nearly forty years as the best teller of a story in Europe, – and that there was certainly nobody like him in that respect.

When the Prince was gone we went to bed. In the morning Lord John Russell drove me back to London in his cabriolet, much amused with what I had seen and heard. – But I must stop. Thank you for your kind little note. Love to my father, sisters, uncle, aunt, and cousins. I forgot to tell my clerk to change the direction of the newspapers.[2] Farewell, – my dearest, – and write to me when you have a few minutes to spare. You cannot think how much I love to see your handwriting on a letter.

Ever yours my love
T B M

Where is Mr. Wilberforce? Some blockhead sends me letters for him without a direc[tion.][3]

TO SELINA MACAULAY, 13 JULY 1831

MS: Trinity College. *Address:* Miss Macaulay; enclosed in cover addressed: Miss Macaulay / Rothley Temple / Mountsorrel / Leicestershire. *Frank:* London July thirteen 1831 / T B Macaulay.

London July 13. 1831

My dearest Selina,

I cannot refrain from sending a line – it must be but a line – to tell you with how much pleasure I have read in your own handwriting a con-

---

[1] Paper torn away with seal.
[2] Zachary Macaulay and his daughters had now left Leamington for Rothley Temple.
[3] Word cut off by mounting of MS.

firmation of what I had heard from others as to the improvement in your health. I am glad that you like my speech. It is very ill-reported, and worse reported, I think, in the Mirror of Parliament[1] than any where else. – Of course I did not correct it. My oldest and most judicious parliamentary friends advise me to keep my speaking and writing distinct; and I thoroughly agree with them. A man who speaks with the press before his eyes generally speaks ill.

Kindest love to my father and Fanny. I have sent a dispatch, private and confidential, as the Downing street cabinet epistles are marked, to Hannah.

Ever yours, my love
T B M

TO HANNAH MACAULAY, 13 JULY 1831

MS: Trinity College. *Address:* Miss H M Macaulay / Private.

London July 13. 1831

My dear dear girl,

I am sorry to find that there is any chance of your having to go to a place which you dislike.[2] I will do all in my power to prevent it. But at any rate do not think that you will miss seeing me. You will go to no place to which, as soon as Parliament rises, I shall not follow you. My dear dear girl, my sister – my darling – my own sweet friend, – you cannot tell how, amidst these tempests of faction and amidst the most splendid circles of our nobles, I pine for your society, for your voice, for your caresses. I write this with all the weakness of a woman in my heart and in my eyes. We have difficulties to pass through. But they are not insurmountable; and, if my health and faculties are spared, I feel confident that, however the chances of political life may turn, we shall have a home, perhaps a humble one, but one in which I can be happy, if I see you happy. – Farewell my dearest, and believe that there is nothing on earth that I love as I love you.

T B M.

[1] *Mirror of Parliament*, 1831, I, 347–51. The *Mirror of Parliament*, published from 1828 to 1841, provided fuller and more detailed reports of parliamentary debates and proceedings than did *Hansard*. Dickens wrote for it, his uncle John Henry Barrow being the editor, and may have reported or at any rate attended one or more of TBM's Reform Bill speeches: see Madeline House and Graham Storey, eds., *The Letters of Charles Dickens*, Oxford, I (1965), 2n. In 'A Parliamentary Sketch' Dickens presents an old County Member who 'has a great contempt for all young Members of Parliament' and 'is of opinion that "that young Macaulay" was a regular impostor' (*Sketches by Boz*).

[2] While Zachary Macaulay was house-hunting in London; in the event Hannah went to the Buxtons: see 27 May 1831.

TO HANNAH MACAULAY, 15 JULY 1831

MS: Trinity College. *Address:* Miss H M Macaulay / Rothley Temple / Mountsorrel / Leicestershire. *Frank:* London July fifteen 1831 / T B Macaulay. *Published:* Clive and Pinney, *Selected Writings of Macaulay*, pp. 433–4.

Basinghall Street July 15 – 1831

My darling,

I will not try to tell you – because I cannot tell you – how happy your letter made me, and how much I long to see you and talk with you. My father arrived yesterday night. This morning I saw him in excellent health and spirits to all appearance. *Entre nous* Buxton[1] has spoken to Lord Brougham – and Lord Brougham has declared himself eager to serve my father to the utmost either of his own patronage or of any influence which he may have over others. But in these times of competition and of strict retrenchment Lord Brougham, even if he be sincere, – which I do not dispute – may not find it easy to fullfil his promises.

The rage of faction at the present moment exceeds any thing that has been known in our time. Indeed I doubt whether, at the time of Mr. Pitt's first becoming Premier, – at the time of Sir Robert Walpole's fall, or even during the desperate struggle between the Whigs and Tories at the close of Anne's reign, the rage of party was so fearfully violent. Lord Mahon said to me yesterday that friendships of long standing were every where giving way, – and that the schism between the reformers and anti-reformers was spreading from the house of Commons into every private circle. Lord Mahon himself is an exception. He and I are on excellent terms. But Praed and I become colder every day. His silly, conceited, factious conduct has disgraced him even more than his bad speaking.[2]

The scene of Tuesday night[3] beggars description. I left the House at about three, in consequence of some expressions of Lord Althorpe's which indicated that the ministry was inclined to yield. I afterwards much regretted that I had gone away; not that my presence was necessary; but because I should have liked to have sate through so tremendous a storm. Towards eight in the morning the Speaker was almost fainting. The ministerial members however were as true as steel. They furnished the

---

1 (Sir) Thomas Fowell Buxton (1786–1845: *DNB*), a wealthy brewer and an Evangelical, M.P. for Weymouth, 1818–37. Buxton was the leader in Parliament of the effort to abolish slavery and thus closely associated with Zachary Macaulay.

2 When the motion was made to go into committee on the Reform Bill, Praed was among the leaders of the Tory effort to adjourn the debate, producing repeated divisions. He was also prominent in arguing that boroughs subject to disfranchisement had a right to be heard by counsel at the bar of the House.

3 I.e., 12 July: the debate on the motion to go into committee lasted until 7:30 a.m.: 'There was much disorder and violence' (Lord Ellenborough in A. Aspinall, ed., *Three Early Nineteenth Century Diaries*, 1952, p. 104).

ministry with the resolution which it wanted – "If the noble lord yields," said one of our men – "all is lost." Old Sir Thomas Baring sent for his razor, and Benett,[1] the Member for Wiltshire, for his night-cap, and they were both resolved to spend the whole day in the House rather than give way. If the opposition had not yielded in two hours half London would would [hav]e[2] been in Old Palace Yard.

Since Tuesday night the opposition have been rather cowed. But their demeanour, though less outrageous than at the beginning of the week, indicates what would in any other times be called extreme violence. I have not been once in bed till three in the morning since last Sunday.

To morrow we have a holiday. I dine at Lansdowne House. Next week I dine with Littleton[3] the Member for Staffordshire and his handsome wife.[4] He told me that I should meet two men whom I am curious to see, Lord Plunkett and the Marquess Wellesley – let alone the Chancellor who is not a novelty to me.

I am ashamed to send you so dull a letter. But if it gratifies you half as much as the sight of your handwriting about the most insignificant thing gratifies me, you will read even this trifling with pleasure. Kindest love to my Uncle, Aunt, sisters, and Cousins.

Ever yours, my own love,
T B M

TO HANNAH MACAULAY, 18 JULY 1831

MS: Trinity College. *Address:* Miss H M Macaulay / Rothley Temple / Mountsorrel / Leicestershire. *Frank:* London July eighteen 1831 / T B Macaulay.

London July 18. 1831

My darling,

On Saturday I dined at Lansdowne House. We had a small and very pleasant party. Mackintosh was there, and there was a good deal of conversation – chiefly about books. Lord Lansdowne and Mackintosh told me some good stories about Bozzy. Both of them knew him; and a most eminent fool he seems to have been by their account as well as by his own. The last time that Mackintosh saw him was at a tavern – sitting dead drunk at a table. The waiter said that Mr. Boswell had dispatched seventeen glasses of brandy and water that evening. When the fellow

---

[1] John Benett (1773–1852: *Boase*), M.P. for Wiltshire, 1819–32; for South Wiltshire, 1832–52.

[2] Obscured by seal.

[3] Edward John Littleton (1791–1863: *DNB*), afterwards first Baron Hatherton; in Parliament since 1812; Chief Secretary for Ireland, 1833–4.

[4] Hyacinthe Mary (1789–1849), illegitimate daughter of Lord Wellesley.

first came back from his travels he was so full of Paoli,[1] and of the war between the Corsicans and the Genoese that he was nicknamed Corsica Boswell. This name he took to himself proudly, and literally, or almost literally, bound it like frontlets between his eyes.[2] At the Shakspeare Jubilee he appeared among the crowds that filled Stratford on Avon with an enormous placard on his hat bearing the inscription "Corsica Boswell."[3]

One story suggests another. Lord Holland told me of a droll mistake made by a waiter at the City of London Tavern. During the short peace which followed the Treaty of Amiens there was a great dinner and among the Toasts given was "The Three Consuls of the French Republic." Buonaparte, you know, was First Consul, and Cambacerès[4] and Lebrun[5] the Second and Third. The waiter who knew nothing of the French Constitution gave out "The three per Cent Consols of the French Republic."

We chatted about novels. Everybody praised Miss Austen to the skies. Mackintosh said that the test of a true Austenian was Emma. "Every body likes Mansfield Park. But only the true believers – the select – appreciate Emma." Lord and Lady Lansdowne extolled Emma to the skies. I had heard Wilber Pearson[6] call it a vulgar book a few days before.

But what do you care for all this? Or to what end do I go on chattering thus? Only, my darling, that I may say something to you – just as I used to stay dawdling about you in the drawing-room in Great Ormond Street – making bad puns and bad rhymes, and talking all sorts of nonsense. When shall we talk nonsense together again? My dear dear girl I have read your letter which I received last Friday over and over till I have got it by heart; yet I go on reading it still. Farewell my darling. Give my kindest love to Selina and Fanny – to my Aunt, Uncle, and Cousins.

Ever yours, dearest,

T B M

---

[1] Pasquale de Paoli (1725–1807), Corsican patriot and the hero of Boswell's *An Account of Corsica*, 1768.

[2] Cf. Deuteronomy 6: 8.

[3] Croker's edition (II, 71) also tells this story, but it is not true: see Frederick A. Pottle, *James Boswell, The Earlier Years: 1740–1769*, New York, 1966, p. 427.

[4] Jean Jacques, Duc de Cambacérès (1753–1824).

[5] Charles François Lebrun, Duc de Plaisance (1739–1824).

[6] William Wilberforce Pearson (1809?–1861), son of the surgeon John Pearson, was then at Trinity College, Cambridge, from which he graduated in 1832.

TO HANNAH MACAULAY, 20 JULY 1831

MS: Trinity College. *Address:* Miss H M Macaulay / Rothley Temple / Mountsorrel / Leicestershire. *Frank:* London July twenty 1831 / T B Macaulay. *Published:* Clive and Pinney, *Selected Writings of Macaulay*, pp. 435–6.

Library of the House of Commons / July 20. 1831

My love,

Here I am sitting, waiting for the beginning of the debate on the reform bill. Did you ever see our library? If not let me describe it to you. A handsome Gothic Room, about forty five feet by twenty five, very neat – with a handsome carpet in the centre and thick matting all round, – two immense tables with all conveniences for writing – two fire-places, which, as you may conceive, are now filled only with shavings and tattered scraps of paper, – book cases all round filled with journals of the two Houses, Statutes at large, and various political and historical works. The window at the end, – a Gothic bow-window, – looks out on a small plot of grass planted with elms. Beyond lies the Thames with its boats and barges – and on the other side the Archbishop's palace at Lambeth. In sunny days the view is very pretty. This is a dull day, – all but rainy – and the prospect has nothing alluring. Then for company. In the bow-window sits Sir James Grahame talking to Tom Duncombe[1] – a very honest good-natured fellow Tom; but none of the soberest. At the other end of the room, Lieutenant Gordon preaching to Henry Maxwell,[2] – a very dishonest ill-natured fellow Gordon, though one of the most canting.[3] See how antitheses drop from my pen in its most rapid and unstudied movements. Robinson[4] the Member for Worcester – a bore – is writing at one table – and Mr. Macaulay Member for Calne – no bore – but a very promising young gentleman and a rising speaker – is writing at the other. The door opens while I am writing and in comes another bore – that stupid Irishman Ruthven.[5] "Macaulay" – who calls Macaulay? – Sir James Grahame. What can he have to say to me? Take it dramatically –

Sir J G – Macaulay.

Macaulay – What?

---

[1] Thomas Duncombe (1796–1861: *DNB*), Radical M.P., 1826–61.

[2] Henry Maxwell (1799–1868), afterwards seventh Baron Farnham; Tory M.P. for Cavan, 1824–38.

[3] Gordon was a fanatical anti-Catholic; he undertook a 'mission to Ireland in company with Baptist Noel, announcing himself the Luther, and his gentler colleague the Melancthon, of a second Reformation' (Teignmouth, *Reminiscences*, I, 212).

[4] George Richard Robinson (1781?–1850), a Newfoundland merchant, Chairman of Lloyd's, and Whig M.P. for Worcester, 1826–37; for Poole, 1847–50.

[5] Edward Southwell Ruthven (1772–1836: *DNB*), M.P. for Downpatrick, 1830–2; for Dublin, 1832–6.

Sir J G – Whom are you writing to that you laugh so much over your letter?

Macaulay – To my constituents at Calne to be sure. They expect news of the Reform bill every day.

Sir J G – Well writing to constituents is less of a plague to you than to most people, to judge by your face.

Macaulay – How do you know that I am not writing a billet doux to a lady?

Sir J G – You look more like it by Jove.

Cutler Fergusson[1] MP for Kircudbright. Let Ladies and Constituents alone, and come to the House. We are going on the case of the Borough of Great Bedwin[2] immediately. – So away goes Sir John Graham – and away must I go too. And why do I sit writing this nonsense? And why do I not tear it up now that it is written? – Because no[thing][3] is worthless which affection send[s to][3] affection, and therefore nothing can be worthless which I send to you, my darling.

My uncle will be surprised if you tell him of our library. It has been established, I think, since his time.

We are cruelly worked. I never get to bed till three in the morning – and "Wednesday shines no Sabbath to our toils."[4] Lady Holland has asked me out on Saturday to recruit, and I have accepted her invitation.

Kindest love to Selina, Fanny, my Uncle, aunt, and Cousins.

Ever yours, dearest,
T B M

TO HANNAH MACAULAY, 23 JULY 1831

MS: Trinity College. *Address:* Miss H M Macaulay.

London July 23. 1831

My darling,

I will not let another day pass without sending you a few lines, however little they may be worth. My life is passed in the House of Commons, – and what takes place in the House of Commons you may learn from the newspapers better than from any correspondent – little characteristic anecdotes excepted, and of those the past week has not been very fertile.

You have probably read the proceedings respecting Bingham Baring.[5]

---

[1] Robert Cutlar Fergusson (1768–1838: *DNB*), M.P., 1826–34; Judge Advocate-General, 1834–8.   [2] See *Hansard*, 3rd Series, v, 92.   [3] Paper torn away with seal.
[4] Cf. Pope, 'Epistle to Dr. Arbuthnot,' line 12.
[5] William Bingham Baring (1799–1864: *DNB*), afterwards second Baron Ashburton; M.P., 1826–48; he was accused of having abused a Mr and Mrs Deacle when they were arrested

I was, from my knowledge of him, fully convinced that the charge against him was unfounded even before the discussion. Not a doubt can now exist in any unprejudiced mind. The low rancour of the Times is worthy of the Times.[1] I have been much interested by the matter. He was under the gallery, – poor fellow – during the debate. He looked ten years older than when I saw him last. The base persecution to which he has been subjected had evidently made him ill in body as well as in mind. The triumphant vindication of his character has, I am glad to hear, quite restored his cheerfulness.

I have not for a fortnight been in bed till three o'clock in the morning till last night; – when, finding that there was little chance of a division, I paired off at twelve with Lord Mahon, and drove away in his cabriolet from the House – so that I had the pleasure of hearing one o'clock strike as I got into bed.

To night I go to Holland House, having received a most gracious invitation thither from her Ladyship. To morrow I dine with Littleton. You wanted me to send you an account of the dinner some days ago. You quite mistake your man. I have not the gift of prophecy. I leave it to Henry Drummond and Irving[2] to predict dinners before they take place. My humbler vocation is to describe them after I have eaten them.

You are so grateful for my letter from our library that I must, I think, send my next from our smoking-room; and [then?][3] travel over all the offices belonging to the House of Commons. – Tell me what you are reading, my darling. I should be glad to hear that you had taken some pleasant book of real merit in hand – Burnet's History of his Own Time[4] for example. It is very amusing, and, if it is not at the Temple, it will be either at Matthew's or at the Vicarage. But I mention it merely as an example. Kindest love to my Uncle, Aunt – sisters and Cousins.

Ever yours, my love.
T B M

for inciting to riot during disturbances in Hampshire the preceding November. In June Deacle brought suit for false arrest and was awarded £50 for battery. This led to the debate in the Commons, but the motion for papers in the case was negatived without a division, 21 July: see *Hansard*, 3rd Series, v, 146–74.

[1] *The Times* prints several items on the case; for 'low rancour' see especially that of 18 July.
[2] Edward Irving (1792–1834: *DNB*), the friend of Carlyle, had made a London sensation in 1822 as a preacher. Zachary Macaulay was on friendly terms with him but saw that he was unstable. With Drummond, Irving had taken up the study of unfulfilled prophecy; later his church was notorious for the phenomenon of speaking in the 'unknown tongues.' Irving was at length excluded from his London church and condemned for heresy by the presbytery of Annan. He continued to minister to a much-reduced congregation, but was unable to maintain control of it, was deposed, and died not long after.
[3] Word cut off by mounting of MS.
[4] Gilbert Burnet, *History of His Own Times, 1660–1713*, 2 vols., 1724–34; TBM's copy is item 326 in the catalogue of the sale of his library.

TO HANNAH MACAULAY, 25 JULY 1831

MS: Trinity College. *Address:* Miss H M Macaulay / Rothley Temple / Mountsorrel / Leicestershire. *Frank:* London July twenty five 1831 / T B Macaulay. *Partly published:* Trevelyan, I, 234–5.

London July 25 – 1831

My dearest girl,

I sit down with a swelled eye and face to write to you. Perhaps the dulness of my indisposition may communicate itself to my letter. However I will do my best. On Saturday evening I went to Holland House. There I found the Dutch Ambassador M. de Weissembourg[1] – Mr. and Mrs. Vernon Smith[2] – and Admiral Adam,[3] a son of old Adam who fought the duel with Fox – Palmer,[4] the Member for Reading – Allen, – her Ladyship's Atheist in ordinary, – and others of less note. We dined like Emperors, and jabbered in several languages. I talked French to the Dutchman and got on with him pretty well. Her ladyship, for an *esprit fort*, is the greatest coward that I ever saw. Her general manner is so unfeminine that her fears have none of the excuse which may be pleaded for those of a delicate woman. The last time that I was there she was frightened out of her wits by the thunder. She closed all the shutters – drew all the curtains, – and ordered candles in broad day to keep out the lightening – or rather the appearance of the lightening. On Saturday she was in a terrible taking about the cholera, – talked of nothing else – refused to eat any ice because somebody said that ice was bad for the cholera – was sure that the cholera was at Glasgow – and asked me why a *cordon* of troops was not instantly placed round that town to prevent all intercourse between the infected and the healthy spots. I told her in the first place that I did not believe that the cholera was there; and in the next place that no power existed in any quarter to intercept the communication between different parts of the country. She went maundering on however the whole evening about it, and seemed really quite alarmed and dejected. Lord Holland made light of her fears. He is a thoroughly good-natured, open, sensible, man, – very lively – very intellectual – well read in politics and in the lighter literature both of ancient and modern times. He sets me more at ease than almost any person that I know, by

---

[1] The name is clear in the MS, but I do not know who TBM can mean: the Dutch ambassador in 1831 was Anton Reinhard Falck.

[2] Robert Vernon Smith (1800–73: *DNB*), afterwards first Baron Lyveden, the son of Sydney Smith's brother Robert; M.P., 1829–59, he held office under Grey, Melbourne, Russell, and Palmerston. He married, in 1823, Emma Mary, daughter of the second Earl of Upper Ossory.

[3] Admiral Sir Charles Adam (1780–1853: *DNB*), son of William Adam (1751–1839: *DNB*), whose duel with Fox occurred in 1779.

[4] Charles Fyshe Palmer (1769?–1843), Whig M.P. for Reading from 1818.

a certain good-humoured way of contradicting that he has. He always begins by drawing down his shaggy eyebrows, making a face extremely like his uncle, wagging his head and saying – "Now do you know – ? Mr. Macaulay, I do not quite see that. How do you make it out?" He tells a story delightfully, and bears the pain of his gout and the confinement and privations to which it subjects him with admirable fortitude and cheerfulness. Her ladyship is all courtesy and kindness to me. But her demeanour to some others – particularly to poor Allen – is such as it quite pains me to witness. I can almost believe a story that Empson told me about her. She had a quarrel with Allen at Rome about some trifle. She ordered the carriage, made him get into it with her, and told the coachman to drive to the Monte Sacro – about four miles from the city. She then put the offender out, drove away, and left him to walk back by himself under a burning sun to their house in Rome. Yet I can scarcely pity the man. He has an independent income – and if he can stoop to be ordered about, as he is ordered about, like a foot man, that he may be able to drink champagne and eat made dishes, I cannot so much blame her for the contempt with which she treats him.

Do not shew or repeat – but of course you will not – to any but those in whom you can place entire confidence what I say about this violent, weak, imperious, woman. To me she behaves as well as it is in her nature to behave to any body: and it is not my business to publish to the world the foolish and worse than foolish conduct which, but for her hospitality, I should have no opportunity of observing.

There are all sorts of stories about her. On one occasion, it is said, she was going to the opera with Lord Kinnaird.[1] He wore his hat in the carriage. She drew the check-string. The coach stopped. The footman came to the door. "My lord, you must alight," – said she. "I cannot suffer a gentleman to wear his hat in the carriage with me." –

Another time, they say, she was sitting by while her husband and poor Tom Sheridan[2] were playing at chess. [She][3] called out "Lord Holland, – go and bring my handkerchief. I have left it on the table in my dressing room." Lord Holland, who was absorbed in his game, did not attend to her. She repeated her commands in a louder voice. He said that he would go presently. She became so violent however that he was forced to leave the chess-board and perform the errand. "Lady Holland," said Tom Sheridan, "if I had been your husband, I would have seen you ——— before I would have gone." – From such services as these my Lord is now dispensed by his gout. But poor Allen is really treated like a negro slave. "Mr. Allen, – go into my drawing-room and bring my reticule." "Mr. Allen, go and see what can be the matter that they do not bring up

---

[1] Charles Kinnaird (1780–1826: *DNB*), eighth Baron Kinnaird.
[2] Thomas Sheridan (1775–1817: *DNB*), the dramatist's son.   [3] Word obscured by seal.

dinner." "Mr. Allen, there is not turtle soup enough for you. You must take gravy soup or none." – But I have rambled on so long about this singular woman that I have left myself no room for any thing else – and I have a great deal more to tell. Perhaps I may write again to morrow. Kindest love to all at the Temple.

Ever yours, my own love,

T B M

TO HANNAH MACAULAY, 26 JULY 1831

MS: Trinity College. *Address:* Miss H M Macaulay / Rothley Temple / Mountsorrel / Leicestershire. *Frank:* London July twenty six 1831 / T B Macaulay. *Partly published:* Trevelyan, I, 235–8.

Library of the House of Commons / July 26. 1831

My darling,

Here I am seated, waiting for the debate on St Germains[1] with a very quiet party, – Lord Milton,[2] Lord Tavistock, George Lamb and Wyse[3] the Member for, I think, Tipperary. But instead of telling you, as in my former letter from this place, in dramatic form, my conversations with Cabinet Ministers, I shall, I think, go back two or three days, and complete the narrative which I left imperfect in my epistle of yesterday.

On Sunday I dined at Littleton's. I went dressed to Golden Square at five and staid there talking with Margaret and my father till a quarter after seven. Then I sallied forth – took a cabriolet – and at half after seven was set down at Littleton's palace, – for such it is, – in Grovesnor Place. It really is a noble house – four superb drawing-rooms on the first floor, handsomely furnished, and hung round with some excellent pictures – a Hobbima, the finest by that artist in the world, it is said, and Lawrence's charming portrait of Mrs. Littleton.[4] The beautiful original, by the bye, did not make her appearance. We were a party of gentlemen. But such gentlemen! Listen and be proud of your connection with one who is admitted to eat and drink in the same room with beings so exalted. There were the two Chancellors – Lord Brougham and Lord Plunkett. There was Earl Gower[5] – Lord St Vincent[6] – Lord Seaford[7] – Lord Duncannon

---

[1] See *Hansard,* 3rd Series, v, 343–63.

[2] Charles William Wentworth Fitzwilliam (1786–1857: *DNB*), styled Viscount Milton; afterwards third Earl Fitzwilliam; M.P., 1807–33.

[3] (Sir) Thomas Wyse (1791–1862: *DNB*), M.P. for Tipperary, 1830–2.

[4] Exhibited Royal Academy, 1822; engraved, 1827.

[5] George Granville Leveson-Gower (1786–1861), styled Earl Gower; afterwards second Duke of Sutherland.

[6] Edward Jervis Ricketts (1767–1859), second Viscount.

[7] Charles Rose Ellis (1771–1845: *DNB*), first Baron.

– Lord Ebrington[1] – Sir James Graham – Sir John Newport[2] – the two
Secretaries of the Treasury, Rice and Ellice[3] – Slaney[4] Member for
Shrewsbury, George Lamb, Denison, and half a dozen more Lords and
distinguished Commoners, not to mention Littleton himself who has no
very low opinion of himself. Indeed, though I like him in the main,
I must say that he has a little of that pride of wealth which in a *nouveau
riche* we expect, but which seems singular in the head of an old and honourable family. He has once or twice taken occasion to tell me that he and his
family have between thirty and forty thousand a year in Staffordshire,
and was so enraptured on my saying something civil about his house that
he insisted on shewing me all its beauties and actually carried me into the
nursery still filled with the slops of his children. Till last year he lived in
Portman Square. When he changed his residence his servants gave him
warning. They could not, they said, consent to go into such an unheard
of part of the world as Grosvenor Place. I can only say that I have never
been in a finer house than Littleton's – Lansdowne House excepted – and
perhaps Lord Milton's which is also in Grosvenor Place.

In one respect I profited by my host's ostentation of wealth: for he
gave me a dinner of dinners – a feast of fat things and wines upon the
lees well refined.[5] First came a course of turtle – then milk punch, – the
West Indian concomitant of turtle – then all sorts of fish, all sorts of made
dishes, wines of which I had never heard the names – particularly all
those fine intermediate wines which form the connecting link between
Hock and Burgundy, snipes as the sand on the sea shore – much ice and
many peaches.

I talked with Denison and with nobody else. I have found out that the
only real use of conversational powers is to put them forth in tête à tête.
A man is flattered by your talking your best to him alone. Ten to one he
is piqued by your overpowering him before a company. Denison was
agreable enough. I heard only one word from Lord Plunkett, who was
remarkably silent. He spoke of Doctor Thorpe,[6] and said that, having
heard the Doctor in Dublin, he should like to hear him again in London.
"Nothing, easier," quoth Littleton; "his chapel is only two doors off;
and he will be just mounting the pulpit." "No" said Lord Plunkett;

[1] Hugh Fortescue (1783–1861), styled Viscount Ebrington to 1841; afterwards second Earl
Fortescue; Whig M.P., 1804–39.
[2] Sir John Newport (1756–1843: *DNB*), first Baronet; Whig M.P., 1803–32.
[3] Edward Ellice (1781–1863: *DNB*), wealthy official of the Hudson's Bay Company; M.P.,
1818–26; 1830–63; Whig whip in the House of Commons; Joint Secretary of the Treasury,
1830–2; Secretary at War, 1833–4.
[4] Robert Slaney (1792–1862: *DNB*), Whig M.P. for Shropshire, 1826–35; 1837–41; 1847–62.
[5] Isaiah 25: 6.
[6] Dr William Thorpe (1778–1865: *Boase*), then Chaplain of the Lock Hospital, was an
Evangelical and a friend of Zachary Macaulay.

"I can't lose my dinner." An excellent saying though one which a less able man than Lord Plunkett might have uttered. "Aye," said George Lamb; "if men will preach just when turtle soup is coming in, what can they expect but to preach to empty pews."

At midnight I walked away with George Lamb and Slaney – and went – where for a ducat? To bed – says Miss Hannah. Nay, my sister, not so; but to Brookes's.[1] There I found Sir James Macdonald – Lord Duncannon, who had left Littleton's just before us; and many [other?][2] Whigs, and ornaments of human nature. As Macdonald and I were rising to depart we saw Rogers, and I went to shake hands with him. You cannot think how kind the old man was to me. When Macdonald told him that I would not go without speaking to him, he quite cried with emotion. He shook my hand over and over, – told me that Lord Plunkett longed to see me in [a q][3]uiet way, that he would arrange a breakfast party in a day or two for that purpose and let me know. Rogers had just been at Talleyrand's, and had seen the French King's speech[4] which had arrived that evening; so that I heard the news some hours before the public.

Away I went from Brookes's – but whither. To bed now, I am sure, says little Ann. No, my darling, but on a walk with Sir James Mac[don][2]ald to the end of Sloane Street, talking about the ministry – the reform bill, – and the East India question. Every body flatters me from morning to night – and yet they cannot make me half so proud of any thing as I am of your sweet affection, my dear, dear sister. Farewell, my love. Kindest love to all at the Temple.

Ever yours dearest
T B M

TO HANNAH MACAULAY, 30 JULY 1831

MS: Trinity College. *Address:* Miss H M Macaulay / Rothley Temple / Mountsorrel / Leicestershire. *Frank:* London July thirty 1831 / T B Macaulay. *Partly published:* Trevelyan, I, 238.

House of Commons / Smoking Room – / Saturday –

My darling,

The newspapers will have explained the reason of our sitting to day.[5] At three this morning I left the house. At two this afternoon I have returned to it – the thermometer at boiling heat – and four hundred and

---

[1] TBM was elected to Brooks's in December 1830, being proposed by Lord Lansdowne and Lord King (*Memorials of Brooks's*, 1907, p. 116).

[2] Letter torn.   [3] Paper torn away with seal.

[4] At the opening session of the new Assembly, 23 July.

[5] To carry on the discussion of the Reform Bill in committee.

fifty people, stowed together like negroes in the pious John Newton's slave-ship.[1] I have accordingly left Sir Francis Burdett on his legs, and repaired to the smoking room. Shall I describe it to you? A large, square wainscotted, uncarpeted, place with tables covered with green baize and writing materials. On a full night it is generally thronged towards twelve o'clock with smokers. It is then a perfect cloud of tobacco fume. There have I seen – (tell it not to the West Indians –) Buxton blowing fire out of his mouth. My father will not believe it. He holds smoking, eating underdone meat, liking high game, – lying late in a morning, – and all things which give pleasure to others and none to himself to be absolute sins. – Is not that an undutiful reflection?

At present, however, our smoking room is pure enough from smoke to suit my father himself. All the doors and windows are open; – officers of the house and strangers are seen m[o][2]ving to and fro through the [surro][2]unding passages. Benne[tt][2] the Member for Wiltshire is writing at one table – O'Connell and I at another. But I must stop. Here comes Sir William Ingleby[3] to say that Burdett is up.

Get Blackwood's new number. There is a description of me in it. What do you think he says that I am – "a little, splay footed, ugly, dumpling of a fellow with a mouth from ear to ear."[4] Conceive how such a charge must affect a man so enamoured of his own beauty as I am. Farewell, my darling. Kindest love to all at Rothley, and warmest congratulations on the happy event which has taken place there.

Ever yours, my love,
T B M

To morrow I breakfast at Rogers's.

TO HANNAH MACAULAY, 3 AUGUST 1831

MS: Trinity College.

London August 3. 1831

My love,

I do not think that, since you left London, I have suffered so long a time to pass without writing to you. I have been very busy, and still am so.

---

[1] John Newton (1725–1807: *DNB*), once a captain in the slave trade, where he enforced strict sabbath observance on his crew; one of the founders of the Evangelical revival in the Church of England.

[2] Paper torn away with seal.

[3] Sir William Amcotts-Ingilby (1783–1854: *Boase*), M.P. for Lincolnshire, 1823–34.

[4] 'Noctes Ambrosianæ,' *Blackwood's*, xxx (August 1831), 410: 'an ugly, cross-made, splay-footed, shapeless little dumpling of a fellow, with a featureless face too – except indeed a good expansive forehead – sleek puritanical sandy hair – large glimmering eyes – and a mouth from ear to ear.'

But I steal a few minutes during an examination in Quality Court[1] to write a line or two. I breakfasted with Rogers the other day. Nobody was there but Sharp, Lord Plunkett, a stupid silent nephew of our host, – and Luttrell, who was extremely amusing. I liked Lord Plunkett. He is, to be sure, very ugly – but with a strong expression of intellect in his strong coarse features and massy forehead. We had much pleasant talk – and several good stories. One in particular amused me a good deal. An inquisitive lady was boring Canning with questions. – 'And why have they shut one of the gates into the Park at Spring Gardens. The passage is only half as wide now as it used to be. Why is that, Mr. Canning." Canning answered with the gravest face. "It had really become necessary. Such very fat people used to go through."[2]

Rogers has added some fresh curiosities to his collection – a good Claude, and a Guido of the very highest merit. He has two very remarkable reliques – the original deed by which Milton sold the copyright of the Paradise Lost signed by the poet himself – and the original deed by which Dryden contracted to translate the Eneid – signed by Dryden himself and witnessed by Congreve.

On Monday Empson sent to tell me that, if I had any ladies to oblige, he could give them room to see the procession on the Thames[3] from his chambers.[4] I took Margaret and Sarah Anne. We mounted his leads which overlook the Temple Gardens and the river. The sight was really noble. The whole Waterloo Bridge on the West – the whole of Blackfriar's Bridge on the East was one solid mass of human beings. The Southwark Bridge beyond Blackfriar's Bridge was equally crowded. The whole shore was one mass of people. The whole terrace before Somerset House was a sea of heads. The river looked like a street. Two lines of barges and large boats were drawn at the distance of about two hundred feet from each other through the middle of the stream – all blazing with flags – all covered with men and women – decks, masts, shrouds, and all. Through this street the train of royal barges past – the people on each side cheering as the King went by, and bridge after bridge sending up a great shout as he passed under them in succession. All the bells from all the hundred spires and towers of the city were pealing together. The roar of guns was almost incessant. Our prospect extended as far as the balloon on London Bridge and we remained till it went up in signal of the King's arrival. Then down we went to Empson's cold collation – he flirting with Margaret

---

[1] The office of the Lord Chancellor's Secretary of Bankrupts was at 12 Quality Court, Chancery Lane.

[2] This anecdote is in Dyce's *Recollections of the Table-Talk of Samuel Rogers*, ed. Morchard Bishop, 1952, p. 115, where Rogers adds: '(a reply concerning which Tom Moore said, that "the person who does not relish it can have no perception of real wit").'

[3] On the opening of the new London Bridge, 1 August.

[4] 12 Harcourt Buildings, Inner Temple.

all the way down stairs and through the whole repast. The room was filled with damsels eating peaches, grapes, and ices, and of gentlemen indulging their more masculine appetites with pigeon pye and Moselle. Margaret will give you a more copious narrative of our proceedings. Tell me whether it is a better. So I have now lost her too.[1] I think, as I told her, that you and she have treated me as the birds in the nursery song treated the stone

> " There were two birds that sate on a stone
> One flew away, and then there was but one.
> The other flew away and then there was none
> And the poor stone was left all alone."

You ought to write oftener to me now. I am up till three every morning – hallooing, crying *question*, and dividing. Kindest love to all.

Ever yours, my dearest,

T B Macaulay

TO HANNAH MACAULAY, 5 AUGUST 1831

MS: Trinity College. *Address:* Miss H M Macaulay / Rothley Temple / Mountsorrel / Leicestershire. *Frank:* London August five 1831 / T B Macaulay. *Published:* Clive and Pinney, *Selected Writings of Macaulay*, pp. 436–8.

London August 5. 1831

My love,

I need not tell you that I was delighted with your letter which arrived yesterday and with the shorter note which I received to day. I am quite lonely now – except when I am in the House, where indeed I could well spare some of the company: – for the crowd and heat are beyond all endurance. The compression of a slave-ship can hardly be worse. Five hundred people are often there in a space which will not conveniently accommodate more than four hundred, with a thermometer at something less than boiling heat, and this from four or five in the afternoon till midnight and long after. Yet I keep my health, and am still, I blush to say, a dumpling of a fellow, as my friend Blackwood has it.

I said a few words the night before last:[2] – they were merely in reply and quite unpremeditated. They were not ill received. – I feel that much practice will be necessary to make me a good debater on points of detail. But my friends tell me that I have raised my reputation by shewing that I was quite equal to the work of extemporaneous reply. My manner, they say, is cold and wants ease. I feel this myself. Nothing but strong excitement and a great occasion overcomes a certain reserve and *mauvaise honte*

[1] Margaret was leaving London for Rothley Temple.
[2] In committee on the Reform Bill: *Hansard*, 3rd Series, v, 709–11.

which I have in public speaking – not a *mauvaise honte* which in the least confuses me or makes me hesitate for a word – but a *mauvaise honte* which keeps me from putting any fervour into my tone or my action. This is perhaps in some respects an advantage. For when I do warm, I am the most vehement speaker in the House – and nothing strikes an audience so much as the animation of an orator who is generally cold.

I ought to tell you that Peel was very civil, and cheered me loudly – and that impudent leering scoundrel Croker congratulated the House on the proofs which I had given of my readiness. He was afraid – he said – that I had been silent so long on account of the many allusions which had been made to Calne. Now that I had risen again he hoped that they should hear me often.[1] See whether I do not dust that lying varlet's jacket for him in the next number of the Blue and Yellow.[2] I detest him more than cold boiled veal.

After the debate I walked about the streets with Bulwer till near three o'clock. I spoke to him about his novels with perfect sincerity – praising warmly, and criticising freely. He took the praise as a greedy boy takes apple pie, and the criticism as a good dutiful boy takes senna-tea. He has one eminent merit – that of being a most enthusiastic admirer of mine – so that I may be the Hero of a novel yet, under the name of Delamere or Mortimer. Only think what an honour.

Bulwer is to be editor of the New Monthly Magazine.[3] He begged me very earnestly to give him something for it. I would make no promises; for I am already over head and ears in literary engagements. But I may possibly now and then send him some trifle or other. At all events I shall expect him to puff me well. I do not see why I should not have my puffers as well as my neighbours.

Write to me, my love – and make Margaret write – and tell me all about the books that you read, the company that you see, the quarrels between the Temple, the Vicarage, and the Grange, – the mysteries, the secrets, and all the other delightful things which make Rothley so happy a place. I am glad that you have read Madame de Stael's Allemagne.[4] The book is a foolish one in some respects – but it abounds with information and shews great mental power. She was certainly the first [wom]an[5] of her age – Miss Edgeworth, I think, the second, and Miss Austen the third.

But I must give over this idle rattling. Kindest love to all.

Ever yours, my love,

T B M

---

[1] *Hansard*, 3rd Series, v, 715–16: but the report does not give the remarks that TBM mentions.   [2] The Whig colors, used on the cover of the *ER*.

[3] The first number of the *New Monthly* under Bulwer appeared in November 1831. There is no evidence that TBM wrote anything for the magazine.

[4] *De l'Allemagne*, 1813.   [5] Paper torn away with seal.

TO MARGARET MACAULAY, 6 AUGUST 1831

MS: Morgan Library. *Address:* Miss M Macaulay / Rothley Temple / Mountsorrel / Leicester-shire. *Frank:* London August six 1831 / T B Macaulay.

London August 6. 1831

My dearest girl,

I have but very few minutes at my disposal this morning. But I cannot defer sending a few lines in answer to your sweet letter. Indeed, my dear Margaret, you cannot love me better than I love you, or find more pleasure in my society than I find in yours. Gratitude is no feeling for those who love each other as we love each other. Your happiness is my happiness, and I deserve no praise or thanks for promoting it. The affection which I bear to you and Hannah is the source of the greatest enjoyment that I have in the world. It is my strongest feeling. It is that which will determine the whole course of my life. It has made me a better man and a far happier man than any thing else could have made me. The very regret which I feel for your absence is a more delightful sensation than the pleasure which I take in other people's society. I was thinking this morning till the tears came into my eyes of the time when you and she were what Mary's babies now are, and I a boy of eleven – how fond I was of you then, – and how little I foresaw what we should one day be to each other. The pleasures of dissipation end in disgust – those of vanity pall with repetition. Ambition itself passes away. But my love for my sweet sisters and friends becomes stronger and stronger from day to day and from hour to hour. Having been the most restless and aspiring of human creatures, I feel that I could, not only without regret, but with perfect cheerfulness and satisfaction, retire, in their society, to an obscurity in which my name should never be heard. Wealth, power, fame, have become as nothing to me compared with their most sweet and precious affection. My dearest, I have said more than it is my habit to say on this subject. But your letter has drawn it from me. I am glad that you think so well of Selina, and sorry that Lydia[1] is losing her beauty. When that is gone, I fear there will be little that is of any value left. By the time that you receive this you will have been talked to death by Jane – and will be in six or sev[en][2] plots and quarrels. Pray let me know who has been backbiting whom – and who has reported the backbiting to the person backbitten – whether the Vicarage is at peace with the Grange, or the Grange with the Temple – whether Grandmamma still abuses Miss Rose – whether Matthew has cheated his sister out of another broach – and how

[1] Lydia, the eldest daughter of Lydia Babington Rose, was regarded as the beauty of Rothley.
[2] Paper torn away with seal.

85

many dozens of those innumerable and eternal Miss Sykeses[1] are making mischief at Rothley this year.

Farewell – My love. Do not shew this letter except to Hannah. Again, my love, farewell.

Ever yours

T B M

TO HANNAH MACAULAY, 9 AUGUST 1831

MS: Trinity College. *Address:* Miss H M Macaulay / Rothley Temple / Mountsorrel / Leicestershire. *Frank:* London August nine 1831 / T B Macaulay.

London August 9. 1831

My love,

I have only time to say that, if it is perfectly convenient to my uncle and aunt, I think of going to the Temple on Wednesday the 17th for a week. I have spoken to the Secretary of the Treasury[2] who promises to find me a pair – and the state of bankrupt business is such that I shall, I hope, be able to absent myself [from][3] London without inconvenience. I am knocked up by the late hours and by the excessive heat of the season. I should indeed, but for some bankrupt commissions which cannot be postponed, take flight from London earlier.

Learn whether my visit will be productive of any inconvenience to my uncle and aunt. If you have any reason to think that it will incommode them, say nothing to them about it. I will go to Sir George Hampson[4] who has been pressing me very warmly to recruit my forces with him at Brighton. Many thanks, my darling, for your kind letter. Love to all.

Ever yours most tenderly

T B M

TO HANNAH MACAULAY, 11 AUGUST 1831

MS: Trinity College. *Address:* Miss H M Macaulay / Rothley Temple / Mountsorrel / Leicestershire. *Frank:* London August eleven 1831 / T B Macaulay.

London August 11 – 1831

My love,

It is with difficulty that I write these lines. I have been wretchedly ill since I wrote last; and – though convalescent, am still on my sofa as weak

[1] The Sykes family of Hull was intricately connected with the Clapham Sect; the wife of the elder Henry Thornton was a Sykes, as were Mrs Matthew Babington and Mrs Henry Venn.
[2] Edward Ellice.
[3] Word obscured by stain from seal.
[4] Sir George Francis Hampson (1789–1833), eighth Baronet, a barrister.

as a child. I have had a violent, though happily short, attack of the influenza – grippe – cholerine – English cholera – or whatever else you chuse to call it. After four and twenty hours of very sharp suffering the complaint very rapidly subsided, and I am now labouring under no inconvenience but that of extreme languor. On Wednesday you may expect to see me at the Temple for a week. Thank my aunt and uncle from me in the warmest manner for their kindness. I cannot tell you, my darling, how happy I feel in the thought of seeing you again.

George's care and kindness have been what, without my mentioning them, you would suppose them to have been. I cannot write more at present. Love to all.

Ever yours, dearest,

T B M.

TO HANNAH MACAULAY, 12 AUGUST 1831

MS: Trinity College. *Address:* Miss H M Macaulay / Rothley Temple / Mountsorrel / Leicestershire. *Frank:* London August twelve 1831 / T B Macaulay. *Published:* Clive and Pinney, *Selected Writings of Macaulay*, pp. 438–9.

London August 12 – 1831

My love,

I am recovering, but slowly; – and am still under sentence of confinement and starvation. It is three days since I have tasted any food except milk and water – except indeed that this morning I ate three mouthfuls of bread. I am on my sofa – as weak as Mary's baby and quite solitary. The treasury has found me a pair for a fortnight – to wit – my uncle's old colleague Sam Smith.[1] I still expect to be with you next Wednesday. I fear or perhaps I should say I hope that I shall come down to you thinner than I have been for a long time.

Write to me my darling – and since I cannot have your society during this time of weakness and seclusion let me have your handwriting.

I shall not be sorry to be out of the way of the miserable proceedings in the House of Commons.[2] One is ashamed to support such a government – and, in my situation, I cannot attack it. The weakness, dulness, cowardice, and tergiversation of the ministers – those I mean who sit in the House of Commons, – have begun to disgust their most devoted friends. I will tell you instances of their fatuity and infirmity of purpose

---

[1] Samuel Smith (1745–1834), a London banker, brother of John Smith; M.P., 1780–1832; from 1790 to 1818 he sat for Leicester.

[2] The Committee on the Reform Bill lasted for forty nights, not concluding until 7 September; the tactics of the opposition were obstructive, so that 'night after night had been wasted with an objectless discussion, which only irritated the country and wearied the Government' (Spencer Walpole, *A History of England*, II [1878], 651).

when we meet which are absolutely astounding. Do not trumpet what I say to every body. But nothing can save them from ruin if they do not speedily alter their course. The Chancellor has written to me a private letter expressing this opinion in language much stronger than what I am now using, and intreating me to put myself forward to defend them. He must feel the pressure of the danger strongly, when he treats me with so much civility. – But my course is taken; – indeed the cholera has settled it [wi]¹thout any reference to my pleasure. [And i]t¹ is no business of mine whether [they]² stand or fall. There is not one of them [in]² the House of Commons except Lord Althorp who is not either useless or worse than useless³ – and I do not see that it would be either for my interest or my honour to thrust myself between them and the public contempt. This, I repeat, is secret. What I mean by secret I leave it to your discretion to judge.

Love to all.

Ever yours my darling
T B M

TO HANNAH MACAULAY, 13 AUGUST 1831

MS: Trinity College. *Address:* Miss H M Macaulay / Rothley Temple / Mountsorrel / Leicestershire. *Frank:* London August thirteen 1831 / T B Macaulay.

London August 13 – 1831

My love,

I am going on very well – and have to day got as far as to dine on two poached eggs – the largest quantity of solid food that I have swallowed since Tuesday. My appetite is indeed good – and too good to be fully gratified. I need not tell you how I feel your kind expressions. Indeed, my love, to have had you near me would, at some moments, have been a great comfort to me.

I have done Margaret's bidding about the letter which she sent, and have, like the good Samaritan, one letter only being altered, "taken out two pence and given them to the *post.*"⁴

On Wednesday you will see me, I hope. I shall breakfast with you if

---

¹ Paper torn away with seal.   ² Word obscured by stain from seal.
³ Brougham praised Althorp's knowledge of the details of the Reform Bill and 'of all the numberless matters connected with it, which was almost supernatural. The others knew it so ill, and got into such scrapes when opposed to the most formidable opposition of Croker chiefly (who had something like his mastery of the subject), that it became quite necessary to prevent them from speaking – or what was then called "to put on the muzzle" – and A. really did the whole' (quoted in J. R. M. Butler, *The Passing of the Great Reform Bill*, 1914, pp. 277–8).
⁴ Cf. Luke 10: 35.

I can manage it – not by travelling all night, but by leaving London at
two on Tuesday after bankrupt business – sleeping at Leicester for a few
hours and coming to the Temple in a post chaise on Wednesday morning.[1]
Kindest love to all.

Ever yours dearest
T B M

TO HANNAH MACAULAY, 29 AUGUST 1831

MS: Trinity College. *Address:* Miss H M Macaulay / M Babington's Esq / Rothley / Mountsorrel / Leicestershire. *Frank:* London August twenty nine 1831 / T B Macaulay. *Published*
Clive and Pinney, *Selected Writings of Macaulay*, pp. 439–42.

London August 29. 1831

My darling,

Here I am again settled, sitting up in the House of Commons till three
o'clock five days in the week, and getting an indigestion of great dinners
on the remaining two. I dined on Saturday with Lord Althorpe and
yesterday with Sir James Graham. Both of them gave me exactly the
same dinner; – and, though I am not generally copious on the repasts
which my hosts provide for me, I must tell you, for the honour of official
hospitality, how our ministers regale their supporters. Turtle, turbot,
venison, and grouse, formed the principal part of both entertainments – the effect of which is that I had the heartburn all last night,
and have solemnly vowed never to eat of such a variety of good
things again.

Lord Althorp was extremely pleasant at the head of his own table.
We were a small party – Lord Ebrington, Hawkins, Captain Spencer,[2]
Stanley, and two or three more. We all of us congratulated Lord Althorpe
on his good health and spirits. He told us that he never took exercise now,
that from his getting up till four o'clock he was engaged in the business
of his office – that at four he dined, went down to the house at five, and
never stirred till the house rose, which is always after midnight, – that
he then went home, took a basin of arrow-root with a glass of sherry in it,
and went to bed – where he always dropped asleep in three minutes.
"During the week," said he, "which followed my taking office I did not

---

[1] Empson wrote to Napier, 16 August, that 'I saw M[acaula]y on Saturday for an hour, but
he had been very ill for 4 days with our cholera simplex and leaves Town to day *on a pair*
(not a chaise and pair) for a fortnight to recruit Mind and Body at his Uncle Babington's in
the Country. His mind is chiefly sore with Spleen at the way in which he, naturally enough
exaggerating the mismanagement of Ministers in H.C., looks at our and indeed at our
general Politics' (MS, British Museum).
[2] Althorp's brother, Captain Frederick Spencer (1798–1857: *DNB*) entered the navy, 1811;
succeeded his brother as fourth Earl Spencer, 1845; M.P., 1831–4; 1837–41.

close my eyes for anxiety. Since that time I have never been awake a quarter of an hour after taking off my clothes."

Stanley laughed at Lord Althorp's arrow-root and recommended his own supper – cold meat and warm negus – a supper which I will certainly begin to take when I feel a desire to pass the night with a sensation as if I was swallowing a nutmeg-grater every third minute.

We talked about timidity in speaking. Lord Althorp said that he had only just got over his apprehensions. "I was as much afraid," he said, "last year as when first I came into parliament. But now I am forced to speak so often that I am quite hardened. Last Thursday I was up forty times." I was not much surprised at this in Lord Althorp – as he is certainly one of the most modest men in existence. But I was surprised to hear Stanley say that he never rose without great uneasiness. "My throat and lips," he said, "when I am going to speak are as dry as those of a man who is going to be hanged." Nothing can be more composed and cool than Stanley's manner. His fault is on that side. A little hesitation at the beginning of a speech is graceful; and many eminent speakers have practised it merely in order to give the appearance of unpremeditated reply to prepared speeches. Stanley speaks like a man who never knew what fear or even modesty was. Tierney, it is remarkable, who was the most ready and fluent debater almost ever known, made a confession similar to Stanley's. He never spoke, he said, without feeling his knees knock together when he rose.

Sir James Graham's official house[1] is much finer than Lord Althorp's, and indeed than Lord Grey's. It is really a palace. The rooms in which we dined and took coffee look out on St James's park. They are very handsome and are hung round with paintings from which the prints in Cook's Voyages were taken – of scenes in Otaheite and New Zealand. Cook's Voyages, you are aware, were undertaken under the direction of the Admiralty.

Lord Althorp was at Graham's. James[2] the member for Carlisle, the Attorney and Solicitor General,[3] and the Lord Advocate were also there. There was a little more constraint than at Lord Althorp's, who is simplicity itself. I came away with Jeffrey who brought me in his carriage to the entrance of Gray's Inn.

My opinion of Lord Althorp is extremely high. In fact his character is the only stay of the ministry. I doubt whether any person has ever lived in England who, with no eloquence, no brilliant talents, no profound

---

[1] At the Admiralty.
[2] William James (1791–1861: *Boase*), M.P. for Carlisle, 1820–6, 1831–5; for East Cumberland, 1836–47.
[3] Sir William Horne (1775–1860: *DNB*), Solicitor-General, 1830–2; Attorney-General, 1832–4.

information, – with nothing in short but plain good sense and an excellent heart, possessed as much influence both in and out of Parliament. His temper is an absolute miracle. He has been worse used than any minister ever was in debate; and he has never said one thing inconsistent, I do not say with gentlemanlike courtesy, but with real benevolence. His candour is absolutely a vice in debate. He is perpetually shewing excuses and ways of escape to his adversaries which they would never find of themselves. Lord North perhaps was his equal in suavity and good nature. But Lord North was not a man of strict principles. His administration was not only an administration hostile to liberty; but it was supported by vile and corrupt means – by direct bribery, I fear, in many cases. Lord Althorp has the temper of Lord North with the principles of Romilly. If he had the oratorical powers of either of those men, he might do any thing. But his understanding, though just, is slow; and his elocution painfully defective. It is however only justice to him to say that he has done more service to the Reform Bill even as a debater than all the other ministers together, Stanley excepted. Graham is either afraid or idle. Grant and Palmerston[1] are idle, and, I suspect, not very hearty. Lord John Russell gives all that he has – to wit two mites which make a farthing. I must in fairness say, however, that Lord John made a better speech on Saturday than any that I have heard from him for a long time.

We are going, – by *we* I mean the Members of Parliament who are for reform – , as soon as the Bill is through the Commons, to give a grand dinner to Lord Althorp and Lord John Russell as a mark of our respect. Some people wished to have the other Cabinet Ministers included. But Grant and Palmerston are not in sufficiently high esteem among the Whigs to be honoured with such a compliment. Where we [are to][2] hold our festivities – whether at the Albion or the City of London Tavern,[3] or whether we shall go to Greenwich to eat white-bait is undecided.

But I must stop. Kindest love to all at the Temple.

Ever yours, my love

T B M

---

[1] Henry John Temple (1784–1865: *DNB*), third Viscount Palmerston, in Parliament and in office since 1807; Foreign Secretary under Grey; Prime Minister, 1855–8; 1859–65.

[2] Paper torn away with seal.

[3] In Bishopsgate Street, as was the London Tavern, with which this is sometimes confused.

TO GEORGE RAWSON,[1] 2 SEPTEMBER 1831

Text: Leeds *Mercury*, 10 September 1831.

London, Sept. 2d, 1831.

My dear Sir,

I have received your communication, and I thank you most cordially for the friendly and courteous manner in which it is expressed.

With respect to the mitigation of public burdens, the abolition of slavery, and the principles which ought to regulate our intercourse with Foreign States, my opinions strictly coincide with those which are professed by the Association. I am decidedly opposed to all monopolies, and in particular to that great monopoly which will in a few months come under the consideration of Parliament, the monopoly of the East India Company. A free trade with China, and a fundamental change in the Corn-Laws will be, I hope and believe, among the earliest fruits of the Reform Bill.

My opinions on the subject of Parliamentary Reform I have avowed in the House of Commons. They are unchanged, and, I believe, unchangeable. But on the subject of the Ballot I have never yet expressed my sentiments publicly. In fact till lately my opinions on that subject have been in a fluctuating state: and I can even yet scarcely venture to say that they are absolutely fixed. I will, however, lay them before you with perfect sincerity; though they are, I fear, too moderate to please either party.

Most of the arguments which are urged against the Ballot I consider as fallacies. Greatly as I revere the intellectual powers of some of the statesmen who use those arguments, they have not convinced me that there is any thing in secret voting inconsistent with rectitude and manly spirit. I have never been able to understand why it should be considered as more un-English in an elector to vote in secret, under the protection

---

[1] Rawson was secretary of the 'Leeds Association for Promoting, within the County of York, the Free Return of Fit Representatives to Parliament.' At the meeting of the Association on 29 August TBM had been proposed as a candidate to represent Leeds in a reformed Parliament (Leeds *Intelligencer*, 1 September). Rawson then sent an inquiry in the name of the Association to TBM, to which this letter is a reply, asking 'his opinions on the several points contained in the following resolution, which forms the basis of the Association: –

> "That the principles by which the Association shall be guided are, such a Reform of the Representative System, (including the vote by Ballot) as shall rescue the Elector from corrupt influence and identify the House of Commons with the interests of the people, – Reduction of Taxation, with rigorous Economy in the Public Expenditure, – extinction of all Monopolies, – the total Abolition of Colonial Slavery, – and Non-Interference with the internal affairs of Foreign States"'   (Leeds *Mercury*, 10 September).

On 3 September the Leeds *Mercury* took up the action of the Leeds Association and brought before the public the proposal that TBM should stand for Leeds when the time came.

of the ballot, than to vote against his conscience for want of the protection of the ballot.

The objections to this mode of voting seem to me to be slight; its advantages on the other hand to be obvious and considerable. It would clearly diminish the expense of elections. It would, at least in large constituent bodies, extinguish corruption. It would protect the voter from ejectments like those of the Duke of Newcastle[1] on the one hand, and from outrages like those of the mob of Wigan[2] on the other.

I am therefore favourable to the ballot. Yet I cannot but remember that this is a question which has but very recently begun to excite general attention. This is a question on which I have the misfortune to differ from many of the most virtuous and enlightened public men in England, from the majority of the parliamentary supporters of the Reform Bill, and from almost every member of the cabinet by which that Bill has been brought forward. It is therefore, I think, a question which ought to be treated in a mild and tolerant spirit, – a question which ought rather to be left to work its way by the force of reason and by the progress of time, than to be violently hurried forward, at the risk of disuniting those sincere reformers on whose hearty union the safety of the state depends.

I do not indeed consider this point as by any means so important as the other points to which reference is made in the fourth resolution of the Association. I think secret suffrage desirable; but I do not think it essential to good government. And I am firmly persuaded that the great measure now in progress through parliament will, by its indirect operation, mitigate or remove many of those evils against which the ballot is, in the opinion of many most respectable persons, the only security.

In short, I am a supporter of the ballot. But I do not consider the question of the ballot as one of those vital questions which ought to be pressed forward at all risks, and which draw impassable lines of distinction between parties.

Permit me again to assure you of the grateful sense which I entertain of your personal kindness towards myself, and of the pleasure which your favourable opinion of my public conduct has given to me. / Believe me, my dear Sir,

Your most faithful servant,

T. B. Macaulay.

To George Rawson, Esq.

---

[1] Following the election at Newark in 1829 the Duke ejected thirty-seven of his tenants for voting against his candidate, Michael Sadler.

[2] The mob took over the town during the general election of May 1831, and troops had to be called out to put down the riot.

TO HANNAH MACAULAY, 3 SEPTEMBER 1831

MS: Trinity College. *Address:* Miss H M Macaulay / M Babington's Esq / Rothley / Mount-sorrel / Leicestershire. *Frank:* London September three 1831 / T B Macaulay.

London Septr. 3 – 1831

My darling,

Though I am very busy your kind letters and those of Chitapet[1] must be acknowledged. I am advancing with my review pretty successfully. I do not think that I have left Croker a leg to stand on.

I have been engaged for some days past in a negotiation which, I think, is on the point of terminating favourably. The liberal party at Leeds have applied to me proposing, if my political views coincide with theirs, to bring me in free of expense at the next general election. The seat is a most honourable one – a city of probably a hundred thousand inhabitants, with vast wealth and vast influence. I have had some correspondence with them on the subject of the ballot. Next Monday they are to hold a meeting where the matter will be settled. As soon as I know their decision you shall know it. The leading men are strongly for me. But I fear that my opinions are too moderate for some among the rank and file of the party. – This is for the present a secret.

I have read Mrs. Gore's Manners of the Day[2] since I came to London. I like it much. The style I think very lively and poignant. The story is nothing. As to the characters Lady Mordaunt and her daughter Lilfield are the best. The heroine is a slamikin – her friend Lady Theodosia a swank – Miss (I forget her name) the Irish beauty a sheel – Lord Willersdale a sawney and Lord Barton a spooney.

Yesterday I got Honor O'Hara.[3] It looks amusing. But I shall be a month in finishing it.

By way of consoling you for the conciseness of my letter I send you a poetical epistle which I received the other day by post. The writer – the queerest looking ragged, grinning, wretch that ever you [sa]w[4] – came yesterday to enforce the [ap][4]plication contained in the letter. [I][4] gave him a shilling for the fun that he had afforded me.

Next week we shall have the Coronation, and I dine at Stanley's, so there will be matter for letters.

Ever, dearest, yours

T B M.

Kindest love to all. Chitapet is very kind to write so often.

---

[1] One of TBM's pet names for Margaret.
[2] *Women as They Are, or Manners of the Day*, 3 vols., 1830.
[3] Anna Maria Porter, *Honor O'Hara*, 3 vols., 1826.   [4] Paper torn away with seal.

TO HANNAH MACAULAY, 7 SEPTEMBER 1831

MS: Trinity College. *Extract published:* Trevelyan, I, 245.

London Septr. 7. 1831

My love,

I send off half my article, or rather more than half, to Edinburgh to day. I have – though I say it who should not say it – beaten Croker black and blue. Impudent as he is, I think he must be ashamed of the pickle in which I leave him.

I have read Pinmoney[1] while undressing and getting to bed during the last week. What a strange way novellists have of repeating themselves. Pinmoney is nothing but an Echo of the Manners of the Day. I like it well enough. But not so well as its predecessor. Perhaps, if I had read Pinmoney first my judgment would have been different. It is a twice told tale. Both novels begin with a marriage. The plot of both consists in the imprudence of a well meaning married woman, – the estrangement of an affectionate husband by the mistakes of the wife, – and the reconciliation. Lord Calder is Stanhope. Lady Sophia answers to Lady Theodosia. In both novels too there is a dashing hot headed brother who interferes between the heroine and the designing lover.

The moral is absurd. What had Lady Rawleigh's playing at Écarté without knowing what she was about, to do with her having Pin Money? And as to tradesmen's bills, was she less likely to run them up when she had not a fixed sum to spend than when she had? She is cheated by her friend as to the price of an Opera Box. But this imposition or mistake – whichever it was – might as well have taken place if she had been spending Sir Brooke's money as when she was spending her own. To charge on Pin-Money the bad consequences which follow from having vicious friends and expensive tastes, – and from meeting with unforeseen accidents, is quite absurd. Mrs. Gore might as well have attributed the conjugal infelicity of her hero and heroine to Sir Brooke's being a baronet as to his wife's having a separate purse. You see that, like Mr. Smith, I always stand up for the ladies.[2]

I must stop. Kindest love to all. Thank dear Chitapet for her letter. She has answered my last criticisms on [. . . .][3]

[1] Mrs Gore, *Pinmoney*, 3 vols., published in June 1831.
[2] See Fanny Burney, *Evelina*, Letter 44.
[3] The rest is missing.

TO MACVEY NAPIER, 7 SEPTEMBER 1831

MS: British Museum. *Address:* Macvey Napier Esq / Castle Street / Edinburgh. *Frank:*
London September seven 1831 / T B Macaulay. *Mostly published:* Napier, *Correspondence*,
p. 119.

London Septr. 7. 1831

My dear Napier,

I send off to day the first part of my article. The rest will follow early
in next week at the latest. I send the first part separately, because it is
absolutely necessary that I should see the proofs of it. It is an exposure of
Croker's monstrous blunders; and we must not, in censuring his inaccuracy, be ourselves inaccurate.

I have not been able to find the date of Sir William Forbes's death.[1]
Oddly enough it is not in the annual register. You at Edinburgh can have
no difficulty. I should be glad if you would insert it – taking of course
particular care to be quite accurate.

As to the latter part of the article, though I should wish if possible to
see the proofs, mistakes will be comparatively of little importance.

Our work on the Committee is over. To-morrow I go to the Coronation.

Ever yours
T B Macaulay

TO HANNAH MACAULAY, 9 SEPTEMBER 1831

MS: Trinity College. *Address:* Miss H M Macaulay / Rothley Temple / Mountsorrel /
Leicestershire. *Frank:* London September nine 1831 / T B Macaulay. *Mostly published:*
Trevelyan, I, 243–5.

London September 9. 1831

My love,

I scarcely know where to begin or where to end my story of the magnificence of yesterday. No pageant can be conceived more splendid. The
newspapers will happily save me the trouble of relating minute particulars.
I will therefore give you an account of my own proceedings, and mention
what struck me most. I rose at six. The cannon awaked me, and as soon
as I got up, I heard the bells pealing on every side from all the steeples
in London. I put on my court-dress and looked a perfect Lovelace in it.
At seven the glass coach which I had ordered for myself and some of my

---

[1] 'Mr Croker informs us, that Sir William Forbes of Pitsligo, the author of the Life of Beattie,
died in 1816. A Sir William Forbes undoubtedly died in that year – but not the Sir William
Forbes in question, whose death took place in 1806' ('Boswell's Life of Johnson,' *ER*,
LIV, 2).

friends came to the door. I called in Hill Street for William Marshall,[1]
M P for Beverley, and in Cork Street for Strutt the member for Derby
and Hawkins the member for Tavistock. Our party being complete we
drove through crowds of people and ranks of horse-guards in cuirasses
and helmets to Westminster Hall, which we reached as the clock struck
eight.

The House of Commons was crowded. There must have been four
hundred members present, and the aspect of the assembly was very
striking. The great majority were in military or naval uniforms. All
officers in the militia or the yeomanry, and all the Deputy-Lieutenants
of Counties wore their military garb. The ministers were in their official
suits of purple and gold. There were three or four Highland Chiefs in
Kilts, plaids and philibegs with eagle's plumes in their hats, dirks and
pistols at their sides, and claymores in their hands. The Speaker came at
nine in his robes of State, covered with gold embroidery. After prayers
we went out in order by lot, the Speaker going last. My county, Wiltshire,
was among the first drawn so I got an excellent place, next to Lord Mahon,
who is a very great favourite of mine, and a very amusing companion,
though a bitter Tory.

Our gallery was immediately over the great altar. The whole vast
avenue of lofty arches was directly in front of us. In the centre of the
Abbey, where the nave and transept cross each other, were several raised
steps, covered with a Brussels carpet. On these steps a footcloth of yellow
silk was spread, and the throne and footstool for the king were in the
centre of this cloth. The Queen's throne was a few steps lower. The Chair
in which the Kings are crowned is different from the Throne. They are
not enthroned till after they have been crowned. The Coronation Chair
I have seen a hundred times. It is one of the shews of the Abbey, six
hundred years old at least; and quite mouldering. The seat is placed on
a stone which Edward the First brought from Scotland as a trophy. Stone
and wood however were now completely covered with cloth of gold and
satin. All the pavement of the Abbey was covered – with blue cloth and
red cloth in the less conspicuous parts, – with rich carpeting in the place
where the ceremony was to be performed. Vast galleries hung with red
cloth were extended between the pillars, and some were hung at a dizzy
height far above our heads.

Gradually the body of the Abbey filled with Peers, Peeresses, and
Judges, and Bishops, all in full robes, the Peers and Peeresses with coronets in their hands. Our gallery was quite full, and was, I understand,
one of the most brilliant objects in the Abbey. On our right hand was

[1] William Marshall (1796–1872: *Boase*), M.P. for various constituencies, 1826–68, including
Beverley, 1831.

a gallery filled with the foreign Ambassadors and their ladies. There were Talleyrand, Washington Irving,[1] the Duchess de Dino[2] – the Princess Lieven,[3] and a crowd of others. All the uniforms and orders of Europe might be seen there. Other galleries in our neighborhood were occupied by charming English women, who outbloomed the ladies of the Corps Diplomatique most indisputably.

At eleven the guns fired, the organ struck up, and the procession entered. I never saw so magnificent a scene. All down that immense vista of gloomy arches there was one blaze of scarlet and gold. First came heralds in coats stiff with embroidered Lions, Unicorns and harps, then nobles dressed in Ermine and velvet bearing the Regalia – with pages in rich dresses carrying their coronets on cushions – then the Dean and Prebendaries of Westminster in rich Copes of Cloth of gold, – then a crowd of beautiful girls and women – or at least of girls and women who at a distance looked altogether very beautiful attending on the queen. Her train of purple velvet and ermine was borne by six of these fair creatures. All the great officers of state in full robes. The Duke of Wellington with his marshal's staff – the Duke of Devonshire with his white rod, Lord Grey with the Sword of State – and the Chancellor with his seals came in procession. Then all the Royal Dukes with their trains borne behind them, and last the King leaning on two Bishops. – I do not, I dare say, give you the precise order. In fact it was impossible to discern any order. The whole Abbey was one blaze of gorgeous dresses, mingled with lovely necks and faces.

The Queen behaved admirably, with wonderful grace and dignity – the King very ill and awkwardly. The Duke of Devonshire looked as if he came to be crowned instead of his master – I never saw so princely a manner and air. The Chancellor looked like Mephostopheles behind Margaret in the Church.[4]

The ceremony was much too long, and some parts of it were carelessly performed. The Archbishop[5] mumbled. The Bishop of London[6] preached, well enough indeed, but not so effectively as the occasion required; and, above all, the low, clumsy bearing of the King made the foolish parts of the ritual appear monstrously ridiculous, and deprived many of the better parts of their proper effect. Persons who were at a distance perhaps did not feel this. But I was near enough to see every turn of his finger and every glance of his eye. The moment of the crowning was extremely fine. When

---

[1] Washington Irving (1783–1859), the author, was then secretary to the American embassy in London.

[2] Dorothea, Duchesse de Dino (1792–1862), Talleyrand's mistress, the wife of his nephew; she presided over his house in London.

[3] Dorothea Christophorovna, Princesse de Lieven (1785–1847), wife of the Russian ambassador.   [4] *Faust*, Part 1, scene 20.

[5] William Howley (1766–1848: *DNB*), Archbishop of Canterbury from 1828.

[6] Charles James Blomfield (1786–1857: *DNB*), Bishop of London, 1828–56.

the Archbishop placed the crown on the head of the King, the trumpets sounded, – the whole audience cried out God save the King. All the Peers and Peeresses put on their coronets, and the blaze of splendour through the Abbey seemed to be doubled.

The King was then conducted to the raised Throne, where the Peers successively did him homage, – each of them kissing his cheek and touching the Crown. Some of them were cheered which I thought indecorous in such a place and on such an occasion. The Tories cheered the Duke of Wellington, and our people, in revenge, cheered Lord Grey and Brougham.

You will think this a very dull letter for so great a subject. But I have only had time to scrawl these lines in order to catch the post. I have not a minute to read them over. I lost yesterday and have been forced to work to day. If I find time I will tell you more to morrow.

Ever yours

T B M

TO HANNAH MACAULAY, 13 SEPTEMBER 1831

MS: Trinity College. *Address:* Miss H M Macaulay / Rothley Temple / Mountsorrel / Leicestershire. *Frank:* London September thirteen 1831 / T B Macaulay. *Published:* Clive and Pinney, *Selected Writings of Macaulay*, pp. 442–3.

London Septr. – 13 – 1831

My love,

I am in high spirits at the thought of soon seeing you all in London and of being again one of a family – and of a family which I love so much. It is well that one has something to love in private life. For the aspect of public affairs is very menacing – fearful, I think, beyond what people in general imagine. Three weeks however will probably settle the whole, and bring to an issue the question, Reform or Revolution. One or the other I am certain that we must and shall have. I assure you that the violence of the people, the bigotry of the Lords, and the stupidity and weakness of the ministers, alarm me so much that even my rest is disturbed by vexation and uneasy forebodings – not for myself; for I may gain and cannot lose, – but for this noble country which seems likely to be ruined without the miserable consolation of being ruined by great men. All seems fair as yet, and will seem fair for a fortnight longer.[1] But I know the danger

---

[1] The Reform Bill went up to the House of Lords on 22 September; it was defeated on the second reading, 8 October. TBM's attitude at this time is described in Margaret Macaulay's letter to her cousin Henry Thatcher, 30 September: 'Tom in common with most Whigs is looking extremely blue about the division in the Lords next week. Everyone expects that the Bill will be thrown out, many expect disturbances in consequence, and Tom whose imagination you know often exaggerates evils talks in the strongest manner of the dangers that may be apprehended, and prophesies that blood will flow in this city before the end of the week' (MS, Huntington).

from information more accurate and certain than, I believe, any body not in power possesses – and I know, what our men in power do not know, how terrible the danger is.

All this is strictly confidential. I called on Lord Lansdowne on Sunday. He told me distinctly that he expected the bill to be lost in the Lords, and that if it were lost the ministers must go out. I told him with as much strength of expression as was suited to the nature [of] our connection, and to his age and rank, that if the ministers receded before the Lords, they and the Whig party were lost, – that nothing remained but an insolent oligarchy on the one side and infuriated people on the other – that Lord Grey and his colleagues would become as odious and more contemptible than Peel and the Duke of Wellington. "What could be done?" "Make more peers," said I. Lord Lansdowne objected to such a course with the feeling natural to a nobleman of such ancient descent and such high rank. But why did not they think of all this earlier? Why put their hand to the plough and look back? Why begin to build without counting the cost of finishing? Why raise the public appetite, and then baulk it?

I told him that the House of Commons would address the King against a Tory ministry. I feel assured that it would do so. I feel assured that if those who are bidden will not come, the highways and hedges will be ransacked to form a reforming ministry. To one thing my mind is made up. If no body else will move an address to the Crown against a Tory ministry, – I will. –

This is all strictly secret. I cannot tell you how it vexes and alarms me. Kindest love to all.

Ever yours my dearest
T B M.

TO HANNAH MACAULAY, 15 SEPTEMBER 1831

MS: Trinity College. *Address:* Miss H M Macaulay / Rothley Temple / Mountsorrel / Leicestershire. *Frank:* London September fifteen / 1831 / T B Macaulay. *Published:* Clive and Pinney, *Selected Writings of Macaulay,* pp. 443–5.

London September 15 – 1831

My love,

I have been very busy since I wrote last, moving heaven and earth to render it certain that, if our ministers are so foolish as to resign in the event of a defeat in the Lords, the Commons may be firm and united: – and I think that I have arranged a plan which will secure a bold and instant declaration on our part, if necessary. Lord Ebrington is the man whom I have in my eye as our leader. I have had much conversation with him and with several of our leading county members. They are all staunch: and I will answer for this; – that if the Ministers should betray us, we will be ready to defend ourselves.[1]

We are to have a magnificent dinner in a week or ten days to commemorate the passing of the Bill through the Commons. There will be three hundred Members or thereabouts present. It will cost us, I am sorry to say, three pounds a piece. We are to dine in Stationers' Hall, the Company having lent it to us for the occasion. The Landlord of the Albion Tavern is to furnish the dinner; and, by all that I can hear of that eminent person, we may think ourselves very lucky to get off for 3£ each. Every thing is to be in the first style. Sir Francis Burdett is to take the chair. The Newspapers will be full of it, no doubt, whenever it does take place. There is to be a table for the reporters.[2]

My father has received very kind and ardent assurances from the Chancellor of attention to his interests – ; Lord B[rougham] charges himself absolutely with John's fortune. He told Buxton that, whether he went out or staid in, he would take care to provide for John before he gave up the Seals.[3] He means also, in case a Bill for appointing Commissioners of Public Charities, now under discussion, should pass into a law, to make my father a Commissioner.[4] This will be a 800£ a year.

[1] TBM's plan was to call a meeting of M.P.s at Willis's Rooms to agree on a resolution of support to the ministry; Greville's *Memoirs* for 22 September and 10 October refer to two meetings of this kind but do not mention TBM (II, 201; 206). On 10 October, following the defeat of the Bill in the Lords, Ebrington moved his resolution and was followed by a speech from TBM. The standard accounts do not, apparently, know anything about TBM's role in originating this move, supposing that he in fact did so: see also 17 October 1831.

[2] The dinner, in honor of Lord John Russell and Lord Althorp, was held on 24 September. TBM gave the toast to '"the glorious cause of reform"' (*Morning Chronicle*, 26 September); his speech is briefly summarized in the *Morning Herald*, 26 September.

[3] Brougham made up for the unsatisfactory earlier gift of a living to John Macaulay by appointing him to that of Loppington, Shropshire, worth £270.

[4] Zachary Macaulay received the appointment in December, but not before he and TBM had quarrelled over the good faith of Brougham's promises. Margaret Macaulay, *Recollections*, 1864, writes that 'on Tuesday last [29 November], after a long conversation with Tom, in which he as usual abused him [Brougham] as the most profligate, faithless scoundrel in England, and Papa defended him with his usual warmth, Papa went to see him. I was with Tom at a friend's house, we returned late and found Papa alone in the drawing-room. "Well," said Tom, "what does the Chancellor say about the commission?" "Why, he says there is a hitch," replied Papa. "Ah! I knew it would be so," replied the other, pale with rage; "profligate, unprincipled scoundrel, that he is! You will never get it – I knew he would never give it to you. I am not disappointed." Papa was very much displeased indeed at this and similar language. Told him he was unfair and would not allow for the difficulties which encompassed such men, that he did not judge as he would be judged, that his prejudice against his Lordship was quite different from his usual manner of feeling and viewing things; that he must insist upon it, that he no more went about talking in the violent manner in which he had spoken, and so on; he was extremely angry. Tom's voice trembled with passion and agitation. He said he was sorry that he had spoken in that manner, but could not restrain himself every time he spoke of him from using the most violent expressions of contempt and hatred. He begged Papa to relate what had passed. "It

He is negociating with Lord Goderich an arrangement which will secure
to Henry the place, (not in itself, I think, very desirable,) of Commissioner
of Prizes at Sierra-Leone.[1]

My father seems to wish that you were in town. I asked him to day
when you were to come up. He said; "I wish them to come immediately
but I do not like to interfere with their pleasures. I have hinted what
I desire. But they seem to like the country." Do not mention to him what
I tell you. But make your arrangements as you think best under these
circumstances.

Farewell, my dear, dear, love. How delightful it is in the middle of
intrigues and tumults and ambitious competitions [to][2] feel that there are
some whose [affec][2]tion is unalterable. Lord [Byron told?][2] his sister in
the midst of his tro[uble][2]

["Th]ere[2] yet are two things in my destiny
A world to roam through, – and a home with thee."[3]

Go the world as [it][2] will – rise or fall who may, – a quiet home with
those who are dearest to me will at last be within my reach: – and to that
home I shall carry the best lesson which a man can learn in the great
world – to despise it.

Not that I have any special reason for cynicism at this moment. I
receive warm assurances of the enthusiasm in my favour at Leeds. But I
must stop. Kind loves to every body.

Yours ever, darling

T B M

Thank Margaret for her letter.

---

seems," said Papa, "that Brougham is accused of favouritism." – "Has he the effrontery
to say that?" returned Tom. – "There, again, Tom! I really must insist on hearing no
more of such language." – "Well, I am sorry, I am sorry; but I must tell you that I do not
believe one single word Lord B. says."...I followed Tom down stairs, and blamed him
for not having endeavoured to soothe Papa. After having talked over the business, I proposed to him to go up stairs, and say that he was sorry he had been so warm, but really
he was so hurt and vexed about it that he could not help it. He went accordingly; and coming
down in a few minutes, said he had done as I advised' (pp. 61–3).

1 Henry's appointment as Commissioner of the Mixed (i.e., English and Spanish) Court of
Arbitration at Sierra Leone was gazetted on 6 January 1832; on 22 November 1831 Margaret
Macaulay wrote that 'Henry's Commission is gone out to him and we hear that the person
above him is coming home in which case Henry will step into his place and an income of
three thousand a year' (to Mrs John Cropper: MS, Huntington). Selina Macaulay, Diary,
3 June 1833, states more soberly that Henry's place was worth £2,000 a year, 'with a retiring
pension, after seven years' service, of 750 £ a year.' In his letter to Brougham following
the quarrel with TBM (note 4, above), Zachary Macaulay pointed out that Henry's appointment could not be made evidence of Brougham's favoritism, for 'the place was in Lord
Goderich's gift, and was asked for through Mr. C. Grant; he must however acknowledge
the kindness with which Lord B. had interfered to remove such obstacles as stood in the
way' (Margaret Macaulay, *Recollections*, 1864, p. 65).   2 Paper torn away with seal.
3 Byron, 'Epistle to Augusta,' stanza 1; written in 1816 but first published by Moore, *Letters
and Journals of Byron*, II (1831), 36.

TO [THE LEEDS ASSOCIATION], 5 OCTOBER 1831

MS: University of Iowa. *Address:* E: Baines Esq Junior[1] / Leeds. *Frank:* London, October five 1831 / T B Macaulay. *Published:* Leeds *Mercury*, 8 October 1831.

London October 5 – 1831

Gentlemen,

It is not easy for me to express the feelings of pride and pleasure with which I have read your requisition[2] and looked over the long series of respectable names attached to it. The trust which you have offered to me is one which, young as I am in public life, and unconnected as I am with your town, I should have thought it the height of presumption to solicit. It is one which I should consider as an ample reward for a long course of laborious public service. Should you place me in the high and honourable situation of your representative it shall be my constant endeavour to vindicate your choice by steadily adhering to those public principles to which alone, as I well know, I am indebted for your favour.

What those public principles are I need not here state at length. I have to the best of my power supported the reform-bill introduced by his Majesty's ministers; – and I shall always be ready to support every measure which may appear to me necessary to secure the freedom and purity of election.

I am firmly convinced that the system of slavery which exists in our colonies is inconsistent with religion, with morality, and with sound policy, and that it is the duty of the legislature to take measures for the early and complete extinction of that great evil. Such measures will

---

[1] (Sir) Edward Baines (1800–90: *DNB*), son of Edward Baines (1774–1848: *DNB*); the elder Baines was, from 1801, proprietor of the Leeds *Mercury* and had made it the leading provincial newspaper in England; his son Edward was editor. The Baineses were Dissenters and prominent in the Whig politics of Yorkshire. TBM would already have known the eldest son, Matthew Talbot Baines (1799–1860: *Boase*), B.A., Trinity, 1820; President of the Union, 1818; and on the Northern Circuit from 1825.

[2] 'We, the undersigned inhabitants of the Borough of Leeds, who, under the Reform Bill, shall possess the elective Franchise, considering you to be eminently qualified to represent the Borough in the House of Commons, by the great and diversified talents you have displayed in Parliament, the Soundness and Liberality of your Political Principles, and the Service you have rendered to the Country by your eloquent and powerful advocacy of that great Measure which confers the Franchise upon this and other populous and wealthy Towns, respectfully request that you will allow yourself to be put in Nomination at the first Election of Members for Leeds, and we promise to give you our zealous, free, and independent Support. / [Signed by One Thousand Three Hundred and Four persons qualified to vote for Members for the Borough of Leeds]' (Leeds *Mercury*, 8 October). This requisition was presented to TBM in London on 5 October by a delegation from Leeds, to whom TBM replied by reading the letter printed here. He then gave the MS to the elder Baines to be sent to his son at Leeds for publication in the *Mercury* and provided the frank for the cover. The elder Baines's covering note to the Leeds Association calls TBM's reply 'very satisfactory' (MS, University of Iowa).

always have my warmest support. I shall at the same time be ready to concur in every regulation which may be necessary for the protection of those British labourers who are so situated that they can scarcely be considered as free agents.

A great and extensive reform in the whole system of our civil and criminal jurisprudence ought to be, and, I trust, will be the consequence of reform in the representation.

To mitigate as far as possible the public burdens and to distribute them judiciously will be among the first duties of the parliament. It will be in an especial manner the duty of those who may, under the new system, represent the great manufacturing towns to attack those monopolies by which far more than by direct taxation the difficulties under which the country now lies have been produced. I conceive, in particular, that the whole system of the corn-laws requires a complete revision, and that the vast market of the East ought, with as little delay as possible, to be thrown open to English industry and enterprise.

A reformed House of Commons will undoubtedly take into its most serious consideration the state of Ireland. I shall assuredly support, to the best of my ability, any measure which may appear to me likely to improve the moral and physical condition of a people suffering under the effects of many ages of misgovernment.

I trust that it will be in my power shortly to visit Leeds, to return thanks personally to those who have honoured me with their confidence, and to return full and explicit answers to those questions which electors are entitled to ask of every man who solicits a public trust at their hands. I will, therefore, at present only repeat that I feel the deepest gratitude for your kindness, and that if your choice shall fall on me my time, and whatever talents I possess, shall be devoted to your service. / I have the honour to be, / Gentlemen

Your most faithful Servant
T B Macaulay

TO THOMAS FLOWER ELLIS, 17 OCTOBER 1831

MS: Trinity College. *Address:* T F Ellis Esq. *Published:* Clive and Pinney, *Selected Writings of Macaulay*, pp. 445–7.

London October 17. 1831

My dear Ellis,

I should have written to you long ago – but that I mislaid your letter and forgot your direction. When shall you be in London? Of course you do not mean to sacrifice your professional business to the work of numbering the gates and telling the towers of boroughs in Wales.[1] What you mean by saying that you are hard worked, I do not very well understand. I should have thought that your duties would be very easy.

You will come back, I suppose, with your head full of ten-pound householders instead of ἥρωες, and of Caermarthen and Denbigh instead of Carians and Pelasgians.[2] I expect to hear you talk of nothing but limits and population returns. Is it true, by the bye, that the Commissioners are whipped on the boundaries of the boroughs by the beadles, in order that they may not forget the precise line which they have drawn? I deny it wherever I go, and assure people that some of my friends who are in the Commission would not submit to such degradation. Indeed I believe that the story originates solely in the circumstance that Bellenden Kerr[3] has been horsewhipped at every place to which he has yet gone.

You must have been hard-worked indeed and soundly whipped too, if you have suffered as much for the reform-bill as we who debated it. I believe that there are fifty members of the House of Commons who have done irreparable injury to their health by attendance on the discussions of this Session. I have got through pretty well. But I look forward, I confess, with great dismay to the thought of recommencing; particularly as Wetherell's cursed lungs seem to be in as good condition as ever.

As to myself – I have every reason to be gratified by the manner in which my speeches[4] have been received. To say the truth the station which I now hold in the house is such that I should not be inclined to quit it for any place which was not of considerable importance. My modesty, –

---

[1] Ellis was one of twenty commissioners appointed to report on the boundaries of the boroughs of England and Wales.

[2] Ellis was writing a review of vol. 1 of Thomas Arnold's edition of Thucydides (1830) for the SDUK's *Quarterly Journal of Education*, IV (July 1832), 142–60.

[3] Charles Henry Bellenden Ker (1785?–1871: *DNB*), a barrister, and, with Ellis, among the most active members of the SDUK.

[4] On the Reform Bill, 20 September, *Hansard*, 3rd Series, VII, 297–311; and on Lord Ebrington's motion, 10 October, *ibid.*, VIII, 390–9. Of the first of these speeches, Empson reported to Napier that TBM 'outdid himself on Tuesday. I staid to hear him. He is a most extraordinary being' ([23 September]: MS, British Museum). The same speech is interestingly described by a correspondent of the New York *Observer*: 'a little man, of small voice, affected utterance, clipping his words, and hissing like a serpent, succeeded in gaining the floor.... "Mr. Macaulay" – "Mr. Macaulay" – went quick around among the spectators, in a low, but animated voice.... The house was still for the first time in the evening, and each fixed his eye upon the little man – Thomas Babington Macaulay. And surely I thought them very simple to be so attracted by such an unpromising beginning – and utterly perverted in taste to be able even to endure such affected, intolerable elocution.... Fortunately, however, these spasmodic symptoms gradually wore off, as the fire of argument kindled up his soul, and the more proper shapes of human speech by equal degrees formed upon his tongue, and flowed from his lips. In fifteen minutes he had wrapped himself in the Reform Bill, as in a mantle, and thrown its brilliant and attractive forms over him, in the most graceful and befitting forms, – and himself stood up, thus invested, challenging and receiving universal admiration' (quoted in Leeds *Mercury*, 21 January 1832).

which, as you well know, is my great weakness, will not allow me to repeat all the compliments which I have received. You will see my two last speeches excellently reported and corrected by myself in the Mirror of Parliament.

What you saw about my having a place was a blunder of a stupid *reporther's*. Croker was taunting the government with leaving me to fight their battle and to rally their followers; and said that the honourable and learned member for Calne, though only a practising barrister in title, seemed to be in reality the most efficient member of the government.[1] *Entre nous* they would have made a poor hand of it without me. Our meeting at Willis's rooms and Lord Ebrington's motion were wholly brought about by me. I really believe that, but for the stir which I made among our county-members, the ministers would have resigned. This is all in the strictest confidence. You shall hear particulars when we meet.

By the bye – my article on Croker has not only smashed his book,[2] but has smashed the Westminster Review incidentally. The utilitarians took on themselves to praise the accuracy of the most inaccurate editor that ever lived – and gave as an instan[ce][3] of it a note in which, as I have shewn, he makes a mistake of twenty years and more.[4] John Mill[5] is in a foaming rage, and says that they are in a worse scrape than Croker: – John Murray[6] says that it is a damned nuisance: and Croker looks across the House of Commons at me with a leer of hatred which I repay with a gracious smile of pity. Most of the readers of the Edinburgh Review are as much pleased to see Croker trounced as the spectators on a memorable occasion at Covent Garden Theatre were to see Westmacott[7] beaten; – and are on my side without knowing why. You will see that I have stolen a hint from you to embellish my article. –

[1] In reply to TBM's speech of 20 September Croker sarcastically complimented him upon his imminent promotion to 'some high station of the Ministry' and expressed his surprise that TBM, 'notwithstanding his great talents, has hitherto had little other opportunity of displaying them, than in the humbler station of a practising barrister' (*Hansard*, 3rd Series, VII, 311–12).

[2] In the first fifty years following its publication 'more than sixty thousand copies (not including those of the many American editions) were disposed of' (Myron F. Brightfield, *John Wilson Croker*, Berkeley, 1940, p. 306).

[3] Paper torn away with seal.

[4] The reference is to a note regarding an anecdote reported by Sir Joseph Mawbey: see *Westminster Review*, xv (October 1831), 387; and TBM's review of Croker, *ER*, LIV, 7.

[5] TBM may or may not have known that Mill ceased to write for the *Westminster Review* in 1828.

[6] John Murray (1778–1843: *DNB*), whose firm published Croker's book. 'Murray told an acquaintance of Tom's that his review had spoiled the sale of the book....Murray in his energetic language says it is "a cursed business"' (Hannah to Fanny Macaulay, [October? 1831]: MS, Huntington).

[7] Charles Molloy Westmacott (1787?–1868: *Boase*), editor of the *Age*; he was beaten, on 16 October 1830, by Charles Kemble in the lobby of Covent Garden for printing abuse of Kemble's daughter Fanny. The spectators refused to give any assistance to Westmacott.

I am ashamed to have said so much about my self. You will think me as great an egotist as Sir John Malcolm.[1] But you asked for news about me. No request is so certain to be granted, or so certain to be a curse to him who makes it as that which you have made to me.

Ever yours
T B Macaulay

TO MACVEY NAPIER, 29 OCTOBER 1831

MS: British Museum. *Address:* Macvey Napier Esq / Edinburgh. *Frank:* London October twenty nine 1831 / T B Macaulay. *Mostly published:* Napier, *Correspondence*, pp. 119–20.

London October 29. 1831

Dear Napier,

Have the kindness to let me know what is the longest time that you can possibly give me for the next Number. Lardner is very desirous to bring out my book about France – and I wish to finish at least the first part of it for him, before I do any thing else.

I will at all events give you a paper on John Bunyan.[2] Longman has sent me Southey's edition and a beautiful edition it is.

I must, I fear, give up all hope of being able to do any thing about Lord Nugent's Book.

Lord Kerry tells me that the neologian article about German divinity[3] was written by Tom Moore, and that Tom Moore himself owned it to him. I should never have thought it. It is rather a perilous enterprise for Moore. He knows, I believe, scarcely a word of German. The article has given offence – but not so much as I had expected.

It is of the greatest consequence that we should bestir ourselves. I hope that the Lord Advocate who is now taking a holiday will do something during the prorogation. It is vain, I fear, to talk about Sydney.

Ever yours truly
T B Macaulay

[1] Sir John Malcolm (1769–1833: *DNB*), administrator and diplomat in the service of the East India Company; Governor of Bombay, 1826–30; Tory M.P., 1831–2. TBM's essay on Clive nominally reviews Malcolm's *Life of Clive*.

[2] 'Southey's Edition of the Pilgrim's Progress,' *ER*, LIV (December 1831), 450–61; Southey's edition was published in 1830.

[3] 'State of Protestantism in Germany,' *ER*, LIV (September 1831), 238–55.

TO MACVEY NAPIER, 1 NOVEMBER 1831

MS: British Museum. *Address:* Macvey Napier Esq / Edinburgh. *Frank:* London November
one 1831 / T B Macaulay. *Extract published:* Myron F. Brightfield, *John Wilson Croker*,
Berkeley, 1940, p. 301.

London Nov 1. 1831

Dear Napier,

I received your letter and the inclosed bill yesterday. I am very sorry
to hear that you have been unwell. I wrote on Saturday to ask what time
you can allow me for the next Number. I hope that when you answer
that question you will send me a good account of yourself.

I should like to write a short article on Hampden – that is to say if
Lord N[ugent]'s book be one which I can praise with a safe conscience.[1]
But on that subject I can promise nothing till I have seen it, and till I have
had some talk with Lardner, who is just now expected in London. He has
been wandering over the Continent.

My article on Johnson takes here greatly. Blackwood has some abuse
of it, I see, and some futile objections.[2] The Quarterly which comes
out to morrow will, I have no doubt, say something on the subject.[3]
Lockhart, I hear, has been much vexed, and so has John Murray.

Ever yours
T B Macaulay

TO MACVEY NAPIER, 19 DECEMBER 1831

MS: British Museum. *Address:* Macvey Napier Esq / Castle Street / Edinburgh. *Frank:*
London December nineteen 1831 / T B Macaulay.

London Decr. 19 –

Dear Napier,

Our sittings are over for a time; and I have leisure to think about the
Edinburgh Review. In three or four days I will send off a short article on
John Bunyan.

Whether I shall or shall not be able to review Lord Nugent's book
for this Number depends on your arrangements as to time. If, as I think

1   TBM reviewed it in 'Lord Nugent's Memorials of Hampden,' *ER*, LIV (December 1831),
    505–50. Margaret Macaulay wrote on 25 November that 'Lord Nugent is bringing out a
    Life of Hampden, which he tells Tom he shall send him, with his favourite passages *marked*'
    (*Recollections*, p. 221). The book was not published until 19 December.
2   Wilson, using notes furnished by Croker, replied to TBM's review in 'Noctes Ambrosianæ,'
    Blackwood's, XXX (November 1831), 829–38.
3   The article on Croker's *Boswell*, *Quarterly Review*, XLVI (November 1831), 1–46, takes no
    particular notice of TBM's attack but praises the quality of Croker's editing. The reviewer
    was John Gibson Lockhart (1794–1854: *DNB*), Scott's son-in-law and biographer, and
    editor of the *Quarterly*, 1825–53.

you said, you do not publish till the middle of January, I can let you have an article by the 8th or 10th. If that will not do, the subject must stand over till the following Number.

You will read all our news in the papers. We had a glorious majority[1] — and as great a superiority, I think, in the debate as in the division.

Ever yours truly

T B Macaulay

TO MACVEY NAPIER, [*3?*][2] JANUARY 1832

MS: British Museum. *Address:* Macvey Napier Esq | Castle Street | Edinburgh. *Frank:* London January three 1832 / T B Macaulay. *Published:* Napier, *Correspondence*, p. 120.

London Jan 2 —

Dear Napier,

I send back the sheets. On the whole I wish, — that is, unless you object strongly to it — that the last paragraph should stand.[3] I admire Dryden. But I do not think him a man of a creati[ve][4] mind. He had great fertility, great command of language, great skill [in][4] versification. But I do not think that he had, in the high sense of the word, any originality. I do not dispute that his works are more valuable than those of Bunyan. But I do not think that they shew so much creative power. I should say the same of Pope as compared with Defoe. I allow that Pope's works are more valuable than Defoe's. But I think that Defoe had more originality, more native power of imagination than Pope.

I am delighted to hear that Empson has given you an article about the Prince's Travels.[5] I have no doubt that it will be good. I am getting on

---

[1] The third Reform Bill was introduced on 12 December; in the division of 17 December on the second reading the majority for the bill was one hundred and sixty-two. TBM spoke in the debate on 16 December (*Hansard*, 3rd Series, IX, 378–92). Of this speech, which was also published separately, Margaret Macaulay writes, *Recollections*, p. 255, that 'people unite in calling it more Parliamentary, moderate, and statesmanlike, than any of his previous speeches, though less brilliant. It was spoken a day sooner than was intended and the last touches were not put to it, but he was called up by some observations of Lord Mahon's on the Leeds business.' Hobhouse reports how it seemed to one not in the family: 'Lord Mahon made a good speech; but, alluding to Macaulay, who had just sauntered into the House, drew up that extraordinary young man, who made one of his best speeches – indeed, one of the best I ever heard' (Lord Broughton, *Recollections of a Long Life*, ed. Lady Dorchester, 6 vols., 1909–11, IV, 155). Mahon had reproached TBM for approving the ballot in his letter to the Leeds Association of 2 September, and for other indications that he was being carried away by 'the revolutionary torrent' (*Hansard*, 3rd Series, IX, 377–8).

[2] The letter was perhaps written on 2 January and not mailed until 3 January; but since both postmark and frank agree on 3 January, 2 January may be TBM's mistake.

[3] TBM admits only Bunyan and Milton to the rank of 'great creative minds' in the latter half of the seventeenth century (*ER*, LIV, 461).   [4] Paper torn away with seal.

[5] 'Tour in England, Ireland, and France, By a German Prince,' *ER*, LIV (December 1831), 384–407.

very fast with Hampden. I fear that it will be longer than most of my articles – above thirty pages. –

Croker has put forth a silly little pamphlet[1] in defence of himself against the Edinburgh Review – partly Blackwood's and partly his own. I do not know whether it is sold. It lies on the table of the Athenæum. I can blow it to atoms in a note which will not be, I think, longer than a page or a page and a half.

Ever yours
T B Macaulay

TO MACVEY NAPIER, 9 JANUARY 1832

MS: British Museum. *Address:* Macvey Napier Esq / Castle Street / Edinburgh. *Frank:* London January nine 1832 / T B Macaulay. *Mostly published:* Trevelyan, I, 248–9.

London Jany. 9. 1832

Dear Napier,

I have been so much engaged by bankrupt business, – as we are winding up the affairs of many estates[2] – that I shall not be able to send off my article about Hampden till Thursday the 12th. It will be, I fear, more than forty pages long. As Pascal said of his eighteenth letter, I would have made it shorter, if I could have kept it longer.[3] You must indulge me however. For I seldom offend in that way.

It is in part a narrative. This is a sort of composition which I have never yet attempted. You will tell me, I am sure, with sincerity how you think that I succeed in it.

Lord Nugent's book, *entre nous*, is dreadfully heavy. I have said as little about it as I decently could.

Ever yours
T B M

1 'Answers to the Edinburgh Reviewer of Croker's Boswell, selected from Blackwood's Magazine,' privately printed, 1831.
2 The Bankruptcy Commission ceased to act on 11 January.
3 *Lettres Provinciales*, XVI.

TO UNIDENTIFIED RECIPIENT, [6?–10? JANUARY 1832][1]

MS: Columbia University.

[London]

I should have very great pleasure both in dining with you and in meeting Mr. Shepherd.[2] But I expect to leave London for a few days between the expiration of our jurisdiction in Bankruptcy and the meeting of parliament. It will therefore be out of my power to dine with you on Friday.

Ever yours
T B Macaulay

TO MACVEY NAPIER, 19 JANUARY 1832

MS: British Museum. *Address:* Macvey Napier Esq / Castle Street / Edinburgh. *Frank:* London January nineteen 1832 / T B Macaulay. *Published:* Napier, *Correspondence*, p. 121.

London Jany 19 – 1832

Dear Napier,

I am heartily glad that you like my article. I was, and [in][3] spite of your commendations still [am, a][3] little afraid about it, as it was written so quickly that I had no time for careful revision.

I will try the life of Lord Burleigh,[4] if you will tell Longman to send me the book. However bad the work may be, it will serve as a heading for an article on the times of Elizabeth.

On the whole I thought it best not to answer Croker. Almost all the little pamphlet which he published – or rather printed, for I believe it is not for sale, – is made up of extracts from Blackwood. And I thought that a contest with your [g][3]rog-drinking, cock-fighting, cudgel playing, Professor of Moral Philosophy[5] would be too degrading. I could have demolished every paragraph of the defence. Croker defended his θνητοι φιλοι[6] by quoting a passage of Euripides which, as every scholar knows,

---

[1] The expiration of the Bankruptcy Commission on 11 January, the meeting of Parliament on 19 January, and the reference to the Friday between those dates, indicate that TBM is writing not earlier than Friday, 6 January, nor later than Tuesday, 10 January.

[2] Probably William Shepherd (1768–1847: *DNB*), Unitarian minister at Liverpool, author, and close friend of Brougham.   [3] Covered by seal.

[4] Edward Nares, *Memoirs of the Life and Administration of the Right Honourable William Cecil, Lord Burghley*, 3 vols., 1828–31; reviewed by TBM in 'Nares' Memoirs of Lord Burghley – Political and Religious Aspects of his Age,' *ER*, LV (April 1832), 271–96.

[5] John Wilson.

[6] Croker's conjecture for the meaning of the initials θφ in Johnson's prayers and meditations for 4 April 1779. Croker translated the phrase as 'departed friends'; TBM observed that 'no schoolboy could venture to use the word θνητοι in the sense which Mr Croker ascribes to it without imminent danger of a flogging' (*ER*, LIV, 10). In reprinting the essay on

is corrupt, which is nonsense and false metre if read as he reads it, and which Markland[1] and Matthiæ[2] have set right by a most obvious correction. – But, as nobody seems to have read his vindication, we can gain nothing by refuting it.

Ever yours
T B Macaulay

TO UNIDENTIFIED RECIPIENT, 21 [JANUARY? 1832?][3]

Text: [Thornton Hunt, ed.], *The Correspondence of Leigh Hunt*, 1862, I, 265–6.

Gray's Inn, Saturday, 21st June.

Sir, –

I will with great pleasure give to the plan which you have communicated to me any little advantage which it may derive from my name.[4] I wish to subscribe for one copy of the poems, and I heartily wish that it were in my power to do more. I do not know Mr. Leigh Hunt by sight; I dissent from many of his opinions; but I admire his talents – I pity his misfortunes – and I cannot think without indignation of some part of the treatment which he has experienced. – I have the honour to be, Sir, your faithful servant,

T. B. Macaulay.

Croker TBM added a note saying that 'an attempt was made to vindicate this blunder by quoting a grossly corrupt passage from the 'Ικέτιδες of Euripides' (*Essays*, 1843, I, 365). Croker had the last word in the third edition of his Boswell, 1848, pp. 626–7, pointing to another passage in his favor in Euripides' *Hercules Furens*. A long note on the question appears in G. B. Hill, ed., *Johnsonian Miscellanies*, Oxford, 1897, I, 89–90.

[1] Jeremiah Markland, ed., *Euripidis Drama Supplices Mulieres*, 1763.
[2] August Matthiae, ed., *Euripidis Tragoediae*, 10 vols., Leipzig, 1813–37.
[3] The date in the printed text is clearly wrong, since 21 June did not fall on a Saturday in any of the years that TBM lived in Gray's Inn; 21 January 1832 is a Saturday, and the promotion of a subscription for Hunt's poems was going on in that month.
[4] TBM is one of the signers of the prospectus for the publication of Hunt's poems by subscription in the *Athenaeum*, 18 February 1832, p. 114. In January Hunt's friend John Forster had asked Bulwer to speak to TBM for his support (Sadleir, *Bulwer: A Panorama*, p. 293). Leigh Hunt (1784–1859: *DNB*), the poet, critic, editor, and friend of Byron, Shelley, and Keats, was in perennial financial difficulty; the publication of the *Poetical Works of Leigh Hunt*, 1832, provided only temporary relief. In 1847, TBM was instrumental in getting a pension for Hunt.

TO MACVEY NAPIER, 1 FEBRUARY 1832

MS: British Museum. *Mostly published:* Napier, *Correspondence,* pp. 121–2.

London Feby. 1. 1832

My dear Napier,

I wrote a few lines to you yesterday from Empson's Chambers. But I cannot defer sending a few more to tell you how sincerely I sympathise with your affliction.[1] During the last few months I have my self, for the first time in my life, felt the pain of such separations; and I have learned how little consolation can do, and how certain is the healing operation of time.

I am glad to hear that my articles are liked at Edinburgh. I have been laid up for a fortnight,[2] and therefore know little of what is said here. But what I have learned is favourable. As to Carlyle,[3] or Carlisle, or whatever his name may be, he might as well write in Irving's unknown tongue at once. The Sun newspaper, with delicious absurdity, attributes his article to Lord Brougham.[4] Of Empson's articles I rather prefer that on the Game Laws.[5] But they are both well done. The article on Portugal[6] I think very good.

Ever yours truly
T B Macaulay

---

[1] Perhaps the death of a child; Carlyle wrote to Napier, on 6 February, that 'the hand of Death has been busy in my circle, as I learn that it has been in yours' (Napier, *Correspondence,* p. 122).

[2] 'Tom has been keeping his Chambers for nearly a week with Lumbago and George has been very kindly attending him' (Margaret to Frances Macaulay, [28 January 1832]: MS, Huntington).

[3] Thomas Carlyle (1795–1881: *DNB*), the essayist and historian. TBM is referring to his 'Characteristics,' *ER,* LIV (December 1831), 351–83. In 1840 TBM considered reviewing Carlyle's *Chartism* (1839) for the *ER* (Empson to Napier, 10 February [1840]: MS, British Museum) but did not do so – wisely, no doubt, in view of his utter lack of sympathy for Carlyle. TBM's antipathy was fully reciprocated; Carlyle's judgment in his Journal, 14 March 1848, that TBM's was an 'essentially irremediable, commonplace nature' is typical (J. A. Froude, *Thomas Carlyle, A History of His Life in London, 1834–1881,* New York, 1910, I, 369).

[4] 'The most eloquent, the most animated essay in this very superior number, is one entitled "Characteristics,"...every line bears traces of a master-spirit....we cannot but fancy that we recognize the masculine and subtle intellect of Lord Brougham' (*Sun,* 30 January).

[5] 'The New Game Laws,' *ER,* LIV (December 1831), 277–311.

[6] 'Recent History, Present State, and External Relations of Portugal,' *ER,* LIV (December 1831), 407–49, was by Henry Rich.

TO UNIDENTIFIED RECIPIENT, [25? FEBRUARY 1832][1]

Text: Leeds *Intelligencer*, 1 March 1832.

[London]

Sir,

The letter respecting which you enquire has never reached me.[2] Had I received it I should have instantly acknowledged it. To your question, my answer is this. I think that the Established Church of Ireland requires a complete reform, and that it is both just and expedient that a large portion of the ecclesiastical property in that country should be applied to public purposes. To what public purpose this fund may with most advantage be applied, is a question which requires much consideration, and respecting which I must decline giving any pledge. I think it right, however, to add, that in any new arrangement which may be made respecting the Irish Church, it seems to me just and politic that strict respect should be paid to existing interests. So strong and decided is my opinion on this subject, that I would far rather pass my whole life out of Parliament, than be a party to a measure which should turn the present incumbents out of their benefices. I should consider such a measure as a distinct act of robbery, and no such act will I ever, under any circumstances, or for any object, be concerned in. The insecurity of property is, I am convinced, a far greater evil than the heaviest of public burdens. It appears to me, therefore, that before we can with propriety apply the revenue of any benefice to the purposes of the state, we must either wait for the death of the existing incumbent, or compensate him for the loss which he sustains by buying up his life interest. Whether you will approve of these opinions I know not, but I trust that I shall not suffer in your esteem on account of the frankness with which I have declared them.[3]

I am, etc.

T. B. Macaulay

[1] TBM's letter was received in Leeds on Monday, 27 February (Leeds *Intelligencer*, 1 March); 25 February seems the most likely date for his reply.

[2] William Cobbett (1762–1835: *DNB*), the journalist and politician, delivered a series of political lectures in Leeds between 23 and 28 February, the last of which was devoted to the subject of the Irish Church, the payment of tithes being then the most urgent Irish question. He had earlier caused a letter to be sent to TBM inquiring whether he supported the petition from Leeds in January asking Parliament to appropriate Irish Church revenues to Irish poor relief. To this no answer had been received. On his arrival in Leeds Cobbett recommended that the question be put to TBM again – by whom is not stated. TBM's letter is a reply to this second inquiry (Leeds *Intelligencer*, 1 March).

[3] 'At the conclusion of this letter there was a burst of disapprobation and cries of "No Macaulay," but Mr. Cobbett checked this expression of feeling, observing that he wished them to consider the matter well before they decided. For his part, he commended Mr. Macaulay's frankness, though he disapproved of his opinions' (Leeds *Intelligencer*, 1 March).

TO MACVEY NAPIER, 6 MARCH 1832

MS: British Museum.

London March 6 – 1832

Dear Napier, –

I will set to work on Lord Burghley without delay. But what with the House in the evening and the West India Committee[1] in the morning, I have scarcely any time. I cannot promise to be ready before the end of the first week of April.

Ever yours truly
T B Macaulay

TO JOSEPH LEES,[2] 15 MARCH 1832

Text: Composite from Leeds *Mercury,* 7 April and Leeds *Intelligencer,* 12 April 1832. *Address:* Joseph Lees, Esq. Committee Room, Political Union, Leeds.

London March 15, 1832.

Sir,

I highly approve of the resolution which has been formed by the gentleman in whose name you have written, not to support any candidate who will not explicitly and frankly avow his sentiments upon the question of tithes. On this, and on every subject, my opinions, whether popular or unpopular, shall be openly and fearlessly stated.

I will answer your questions as shortly and clearly as I can.

To the first I say, that in my opinion part of the Church revenues is private property, and part public property. An advowson which has come, by purchase or by inheritance, into the hands of an individual, seems to me just as much his property as his house. It may be taken from

---

[1] On 15 December 1831 TBM was appointed a member of the select committee on the commercial state of the West Indian Colonies. Among the witnesses before the committee were Zachary Macaulay's old antagonists, James MacQueen and Joseph Marryatt.

[2] The secretary of the Leeds Political Union, formed in November 1831, on the model of the Birmingham Political Union, to promote reform. Lees wrote to all three candidates – TBM, Sadler, and Marshall – on 13 March stating that the Union would support no candidate who would not 'explicitly and frankly' avow his sentiments on Irish tithes, and putting the following questions:

'Do you consider the revenues of the Church to be public or private property?

What is your opinion respecting the appropriation of a part of the immense wealth of the Church to the necessities of the state?

What is your opinion of the Leeds Petition respecting Irish Tithes, and their appropriation to the *Poor,* the Clergy, and the Church equally?

In your opinion, ought there to be a commutation or an abolition of the Tithes in Ireland?

In your opinion, ought the present incumbents to receive the whole or any part of their present incomes during life?'   (Leeds *Mercury,* 7 April).

him for public purposes, just as his house may be taken from him in order to make a canal or a rail road, but, as in the case of his house, so in the case of his advowson, full compensation ought to be given. There are, however, if I am rightly informed, very few advowsons of this kind in Ireland.

The revenues of Bishoprics, of Deans and Chapters, of benefices to which the Crown nominates, are, in my opinion, strictly public property, and may, without injustice to any human being, be applied by the legislature to public purposes, as soon as the existing interests expire. Almost all the Church property of Ireland is of this latter kind. The revenues of the Church of Ireland are therefore, in my judgment, public property.

To the second question I answer that a considerable portion of the church property ought, in my opinion, to be applied to public services, due regard being had to existing interests.

To the third question I answer that in my opinion it is of little consequence to us now what may have been the distribution of the tithes seven hundred years ago. Whatever may have been the original distribution, we know that for some centuries the tithes have not been equally divided between the church, the clergy, and the poor – and that no advowson or presentation has for some centuries been bought or sold with the understanding that the tithes were to be so divided. The claim, if it ever existed, has been dormant for many generations. The discussion of it may now amuse antiquarians – but it is, I think, not a subject worthy of the grave consideration of statesmen.

Consider, too, that if the tithes are to be now appropriated to their own original purposes, the clergyman's third will, both in England and Ireland, go to the Catholic Priest: for it was for the support of the Catholic religion that tithes were originally instituted in this country. We cannot apply the tithe to its original uses without establishing the Catholic religion again.[1]

I by no means say that it may not be very proper to apply a large part of the church property of Ireland to the relief of the poor. But if this is done, it ought to be done because it is useful and humane to do it, and not from any regard to a law which, if it ever existed, has been obsolete for many hundreds of years.

The fourth question I am not sure that I quite understand. I do not know what is meant by the abolition of tithe as contra-distinguished from commutation. The mode of collecting the tithe may be changed. The appropriation of the tithe may be changed, but the tithe itself cannot be abolished. That part of the produce which the clergyman receives must

---

[1] 'Here several voices indulged in expressions of disapprobation, but the Chairman entreated that order might be kept; and the Secretary requested those who bawled out "We won't have it," to pay especial attention to the following sentence of Mr. Macaulay's letter' (Leeds *Intelligencer*, 12 April).

always remain. Somebody must have it. If nobody else takes it, the land-lord, who clearly has no right to it, will take it. Indeed all the preceding questions imply that the tithe is to remain, though collected and appro-priated on new principles. If tithe is abolished, it cannot be appropriated to the necessities of the state, to use the words of the second question; or appropriated to the poor, the clergy, and the church equally, to use the words of the third question.

To the last question I answer that the present incumbents ought, in my opinion, to receive the whole of their revenues during life. If their life interest be not property they have no claim whatever. If it be, as I believe it to be, property in the strictest sense, they have a claim to the whole.

Whatever you may think of these answers, you will, I trust, be of opinion that they are frank and explicit. / I have the honour to be, Sir,

Your most obedient Servant,

T. B. Macaulay.

TO RALPH TAYLOR,[1] 16 MARCH 1832

Text: 'Alfred' [Samuel Kydd], *History of the Factory Movement*, 1 (1857), 148–50.

London, March 16th, 1832.

Sir,

I am decidedly favourable to the principle of Mr Sadler's bill.[2] That is to say, I think that the hours of labour of children ought to be regulated. But I see, I confess, some strong objections to the machinery by which Mr Sadler proposes to effect this object; and I know that some of the most zealous and intelligent friends of the working classes, both in and out of parliament, agree with me in thinking, that if the bill now before us should pass into a law without great modifications, its effect would be most seriously to injure the labourers of our manufacturing districts. There is a strong and general feeling in the House of Commons, that something ought to be speedily done for the protection of the children. There is also,

---

[1] Parson and White, *Leeds Directory*, 1830, lists a Ralph Taylor, cloth drawer; the Leeds *Intelligencer*, 21 June 1832, however, identifies the Ralph Taylor who was among the dissi-dents at TBM's speech on 15 June as a surgeon. He was in any case secretary of the Leeds Committee for Promoting the Ten Hours Bill. Taylor is reported as asking TBM, during his speech at Leeds, 7 September 1832, whether he would support the trades unions (the answer was yes); later, he is indignantly identified by the *Mercury* as the person who, on 10 December, supplied bludgeons to the mob at the hustings, bludgeons that had been manufactured on 'a Sunday' (8 and 11 December).

[2] Introduced 15 December 1831; it proposed to limit the labor of children under nine to ten hours a day. On the second reading, the day of this letter, it was referred to a select com-mittee and did not come before this Parliament again.

I think, a general feeling that the details of Mr Sadler's bill have not been well considered. The government will, I believe, take the question up: and I hope and trust, that before the end of this session, we shall have a law which will accomplish your object in an unexceptionable manner. Permit me to add one word on the subject of the Order in Council, which has been sent to St Lucie.[1] That Order, as you justly say, has provided that a slave shall be forced to work only nine hours a day, and only five days a week. But you forget, I think, that the slave has to find his own subsistence besides. The time which is secured to him is not holiday time. He must cultivate his own provision-ground during the hours when he is absent from his master's sugar plantation. The labour of the slave which the Order in Council limits, is a forced labour, and an unpaid labour. He may work eighteen hours a day voluntarily, and for hire if he pleases. The Order does not in the least restrict him from performing any quantity of work which it may be his own pleasure to perform. There is, therefore, not the slightest analogy between the case of a freeman of mature years. The law ought to limit the hours of forced labour of the slave: – and why? Because he is a slave. Because he has no power to help himself. But the freeman cannot be forced to work to the ruin of his health. If he works over hours, it is because it is his own choice to do so. The law ought not to protect him; for he can protect himself.

The case of a child bears a nearer analogy to the case of a slave. The child may have cruel parents, or may be in the power of those who are not his parents. It is therefore just and reasonable, that the law should extend to the child a protection similar to that which it extends to the slave. But the reason for this protection ceases as soon as the child becomes his own master, and is capable of contracting on his own behalf. The Order in Council to which you refer, limits the hours during which free negroes are to work. And in the same manner I would limit the hours of labour for a child of thirteen or fourteen. But why the hours of labour of a youth in his twentieth year should be limited, as proposed by Mr Sadler's bill, I cannot understand.

I earnestly hope that we may be able to come to a speedy and satisfactory adjustment of this question. / I have the honour to be, Sir,

Your most obedient servant,
T. B. Macaulay

[1] The last effort to make the policy of 'amelioration' effective, a revised Order in Council, of 2 November 1831, stiffened the existing regulations for the treatment of slaves in the Crown Colonies, including St Lucia. One provision fixed the length of time that a slave could be compelled to work.

TO MACVEY NAPIER, 21 MARCH 1832

MS: British Museum.

London March 21 / 1832

Dear Napier,

I send you by the mail of this day Malden's article on slavery.[1] It is, I think, not ill executed: but you must judge for yourself. It is not the subject which I wished him to take. He is a man of very profound classical knowledge, and quite competent to exhibit that knowledge in an interesting manner. I have spoken to him about the 2nd vol. of Niebuhr. The review of the 1st vol. was so bad that I hope the 2nd will not be intrusted to the same hand. If it is not engaged I know nobody who would be likely to do it better than Malden.[2]

If you think fit to print Malden's article, and have time to send a proof to London, put it under a frank to me.

Ever yours
T B Macaulay

TO MACVEY NAPIER, 3 APRIL 1832

MS: British Museum. *Address:* Macvey Napier Esq / Castle Street / Edinburgh. *Frank:* London April three 1832 / T B Macaulay.

London April 3 – 1832

Dear Napier,

I send Malden's article. He has added a passage which I do not much like. You will judge of it for yourself. I am sorry to say that ever since last Thursday I have be[en][3] prevented from writing by an in[flammation?][3] in one of my eyes. To day I am much better – indeed all but quite well. But I find that after writing a page, I must pause for half an hour. Nothing in this vexatious attack plagues me so much as the thought of the inconvenience which it may possibly produce to you. I will go on as fast as I can. But if you can get your Number out without me, do so by all means.

Ever yours
T B Macaulay

---

[1] 'Jeremie on Colonial Slavery,' *ER*, LV (April 1832), 144–81.
[2] The second volume of the English translation of Niebuhr appeared *c*. 17 March. Malden reviewed it in 'Niebuhr's Roman History,' *ER*, LVI (January 1833), 267–312.
[3] Paper torn away with seal.

TO [JOSEPH LEES], 9 APRIL 1832

Text: Leeds *Mercury*, 14 April 1832.

London, April 9th, 1832.

Sir,

I am most highly gratified by the resolution which you have transmitted to me.[1] I rejoice in it still more on public than on private grounds.
I see in it a refutation of the calumnies of those enemies of Reform, who
have so often asserted that no person would be able to find favour with
a popular constituent body, unless he were disposed to court that favour,
by abject and unreasoning servility. I, on the contrary, have always been
firmly convinced, that the confidence of the English people is to be
obtained not by a sycophancy, which degrades alike those who pay and
those who receive it, but by rectitude and plain dealing. It gives me the
greatest pleasure to learn from your letter, that in this opinion I am not
mistaken. / I have the honour to be, Sir,

Your most faithful Servant,

T. B. Macaulay.

TO MACVEY NAPIER, 11 APRIL 1832

MS: British Museum. *Address:* Macvey Napier Esq / Castle Street / Edinburgh. *Frank:*
London April eleven 1832 / T B Macaulay.

London Wednesday

Dear Napier,

I fully expected, as I told you, to finish to day at the very latest. My eye
has, I am sorry to say, given me another warning – and I must in consequence wait till to morrow. To morrow I shall send off an article of,
I suppose, about thirty pages, very desultory, and, in all respects, I fear,
very indifferent.

To night, I think, the Lords will certainly divide.[2]

Ever yours

T B Macaulay

---

[1] A resolution of thanks following the reading of TBM's letter of 15 March on the Irish tithes
at a meeting of the Leeds Political Union, 5 April.

[2] The division on the second reading of the Reform Bill in the House of Lords did not take
place until 14 April, when the Bill received a majority of nine.

TO MACVEY NAPIER, 12 APRIL 1832

MS: British Museum. *Address:* Macvey Napier Esq / Castle Street / Edinburgh. *Frank:* London April twelve 1832 / T B Macaulay. *Published:* Napier, *Correspondence*, p. 127.

London April 12 / 1832

Dear N,

I send off by this mail an article which if you put into the fire you will, I think, do no more than justice. Pray, if you print it, take care of the typography. For it has no need of printer's faults in addition to those which it already has. – You will see that I have huddled it up at the end.

Ever yours

T B Macaulay

TO MACVEY NAPIER, 18 APRIL 1832

MS: British Museum. *Address:* Macvey Napier Esq / Castle Street / Edinburgh. *Frank:* London April eighteen 1832 / T B Macaulay. *Published:* Napier, *Correspondence*, p. 127.

London April 18 – 1832

Dear N,

I am glad to learn that we are likely to see you in London; – and also that you like my article better than I liked it myself. It seemed to me a strange rambling performance.

I think of writing two or three articles, – none of them very long, for the next number. Lord Grey has begged me to review the Speech that Philpotts made on the government scheme of education in Ireland.[1] I think also of reviewing Dumont's life of Mirabeau,[2] unless you are already provided. I have one or two other plans which we can talk over when you come to London. I mention these, lest other applicants should anticipate me.

I am perfectly well at present and in hopes of a short holiday. I will look after Malden and his article on Niebuhr. You are not, I think, likely to find any person better informed on all points of ancient literature than he is. I hope that he possesses the art of giving the spirit and quintessence

---

[1] 22 March (*Hansard*, 3rd Series, XI, 594–615) and published separately. TBM did not review it. Henry Phillpotts (1778–1869: *DNB*), Bishop of Exeter, was perhaps the most energetic and formidable controversialist among the very high Churchmen and very high Tories. He was a veteran antagonist of the *ER*.

[2] Étienne Dumont, *Souvenirs sur Mirabeau*, 1832, the subject of TBM's 'Dumont's *Recollections of Mirabeau* – the French Revolution,' *ER*, LV (July 1832), 552–76. On 28 [March] Margaret Macaulay wrote that she and TBM, the day before, 'walked out and talked a great deal about Mirabeau, who is the prominent person in a very pleasant volume on the revolutionary persons and events, by M. Dumont, and of the Revolution in general' (*Recollections*, p. 244).

of his knowledge without the drossy matter. But this is the rarest of all attainments.

I shall be anxious to hear more about your Raleigh.[1] The story, as you tell it, is indeed a sad one. But this and many other subjects may wait till we meet.

Ever yours
T B M

TO HANNAH AND MARGARET MACAULAY, 7 JUNE 1832

MS: Trinity College.

London June 7 – 1832

My darlings, –

I am sitting in a very handsome well furnished room, with a large window looking out on the Thames; and writing to you with government ink and a government pen on government paper and under a government seal.[2] I have little time to write to day, and little to say except what you will believe without my saying it, how dearly I love and how much I miss you.[3] I am glad that I have business to transact; for I could find it in my heart to whimper as I used to do when I went to school at twelve years old. How two such little gypsies should manage to take such a hold of my heart I do not understand. London looks quite gloomy without you. Gloomy indeed it may well look for it has gone and rained[4] – nay it has done worse – it has gone and thundered and lightened; and over the whole of the broad expanse of the Thames a vast army of mendicant cavalry are performing their evolutions. Do you smoke the meaning of that, little M D?[5]

Be the weather foul or fair I must travel some five hundred miles within the next week. I expect to be elected at Calne on Monday;[6] – and I must

---

1 'Sir Walter Raleigh,' *ER*, LXXI (April 1840), 1–98.

2 TBM is no doubt writing from the office of the Board of Control in Cannon Row. He was appointed one of the Commissioners of the Board, at a salary of £1,200, in the place of Sir James Mackintosh, who died on 30 May. Though the appointment was not gazetted until 21 July, it is noticed in *The Times*, 5 June, and preparations were already made by the date of this letter for the re-election at Calne necessitated, according to the old rule, by TBM's acceptance of a place. The Board of Control, properly the Board of Commissioners for the Affairs of India, represented the Crown in its relations with the East India Company. Established by Pitt in 1784, it was abolished in 1858 on the Company's ceasing to govern.

3 Hannah and Margaret had gone to James Cropper's home in Liverpool.

4 Swift, *Journal to Stella*, 8 February 1710–11. Writing on 9 February, Margaret Macaulay says that TBM called and 'was very pleasant. . . . he quoted an absurd sentence out of *Swift's Journal*, "What do you think it has gone and done? it has gone and rained"' (*Recollections*, p. 230).

5 The language is from Swift's *Journal to Stella*. I cannot explain the riddle about 'mendicant cavalry.'   6 The date of the election was changed to Wednesday, 13 June.

then travel night and day to reach Leeds, where I am to dine at two o'clock on Wednesday.[1] You must not therefore expect me to be a very regular correspondent till I am again settled in London, which will be, I suppose, about the end of next week.

Farewell my dearest girls. Farewell Bird Annie, Nancy, little Anne. Farewell Chitapet. Farewell Preaching Price. I do not know why it is that all our little jokes and nicknames come into my head at once, and almost make the tears come into my eyes. Again and again farewell.

Ever yours my loves,

T B M

TO [ISAAC GOLDSMID?],[2] 7 JUNE [1832][3]

MS: University College, London.

Gray's Inn June 7

My dear Sir,

I am very sorry to say that I am engaged on Wednesday the 20th, and that I shall therefore be forced to deny myself the pleasure of dining with you on that day. / Ever, my dear Sir,

Yours most truly

T B Macaulay

TO HANNAH AND MARGARET MACAULAY, 8 JUNE 1832

MS: Morgan Library. *Address:*[4] Miss Macaulay / J. Cropper Esq / Dingle Bank / Liverpool. *Frank:* London June eight 1832 / T. Hyde Villiers. *Published:* Clive and Pinney, *Selected Writings of Macaulay*, pp. 447–8.

London June 8

My dear Girls, –

To night I set out. When I shall be able to write again I hardly know. I expect not to have a single moment to my self, except

---

[1] TBM was going to Leeds to attend a public dinner in celebration of the passing of the Reform Bill. The occasion was in fact an electioneering opportunity, and was so understood in Leeds; TBM and his fellow Whig candidate, John Marshall, were the principal speakers at the dinner. Because of the change in the date of the Calne election the Leeds dinner was given on Friday, 15 June.

[2] The letter is among the papers of the Goldsmid family.

[3] The only year of TBM's residence at Gray's Inn in which 20 June was a Wednesday.

[4] TBM has written the address on the back of the cover; it was then copied on the front by Villiers, under whose frank the letter was sent.

indeed while I am in the post chaise during the next week. If I can I will snatch a moment or two at Calne on Monday to let you know my movements.

The royal assent was given yesterday afternoon to the English Reform-Bill. It was given by Commissioners.[1] The King unfortunately for himself has been induced by that wretched Court faction which surrounds him to give this proof of his impotent enmity to his ministers and his people. If the matter were merely one of party, I should rejoice at the course which he has taken. It has had this effect – that Lord Grey and the Whigs have all the honor of the reform-bill and the King none of it. If we are to have a quarrel with the Court we shall be far stronger and the Court far weaker than if William the Fourth had on this occasion acted in such a way as to make himself popular throughout the country. I fear – I fear – that he has entered on the path of Charles and Louis. He makes great concessions: but he makes them reluctantly and ungraciously. The people receive them without gratitude or affection. What madness! – to give more to his subjects than any King ever gave, and yet to give in such a manner as to get no thanks! –

Remember to keep to yourselves what I say about politics. In my present situation it would not do for me to promulgate opinions unfavourable to the Prince whom I serve.

I shall expect as soon as my franking privilege returns full details of your journey: – how the Quaker threw Margaret's eggs out of the coach window; – how he sent Hannah's novel after them; – how you met Cook the murderer[2] handcuffed half-way between Liverpool and Leicester; – how you admired the scenery of Matlock and the architecture of Buxton; – how you thundered along the rail-road;[3] – with every etc., as Mrs. Meeke would say. Did you meet any old sinner of a land lady? Were you shewn

[1] An extraordinary number of commissioners – Lords Wellesley, Lansdowne, Brougham, Durham, Grey, and Holland – was present to mark the solemnity of the occasion. The engraving of 'The Reform Bill Receiving the King's Assent by Royal Commission' by S. W. Reynolds, Jr, and William Walker, 1836 (see frontispiece, vol. II, and 8 July 1831), shows TBM among the M.P.s witnessing the ceremony, but the engraving obviously represents an ideal scene – Sir James Mackintosh, who died a week earlier, is also shown – and TBM certainly does not write as though he had seen it.

[2] James Cook, after murdering a Mr Pass in Leicester, fled to Liverpool. He was arrested there on 5 June and returned to Leicester for trial; executed, 10 August.

[3] James Cropper was one of the original promoters of the Liverpool and Manchester Railway. In an undated letter (but doubtless from 1830), Margaret writes of a trip on the railroad that 'our speed in general was between twelve and seventeen miles an hour but they gave us a touch at twenty five which would have been pleasant enough if we had not been on the very verge of a fall forty seven feet deep and unnumbered stones might be on the rail.... The whole of our journey back was spent in a shower of ashes and even hot coals which burnt some of our clothes though we carried umbrellas up the whole way....However I have the satisfaction of thinking I have been the first public journey of the rail road in company with about a hundred people in several carriages chained so close together as to form one compact mass' (to Fanny Macaulay: MS, Huntington).

into any horrible tap-room like that described in Conscience?[1] Were you detained by any villainy on the part of the Coach-proprietors? I shall expect all the conversation that passed in the stage to be detailed dramatically, between inverted commas; – so that I may be able to judge whether my darlings will ever produce a good novel.

But I must stop. Ever, my dear loves, your affectionate friend and brother.

T B M.

[1] Mrs Meeke, *Conscience*, 1814, II, ch. 8.

INDIA BOARD AND M.P. FOR LEEDS
10 JUNE – 26 DECEMBER 1832

1832 Early June
Appointed member of the Board of Control

– June 13
Re-elected for Calne in consequence of accepting office

– June 15
Reform Bill dinner speech at Leeds

– June 22
Appointed to committee of inquiry into East India Company Charter

– July 12
Finishes 'Dumont's *Recollections of Mirabeau*' (*ER*, July)

– September 3–8
Campaigning in Leeds

– October 6–7
Visits Cambridge with Hannah and Margaret

– November 28–December 15
In Leeds for election

– December 8
Appointed Secretary to the Board of Control

– December 11
Margaret Macaulay married

– December 14
Elected at Leeds

TO HANNAH AND MARGARET MACAULAY, 10 JUNE 1832

MS: Trinity College. *Address:* Miss Macaulay / J Cropper's Esq / Dingle Bank / Liverpool.
Partly published: Trevelyan, I, 255–6.

Bath June 10. 1832

My darlings, –

I have just heard from Fanny, who tells me that you had reached Manchester in safety. Everything has gone wrong with me. The people at Calne fixed Wednesday for the election there; – the very day on which I wished to be at Leeds. I shall therefore remain here till Wednesday morning, and read Indian politics in quiet. I am already deep in Zemindars, Ryots, Polygars, Courts of Phousdary, and Courts of Nizamut Adaulut.[1] I can tell you which of the native Powers are subsidiary and which independent, and read you lectures of an hour on our diplomatic transactions at the Courts of Lucknow, Nagpore, Hydrabad, and Poonah. At Poonah, indeed, I need not tell you that there is no Court. For the Paishwa, as you are doubtless aware, was deposed by Lord Hastings in the Pindaree War. Am I not in fair training to be as great a bore as if I had myself been in India? – that is to say as great a bore as the greatest. I know no such pests as those curry-coloured old watering-place Nabobs. Heaven help me! I fear I shall have a good deal to do with them during the approaching year.

I am leading my watering place life here; – that is to say, reading, writing, and walking all day, – speaking to nobody but the waiter, the chambermaid, and Boots, – solitary in a great crowd, and content with solitude. I shall be in London again on Thursday,[2] and shall also be an M P. From that day you may send your letters as freely as ever: – and pray do not be sparing of them. You would not, if you knew how glad I shall be to receive them.

I am ashamed to make you pay for this stuff. But I would gladly pay for any scrap from either of you: – and I do not believe that I love you more than you love me. Write soon, my own little girls. Perhaps in my next, I may tell you something about Bath. Remember me kindly to your hosts.

Ever yours
T B M

[1] Perhaps TBM was reading James Mill's *History of British India*, 1818, where all of these terms will be found defined and discussed.
[2] The day after the Calne election, since TBM did not now expect to go to Leeds; in the event, he did not return to London until 17 June.

TO HANNAH AND MARGARET MACAULAY, 13 JUNE 1832

MS: Morgan Library. *Address:* Miss Macaulay / J Cropper's Esq / Dingle Bank / Liverpool.
Frank: Calne June thirteen 1832 / T B Macaulay.

Calne June 13 – 1832

My dearest girls, –

This is the day of election, and in three or four hours I shall again be
M P. I snatch the only minutes which I shall have to myself till midnight,
to prattle with you on paper. When shall we prattle again face to face, and
make puns on the names of the shopkeepers along the streets?[1] My own
dear sisters, my heart becomes quite heavy when I think for how long
a time we are to be separated.

But this is no day for being heavy. The bells are ringing. Flags are
flying on the housetops. Music is playing in front of the Inn – Macaulay
for ever! Huzza! – Read the inclosed handbill, and you will see how much
honor a prophet may have out of his own country who has none in it.
I shall have I understand to dine with all the élite of all the surrounding
towns.[2] From Chippenham, from Marlborough, yea even from Devizes,
I am told, people are coming to gaze upon and listen to the great patriot.
And I am wishing all the time that I were two hundred miles away,
gazing upon and listening to my own little girls.

But I have been at Bath. I have seen all the spots made classical by
Miss Austen, – the pump-room and the identical bench whereon Miss
Thorpe and Miss Morland discussed the merits of novels,[3] – the nasty
buildings wherein Mrs. Smith lodged,[4] – the street where Captain Went-

---

[1] 'We amuse ourselves sometimes as we walk in the streets in a manner which is, I believe,
quite original, punning upon the names of the shopkeepers as we pass on, in this sort of
manner: "I wish you had more No. 22 for me." The name is *Love*....."Is there any
No. 27 you are afraid of seeing just now?" The name is *Dunn*....this novel diversion is...
particularly favoured by Tom. I have given very simple specimens as the only ones that
occur to me; this kind is held in great contempt, and those only are received with applause
which from being far-fetched show some ingenuity' (Margaret Macaulay, *Recollections*,
p. 243).

[2] Following his election TBM was entertained at a public dinner 'at the Lansdowne Arms,
which was attended by Lord Kerry and nearly all the principal gentlemen of the town.
Several of the Devizes Reformers were also present, and were treated with marked respect'
(*Devizes and Wiltshire Gazette*, 14 June). The same source summarizes TBM's 'eloquent
and energetic speech, in the course of which he contrasted the conduct of the English
people with that of other countries, in any great national undertaking; and observed, that
in no other country was ever such a glorious triumph achieved, as had been gained by the
Reformers in Britain, without one drop of blood having been spilt, or one existing law
violated. He trusted, that under the new Bill of Rights we should have a better system of
Government than we or our fathers had ever known. He stated that the connexion which
now existed between himself and the people of Calne, would shortly terminate; but he
should ever remember with feelings of gratitude and pride, the kindness he had experienced
from them, and that it was by them, that he was introduced into Parliament.'

[3] *Northanger Abbey*, ch. 6.   [4] *Persuasion*, ch. 17.

worth made his proposals to Anne.[1] The assembly room, I own, I did not see. But I climbed the hill whereon the Revd Henry Tilney M A, Miss Tilney, and Catherine held their conversation;[2] – and I did not agree, I must say, with their opinion that the city of Bath might with advantage have been struck out of the landscape. I went to the Abbey where, as you may remember, Mrs. Macmaurice heard so good a sermon that she exclaimed "What a mercy it is that one can go home and forget it all." I heard a very bad sermon; and have most certainly forgotten it all.

I saw Russell Street and the outside of Tom Babington's house: but having a hundred and twenty pounds or so in bank-notes about me, I did not venture in. – But here come the Guild-Stewards and the Burgesses in their best. Here comes the music. Here come the beadles with fine coats and gold-headed staves: and here comes – is it? no – yes – it is Lord Kerry. I had no notion that he was here. I must go and shake hands with him. God bless you, my own dearest girls.

T B M

TO SELINA MACAULAY, 14 JUNE 1832

MS: Huntington Library. *Address:* Miss Macaulay / 44 Bernard Street[3] / Russell Square / London. *Frank:* Birmingham June fourteen / 1832 / T B Macaulay.

Birmingham June 14. 1832

My dear Selina,

I am here on my road to Leeds as fast as I can post. The Leeds people put off their festivities on my account and sent after me to Calne; so that I had no choice. I shall not be in London at the very earliest till Saturday evening. Will you be so kind as to notify this to my clerk; and let him tell the laundress to have every thing in readiness for me from that time, as I cannot be quite certain when I shall come. I must stop.

Ever yours
T B M

---

[1] *Persuasion*, ch. 23.   [2] *Northanger Abbey*, ch. 14.
[3] Where the Macaulay family had been living since the preceding November.

TO GEORGE WAILES,[1] [16 JUNE 1832]

Text: Leeds *Mercury*, 23 June 1832.

I conceive that the new system of representation, so earnestly demanded by the great majority of the nation, ought to have a fair trial. I believe that it will, without the ballot, and without any shortening of the duration of Parliaments, produce good government; but if experience shall prove that tyrannical and illegitimate influence is still exercised over the constituent bodies of England, I shall support the Ballot; and if it shall be found that Parliaments are not sufficiently in harmony with the sense of the people, I shall be of opinion that their duration ought to be abridged. Till the experiment has been fully tried, I am of opinion that we ought to pause.

My opinion is, on the whole, in favour of a property tax, and I fully admit, that if any property tax should be imposed, the fundholder should bear his share; but 1 will not at present pledge myself to support every proposition which may be made for establishing a property tax. I must know what the details of such a measure are to be; I must know what the taxes are for which the property tax is to be a substitute, before I can return a positive answer on that head.

TO HANNAH AND MARGARET MACAULAY, 18 JUNE 1832

MS: Morgan Library. *Address:* Miss Macaulay / J Cropper's Esq / Dingle Bank / Liverpool. *Frank:* London June eighteen / 1832 / T B Macaulay.

London June 18. 1832

My darlings,

On Saturday morning I sent you a newspaper from Leeds. You will have learned from that newspaper my adventures from Wednesday to Friday more fully than I can spare time to detail them.[2] We had a violent

---

[1] A Leeds barrister and Radical (1773?–1854: *Boase*). This text is not properly a letter but the answers to questions that Wailes had tried to put to TBM on the hustings, 15 June; he had been hustled out of range by the Whig crowd before he could do so (Leeds *Intelligencer*, 21 June). The next day Wailes waited on TBM with his questions and received this written reply. The questions were these:

'Will you vote for and advocate
    1. A direct tax upon all tangible property, including the Funds, and a repeal, as far as practicable, of all taxes, more immediately affecting the people?
    2. Election by ballot?
    3. Shortening the duration of Parliaments?'   (Leeds *Mercury*, 23 June).

[2] As reported in the Leeds *Mercury*, 16 and 23 June, and the Leeds *Intelligencer*, 21 June, the Friday, 15 June, that TBM spent in Leeds was a heroic day. After travelling post all night, TBM arrived in Leeds at 11:30 a.m. and met his committee at the Rotunda of the Coloured

struggle and a complete victory. Nothing could exceed the kindness with which my friends treated me. I was lodged, feasted, courted, cheered, and sent off with colours flying to London. I left Leeds on Saturday morning by the mail and reached my chambers early on Sunday.

I have learned from Selina to my great delight that Margaret is well, that your hosts are kind, that the children are pleasant, that the Dingle looks pretty, and that you are both joyous and contented. Dear M D – write a little now and then to poor Presto.[1] – A pun! a pun! – well suited to a Commissioner for the Affairs of India. What city in Hindostan tells the whole history of Desdemona? Do you give it up? Moor-she'd-a-bad. Huzza! How witty!

My loves – I must stop this nonsense. I have found a good many letters which I must answer, – the arrears of my absence. To you I do not write letters, but prattle and talk nonsense, as we used to do, only that I use my pen instead of my tongue. Oh if you knew, my little girls, what a desert this vast city is to me without you! How sweet and perfect a love is that of brothers and sisters when happy circumstances have brought it to its full maturity. And what says the judicious poet?

> My cousin is a bore, –
> My aunt she is a scold, –
> My daughter is too young, –
> My grannam is too old, –

Cloth Hall. The banquet there, postponed from Wednesday to Friday expressly to secure TBM's presence and dedicated to the celebration of the Reform Bill, began at 2:00 p.m. and was climaxed by a speech from TBM. The company then went in procession, accompanied by bands and banners, to the White Cloth Hall yard, to be met by a hostile assembly of Tories and Radicals, who had taken over the hustings erected there. Some scuffling took place, and the Whig leaders retreated to the Hall Keeper's house. A stage coach, named 'The Invincible,' was at length brought into the yard, and from the roof of this, in conditions of near riot before a crowd of 30,000 (*Mercury*), TBM spoke, but not before he had 'stood, in dumb show, for nearly half an hour, making vain essays to address the people, who would not hear him' (*Intelligencer*). The *Intelligencer* also reported that TBM, discouraged by the opposition to him, said 'I assure you, gentlemen, that such scenes of confusion as this are not congenial to my mind. I have, I assure you, no need to join in such scenes of turmoil, and to subject my self to such inconvenience as this.' But these words were probably wished for rather than actually heard by the *Intelligencer*. Following his speech, TBM was forced into a question and answer match with Richard Oastler over Sadler's Factory Bill, and, after his fellow-candidate Marshall had spoken, was called back for yet another speech; by this time he had moved from the roof of the stage coach to the hustings. The Whig crowd then returned, at half-past seven, to the Rotunda of the Coloured Cloth Hall, where TBM spoke again. This concluded the public proceedings of the day, but TBM spent the evening in company at the home of his host, George Rawson, while 'fireworks were displayed in honour of the occasion' (*Mercury*). TBM left Leeds the next morning by the Glasgow Mail.

[1] The names are from the 'little language' of Swift's *Journal to Stella*.

My mistress is a jilt, –
My wife, – ah! bad's the best, –
So give me my little sisters
And plague take all the rest.

And good b'ye and good b'ye again little M D.

Ever yours
T B M

I open my letter to say that I have received your sweet letters, – and hope
to receive many such.

Farewell dearest
T B M

TO HANNAH AND MARGARET MACAULAY, 19 JUNE [1832]

MS: Trinity College.

House of Commons / Library June 19 –
My darlings,

Here I am waiting to be sworn in again as M P for Calne. The Lord
Advocate is writing a letter at my elbow and asking about my Leeds
adventures, Gally Knight,[1] with whom, *soit dit en passant*, I am to dine on
Saturday, is reading opposite to me, and Sir Robert Peel is wandering
up and down through the room staring at the backs of the books. In such
good company I sit down to write to my own sweet sisters. And what to
say? Nothing, at least no news. I am as yet scarcely settled again in
London. No arrangement of the business of our Board has been made;
and indeed the Commission under the authority of which we are to act
has not yet received the impression of the Great Seal. I am therefore as
yet a gentleman at large; and my employments are, reading Indian history
and politics and writing for the Edinburgh Review.

In another week I must go to court, and kiss the King's hand. You
shall have a full and true account of the whole scene. When my official
duties commence, you shall hear what kind of life it is. When I dine out,
you shall hear with whom, on what, and under what circumstances. But
till I go to Court, or have business to do, or have dinners to eat, what can
I tell you except what you know without my telling you, that I love you
dearly and miss you sadly.

---

[1] Henry Gally Knight (1786–1846: *DNB*), Tory M.P., 1824–46; best known for his books
on Norman and Italian architecture.

A pun! A pun for friend Jamie![1] What have I done to the horses that my chief opponents should be an *Ostler*[2] and a *Sadler*. But no matter: my good cause *Marshalls*[3] me the way and *Leeds* me to victory. I must go to be sworn in.

Ever yours, dear girls,
T B M

TO MACVEY NAPIER, 19 JUNE 1832

MS: British Museum. *Published:* Napier, *Correspondence*, pp. 127–8.

London June 19 – 1832

My dear Napier,

I am again in London after a rambling expedition filled with electioneering, speaking, eating, drinking, hallooing, and so forth. Some part of my exploits you may see in the newspapers. I hope to finish an article on Mirabeau by the end of this month or very early in July. The Irish education question must wait. My journey, and my business at the India Board will render it impossible for me to send you more than one review for this Number.

Ever yours
T B Macaulay

TO HANNAH AND MARGARET MACAULAY, 21 JUNE 1832

MS: Morgan Library. *Address:* Miss Macaulay / J Cropper's Esq / Dingle Bank / Liverpool. *Frank:* London June twenty one 1832 / T B Macaulay.

E[ast] I[ndia] Board June 21. 1832

My dearest girls,

To day I had a letter from Nancy, short and sweet. You are seeing sights, it appears, and have no time to write at length. Remember that I shall expect full details concerning the Docks, the Exchange, the Cemetery, the rail-road, the blind men's Chapel and the Quaker's meeting.

[1] James Cropper.

[2] Richard Oastler (1789–1861: *DNB*), steward of the Thornhill estates at Fixby, near Leeds, was the leader in Yorkshire of the campaign for Sadler's Ten Hours Bill. He had been the main challenger to TBM on the hustings at Leeds, 15 June, and continued throughout the Leeds campaign to press TBM for a commitment on factory regulation.

[3] The elder Marshall provided the money for the Whig campaign in Leeds. His son John (1797–1836) was chosen as the local candidate to accompany TBM in the representation of Leeds and came in at the head of the poll; he retired from Parliament on the dissolution in 1835 and died in the next year.

You have not yet told me about your journey by steam. What was the road like? What was the vehicle like? What was the motion like? Were you frightened out of your wits? Have you been on board of any vessels? Have you talked with any Yankees? Do you find them as agreable as those whom Mrs. Trollope describes?[1] Do they spit? Do they turn up their heels? Do they keep on their hats in your presence? Have either of you played Miss Clarissa to the Mr. Smith[2] of any of Mr. Cropper's Captains?[3] What do people say at Liverpool about the East Indian Question?[4] What about the next election, and Lord Sandon?[5] Write, my darlings, write. Give me whole conversations, if you have nothing else to tell. Above all tell me tales of each other. I am sure, Nancy, that Meg is turning a quaker. Let me hear the whole progress of her apostasy. I am sure, my dear Margaret, that Nancy's pertness must have often and often scandalised your kind hosts. Pray tell me how many opportunities she has drawn on herself from Friend Obadiah; and how many sharp things Friend Kerenhappuch has been moved to say to her. My own dear little girls, when shall we talk nonsense to each other again?

I come hither every day: but as yet I have nothing to do. Owing to some hitch about the appointment of the unsalaried Commissioners the Commission has not yet received the great Seal; and I am unable to act. Even when the formal difficulties are got over, and when I am sworn in, I hardly know whether it will be possible or desirable for me immediately to take a very active share in the ordinary business of the office. There are wheels within wheels, – mines under mines, – intrigues crossing intrigues, – which at this moment I have not time fully to explain. In my next letter I may perhaps let you into some of the secret history of the Office. Remember that it is secret history in the strongest sense of the word.

The King is in better temper with the ministers; and there [seems to?][6] be a fair prospect of our going on easily and quietly for the present.

How long is your stay at Liverpool to be? And what are then to be your movements? I am close prisoner till September. At least so I think. But Parliament will rise, I hope, in a month at furthest. I must stop.

Ever yours, my darlings,
T B M

[1] Frances Trollope, *The Domestic Manners of the Americans*, 2 vols., published 13 March 1832.

[2] Perhaps the loutish Mr Smith of Fanny Burney's *Evelina*, though why paired with Clarissa I do not know.

[3] Cropper, Benson and Co. owned 'the first line of packets that sailed on stated days between England and America' (F. A. Conybeare, *Dingle Bank*, p. 6).

[4] The charter of the East India Company was about to be reviewed and revised as the condition of its renewal; on the day after this letter TBM was appointed to the committee receiving testimony on the question: see 4 July 1832.

[5] He was re-elected.   [6] Paper torn away with seal.

TO HANNAH AND MARGARET MACAULAY, 23 JUNE 1832

MS: Trinity College. *Address:* Miss Macaulay / J Cropper's Esq / Dingle Bank / Liverpool.
Frank: London June twenty three / 1832 / T B Macaulay. *Extract published:* Trevelyan, I, 256.

London June 23. 1832

My darlings,

Yesterday I dined at Charles Grant's.[1] His brother Robert was there, and Mrs. Robert,[2] and that loathsome fool William,[3] who sate at my elbow and pestered me with such senseless, dull, absurdity that I was minded to break his head. There was Hyde Villiers, and Lord Sandon, and Elphinstone,[4] the most distinguished of the civil Servants of the East India Company, – a venerable looking man, somewhat broken by Eastern climates, but evidently both a gentleman and a man of talents. There was – who, for a ducat? I give you three guesses. The Duke of Wellington? – No you are out. What should the Duke be doing at the table of a Cabinet Minister? Sir Robert Peel? – Worse and worse, you foolish gypseys, can I never make you comprehend the state of parties? Well then Miss Fanny Kemble?[5] No – no – Miss Fanny Kemble was acting in the Hunchback.[6] Well then shall I tell you? Do you give it up?

---

[1] Charles Grant (1778–1866: *DNB*), afterwards Baron Glenelg, was a Claphamite and a distinguished classicist at Cambridge; entered Parliament, 1811, and first held office in 1813; President of the Board of Control, 1830–4; Colonial Secretary, 1835–9, when he retired under pressure of the general sense of his incompetence. Despite his deficiencies in decision and despatch, Grant was one of the official men whom TBM genuinely liked. Margaret Macaulay wrote, 21 February 1832, that "I do not hear [TBM] speak of any one with such interest and regard. He says he likes him better and better every time they meet. I do not wonder he likes him. Mr. Grant is the perfect model of a gentleman. Highminded, and most highly principled, intellectual, cultivated, with a retiring manner and a countenance expressive of all these qualities, and of something more interesting still' (*Recollections*, p. 235).

[2] Robert Grant married Margaret Davidson, a Scotswoman, in 1829.

[3] William Grant (1793?–1848), younger brother of Charles and Robert; private secretary to Charles at this time. He was a clown, and therefore offensive to TBM. Lord Teignmouth says that once when TBM was 'engaged in attending a council of the India Board on some urgent affair,...Grant entered the chamber and whispered to him that he was particularly wanted, and on Macaulay replying that he could not possibly leave his post, Grant hovered about and renewed his application, till it succeeded, when, proceeding rapidly to a door, he threw it open and pointed to a Yorkshire pie as far preferable to business. Macaulay turned on his heel and hastened promptly back to the Council-chamber' (*Reminiscences*, I, 17–18).

[4] Mountstuart Elphinstone (1779–1859: *DNB*), in the East India Company's service from 1796, held many high appointments, culminating in the governorship of Bombay, 1819–27. At a public dinner in Calcutta, in 1834, TBM said of Elphinstone that 'I never saw any man who carried about him more of the character of greatness than he did' (Arnold, *Public Life of Lord Macaulay*, p. 197); in 1856, after a final visit to Elphinstone, TBM called him 'a great and accomplished man as any that I have known' (Trevelyan, II, 404). Elphinstone and TBM were neighbors in the Albany in the 1840s.

[5] Fanny Kemble (1809–93: *DNB*), the actress.

[6] A comedy by Sheridan Knowles; opened on 5 April at Covent Garden.

Lister,[1] the author of Granby, and his Caroline Jermyn, his Agnes Morton,[2] his wife, and Villiers's sister.[3] Lister is in appearance much the same that I remember him at Cambridge. He talked well, – not brilliantly, – but with sense and information. His wife is decidedly good-looking, with eyes full of vivacity and sentiment, and a charming mouth. Her other features are not very good; and I fear, I fear, that the bloom on her cheeks came from M. Delcroix.[4] She talks very well and pleasantly; but I did not sit near her at dinner, and had very little conversation with her afterwards, as I was forced to go back to the House of Commons, after drinking my coffee.

Àpropos of *Lister* and of Villiers's *sister*, as the judicious poet observes, do you read any novels at Liverpool. I should fear that the good quakers would twitch them out of your hands and appoint their portion in the fire. Yet probably you have some safe place, some box, some bag, some drawer with a key, wherein a marble-covered book may lie for Nancy's Sunday reading.[5] How is that? And if you do not read novels, what do you read? How does Schiller go on? I have sadly neglected Calderon. But whenever I have a month to spare, I shall carry my conquests far and deep into Spanish literature.

I promised you, I think, in my last letter, an account of all our discords and cabals at the India Board. But I have filled my paper and filled my time too. I am just setting off to hear the question about Suttee argued before the Privy Council.[6] Lo[rd][7] W Bentinck,[8] you know, forebade ladies to burn themselves with their husbands. The ladies have in consequence appealed to Cæsar, – that is to the government here. And Drinky[9] – short and shabby – is counsel for the burning. I am going to hear the matter discussed.

[1] Thomas Henry Lister (1800–42: *DNB*), entered Trinity in 1820, but did not graduate; published a number of novels of society, the first and best-known of which was *Granby*, 1826; Registrar-General of England and Wales, 1836–42.

[2] Caroline Jermyn is from Lister's *Granby*; Agnes Morton from his *Herbert Lacy*, 1828.

[3] Maria Theresa Villiers (1803–65), sister of the fourth Earl of Clarendon and styled, after his succession to the title, Lady Theresa; she married, second, Sir George Cornewall Lewis in 1844. From the tone of his subsequent references, TBM was evidently much smitten by her.

[4] Delcroix and Co., perfumers, 158 New Bond Street (*Post Office London Directory*, 1832).

[5] A joke of TBM's; the MS, *c.* April 1832, of a list of miscellaneous literature, partly in Hannah's hand and partly in TBM's, is headed by TBM 'Nancy's List of Books for Sunday reading.' On the reverse is TBM's 'Ode to Nancy Notable on her composing the above list for Sunday reading,' the last stanza of which runs: 'But no! for sermons you don't care / You bellow for Romances. / So it always was – so still it is / So still 'twill be with Nancies. / He who wrote this here libel / Was he that gi'ed you an Italian Bible' (MS, Harvard: verses printed in Margaret Macaulay, *Recollections*, pp. 246–7).

[6] A decree of the Governor-General in 1829 abolishing suttee was appealed against to the King in Council; the appeal was dismissed on 7 July.

[7] Paper torn away with seal.   [8] Governor-General of India: see 10 June 1834.

[9] John Drinkwater. The senior counsel was Stephen Lushington.

I have had a letter from poor old Godwin,[1] the author of Caleb Williams, begging for a place. The letter indeed was to Bulwer, but Bulwer transmitted it to me. I have nothing for him. I have returned a very kind answer however, and I keep the letter to enrich Preaching Price's collection of autographs.

Ever yours, my sweet girls,

T B M

TO HANNAH AND MARGARET MACAULAY, 25 JUNE 1832

MS: Morgan Library. *Address:* Miss Macaulay / J Cropper's Esq / Dingle Bank / Liverpool. *Frank:* London June twenty five 1832 / T B Macaulay.

London June 25 – 1832

My darlings,

On Saturday I dined at Gally Knight's. The party was dull though Sydney Smith was there, – so dull that it was all I could do to keep my eyes open. The dispute at our Board is not yet settled. The history of it is this. Gordon,[2] the Member for Cricklade, a fat, ugly, spiteful, snarling, sneering, old rascal of a slave-driver, is my colleague, as you know. The appointment was, in my opinion, quite unjustifiable. He had always been a Whig, and a violent Whig. When the present ministers came in he asked for one of the Under Secretaryships of State. They were all given. He became angry, and, though he could not with decency oppose the Reform Bill, having always declared himself a zealous reformer, he gave the ministers all the trouble in his power. On their colonial policy, on their financial policy, on their commercial policy, – nay wherever a favourable opportunity offered, even on the details of the Reform Bill, he opposed and harassed them. It was not without much grumbling and reluctance that, on the night of Lord Ebrington's late motion, he voted with them. They have resolved, it seems, to buy him off, and they have stopped his ugly, wide, grinning mouth, with this Commissionership.

He brings into his new situation the same vile temper which he has always displayed in public life. Knowing nothing of the business of the

---

[1] William Godwin (1756–1836: *DNB*), the philosopher and novelist; perpetually in distress for money, he was given a sinecure office by Lord Grey in 1833.

[2] Robert Gordon (1786–1864: *Boase*), M.P., Wareham, 1812–18; Cricklade, 1818–37; Windsor, 1837–41; called the 'Dorsetshire Joseph Hume' and caricatured by HB as 'Bombastes Furioso.' He was appointed to the Board of Control at the same time as TBM, and succeeded him as Secretary, December 1833. Sir Denis Le Marchant, *Memoir of Althorp,* 1876, p. 242, says that TBM told him in later life that 'he used to listen with admiration to [Gordon's] speeches, thinking them eminently clever and persuasive, and hardly venturing to hope that he might one day speak as well.'

Office, he wishes to remodel it all. He has already quarrelled with Charles Grant and with Hyde Villiers, and wishes to draw me to his party. What chance he has of succeeding with me you may judge from this letter.

I am opposed to him, not merely from dislike of his temper and from distrust of his principles, but also on public grounds. It is not merely by an envious, querulous, busy-bodyish disposition that he has been induced to act as he has acted. He differs from Grant and Villiers with respect to the policy which ought to be pursued towards India. We consider him as being, in fact, the creature of the Directors, – a friend to the China mono-poly, – a friend to the existing system of patronage. He as good as told me that he considered himself as placed at the board to be a check on Grant and Villiers. Now I go as far as either Grant or Villiers, nay further than either of them, in my opinions both about the Monopoly and about the patronage.

Gordon's wish is to turn Villiers into a mere copying clerk, and to take on himself, or to divide between himself and me, the business which Villiers now transacts. I have positively refused to concur in a project so absurd and unfair. I have told him that I shall leave it to Grant and Villiers to propose a plan [for][1] the distribution of business, and that to their plan, be it what it may, I shall accede, because I feel that I have not at present sufficient official experience to entitle me to object. If on trial their arrangement shall be found to be susceptible of improvement, I will then support him in recommending an alteration. But I will not make myself ridiculous by proposing to recast the whole system of a Board, before I know what the working of that system is. This I have said quite plainly: and I think it very likely that he will soon quarrel with me, as he has quarrelled with both President and Secretary. Thanks to Meg for her letter.

Ever yours, dear girls,
T B M

Remember that all this is strictly private, and that Cropper's is one of the last houses in England in which any thing relating to the disputes at the India Board ought to be known.

---

[1] Paper torn away with seal.

TO HANNAH AND MARGARET MACAULAY, 27 JUNE 1832

MS: Morgan Library. *Address:* Miss Macaulay / J Cropper's Esq / Dingle Bank / Liverpool. *Frank:* London June twenty seven / 1832 / T B Macaulay.

London June 27 – 1832

My darlings,

> Wherefore come ye not to Court?
> Certie, 'tis the bravest sport

As old Sir David Lindsay sings.[1] Oh if you but knew the pleasure of being admitted to the Royal presence! I cannot keep my elation to myself. I cannot describe my feelings in dull creeping prose. I burst forth in unpremeditated verse, worthy of the judicious poet whom I so often quote.

> I passed in adorning
> The whole of the morning
> When the hand of the King must be kissed,
> > must be kissed.
> I put on my back
> A fine suit of black
> And twelve ells of lace on my wrist
> > on my wrist.
> I went to the levee
> And squeezed through the bevy
> Till I made good my way to his fist
> > to his fist.

But my wing fails me. I must creep in prose for a few lines. At one we assembled in the House of Commons. For this was the day appointed for taking up our address to the King on his escape from the beggar who threw a stone at him the other day.[2] The House looked like a parterre of tulips – all red and blue – like certain Heathen Gods of whom you may have heard.[3] Much gold lace was there and much silver lace – many military uniforms – yeomanry uniforms – navy uniforms, official uni-

---

[1] I can find no such lines in Lindsay's work. It is just possible that TBM is improvising a parody.

[2] At Ascot, on 19 June, a discharged Greenwich pensioner named Dennis Collins threw a stone at William IV and hit his hat; the next day both Lords and Commons moved an address to the King expressing 'horror and indignation at the late atrocious and treasonable attempt upon his Majesty' (*The Times*, 21 June).

[3] Perhaps Jeremiah 10: 9; see also the note on TBM's hymn, 21 July 1830. *The Times*, 28 June, says 'we never remember the house to present so animated an appearance, the members to the number of nearly 300 appearing in full dress, in which those in military costume greatly predominated, from the great proportion of the hon. members wearing the lieutenancy uniform, which very closely resembles that of the staff.'

forms, – and so forth. Then the Speaker rose and walked majestically down stairs to his state carriage, – an old thing covered with painting and gilding of the days of Queen Anne. In this huge conveyance he drove away with the Serjeant at Arms carrying the mace, and the Chaplain[1] carrying his own fat rotundity – quite load enough, I assure you. We came behind in about a hundred carriages. I was in Littleton's, and away we went, at hearse pace, forming a string from Westminster Hall to St James's palace. The carriage stopped. We alighted at the door of a long passage, matted, and furnished only with large wooden benches. Along this passage we went to a stone staircase. On the landing places guards with their swords and carbines were in attendance to slay us if we behaved improperly. At the top of the staircase we passed through two ranks of beef-eaters, blazing in scarlet and gold, to a table, where we wrote our names, each on two cards. One card we left on the table with the page. The other we took with us to give to the Lord in Waiting.

As a member of the House of Commons, I had peculiar advantages. For before the levee we were admitted to present our address. The throne room was however so crowded that while we were going through the ceremony I heard little, and saw nothing. But I mistake – one thing I saw – a great fool with a cocked hat and a coat like that of the fifer of a band, Mr. Edwin Pearson,[2] who was performing his duties as Exon. He condescended to quiz me through his glass, and then to extend his hand and congratulate me on my appointment. "Such instances of elegant breeding," – as Sir William Lucas says, "are not uncommon at the Court."[3] When we had walked out backward, trampling on each other's toes and kicking the skin off each other's shins, the levee began, and we were re-admitted singly to the apartment which we had just left in a body. The King stood near a door. We marched before him and out at a door on the other side, bowing and scraping the whole way. When I came to him, I gave my card to the Lord in Waiting who notified the name to the King. His Majesty put forth his hand. I kneeled, or rather curtseyed, and kissed the sacred object most reverently.[4] Then I walked away backwards bowing down my head like a bulrush, and made my way through the rooms into the street with all expedition.

---

[1] Frederick Lockwood (1803–51: *Boase*), B.A., Trinity College, 1824; Chaplain to the House of Commons, 1828–45; Canon of Canterbury, 1838–51.

[2] Edwin Pearson (1802–83: *Boase*), son of the surgeon John Pearson; at Trinity College, 1822–5, when he is reported as saying that he thought TBM 'decidedly the cleverest man in Cambridge' (Mary Babington to Henry Macaulay, 20 October 1823: typescript copy, Mrs Lancelot Errington). He had just been made an Exon of the Yeomen of the Guard.

[3] *Pride and Prejudice*, ch. 29.

[4] 'The following were presented to His Majesty: Mr. Macaulay, M.P. on his appointment to the India Board, by the Right Hon. C. Grant' (*The Times*, 28 June).

This is a levee: and a stupid affair it is. I had a thousand times rather have one of the quiet walks which I used to have this time year with Margery than cuff and kick my way through these fine people – and I would a thousand times rather kiss my Nancy's lips than all the hands of all the Kin[gs in][1] heaven.

Given from the library of the House of Commons at five in the afternoon. Present Lord Lowther, writing, James Brougham,[2] reading, Pendarves[3] yawning, Sir Ronald Fergusson[4] sealing letters, and Billy Holmes telling lies. / Farewell and farewell

my own darlings
T B M

TO HANNAH AND MARGARET MACAULAY, 29 JUNE 1832

MS: Trinity College. *Address:* Miss Macaulay / J Cropper's Esq / Dingle Bank / Liverpool. *Frank:* London June twenty nine / 1832 / T B Macaulay.

London June 29. 1832

My loves,

I am so busy that I can only write a few lines; yet I write them to shew that, busy or not, I always have my sweet sisters in my mind.

I have begun to work with an energy which makes poor Charles Grant stare. It was with something of the oath kind that he received two reports which I have drawn up within twenty four hours on cases which occupied about a cart load of paper. You know how fast I read: and the President seemed really to think me a conjuror.

Poor Macdonald[5] is dead – suddenly, yet not suddenly. He has for years been so ill that I never reckoned on his living three months. But yesterday night he was out at dinner. He was taken ill on his return to his own home; and this morning he expired. His wife was on the road to join him. They were going together to Corfu where he hoped to recruit his health.

He was a very kind and very useful friend to me. I shall always remember him with affection. Poor fellow! The table at which I am writing was his a few weeks ago: and I cannot help being touched when I remember what pains he took to secure his room to me, because it was

[1] Paper torn away with seal.
[2] James Brougham (1780–1833), the Chancellor's brother, M.P., 1829–33.
[3] Edward William Wynne Pendarves (1775–1853: *Boase*), M.P. for Cornwall, 1826–32; for West Cornwall, 1832–53.
[4] General Sir Ronald Ferguson (1773–1841: *DNB*), M.P., 1806–41.
[5] Sir James Macdonald died of cholera on 29 June.

the most agreable in the Office. It is [very?][1] strange that two Commissioners of our board[2] should have died within a month.

Ever yours, my loves,
T B M.

I have Meg's kind letter. Write like mad, both of you.

TO HANNAH AND MARGARET MACAULAY, 2 JULY 1832

MS: Morgan Library. *Address:* Miss Macaulay / J Cropper's Esq / Dingle Bank / Liverpool. *Frank:* London July two 1832 / T B Macaulay. *Partly published:* Trevelyan, 1, 256–8.

London July 2. 1832

My darlings,

I am, I think, a better correspondent than you two put together. I will venture to say that I have written more letters by a good many than I have received – and this with India and the Edinburgh Review on my hands – the life of Mirabeau to be criticised – the Rajah of Travancore to be kept in order, and the bad money which the Emperor of the Burmese has had the impudence to send us by way of tribute to be exchanged for better. You have nothing to do but to gad and to write. Make no excuses: for your excuses are contradictory. If you see sights, describe them: – you have then subjects. If you stay at home, write: for then you have time. Remember that I never saw the cemetery or the rail-road. Be particular, above all, in your accounts of the Quakers. I enjoin this especially on Nancy: for from Meg I have no hope of extracting a word of truth.

I dined yesterday at Holland House. All Lords except myself – Lord Radnor[3] – Lord Poltimore[4] – Lord King[5] – Lord Russell and his uncle Lord John. First course: White soup – spring soup – fricassee of sole, – and salmon. Then roast beef with browned *pratees*[6] – lamb chops and peas – veal cutlets with mushrooms – and sweet bread. Then leveret – green goose[7] – stewed peas – stewed artichokes – jellies – blanc mange – and tarts. After these pickled fish and cheese. Wines – Port, Madeira, sherry, Champagne, Claret, and Majorca wine. Lady Holland was very gracious, – praised my article on Burleigh to the skies – and told me

---

[1] Paper torn away with seal.

[2] I.e., Macdonald and Sir James Mackintosh; the latter died on 30 May.

[3] William Pleydell-Bouverie (1779–1869: *DNB*), third Earl Radnor; Whig M.P., 1801–28; a liberal and friend of Cobbett.

[4] George Warwick Bampfylde (1786–1858), first Baron Poltimore.

[5] Peter King (1775–1833: *DNB*), seventh Baron, a follower of Lord Holland in the House of Lords.

[6] Potatoes.   [7] A young goose (*OED*).

among other things that she had talked on the preceding day two hours with Charles Grant about religion, and had found him very liberal and tolerant. It was, I suppose, the Cholera[1] which sent her ladyship to the only saint in the ministry for ghostly counsel. Poor Macdonald's case was most undoubtedly cholera. It is said that Lord Amesbury[2] also died of cholera – though no very strange explanation seems necessary to account for the death of a man of 84. Yesterday it was rumored that the three Miss Molyneuxes,[3] of whom by the bye there are only two, were all dead in the same way – that the Bishop of Worcester[4] and Lord Barham[5] were no more – and many other foolish stories. I do not believe that there is the slightest ground for uneasiness; though Lady Holland apparently considers the case so serious that she has taken her conscience out of Allen's keeping and put it into the hand of Charles Grant.

I came back to town with Lord King and his wife.[6] He abused the Church the whole way. I have never wondered at his aversion to the Clergy since I was told that Cunningham[7] was curate of his Lordship's parish for about a year.

Here I end my letter – a great deal too long already for so busy a man to write and for such careless correspondents to receive.

Farewell, my own sweet sisters,
T B M.

TO HANNAH AND MARGARET MACAULAY, 4 JULY 1832

MS: Trinity College. *Address:* Miss Macaulay / J Cropper's Esq / Dingle Bank / Liverpool. *Frank:* London July four 1832 / T B Macaulay. *Partly published:* Trevelyan, 1, 258–9.

London July 4. 1832

My darlings,

I am delighted to hear of your proposed tour – but not so well pleased to learn that you expect to be bad correspondents during your stay at Welsh inns. Take ink and pens with you if you think that you shall find

---

[1] The cholera was first reported in London on 13 February.
[2] Charles Dundas (1751–1832: *DNB*), Baron Amesbury, died on 30 June, aged eighty.
[3] The Misses Molyneux, 8 Wyndham Street, Bryanston Square (*Royal Blue Book*, 1832) are still at the same address in 1833; an Emily Molyneux, 'youngest daughter of General Molyneux,' died on 26 June (*Gentleman's Magazine*).
[4] Robert James Carr (1774–1841: *DNB*), Bishop of Worcester, 1831–41.
[5] Charles Noel (1781–1866), third Baron Barham, afterwards Earl of Gainsborough; brother of the first Mrs Thomas Gisborne Babington.
[6] *Née* Lady Hester Fortescue (1784–1873), daughter of the first Earl Fortescue.
[7] John William Cunningham (1780–1861: *DNB*); curate of Ripley, Surrey, 1802; of Clapham, 1809–11; Vicar of Harrow, 1811–61; editor of the *Christian Observer*, 1850–8.

none at the Bard's Head or the Glendower Arms. But it will be too bad if you send me no letters during a tour which will furnish so many subjects. Why not keep a journal and minute down in it all that you see and hear; – and remember that I charge you, as the venerable circle charged Miss Byron, to tell me of every person who "regards you with an eye of partiality"[1] – be he a sleek quaker or a Yankee Ship Captain with his heels in the air and his mouth smoking like a chimney.

I breakfasted this morning with Sam Rogers. Sharp was there, Whishaw, Professor Smyth, and Lord Mahon. We had some pleasant talk. I am to be there again in Friday. On this day week I dine at Guildhall with the Lord Mayor and Corporation of London to celebrate the passing of the Reform Bill.

What can I say more? as the Indians end their letters. – I am writing in a Committee-room of the House of Commons[2] – Stewart Mackenzie[3] in the chair – Sir Alexander Johnstone[4] – on whom be all the curses of bores, – palavering at the table, and Gurney[5] the short-hand-writer scratching close to my ear. What a place for scribbling nonsense to girls! I can think of nothing to say. That Sir Alexander's eternal prosing puts all my imaginations to flight. Did not Lady Holland tell me of some good novel? I remember – Henry Masterton[6] – 3 vols – an amusing story and a happy termination. Smuggle it in next time that you go to Liverpool from some circulating library; and deposit it in some lock-up place out of reach of them that are clothed in drab; and read it together at the curling hour.

My article on Mirabeau will be in the forthcoming Number. I am not a good judge of my own compositions, I fear. But I think that it will be popular.

Ever yours, my darlings,
T B M

---

[1] *Sir Charles Grandison*, 3rd edn, I, 35: 'a gentleman, not inconsiderable in his family or fortune, has already beheld your Harriet with partiality.'

[2] A select committee on the affairs of the East India Company was appointed on 27 January 1832; on being made Commissioners of the Board of Control TBM and Robert Gordon were added to the committee, 22 June.

[3] James Alexander Stewart-Mackenzie (1784?–1843: *DNB*), M.P., 1831–7; Governor of Ceylon, 1837–40; High Commissioner of the Ionian Islands, 1840–3. He succeeded to TBM's place on the Board of Control when TBM was appointed Secretary in December of this year.

[4] Sir Alexander Johnston (1775–1849: *DNB*), President of the Council of Ceylon, 1811–19.

[5] Probably William Brodie Gurney (1777–1855: *DNB*), but possibly his son Joseph (1804–79: *DNB*); the father was official shorthand writer to the Houses of Parliament but was assisted by his son from 1822.

[6] G. P. R. James, *Henry Masterton; or the Adventures of a Young Cavalier*, 3 vols., published early in June.

TO UNIDENTIFIED RECIPIENT, 4 JULY 1832

MS: University of Indiana.

London July 4. 1832

Sir,

Everything that I have seen and heard of your Magazine has given me pleasure: and, if I had time for the purpose, I would most gladly give you any assistance in my power. But the truth is that my engagements, literary, parliamentary, and official, are even now too numerous. It will scarcely, I fear, be in my power to keep all the promises which I have made; and I cannot venture to add to their number.

Accept of my sincere thanks for the kind and flattering tone of your letter, and of my best wishes for the success of your work. / I have the honor to be, / Sir,

Your most faithful Servant
T B Macaulay

TO HANNAH AND MARGARET MACAULAY, 6 JULY 1832

MS: Trinity College. *Address:* Miss Macaulay / J Cropper's Esq / Dingle Bank / Liverpool. *Frank:* London July six 1832 / T B Macaulay. *Partly published:* Trevelyan, I, 258.

London July 6. 1832

My loves, –

Be you Lords or be you Earls
You must write no[1] naughty girls
Be you Foxes, be you Pitts,
You must write to silly chits
Be you Tories, be you Whigs,
You must write to sad young gigs.
Of whatever board you are –
Treasury, Admiralty, War,
Customs, Stamps, Excise, Controul,
Write you must, upon my soul.

So sings the judicious poet. And here I sit in my parlour looking out on the Thames and divided, like Garrick in Sir Joshua's picture,[2] between Tragedy and Comedy – a letter to you and a bundle of papers about Hydrabad, my sweet sisters and the firm of Palmer and Co. late bankers to the Nizam. It is like the choice of Hercules. Indeed I resemble Hercules

---

[1] Thus in MS.   [2] 1761.

in another point. My labour of to day is the same with one of his labours. Guess the joke. Can you? No – Adad – Adad – Adad – poor Stellakins,[1] not you. Why, did not Hercules deal with a bad Hydra, and I have to deal with Hydrabad.

What news? This morning I broke my fast again with Sam Rogers. Sydney and Luttrell were there, and Sydney said one or two good things. By the bye Ellis has written a most capital squib on me in imitation of my style. I will send it to you when the new Edinburgh Review is out. You will hardly understand it fully till then. –

Poor Sir Walter is going back to Scotland by sea to morrow. All hope is over; and he has a restless wish to die at home. He is many thousand pounds worse than nothing. Last week he was thought to be so near his end that some people went, I understand, to sound Lord Althorp about a public funeral. Lord Althorp said, very like himself, that if public money was to be laid out, it would be better to give it to the family than to spend it in one day's shew. The family, I hear, however, are not so ill off. The land is entailed on the eldest son. The daughter is married. And the other children have 5000 £ a piece, the bequest of some relation who died in India.[2]

But what do you care for this stuff? I hardly know why I go on writing – except for writing's sake, and that I may feel a little as if you were near me. Come back – come back to me, my own little darlings; and let the world go as it likes. Let the Whigs sta[y][3] in or be turned out. Let m[oney][3] be abundant or scarce. I do not know how love in a cottage may do with a wife. But I am sure that it would suit me with a sister.

Farewell – dear girls,

T B M.

So here is Nancy's letter. What travellers you are! As the judicious poet sings

> "Pray, Miss, what may you be *ar'ter*?"
> Seeing trees and stones and water.
> Up and down, through all the day,
> On the hills of Wales I stray.
> And at night it is my habit
> For to sup on a Welch rabbit.

---

[1] Cf. Swift, *Journal to Stella*, 14 October 1710.
[2] Scott left London for Abbotsford on 7 July. His debts at his death were £78,000, a sum paid off in 1833. The 'relation in India' was Mrs Scott's brother, who left £20,000 to the four Scott children: see Edgar Johnson, *Sir Walter Scott*, II, 1160; 1269; 1272.
[3] Paper torn away with seal.

And, to please my honoured father,
Who longs to shave my head with lather,
I have bought Welsh wigs for me,
And eke for my dear sisters three.

TO HANNAH AND MARGARET MACAULAY, 10 JULY 1832

MS: Morgan Library. *Address:* Miss Macaulay / James Cropper's Esq / Dingle Bank / Liverpool. *Frank:* London July ten 1832 / T B Macaulay.

London July 10

My loves,

I am so busy that I have only time to inclose [the]¹se letters, and to tell you [th]¹at I love you dearly.

Ever yours, sweet girls,
T B M

TO MACVEY NAPIER, 12 JULY 1832

MS: British Museum.

London July 12. 1832

Dear Napier,

I shall send off my article to day, by a Government frank if I fall in with one, – if not by the mail. It has been hurried to a close as you will see. It is also carelessly written, as you will also see. I hope that you will look well to the printing.

Ever yours
T B M

TO HANNAH AND MARGARET MACAULAY, 12 JULY 1832

MS: Morgan Library. *Address:* Miss Macaulay / J Cropper's Esq / Dingle Bank / Liverpool. *Frank:* London July twelve 1832 / T B Macaulay.

London July 12 – 1832

My dearest girls,

I have but a moment. But I will not pass another day without writing. This morning I received your letters about Wales and about your return to Liverpool, and was charmed with them. By the bye you are unjust to

---

¹ Paper torn away with seal.

Ellis. He repeated the ipecac:[1] lines to me; and I took it for granted that they were his own; – but he never, that I remember, said so and when I asked him about them the other day he told me that they were not his. I will remember to send you his squib when the Edinburgh Review comes out.

Yesterday I dined at Guildhall with the Corporation of London. The Common Council voted 6000 £, for the entertainment to the reformers in the two Houses of Parliament. Eight hundred people sate down to the dinner. The Hall, which you must remember, as I have shewn it to you over and over again, was hung with scarlet cloth and most superbly illuminated. I never saw an artificial light at once so brilliant and so soft. It was really like the sun. The lamps ran along the Gothic tracery of the windows and arches so that the lines of light exactly coincided with the great lines of the architecture. Besides your old friends Gog and Magog[2] a considerable number of figures in armour were ranged round the walls. Banners hung from the roof; – a gorgeous trophy was piled over the Chair of the Lord Mayor. The galleries were occupied by musicians, and there was a splendid display of plate. But the dinner – you will say – what care we for the decorations of the hall? What had you for dinner? The tables, young ladies, were covered with cold things. Every thing was cold except one hundred and sixty tureens of turtle soup, and eighty haunches of venison. Lushington who sate next me dined off cold fowl and ham. But Littleton and I, like Edgar Mortimer and his friend Jackson,[3] agreed cold fowl would be no treat to us, and ate two large dishes of turtle soup apiece. After dinner we had the usual toasts, immense hallooing, stamping, clapping of hands, and thumping of tables. The speeches you will see in the newspapers. I heard scarce [one][4] word of them owing to the incessant din which was kept up in the hall. The sight was magnificent, and I am glad to have been present.[5]

I must stop. My sweet, sweet, girls, farewell, and love me as I love you.

T B M

---

[1] I.e., ipecacuanha, an emetic and purgative. I do not know what lines are meant.
[2] The carved wooden figures so named.
[3] Not identified; probably from one of Mrs Meeke's novels: see 21 July 1832.
[4] Paper torn away with seal.
[5] The scene was painted by Haydon; see 17 July 1833.

TO [HANNAH AND MARGARET MACAULAY, 15? JULY 1832][1]

Text: Trevelyan, I, 259.

A Yankee has written to me to say that an edition of my works is about to be published in America with my life prefixed, and that he shall be obliged to me to tell him when I was born, whom I married, and so forth.[2] I guess I must answer him slick right away. For, as the judicious poet observes,

> Though a New England man lolls back in his chair,
> With a pipe in his mouth, and his legs in the air,
> Yet surely an Old England man such as I
> To a kinsman by blood should be civil and spry.

How I run on in quotation! But when I begin to cite the verses of our great writers I never can stop. Stop I must, however.

Yours
T. B. M.

TO HANNAH AND MARGARET MACAULAY, 16 JULY 1832

MS: Morgan Library. *Address:* Miss Macaulay / J Cropper's Esq / Dingle Bank / Liverpool. *Frank:* London July sixteen 1832 / T B Macaulay.

London July 16. 1832

My darlings,

I am much obliged to Nancy for her sweet letter. – So you saw the Menai Bridge,[3] which I have not seen; – and you have seen the rail-road which I have not seen. Surely you are wiser than all your teachers.[4] But pray, Miss Nancy, have your studies, as well as your travels, gone beyond those of your betters? Have you read Carlos and Wallenstein yet? Or have you got through the Thirty Years War?[5] As to that other lazy baggage, Miss Margaret, she, I will be bound, has not read three lines of

---

[1] The topic of this letter was discussed with Hannah and Margaret sometime before 21 July, by which time they have returned their remarks on it. Trevelyan prints this under date of 6 July, but his text is a composite of 4 July, 6 July, and this undated fragment.

[2] No American edition of TBM's 'works' at this date has been traced; possibly TBM is joking. Seven years later Charles Sumner reported that he had 'spoken with Macaulay about an American edition of his works. He has received no communication from any publisher on the subject, and seemed to be coy and disinclined' (E. L. Pierce, *Memoir and Letters of Charles Sumner*, Boston, II [1878], 70).

[3] The suspension bridge constructed by Thomas Telford, 1819–25.

[4] Cf. Psalms 119: 99.

[5] Schiller, *Don Carlos*, 1787; *Wallenstein*, 1799; and *The History of the Thirty Years' War*, 1789–93.

any printed book since I saw her and her mumps into the stage at the Cross Keys in Wood Street.[1] So you went shopping to Liverpool and came back through a pouring rain. Well says the poet.

> When the Sun shines girls go shopping,
> And when the rain falls they come dropping.

I have been as gay as you. On Friday I went to Lady Grey's rout, and got into the thickest and hottest jam of Duchesses and Countesses in which I ever was in my life. After being squeezed as flat as a pancake by the space of half an hour I went off to vote in the House of Commons.[2]

On Saturday I dined with Rice. He has a handsome house in Mansfield Street; and he had a Polish Prince, a Spanish General, an American Ambassador,[3] and an English Baronet to meet me. The Yankee was endurable; and did not spit much while the ladies remained, nor did he more than once lay his feet on the table. He did to be sure pull up his shirt-collar, – and asked Miss Rice what she called it. He walked away from the house on foot, unlike most other ambassadors that I have seen. But, to be serious, he is an intelligent, agreable, man; and his manners, though not exactly English, are objectionable no further than as they are foreign. They are a little queer; but by no means gross or vulgar.

Yesterday I dined with Lord John Russell at his official House.[4] Lord John is a bachelor, much against his will, I believe.[5] But his house swarmed with women and children as if it had been a lying-in hospital. His sister-in-law Lady William Russell[6] is staying with him while her husband is engaged in a political mission to Portugal. The other sister-in-law Lady Tavistock[7] came very soon after my arrival. I had never seen her before. Lady William I had often met. She is rather a fine woman, and rather a clever woman, but, I think, bold and imperious in manner to a degree quite unfeminine. She is always very [poli][8]te to me; but it is rather the [polite][8]ness of a man than that of a Lady. She kept her children in very good order, and has the character, I believe, of being both a great blue stocking and a great manager in her family.

---

[1] Used by a number of coaches including the Liverpool coach: in *Great Expectations* Pip arrives in London at the Cross Keys.

[2] On the first reading of the Irish Tithes Bill.

[3] There was no American ambassador at this time. TBM must mean Aaron Vail (1796–1878), who served as *chargé d'affaires* in London from 13 July 1832 to April 1836.

[4] Russell, Paymaster-General since June 1831, lived at the Army Pay Office, Whitehall.

[5] Russell first married in 1835.

[6] General Lord George William Russell married Elizabeth Anne Rawdon in 1817: 'her beauty was equalled by her charm of manner and conversation' (*DNB*).

[7] Anna Maria (1783–1857), daughter of Lord Harrington, married Francis Russell, afterwards seventh Duke of Bedford, in 1808.

[8] Paper torn away with seal.

Sir Rufane Donkin[1] dined with us and bored me to death with long campaign stories about Portugal, Spain, and the East Indies. There was his wife too, Lady Anna Maria,[2] who talked rather amusingly. Lastly there was old Sam Rogers, looking like Lazarus half resuscitated, but talking very agreably. But I must bring my letter to an end. Dear, dear girls, when shall I see you again?

Ever yours, my loves
T B M

TO HANNAH AND MARGARET MACAULAY, 18 JULY 1832

MS: Trinity College. *Address:* Miss Macaulay / J Cropper's Esq / Dingle Bank / Liverpool. *Frank:* London July eighteen 1832 / T B Macaulay. *Partly published:* Trevelyan, 1, 260–1.

London July 18. 1832

My darlings,

I have heard from Napier. He speaks rapturously of my article on Dumont, but sends me no money. Allah blacken his face! as the Persians say, – he has not yet paid me for Burleigh.

We are worked to death in the House of Commons, and we are henceforth to sit on Saturdays. This indeed is the only way to get through our business. On Saturday next we shall, I hope, rise before seven, as I am engaged to dine on that day with pretty, witty, Mrs. Lister. I fell in with her at Lady Grey's great crush, and found her very agreable. Her husband is nothing in society. Rogers has some very good stories about their domestic happiness; – stories confirming a theory of mine which, as I remember, made you very angry. When they first married, Mrs. Lister treated her husband with great respect. But when Arlington[3] came out and failed completely, she changed her conduct, and has, ever since that unfortunate publication, henpecked the poor novelist unmercifully. And the case, says Rogers, is the harder, because it is suspected that she wrote part of Arlington herself. It is like the scene in Milton where Eve, after tempting Adam, abuses him for yielding to temptation.[4] But do you not remember that I told you that much of the love of women depended on the eminence of men? And do you not remember how much you resented the imputation? I must take care to write good reviews and to make good speeches, or I shall have a fine time of it with you. Remember, – but of course you will remember, – not to circulate any thing which I may tell you about the ménage of these good people.

[1] General Sir Rufane Donkin (1773–1841: *DNB*), Whig M.P., 1832–41.
[2] Lady Anna Maria Elliot (1786?–1855), Donkin's second wife, just married (5 May).
[3] *Arlington*, 3 vols., published April 1832.   [4] *Paradise Lost*, IX, 1144–61.

Have I any thing else to tell you? I think not. Selina is going to the Temple. And Fanny might as well be going there, as far as I am concerned; for she is going to Kensington,[1] where I shall not be able to see her once in ten days. What are your plans, my loves? And when shall I have any chance of seeing you again? I hope to have a few weeks of holiday early in October. Possibly we may be able to arrange something for that time.

As to the present state of affairs abroad and at home, I cannot sum it up better than in those beautiful lines of the poet.

> Peel is canting and Croker is lying.
> The cholera's raging, the people are dying.
> When the House is the coolest, as I am alive,
> The thermometer stands at a hundred and five.
> We debate in a heat that seems likely to burn us,
> Much like the three children who sang in the furnace.
> The disorders at Paris[2] have not ceased to plague us.
> Don Pedro,[3] I hope, is ere this on the Tagus.
> In Ireland no tithe can be raised by a parson.
> Mr. Smithies[4] is just hanged for murder and arson.
> Doctor Thorpe has retired from the Lock, and 'tis said
> That poor little Squilks[5] will succeed in his stead.

There is a good summary of the news for you.

Ever yours, my own dear little girls

T B M

TO HANNAH AND MARGARET MACAULAY, 21 JULY 1832

MS: Morgan Library. *Address:* Miss Macaulay / J Cropper's Esq / Dingle Bank / Liverpool. *Frank:* London July twenty one 1832 / T B Macaulay. *Partly published:* Trevelyan, 1, 261–2.

London July 21. 1832

My dearest girls,

I am delighted to hear from Meg that you approve of my having followed Mrs. Meeke's precepts at the Guildhall dinner, and from Nancy

---

[1] To the younger James Stephen's house, Hyde Park Gate, which Stephen had loaned to George and Sarah Anne Babington: see 30 July 1832.

[2] On 5 and 6 June, following the death of Casimir Périer.

[3] Dom Pedro, Emperor of Brazil, asserted his daughter's right to be Queen of Portugal against his brother Dom Miguel, and, with British help, succeeded. His forces had just taken Oporto but did little thereafter until the next year.

[4] Jonathan Smithies, executed at Newgate on 9 July.

[5] Trevelyan prints this as 'Wilks,' perhaps thinking of the Rev. S. C. Wilks, whose name may indeed be read 'Squilks.'

that my poetry, or rather, (for I must not, as you accused Ellis of doing, appropriate other people's compositions) the poetry of my judicious friend, gives satisfaction. I am glad also to find that there is no chance of Nancy's turning Quaker. She would indeed make a queer kind of female friend.

What the Yankees will say about me I neither know nor care. I told them the dates of my birth and of my coming into parliament. I told them also that I was educated at Cambridge. As to my early bons mots, my crying for holidays, my walks to school through showers of cats and dogs,[1] I have left all those for the "Life of the Late Right Honourable Thomas Babington Macaulay with large extracts from his correspondence in Two Volumes Quarto by the Very Reverend J Macaulay Dean of Durham, and Rector of Bishopsgate, with a superb portrait from the picture by Pickersgill[2] in the possession of the Marquess of Lansdowne."

As you like my verses, I will some day or other send you a whole rhyming letter. I wonder whether any man ever wrote doggrel so easily as I. I run it off just as fast as my pen can move, and that is faster by about three words in a minute than any other pen that I know. This comes of my schoolboy habit of writing verses all day long. Shall I tell you the news in rhyme? – I think I will send you a regular sing-song gazette.

We gained a victory last night as great as e'er was known.
We beat the opposition upon the Russia loan.[3]
They hoped for a majority, and also for our places.
We won the day by seventy-nine. You should have seen their faces!
Old Croker, when we shouted, looked heavenly blue with rage –
You'd have said he had the cholera in the spasmodic stage.
Dawson was red with ire as if his face was smeared with berries.
But of all human visages, the worst was that of Herries.

[1] When he was at Greaves's school in Clapham TBM used to make 'each several afternoon ...piteous entreaties to be excused returning after dinner, and was met by the unvarying formula, "No, Tom, if it rains cats and dogs, you shall go"' (Trevelyan, I, 29).

[2] Henry William Pickersgill (1782–1875: *DNB*), successor to Lawrence and Phillips as the painter of the eminent.

[3] England and the Netherlands had agreed to bear part of the charge of a loan made to Russia during the Napoleonic Wars, with the stipulation that the obligation should cease if the Netherlands should lose Belgium. The intention was to enlist Russia in maintaining the settlement of 1815. The separation of Belgium and the Netherlands had now come about, but not through Russia, who therefore claimed that England was still obliged to continue to pay the charge. Ministers accepted the liability, as a bribe to Russia to acquiesce in the Belgian settlement. The arrangement was unpopular, partly because its real motive could not be publicly explained, and it had been under attack since January. TBM spoke on the question on 12 July (*Hansard*, 3rd Series, XIV, 293–300).

Though not his friend my tender heart, I own, could not but feel
A little for the misery of poor Sir Robert Peel.
But hang the dirty Tories! and let them starve and pine.
Huzza for the majority of glorious seventy nine.

But I must go down to the House. Even Saturday is no Sabbath to us
now. Farewell, my sweet girls?[1] When shall I see you again?

T B M

TO HANNAH AND MARGARET MACAULAY, 23 JULY 1832

MS: Trinity College. *Address:* Miss Macaulay / J Cropper's Esq / Dingle Bank / Liverpool.
Frank: London July twenty four 1832 / T B Macaulay. *Mostly published:* Trevelyan, I, 262–4.

House of Commons Smoking Room / July 23. 1832

My own loves,

I am writing here at eleven at night in this filthiest of all filthy atmo-
spheres and in the vilest of all vile company, with the smell of tobacco
in my nostrils and the ugly, hypocritical, high-cheeked, gaunt, vulgar,
face of Lieutenant Gordon before my eyes. There he sits writing opposite
to me. To whom, for a ducat? To some secretary of an Hibernian Bible
Society[2] – or to some horrid old woman who gives cheap tracts instead
of blankets to the starving peasantry of Connemara, – or to some good
Protestant Lord who fum fums his Popish tenants. And here sit I, at the
same table, on the same green-baize cloth, writing to the two sweetest
girls in Christendom. Reject not my letter though it may smell of
Havannah cigars and genuine pig-tail. For this is the room –

> The room, but I think I'll describe it in rhyme, –
> That smells of tobacco and chlorate of lime
> The smell of tobacco was always the same
> But the chlorate was brought since the cholera came.

But I must return to prose and tell you all that has fallen out since
I wrote last. I went to dine with the Listers at Knightsbridge. They are in a
very nice house next or almost next to that which the Wilberforces had.[3]

---

[1] Thus in MS.

[2] Gordon was a member of the committee of the London Hibernian Society, founded in 1806
to establish Bible schools in Ireland. A fanatical anti-Catholic, he wished, through the
Society, to 'declare open war against Rome, and cross the Rubicon of avowed reformation'
(Teignmouth, *Reminiscences*, I, 212).

[3] The *Royal Blue Book*, 1832, shows 'Mrs. Lister' only at 12 Wilton Place, Knightsbridge.
Wilberforce had lived, from 1808 to 1821, at Gore House, Kensington, afterwards cele-
brated as the residence of Lady Blessington and Count d'Orsay; the site is now that of the
Albert Hall.

The house is part of one which belonged to Lord Stanley. Old Mrs. Villiers[1] lives with them. We had quite a family party. Except Sir Charles Lemon[2] and a very fine woman, a sister of Lord Minto's,[3] all the party were Villierses and Listers. But no – I forget John Romilly with whom I went. However there was George Villiers,[4] and Hyde Villiers, and Edward Villiers.[5] Charles,[6] who is no favourite of mine, was not there. George and Hyde rank very high in my opinion. I liked their behaviour to their sister much. She seems to be the pet of the whole family: and it is natural that she should be so. Their manners are softened by her presence; and the roughness and sharpness which they have in rather an unpleasant degree in intercourse with men vanishes at once. They seem to love the very ground that she treads on; and she is undoubtedly a charming woman, pretty, clever, lively, polite, and very attentive to me! She seemed to be on a very easy, friendly, footing with her husband, but to keep him in strict order. "She called him Tom. How delightful!"

I was asked yesterday evening to go to Sir John Burke's[7] in order to meet another heroine who was very curious to see me. Whom – do you think? Lady Morgan.[8] I thought, however, that if I went, I might not improbably figure in her next novel and, as I am not ambitious of such an h[onour,][9] I kept away. If I could fall in with her at a great party where I could see unseen and hear unheard, I should very much like to make observations on her. But I certainly will not, if I can help it, meet her face to face – lion to lioness.

That confounded, chattering, blackguard, Gordon, has just got into an argument about the Church with an Irish papist who has seated himself at my elbow: and they keep such a din that I cannot tell what I am writing.

[1] Theresa Parker (1776?–1856), widow of George Villiers, third son of the first Earl of Clarendon.
[2] Sir Charles Lemon (1784–1868: *Boase*), second Baronet, M.P., 1807–12; 1830–57.
[3] Lady Catherine Sarah Elliott (d. 1862), married Sir John Peter Boileau, 1825; she was Lady Donkin's sister.
[4] George Villiers (1800–70: *DNB*), afterwards fourth Earl of Clarendon; at St John's, Cambridge, while TBM was at Trinity; ambassador at Madrid, 1833–9; Lord Lieutenant of Ireland, 1847–52; Foreign Secretary under Aberdeen, Palmerston, Russell, and Gladstone.
[5] Edward Villiers (1806–43), fifth of the Villiers brothers.
[6] Charles Pelham Villiers (1802–98: *DNB*), at Cambridge with TBM; M.P. for Wolverhampton, 1835–98; leader of the anti-corn-law agitation in Parliament.
[7] Colonel Sir John Burke (1782–1847), second Baronet; Whig M.P., 1830–2.
[8] Sydney Owenson, Lady Morgan (1783?–1859: *DNB*), popular novelist and later a leading London hostess. Twenty-five years after this letter TBM did accept an invitation from Lady Morgan, and found her a 'hideous wrinkled little old carcase – eighty five at the least, painted up to the eyes, sinking into dotage, yet retaining all the volubility and levity of youth. How she talked – profanely, indecently, egotistically. I was scandalised and yet amused' (Journal, xi, 116: 11 May 1857).
[9] Paper torn away with seal.

There they go. The Lord Lieutenant[1] – the Bishop of Derry[2] – Macgee[3] – O'Connell – your Bible meetings – your agitation-meetings – the propagation of the Gospel – Maynooth College – the seed of the woman shall bruise the serpent's head.[4] My dear lieutenant, you will not only bruise but break my head with your clatter. Mercy! mercy! – However here I am at the end of my letter, and I shall leave the two demoniacs to tear each other to pieces.

Ever yours, my best sisters.

T B M

TO HANNAH AND MARGARET MACAULAY, 26 JULY 1832

MS: Morgan Library. *Address:* Miss Macaulay / J Cropper's Esq / Dingle Bank / Liverpool. *Frank:* London July twenty six 1832 / T B Macaulay.

London July 26. 1832

My darlings,

The Cholera is all humbug in my opinion. At all events, I a'nt scared. London is thinning fast, and will soon be reduced to its poor stint of fifteen hundred thousand people.

> Alack for woe, and well a day,
> All the folks as I knows has took themselves away;
> To Leicester Selina, to Wales[5] t'ould man,
> And sister Frances to Sarah Anne, –
> Ellis to Calais, and Empson to Lincoln,
> A thing as makes me sad to think on.
> In my mind's eye, I often see 'em,
> As I sits all alone at the Athenæum.
> So I drinks like a fish and I eats like a lion,
> 'Case I likes a wet sorrow much more nor a dry 'un.

The House is still sitting, and sitting twelve hours out of the twenty four. I am forced to be there almost without intermission: for so few members are left that we are in constant danger of being counted out. There is a snug party of forty of us who lay on taxes and pass laws in the quietest manner in the world. I wonder that we have not earned the nickname of the forty thieves.

In two or three days, if there be truth in advertisements, the Edinburgh Review will be out. Villiers has a stomach complaint and keeps his room.

---

[1] Lord Anglesey.
[2] Richard Ponsonby (1772–1853: *DNB*), Bishop of Derry, 1831–53.
[3] William Magee (1766–1831: *DNB*), late Archbishop of Dublin.
[4] Cf. Genesis 3: 15.　　　　　　　　[5] For his work as a charity commissioner.

Tom Duncombe has had a touch of cholera, but is now "odious pert" again. Lord John Russell has left off his wig: but his hair is still thin, and the crown of his head is as bald as a doll's. Don Pedro sends us no news. The Germans are all together by the ears.[1] Lord Nugent is going to the Ionian Islands, as soon as a ship has been built large enough to carry him out. I recommend that the vessel which is to bring us Cleopatra's needle from Egypt[2] should carry his lordship to Corfu. I should think that the machinery which will raise an obelisk of ninety feet long might be sufficient to embark and disembark even the portly form of a Grenville. Lord Henniker[3] is dead. A man has been drowned in the Thames, and them as drownded him is to be hanged.[4] This, I think, is all the news.

A pun! A pun! Who of all the public men of our time has most decidedly surpassed himself during this Session of parliament? Baring – for he has of late been past bearing. You have heard nothing so good as that since you left the Cross Keys in Cheapside, I will be sworn. –

So you are learning to draw. Send me some of your handy work, and let me judge whether you are likely to succeed or not. What do you draw? Screens or flowers, or portraits, or bits of [o][5]ld castles with trees in the corner of the landscape, or cows, or cottages, or lakes, or hill[s][5] or cataracts. Go on and proceed from drawing to painting. For I am not quite of the mind of a great moral poet who says –

> "'Tis according to law
> That young ladies should draw: –
> But it makes a man faint
> That young ladies should paint."

I hope to see your works on the walls of Somerset House, – or rather of the new Gallery which we are going to build for the Royal Academy at Charing Cross.[6] From Margaret I hope to have "an interior with Quakers during an opportunity" – a noble subject for Ostade.[7] From Nancy I am sure we shall have landscapes not inferior to Turner's. But no more nonsense. I must fall to work.

Ever yours, dear girls,

T B M

---

[1] The Germanic Confederation, under pressure from Prussia and Austria, had decreed new repressive measures on 28 June. *The Times*, 26 July, reports a public meeting in London to protest 'the invasion lately made by the Diet of Frankfort on the ancient liberties of the Germanic States.'

[2] This was not brought to London and erected until 1878.

[3] John Minet Henniker-Major (1777–1832), third Baron Henniker, a barrister, died on 22 July.

[4] See *The Times*, 19 and 21 July.   [5] Paper torn away with seal.

[6] The National Gallery, erected 1832–8; the Royal Academy occupied a part of it until 1869.

[7] Adriaan van Ostade (1610–85), Dutch painter.

TO HANNAH AND MARGARET MACAULAY, 30 JULY 1832

MS: Morgan Library. *Address:* Miss Macaulay / J Cropper's Esq / Dingle Bank / Liverpool. *Frank:* London July thirty one 1832 / T B Macaulay. *Partly published*: Trevelyan, I, 264–6.

Library of the House of Commons

July 30 – 1832 – 11 o'clock at night –

My darlings,

Here I am. – Daniel Whittle Hervey[1] is speaking. The house is thin. The subject is dull. And I have stolen away to write to you. Lushington is scribbling at my side. Alderman Thompson, as fat as butter, is reading letters at the next table. No sound is heard but the scratching of our pens and the ticking of the clock. We are in a far better atmosphere than in the smoking room whence I wrote to you last week; and the company is more decent, inasmuch as that beast Gordon, whom Nancy blames me for describing in just terms, is not present.

By the bye, you know doubtless the lines which are in the mouth of every member of parliament, describing the comparative merits of the two rooms. They are, I think, very happy.

> If thou goest into the smoking-room
> Three plagues will thee befall, –
> The chlorate of lime, and the bacco-smoke
> And the captain who's worst of all, –
>> The canting sea captain,
>> The lying sea captain
> The captain who's worst of all.

> If thou goest into the library
> Three good things will thee befall, –
> Very good books, and very good air,
> And M+c++l+y, who's best of all.
>> The virtuous M+c++l+y
>> The prudent M+c++l+y,
> M+c++l+y who's best of all.

Oh! how I am worked. I never see Fanny from Sunday to Sunday. All my civilities wait for that blessed day; and I have so many scores of visits to pay that I can scarcely find time for any of that Sunday reading in which, like my Nancy, I am in the habit of indulging. Yesterday, as soon as I was fixed in my best and had breakfasted, I paid a round of calls to all my friends who had the cholera. Then I walked to all the clubs of

[1] Daniel Whittle Harvey (1786–1863: *DNB*), Radical M.P., 1818–20; 1826–40. On 30 July Harvey spoke both on the Civil List and on the Bribery Bill (*Hansard*, 3rd Series, XIV, 951–2; 958–9).

which 1 am a member, to see the newspapers. The first of these two works you will admit to be a work of mercy; – the second, in a political man, one of necessity. Then, like a good brother, I walked, under a burning sun, to Kensington, to ask Fanny how she did, and staid there two hours. It was very kind of James Stephen to lend Sarah Anne and George his garden and house; but, as the poet says,

> For me, I would not gi'e a fard'en
> For such a house and such a garden.

Then I went to Knightsbridge to call on Mrs. Lister, and chatted with her till it was time to go and dine at the Athenæum. There I dined, and, after dinner, like a good young man, I sate and read Bishop Heber's journal[1] till bed-time. There is a Sunday for you. I think that I excel in the diary line. I will keep a journal like the Bishop, that [my][2] memory may

> Smell sweet and blossom in the dust.[3]

Next Sunday I am to go to Lord Lansdowne's at Richmond, and to sleep there; so that I hope to have something to tell you. But, on second thought, I will tell you nothing – nor ever write to you again – nor ever speak to you again. I have no pleasure in writing to undutiful sisters. Why do you not send me longer letters? When you know that I love the very sight of your handwriting, why do you put me off with little notes, – one to every three letters of mine? But I am at the end of my paper. So that I have no room to scold.

Ever yours, my darlings,
T B M.

TO SELINA MACAULAY, 1 AUGUST 1832

MS: Huntington Library. *Address:* Miss Macaulay / Rothley Temple / Leicester. *Frank:* London August one 1832 / T B Macaulay.

London August 1
Dear Selina,

I never see Fanny, and have heard very little news about you. I am working at Westminster every day from noon till two hours after midnight. My father complains of the want of letters. I write every M[on][4]day, and, if your head does not render it painful, you had better send him a line

[1] Reginald Heber, *Narrative of a Journey through the Upper Provinces of India*, 2 vols., 1828.
[2] Paper torn away with seal.
[3] James Shirley, *The Contention of Ulysses and Ajax*, iii, 24.
[4] Obscured by stain from seal.

now and then. But do nothing to hurt yourself. I hope that you are well. I am sure that you are carefully and kindly looked after. My love to my uncle, Aunt and Cousins.

Ever yours
T B M

TO JOSEPH LEES,¹ [2]² AUGUST 1832

Text: Composite from Leeds *Intelligencer*, 16 August 1832, and Leeds *Mercury*, 18 August 1832.

London, August 3, 1832.

My dear Sir,

I am truly happy to find that the opinion of my friends at Leeds on the subject of canvassing agrees with that which I have long entertained.³ The practice of begging for votes is, as it seems to me, absurd, pernicious, and altogether at variance with the true principles of representative government. The suffrage of an elector ought not to be asked or to be given as a personal favour. It is as much for the interest of constituents to choose well as it can be for the interest of a candidate to be chosen. To request an honest man to vote according to his conscience is superfluous. To request him to vote against his conscience is an insult. The practice of canvassing is quite reasonable under a system under which men are sent to Parliament to serve themselves. It is the height of absurdity under a system under which men are sent to Parliament to serve the public.

¹ TBM's letter, which was read at a meeting of the Leeds Political Union, 14 August, was written in reply to a series of questions put to him by Lees as secretary of the Union: '1. Will you, if returned to Parliament, advocate such an alteration in the Corn Laws as will enable the consumer to have cheaper bread? 2. Will you advocate a strict economy in every department of state...and a total annihilation of all sinecures and useless places? 3. Will you advocate the abolition of Tithes in the fairest way and the shortest time possible? 4. Will you advocate an equalization to a great extent of the Church establishment; and a ceasing to compel any one to pay for the maintenance of any particular doctrine he does not approve? 5. Will you advocate the abolition of all taxes on Knowledge? 6. Will you advocate the abolition of Slavery in every part of the globe? 7. Will you advocate the destruction of all monopolies, particularly the close borough corporations...also the East India and Bank of England monopolies? 8. Will you advocate the establishment of a National Bank...? 9. Will you advocate just and cheap law...? 10. Will you advocate a tax upon all real and funded property...? 11. Will you advocate triennial Parliaments and vote by ballot?' (Leeds *Mercury*, 4 August).
² See note on the date of the next letter.
³ The Leeds *Intelligencer*, 2 August, printed a clumsily-forged letter from TBM in which he is made to say publicly that official duties make it impossible for him to canvass but to add privately that he knows his chances of election are hopeless and therefore will not waste his time on a canvass. The effect of this, the *Intelligencer* says, was to make the Whigs assembled to hear the letter read weep in despair (2 August). The *Mercury* indignantly replied on 4 August that the Leeds Whigs had unanimously agreed with TBM's decision not to canvass. If TBM did write a letter on the subject it has not been found. And, after all, he did aid in the canvassing: see 4 September 1832.

While we had only a mock representation it was natural that this practice should be carried to a great extent. I trust it will soon perish with the abuses from which it sprang. I trust that the great and intelligent body of people who have obtained the elective franchise will see that seats in the House of Commons ought not to be given, like rooms in an almshouse, to urgency of solicitation, and that a man who surrenders his vote to caresses and supplications forgets his duty as much as if he sold it for a bank-note. I hope to see the day when an Englishman will think it as great an affront to be courted and fawned upon in his capacity of elector as in his capacity of juryman. In the polling-booth, as in the jury-box, he has a great trust confided to him – a sacred duty to discharge. He would be shocked at the thought of finding an unjust verdict, because the plaintiff or the defendant had been very civil and pressing; and if he would reflect he would, I think, be equally shocked at the thought of voting for a candidate for whose public character he felt no esteem, merely because that candidate had called on him, and begged very hard, and had shaken his hand very warmly.

I am delighted, though not at all surprised, to find that the enlightened and public-spirited gentlemen in whose name you write agree with me on this subject. My conduct is before the electors of Leeds. My opinions shall, on all occasions, be stated to them with perfect frankness. If they approve that conduct, if they concur in those opinions, they ought, not for my sake, but for their own, to choose me as their member. To be so chosen I should indeed consider as a high and enviable honour. But I should think it no honour to be returned to Parliament by persons who, thinking me destitute of the requisite qualifications, had yet been wrought upon by cajolery and importunity to poll for me in despite of their better judgment.

I will now proceed to answer the questions which you have proposed as plainly and as concisely as I can. To most of them I have formerly replied, and need now reply only by a simple affirmative. I am convinced the Corn Laws ought to be altered in such a manner as may enable the consumer to obtain cheaper bread, – that the strictest economy ought to be observed, – that sinecures ought to be abolished, – that no pension ought henceforth to be given which has not been earned by public service, – that the tithes ought, both in England and Ireland, to be extinguished by a fair commutation, – that slavery ought to be abolished in every part of the empire, – that monopolies ought to be destroyed, – that many parts of our municipal system ought to undergo a revision, – and that a great and extensive reform in the law, with the view of making it cheaper, clearer, and more rational, is indispensably required. I dislike the stamps on newspapers, because I conceive that, in the present state of public feeling, they operate, not only as a tax on sound knowledge, but as a bounty on profligate and inflammatory publications. I heartily hope that they will soon be taken off. I am decidedly favourable to the principle of a bona-fide property tax.

There are some other questions in the paper transmitted to me, which require longer answers. You ask whether I will support "an equalization to a great extent of the Church Establishment, and a ceasing to compel any one to pay for the maintenance of any particular doctrine which he does not approve."

This question seems to involve a contradiction. "An equalization to a great extent of the Church Establishment" implies that there is still to be a Church Establishment. "A ceasing to compel any one to pay for the maintenance of any particular doctrine which he does not approve," implies the complete abolition of the Church Establishment.

There is not, I think, a more perplexing question in the science of politics than the question whether it be or be not desirable that the state should make provision for the religious instruction of the people. In fact, it is a question which does not admit of a general solution. We must look at the circumstances of every particular case. The Americans, situated as they are, judge wisely in having no established religion. The French, on the other hand, judge as wisely in giving a stipend from the revenues of the state to the ministers of opposite religions. Before we can properly decide what course ought to be taken in England, it is necessary that we should take many circumstances into consideration, – the nature of ecclesiastical revenues, – the manner in which those revenues are mixed up with private property, – the state of the public feeling towards the Church. We ought also to consider whether the dislike which is un-doubtedly felt towards the church by a great and respectable party in the country be a curable or an incurable dislike, – whether it proceed from anything essentially bad in the doctrines and constitution of the establish-ment, or from corruptions which judicious legislation might remove. These are matters of which I have thought long and anxiously. It would be impossible for me within the limits to which I must on the present occasion confine myself, to state all the arguments on both sides which have occurred to me. I will therefore simply declare my opinion with-out defending it at length. I think it desirable that the Church of England should be reformed. I do not think it desirable that it should be destroyed.

I have said that I object to monopolies generally; and I know of no reason for making an exception in favour of the Bank. But as the question relating to that corporation is one which I have not minutely studied, – as it is one respecting which very acute and liberal men are divided, – and as it is one which a committee of the House of Commons is still engaged in investigating, – I think it right to suspend my judgment. You must permit me to say that I entertain great doubts about the expediency of establishing a national bank to be conducted under the superintendence of the government and for the profit of the state. That superintendence would, I fear, be careless, and that profit might turn out a loss. Trading governments have seldom performed well either the business of governing or the business of trading. I throw out these merely as my first thoughts. The subject is one which requires much longer consideration than I have been able to give to it.

My opinions concerning the ballot are already before you. They are unaltered. I still continue to think that it is the best mode of voting, – the mode of voting which most completely secures the elector against the legal coercion of the few and against the physical coercion of the many, against ejectments on the one hand and the outrages of mobs on the other. You ask my opinion concerning triennial Parliaments. I think seven years rather too long a term. But I am inclined to think the term of three years too short. At all events, I think that it will be desirable, if the duration of Parliaments is shortened, to abolish the absurd law which provides that a dissolution shall follow the demise of the Crown. That law has, within my own memory, dispersed a parliament which had scarcely sate a year.

But I will frankly confess that I am not disposed at this time to press the introduction of the ballot or any other extensive change in our representative system. We have made a great experiment. Let us pause, at least for a few months, and watch its effects. Till the first elections under the new law shall have taken place, it will be impossible to say how much that law may have indirectly done to remove those evils which produced the feeling in favour of the ballot. Till a session or two has passed it will not be easy to judge whether it be or be not necessary that the representatives of the people should be called to a triennial reckoning. The game is in our own hands. We are sure that we can, if necessary, follow up the great victory which we have won. The delay of a year is nothing in the life of a nation. The events of a year may teach us inestimable lessons. Of this, however, you may be assured, that I will never shrink from any change, however extensive, which experience may prove to be necessary for the good government of the people.

I wish to add a few words touching a question which has lately been much canvassed, – I mean the question of pledges. In this letter, and in every letter which I have written to my friends at Leeds, I have plainly declared my *opinions*. But I think it, at this juncture, my duty to declare that I will give no *pledges*. I will not bind myself to make or to support any particular motion. I will state, as shortly as I can, some of the reasons which have induced me to form this determination. The great beauty of the representative system is that it unites the advantages of popular controul with the advantages arising from a division of labour. Just as a physician understands medicine better than an ordinary man, – just as a shoemaker makes shoes better than an ordinary man, – a person whose life is passed in transacting affairs of State, becomes a better statesman than an ordinary man. In politics, as in every other department of life, the public ought to have the means of checking those who serve it. If a man finds that he derives no benefit from the prescriptions of his physician, he calls in another. If his shoes do not fit him, he changes his shoemaker. If his representatives misgovern him, he can discard them at the next election. But when he has called in a physician of whom he hears a good report, and whose general practice he believes to be judicious, it would be absurd in him to tie down that physician to order particular pills and particular draughts. While he continues to be the customer of a shoemaker it would be absurd in him to sit by and direct every motion of that shoemaker's hand. And in the same manner it would, I think, be absurd in him to require positive pledges and to exact daily and hourly obedience from his representative. My opinion is that electors ought at first to choose cautiously, – then to confide liberally, – and, when the term for which they have selected their member has expired, to review his conduct equitably and to pronounce on the whole taken together.

Consider too that the business of a member of Parliament is the pursuit, not of speculative truth, but of practical good; and that though, in speculation, every truth is consistent with every other truth, yet, in practice, one good measure may be incompatible with another. It is often absolutely necessary to bear with a lesser evil in order to get rid of a greater. For example, I think the Corn Laws an evil. But if there had been in this Parliament a hundred or a hundred and fifty members absolutely bound by pledges to attempt the abolition of the Corn Laws, there would have been a division in the ranks of the reformers: the Tories would have triumphed, and I verily believe, that at the moment at which I am writing, Lord John Russell's bill would have been lost, and the Duke of Wellington would have been Prime Minister. Such cases may and will occur again. Some such cases I can, I think, distinctly foresee. I conceive, therefore, that it is the true wisdom of the electors to choose a representative whom they believe to be honest and enlightened, and, having chosen him, to leave him a large discretion. When his terms expires, when he again presents himself before them, it will be their duty to take a general survey of his conduct, and to consider whether he have or have not pursued that course which has, under all the circumstances, most tended to promote the public good.

If the people of Leeds think fit to repose in me that confidence which is necessary to the proper discharge of the duties of a representative, I hope that I should not abuse it. If it be their pleasure to fetter their members by positive promises, it is in their power to do so. I can only say that on such terms I cannot conscientiously serve them. I hope and feel assured that the sincerity with which I make this explicit declaration will, if it should deprive me of the votes of my friends at Leeds, secure to me what I value far more highly, their esteem.[1] / Believe me, ever, my dear Sir,

Your most faithful Servant,

T. B. Macaulay.

J. Lees, Esq. Leeds.

TO HANNAH AND MARGARET MACAULAY, [2][2] AUGUST 1832

MS: Trinity College. *Address:* Miss Macaulay / J Cropper's Esq / Dingle Bank / Liverpool. *Frank:* London August two 1832 / T B Macaulay. *Extract published:* Trevelyan, I, 267–8.

London August 3. 1832

My sweet M D,

How can you complain of the remissness of Presto as a correspondent? I write twice as many pages to you as you two together write to me? I am delighted to find that you like my review, though I am angry with Margaret for grumbling at my scriptural allusions,[3] and more angry with Nancy for denying my insight into character. It is one of my strong points. If she knew how far I see into her she would be ready to hang herself. No insight into character! An impertinent gypsey!

I have been all day employed in writing a very long letter to Leeds which will, I suppose, be printed. I think it a mighty knowing concern. The worse luck yours! It has occupied me so long that I have scarce two minutes to write to you. However to make you amends, I enclose Ellis's squib. Take care of it. I think it very good. It is an imitation of my style, and particularly of my way of drawing characters and discovering parallels.

---

[1] This letter had a great success: in commenting on it, the *Spectator* prophesied of TBM that 'if he can but wait for honours until they wait on him, which they infallibly will do – he will before many years pass, occupy the most distinguished station in the empire that a subject can occupy' (quoted in Leeds *Mercury*, 1 September 1832).

[2] Postmark and frank both confirm 2 August. In the frank TBM first wrote 'three'; this is overscored and 'two' accompanied by the initials 'TBM' substituted.

[3] TBM alludes to or quotes Luke 14: 10, Joshua 9: 21, and Psalms 129: 7 in the first two pages of the essay on Mirabeau (*ER*, LV, 552–3).

You know, I suppose, that Sir Gregory Lewin,[1] – the butt of the Northern Circuit, was a sailor in his youth, and that he broke his promise of voting for Lord Cavendish at Cambridge[2] in order, as was surmised, to please the late Chancellor[3] with whom he has some connection. / Ever, dearest, sweetest, girls,

Yours
T B M

TO HANNAH AND MARGARET MACAULAY, 6 AUGUST 1832

MS: Trinity College. *Address:*[4] Miss Macaulay / J. Cropper Esq / Dingle Bank / Liverpool. *Frank:* London August six 1832 / T Hyde Villiers.

London August 6. 1832

My sweet girls,

So you think that I am really angry. If you will not let me quarrel with you for being bad correspondents I shall quarrel with you for thinking that I could be out of temper with you. How long is it, you foolish chits, since I was angry with either of you in earnest? But if you knew how much I love the sight of your handwriting you would not be sparing of it.

On Saturday evening, after a week of hard work, I went to Holland House and dined there. The Chancellor was there, in great spirits and talking wildly and merrily. There was his daughter-in-law, Miss Spalding,[5] a smart, good-looking, fashionable, chattering, damsel, with whom I had much discussion touching the exhibitions, the new Picture Gallery,[6] the Palace at Pimlico,[7] Brighton, Ramsgate, and so forth. There was George Lamb and his wife,[8] – a lady about whom a strange scandalous story was

---

1 Sir Gregory Allnutt Lewin (1794?–1845), on the Northern Circuit from 1822; Q.C., 1843; Recorder of Doncaster, 1842–5. He was in the navy, 1808–18, before going to Cambridge. 'Sir Gregory was...the author of *Lewin's Crown Cases* – two little volumes containing much more amusing matter than any other law-books. The marginal notes are amazing, such as "Hay may be stolen in any county;" "Possession in Scotland is evidence of stealing in England." Macaulay was very fond of these reports, and would go to Ellis's chambers in the Temple for the sake of reading in them and enjoying them with him' (Pollock, *Personal Remembrances*, 1, 97–8).

2 In May 1831.   3 Lyndhurst.

4 TBM has written the address on the back of the cover; it was then copied on the front by Villiers, under whose frank the letter was sent.

5 Marian Dora, daughter of the Mrs Mary Anne Spalding whom Brougham married in 1819; Miss Spalding married Sir Alexander Malet in 1834.

6 The planned National Gallery.

7 Buckingham House was being reconstructed as Buckingham Palace for George IV by Nash. Pimlico is defined, in 1831, as 'a district of *Westminster*, that commences at Buckinghamgate, and extends to Chelsea' (James Elmes, *Topographical Dictionary*).

8 Caroline Rosalie Adelaide St Jules, who married George Lamb in 1809. Her mother, Lady Elizabeth Foster, married the fifth Duke of Devonshire as his second wife, also in 1809.

circulated twelve or thirteen years ago, of which the Chancellor was the hero. God knows whether it was true or false. At all events she is older now – perhaps wiser – certainly plainer; and nothing could be more quiet and less lover-like than her demeanour and that of her rumoured admirer. There was Senior[1] the political œconomist, who sate very quiet, and who, as soon as he had departed, was pronounced a bore by Lady Holland. There was Miss Fox,[2] the paragon of maiden aunts, – Allen, of course, the model of humble companions, – Lord John Russell, Colonel Fox, Lady Mary,[3] and the most agreable of companions, Luttrell.

I slept there; and the next day, Sunday, lay in bed till near eleven. It was the first good night's rest that I had enjoyed for a week. After breakfast, which ended towards Litany-time, we sate in the library talking and reading. I had intended to call on Fanny at Kensington: but the rain was canine and feline; and, as I was fixed in my best, I did not chuse to spoil my outer man by walking a mile through the shower. Her ladyship summoned me in the afternoon to her dressing room to read to her and Mrs. Lamb. The work which she gave me to read was interesting, if not in itself, yet for the sake of the writer. It was a manuscript History of Holland House by Sir James Mackintosh.[4] Few houses are so remarkable, or would furnish so much matter to the historian. I may perhaps have told you that it was the scene of a very romantic secret courtship of the famous Duke of Ormond, – that it belonged to the Earl of Holland who, after trimming between Charles the First and the long Parliament, was at last beheaded by sentence of the High Court of Justice, – that Ireton and Cromwell used to consult there, – that William the Third visited it and at one time was inclined to turn it into a royal residence. He preferred however the neighbouring villa of the Earl of Nottingham; and converted it into Kensington palace. Lady Warwick, the wife of Addison, lived there. Addison died there. The room into which he summoned Lord Warwick, the Captain of the Mohawks of those brutal times, to shew him how a Christian could die, still exists. Tickell wrote some very picturesque lines about the House and gardens. Atterbury's daughter afterwards lived there, and that clever, eloquent, intriguing prelate, was a frequent visitor. It passed, some years after, to Henry Fox, the first Lord Holland, and from him descended to the present possessor, in whose time it has

---

[1] Nassau Senior (1790–1864: *DNB*), a barrister and writer, an authority on economic subjects; a member of the Poor Law Commission, his report became the basis of the new Poor Law of 1834. He was a familiar figure in high Whig society, and, after 1840, a regular contributor to the *ER*.

[2] Caroline Fox (1767–1845), Lord Holland's sister; she lived nearby at Little Holland House.

[3] Lady Mary Fox (1806–91), Lord Holland's surviving daughter, married the third Baron Lilford in 1830.

[4] The MS, 'Some Account of Holland House,' *c.* 1827, is among the Holland House papers now in the British Museum.

probably been frequented by a greater number of distinguished literary and political characters than have ever met in any other mansion in England.[1]

Mackintosh's manuscript goes down only to the death of Addison or thereabouts: and Lady Holland was very urgent with me to continue it. Dr. Chambers, who came to look after her ladyship's health, interrupted our reading. She told me that I was one of her prime favourites, that it was very good in her to spare me to Lord Lansdowne, that I must come again next Saturday, and stay till Monday, and at last sent me off to Richmond in a one-horse-fly.

I went, through rain and wind, to Lord Lansdowne's beautiful villa on Richmond hill. You remember the situation well, I make no doubt. There I found a party assembled, my Lord, and my Lady, and my Lady Louisa,[2] and Lord Minto,[3] and Lady Minto,[4] and that hideous old bore Lady Davy,[5] and Spring Rice, and his son Stephen,[6] and Labouchere,[7] and Adam,[8] a very famous lawyer. We had a very agreable evening, and much pleasant talk, particularly when the guests who were not to sleep at Richmond had departed and only the Rices and I were left. This morning the sun was bright, and the lawn, and the wood and the Thames looked beautiful. The view from the villa, however, is not quite so fine as I had expected. The grounds of the Duke of Buccleugh lie just below; and the high trees which screen his house shut out Lord Lansdowne from the prospect which we have so often admired together. I breakfasted and came back with Rice to pass another week in working like a slave. If this week brings us to the end of our labour I shall not repine.

What are your plans? Let me only know positively at what time or about what time you must leave Liverpool and, if I can, I will come to escort you to the Temple. –

Ever, my own darlings, yours affectionately
T B M

---

1 For the details of this history, see the Earl of Ilchester, *The Home of the Hollands, 1605–1820*, 1937.

2 Lord Lansdowne's only daughter (d. 1906), married James Kenneth Howard in 1845.

3 Gilbert Elliot (1782–1859: *DNB*), second Earl of Minto, Whig M.P., 1806–14; Ambassador to Berlin, August 1832–4; First Lord of the Admiralty, 1835–41.

4 Mary Brydone (1786–1853), married Lord Minto in 1806.

5 Jane Kerr (1780–1855: *DNB*), after the death of her first husband, Sir Shuckburgh Apreece, married Sir Humphry Davy in 1812. After Davy's death, in 1829, she continued to be an assiduous hostess in London and Rome. Margaret Macaulay writes that TBM called Lady Davy 'an intolerable woman, always talking of Greek, and Latin...she once talked to him for half an hour about the dreadful loss Livy and Tacitus would be. "I would bear the loss" said he, "for a hundred pounds, and I believe it would be a rather greater one to me than to Lady Davy"' (*Recollections*, p. 206).

6 Stephen Spring Rice (1814–65), Spring Rice's only son.

7 Henry Labouchere (1798–1869: *DNB*), afterwards Baron Taunton; Whig M.P., 1826–59; held various offices under Grey, Melbourne, Russell, and Palmerston.

8 Presumably William Adam (1751–1839: *DNB*), Whig politician and lawyer, Lord Chief Commissioner of the Scottish Jury Court from 1816.

TO LORD MAHON, 8 AUGUST 1832

MS: Stanhope Papers, Chevening. *Mostly published:* Trevelyan, 1, 266n.

London August 8. 1832

My dear Lord Mahon,

Nothing would give me more pleasure than to accept your invitation. But we [are] now strictly on duty. No furloughs, even for a dinner engagement or a sight of Taglioni's legs,[1] can be obtained. It is very hard to keep forty members in the House. Sibthorpe[2] and Leader[3] are on the watch to count us out: and from six till two we never venture further than the smoking room without apprehension. In spite of all our exertions, the end of the Session seems further and further off every day.

If you would do me the favour of inviting Sibthorpe to Chevening Park,[4] you might be the means of saving my life, and that of thirty or forty more of us who are forced to swallow the last dregs of the oratory of this Parliament; – and nauseous dregs they are. / Ever, dear Lord Mahon,

Yours very truly

T B Macaulay

TO SELINA MACAULAY, 8 AUGUST 1832

MS: Trinity College. *Address:* Miss Macaulay / Rothley Temple / Leicester. *Frank:* London August eight 1832 / T B Macaulay.

London August 8 – 1832

Dearest Selina,

I was delighted to receive your letter. Yet I was almost sorry that it was so long, as I feared that so much writing might not agree with you. I am very glad to find that my last article is liked at the Temple, and very much amused by your account of Arthur's[5] premature valetudinarianism. I suppose that when he learns his book well he is treated to senna-tea, and is allowed, on his birth-day, to chuse whether he will have black dose or blue pill. What an education for a child! I should not wonder if the poor little girl who died last year[6] had been physicked to death by that absurd Malade Imaginaire our cousin.

---

[1] Marie Taglioni (1804–84: *DNB*), the most celebrated ballerina of the century, created a London sensation in 'La Sylphide,' first produced at Covent Garden on 26 July.

[2] Colonel Charles DeLaet Waldo Sibthorp (1783–1855: *DNB*), Tory M.P. for Lincoln, 1826–32; 1835–55; a violent reactionary, his politics and his appearance were equally extravagant and made him a favorite with the caricaturists.

[3] Nicholas Philpot Leader (1773–1836), M.P. for Kilkenny, 1830–2.

[4] The Stanhope estate, near Sevenoaks.

[5] Probably Thomas Arthur Babington (1820–96), eldest son of Thomas Gisborne Babington.

[6] Julia Mary, daughter of Thomas Gisborne Babington, died on 16 June 1831.

The only physic that I take is port wine at four in the afternoon and tea at midnight. Our sittings are really merciless. We never rise till two in the morning; and business seems to multiply upon us every day – hills on hills – Alps above Alps.[1] Three weeks ago we expected to have been up by the fifth of August. Last week we hoped to have been up by to day. On Monday last we hoped to have been up by Friday. Now I shall be content if our work is over by next Tuesday.

You have said nothing about the article on Mrs Trollope.[2] What do you think of it? I think it one of Empson's best. –

I am glad to hear of the success of our fat cousin. In return for the news of his being provided for, I will tell you that our man – the poor old fellow whom you and Fanny could not bear, – has got a place. He quite moved my heart with his crying about his wife and children. So I had no choice except to provide for him myself or to get somebody else to take him. I have effected the latter without telling more than the ordinary and lawful quantity of untruth. What would my uncle say to that expression? But I think that a good casuist would allow it to be quite just. For suppose that the practice of telling stories in giving characters to servants has become so general that nobody believes more than half the good which you say, you are then bound to say twice as much in a servant's favour as is true. For your object ought to be to produce a just impression on the mind of your hearer. And if he will believe only half [of] what you say, you must say double of what is true in order to produce a just impression.

But I must go to make a House; – no easy business in the empty state of London, I assure you.

Ever yours affectionately
T B M

TO HANNAH AND MARGARET MACAULAY, [9][3] AUGUST 1832

MS: Morgan Library. *Address:*[4] Miss Macaulay / J. Cropper's Esq. / Dingle Bank / Liverpool. *Frank:* London – August Nine – 1832 / G. Lamb. *Mostly published:* Trevelyan, I, 268–70.

London August 16. 1832

My darling girls,

We begin to see a hope of liberation. To morrow or on Saturday at furthest, we expect to finish our business. I did not reach home till four

---

1 Cf. Pope, *Essay on Criticism*, line 232.
2 William Empson, 'The Americans and Their Detractors,' *ER*, LV (July 1832), 479–526.
3 TBM has clearly dated this 16 August, perhaps thinking ahead to the prorogation of Parliament on that day. Both internal evidence and the evidence of the frank make 9 August certain.
4 TBM has written the address on the back of the cover; it was then copied on the front by George Lamb, under whose frank it was sent.

this morning after a most fatiguing and yet rather amusing night. What passed will not find its way into the papers as the gallery was locked during most of the time. So I will tell you the story.

There is a bill before the House prohibiting the processions of Orangemen which have excited a good deal of irritation in Ireland. This bill was committed yesterday night. Shaw[1] the Recorder of Dublin, an honest man enough, but a great fool and a bitter Protestant fanatic, complained that it should be brought forward so late in the Session. Several of his friends he said – in particular Serjeant Lefroy[2] – had left London believing that the measure had been abandoned. It appeared however that Stanley and Lord Althorp had given fair notice of their intention; so that if the absent members had been mistaken, the fault was their own; – and the house was for going on. Shaw said warmly that he would resort to all the means of delay in his power, and moved that the Chairman should leave the chair. The motion was negatived by 40 votes to 2. Then the first clause was read. Shaw divided the house again on that clause. He was beaten by the same majority. He moved again that the Chairman should leave the Chair. He was beaten again. He divided on the second clause. He was beaten again. He then said that he was sensible that he was doing very wrong; that his conduct was very unhandsome and vexatious; that he heartily begged our pardons; but that he had said that he would delay the bill as far as the forms of the house would permit; and that he must keep his word. Now came a discussion by which Nancy, if she had been in the ventilator, might have been greatly edified, – touching the nature of vows; – whether a man's promise given to himself, a promise from which nobody could derive any advantage and which everybody wished him to violate, constituted an obligation. Jephtha's daughter was a case in point, and was cited by somebody sitting near me. Peregrine Courtenay[3] on one side of the House and Lord Palmerston on the other attempted to enlighten the poor Orangeman on the question of casuistry. They might as well have preached to Percival[4] or to any other madman out of St Luke's. "I feel," said the silly creature, "that I am doing wrong – acting very unjustifiably. If gentlemen will forgive me, I will never do so again. But I must keep my word." We roared with laughter every time that he repeated his apologies. The orders of the house do not enable any person absolutely to stop the progress of a bill in Committee; but they enable

---

[1] (Sir) Frederick Shaw (1799–1876: *DNB*), Recorder of Dublin, 1828–76; Tory M.P. for Dublin, 1830–2; for the University of Dublin, 1832–48.

[2] Thomas Langlois Lefroy (1776–1869: *DNB*), Tory M.P. for the University of Dublin, 1830–41.

[3] Thomas Peregrine Courtenay (1782–1841: *DNB*), Tory M.P. for Totnes, 1810–32. He published *Memoirs of Sir William Temple* which TBM reviewed in 1838, calling Courtenay 'an industrious and useful official man, and...an upright and consistent member of Parliament' (*ER*, LXVIII, 113).   [4] I.e., Spencer Perceval.

him to delay it grievously. We divided seventeen times; and between every two divisions this veracious Irishman made us a speech of apologies and self-condemnation. Of the two who had supported him at the beginning of his freak one soon sneaked away. The other, that hairy, filthy, blackguard, Sibthorpe, staid to the last, – not expressing remorse, like Shaw, but glorying in the unaccommodating temper which he shewed and on the delay which he produced. At last the Bill went through. Then Shaw rose, congratulated himself that his vow was accomplished, and said that the only atonement which he could make for conduct so unjustifiable was to vow that he would never make such a vow again, promised to let the bill go through its future stages without any more divisions, and contented himself with suggesting one or two alterations in the details. "I hint at these amendments" he said. "If the Secretary for Ireland approves of them I hope he will not refrain from introducing them because they are brought forward by me. I am sensible that I have forfeited all claim to the favour of the house. I will not divide on any future stage of the Bill." We were all heartily pleased with these events. For the truth was that these seventeen divisions occupied less time than a real hard debate on the bill would have occupied, and were infinitely more amusing. The oddest part of the business is that Shaw's frank good natured way of proceeding, absurd as it was, has made him popular. He was never so great a favourite with the house as after harassing it for two or three hours with the most frivolous and vexatious opposition. This is a curious trait of the character of the House of Commons.

Perhaps you will find this long story which I have not time to read over again very stupid and unintelligible. But I have thought it my duty to set before you the evil consequences of making vows rashly and adhering to them superstitiously. For in truth, my Christian brethren, or rather my Christian sisters, let us consider etc. etc. etc. But I reserve the sermon on promises which I had intended to preach for another occasion.

Good bye, my own darlings

T B M.

TO ZACHARY MACAULAY, 10 AUGUST 1832

Text: From MS in possession of Mr C. S. Menell, who furnished transcript. *Published:* Knutsford, *Zachary Macaulay*, pp. 468–9.

London. August 10. 1832

My dear Father,

To day we meet for the last time previous to the prorogation. We shall adjourn till Thursday. By that day the Lords will have passed our last batch of bills, and we shall then be dismissed with a speech from the Throne.

The W[est] I[ndian] Committee of the House of Commons met today to consider their report.[1] Graham has become a perfect Aldermanbury-man.[2] He told me yesterday that he had never troubled himself about the question till this report, that he did not at all like being put into the Chair of the Committee – but that he had been delighted and surprised by the results of the inquiry – and was so much fascinated by the subject that he could think of nothing else. "I am quite convinced," he said, "that if a proper system had been pursued since 1823, slavery might already have been extinguished without the least danger of commotion."

The Lords Committee, I understand, mean to present the evidence without any report.[3] But Sir James tells me that Lord Harewood,[4] Lord St Vincent,[5] and Lord Howard de Walden,[6] the son-in-law of Lord Seaford, have all, to his knowledge, declared themselves decidedly for emancipation as necessary to the safety of their own property.

Ever yours,
T B M

TO JOSEPH LEES, 10 AUGUST 1832

Text: Composite from Leeds *Intelligencer*, 16 August 1832, and Leeds *Mercury*, 18 August 1832.

London, August 10, 1832.

My dear Sir,

I am glad to find that our opinions respecting the church differ only in appearance.[7] I should say that the Incumbent of a Crown-living, who is supported by tithes or by the produce of an estate for which the tithes

---

[1] TBM was not a member of this committee, appointed to consider measures for the abolition of West Indian slavery; its report, 11 August, came to no definite conclusion (*Parliamentary Papers*, 1831–2, xx, 3–4).

[2] The offices of the Anti-Slavery Society were at 18 Aldermanbury Street. Sir James Graham was chairman of the committee.

[3] This is, in fact, what the committee did, 9 August (House of Lords *Journals*, 1831–2, Appendix 2).

[4] Henry Lascelles (1767–1841: *DNB*), second Earl of Harewood; Tory M.P., 1796–1820.

[5] Edward Jervis (1767–1859), second Viscount St Vincent.

[6] Charles Augustus Ellis (1799–1868: *DNB*), sixth Baron; he was the son, not son-in-law, of Lord Seaford, and succeeded as the second Baron in 1845. His father was for many years the leader of the West Indian interests in Parliament.

[7] In reply to TBM's letter of [2] August, Lees wrote that the Political Union proposed a plan leaving the Church most of its revenues but without 'any rate upon the community' and that he regretted TBM's introducing the subject of pledges when it had not been raised, for his remarks threw 'a gloom over the opinions you had previously expressed' (Leeds *Intelligencer*, 16 August). TBM's answer was read at the meeting of the Political Union, 14 August, and received with 'the loudest plaudits' (Leeds *Mercury*, 18 August 1832).

have been commuted, is supported in part by people who differ from him in religious opinions. The fund from which he is paid is the property of the nation. The nation consists partly of dissenters; but the fund is employed solely to maintain churchmen. It may therefore, I think, in such a case, be said without impropriety that dissenters contribute to the support of a religion which is not their own. You will perceive that the difference between us is merely verbal. As to the substance of the question we are agreed.

I was perfectly aware that the avowal of my feelings on the subject of pledges was not likely to advance my interest at Leeds. I was perfectly aware that many of my most respectable friends were likely to differ from me. And therefore I thought it the more necessary to make, uninvited, an explicit declaration of my opinions. If ever there was a time when public men were in an especial measure bound to speak the truth, the whole truth, and nothing but the truth, to the people, this is that time. Nothing is easier than for a candidate to avoid unpopular topics as long as possible, and, when they are forced on him, to take refuge in evasive and unmeaning phrases. Nothing is easier than for him to give extravagant promises while an election is depending, and to forget them as soon as the return is made. I will take no such course. I do not wish to obtain a single vote under false pretences. Under the old system I have never been the flatterer of the great. Under the new system I will not be the flatterer of the people. The truth, or what appears to me to be such, may sometimes be distasteful to those whose good opinion I most value. I shall, nevertheless, always abide by it, and trust to their good sense, to their second thoughts, to the force of reason, and to the progress of time. If, after all, their decision should be unfavourable to me, I shall submit to that decision with fortitude and good humour. It is not necessary to my happiness that I should sit in Parliament. But it is necessary to my happiness that I should possess, in Parliament or out of Parliament, the consciousness of having done what is right.

Remember me kindly to all our friends, and believe me ever, / My dear Sir,

Yours most faithfully,
T. B. Macaulay.

Joseph Lees, Esq., Leeds.

TO JOHN SMITHSON,[1] 11 AUGUST 1832

Text: Composite from Leeds *Intelligencer*, 16 August 1832, and Leeds *Mercury*, 18 August 1832.

London, August 11, 1832.

Sir,

I feel greatly obliged to you for the very kind manner in which you have applied to me for explanations touching a part of my letter. I will do my best to make my meaning perfectly clear.

You say that by refusing to be pledged I neutralize what I have said about my opinions. Here I differ from you. In stating my opinions I have given by implication one pledge, which I have no objection to give directly. That pledge is that I will, if I should sit in parliament, take the course which shall appear to me most likely to promote the success of those opinions. But, as I have said, I will not pledge myself to particular votes, because conjunctures may arise in which it may be necessary to abstain from pressing desirable measures, lest other measures even more desirable should be endangered.

If the only question which a member of parliament had to consider were this, – "What would it be best for the country to do?" – your arguments would be unanswerable. But the question which a member of parliament has to consider is this – "What is the best arrangement for the country to which I can induce six hundred and fifty-seven other persons to accede?"

You tell me that you are a member of the Council of the Leeds Political Union. I am quite sure, therefore, that I can appeal to your own experience on this point. I am quite sure that every man who has had to act in concert with others will understand my meaning. I know nothing of the internal history of the body to which you belong. But I would venture to assert that you must, many and many a time, have found it necessary to yield things which you thought desirable and to comply with things which you did not think desirable. I have no objection to say plainly that there were parts of the Reform Bill which I disliked much. I disliked schedule B.[2] I should have greatly preferred having a larger schedule A[3] and no schedule B. I disliked the clause which reserved the rights of the freemen in perpetuity. I disliked the partition of the counties.

But what then? Was I, because I differed from the authors of the bill

---

[1] Smithson, a 'joiner, cabinet maker, furniture broker and appraiser' (White and Parson, *Leeds Directory*, 1830), wrote to TBM on 9 August complaining that his refusal to be pledged 'neutralized' all of his statements. TBM's reply was read by Smithson at the meeting of the Leeds Political Union, 14 August (Leeds *Intelligencer*, 16 August).

[2] The list of boroughs which were to have only one member.

[3] The list of boroughs which were to be disfranchised.

on a few points of this kind, to sow dissension among men engaged in the greatest work ever undertaken for the public good? Was I to play the game of the enemies of all reform? Surely not.

You refer particularly to the taxes on knowledge.[1] "If,"say you," Your mind is made up for abolition, why not say so?" I will most willingly say so. My mind is made up for the abolition of those taxes. But I will not positively pledge myself to vote for or to bring forward a motion for their abolition; and I think that I can easily show you why I refuse to give such a promise.

You are aware that a motion was made, a few weeks ago, on this very subject.[2] It was made by Mr. Bulwer, and supported by Mr. Hume. I was then out of Parliament, having vacated my seat by accepting Sir James Mackintosh's place at the India Board. Mr. Bulwer and Mr. Hume were desirous, I believe, of completely abolishing these taxes. But was the motion a motion for complete abolition? Not at all. It was merely a motion for a commutation, and a commutation by no means free from objections. It was proposed to substitute a postage on newspapers for the stamp-duty. This postage would have been a tax on knowledge. Yet I think that Mr. Bulwer was not to be blamed for framing his motion thus. He probably conceived that there were many persons who disliked the tax, and who were yet very unwilling to concur in any measure which might produce a falling off in the revenue. He framed his proposition therefore, not according to his views of what might in itself be desirable, but according to his views of what might be practicable. In my opinion no member of Parliament can be useful to the public, unless he is at liberty to exercise this kind of discretion, and to shape his course with constant reference to existing circumstances. I should have thought it most inexpedient to introduce measures about the corn laws or the church, while the reform bill was depending.

Now suppose that the Government were in the next Parliament to bring forward excellent plans relating to the Church, the Corn Laws, the East Indies, and Negro Slavery. Suppose, (I am merely putting an imaginary case,) that there was among the members of this Government and its supporters a strong difference of opinion respecting the newspaper stamps. Suppose that some person, whose only object was to set the ministers and their friends at variance, and to stop the progress of their useful measures, were to bring forward a proposition for the repeal of taxes on knowledge, without the least hope or intention of carrying it, but solely with the view of producing embarrassment and dissension.

---

[1] The duties on newspapers, advertisements, and paper, not finally abolished until 1861.
[2] 14 June; Bulwer received no support and withdrew his motion (*Hansard*, 3rd Series, XIII, 619–34). Hume did not speak in this debate, but on 7 December 1831 he had presented a petition against the taxes and argued for their abolition (*Hansard*, 3rd Series, IX, 102–4).

I say explicitly that I should doubt whether I ought to vote with him, and that if I believed that, by voting with him, I should endanger the salutary measures then in progress, I would not vote with him. But if I give a positive pledge to vote for the abolition of taxes on knowledge, how can I exercise any discretion? How can I take circumstances and times into consideration? I may feel that I am not doing any real good. I may feel that I am doing positive harm. But I am bound, and I must vote according to my promise.

I hope that I have now made my meaning clear. I pledge myself to a general line of conduct. But I will not pledge myself to particular votes. I do not think it for your interest that I should so pledge myself. I feel that I cannot serve you so usefully unless I am allowed a certain discretion, – unless I am at liberty to shape my conduct with a view, not only to general principles of legislation, but to the varying circumstances of every day. I might easily have abstained from saying any thing on this subject. But I thought it, and I think it my duty to speak out. If we differ, you will, I am sure, do the same justice to my motives which I render to yours.

Believe me, Sir, your most faithful Servant,

T. B. Macaulay.

J. Smithson, Esq., No. 1, Calls, Leeds.

TO HANNAH AND MARGARET MACAULAY, 11 AUGUST 1832

MS: Trinity College.

London August 11. 1832

My sweet girls,

A thousand thanks for your charming letters – and send me many such. To day our labours are to end. At three we meet, and dispatch the last remains of our business. Then I am off for Holland House till Monday. On Monday I shall come back to utter solitude, to this wilderness of London, deserted by all the aristocrats. There will be, to be sure, a small circle of official men, Labouchere, Villiers, Francis Baring,[1] Rice, and a few more. We intend to hold a weekly feast at Grillon's[2] – a kind of junior cabinet dinner, – and to settle affairs of state and abuse our masters. Most even of the official men are taking holiday. Grant is going

---

[1] Francis Baring (1796–1866: *DNB*), afterwards first Baron Northbrook, M.P. for Portsmouth, 1826–65; Chancellor of the Exchequer, 1839–41; First Lord of the Admiralty, 1849–52. He belonged to the Evangelical branch of the Barings and had been a pupil of John Venn's at Clapham and of Farish at Cambridge.

[2] Grillon's or Grillion's Hotel, 7 Albemarle Street; TBM's group was not connected with those M.P.s called Grillon's Club, who, until 1860, also met at Grillion's Hotel.

to Scotland, – Gordon to Brighton, I believe, – Lord Howick has married a wife and therefore he cannot come.[1] I have put off my holiday for the present. I mean to take it when I can take it with most pleasure to you. When do you think of leaving Liverpool.

Whatever you may hear about my chances at Leeds, I believe them to be by no means good. I bear the suspense, however, and shall bear the result, with the most immoveable philosophy. I am quite sure that to be beaten will not give me half so much uneasiness as I have felt about a tooth-ache of my Nancy's, or about Margaret's mumps.

But I must stop – I am going to Holland House. I wrote these few lines only because, if you love me as much as I love you you will like even to see my handwriting.

Farewell, my own darlings,

T B M

TO HANNAH AND MARGARET MACAULAY, 14 AUGUST 1832

MS: Trinity College. *Address:* Miss Macaulay / J Cropper's Esq / Dingle Bank / Liverpool. *Frank:* London August fourteen 1832 / T B Macaulay. *Partly published:* Trevelyan, I, 266–7.

London August 14. 1832

My dearest girls,

Our work is over at last, not, however, till it has half killed us all. On Saturday we met for the last time, I hope, on business. When the House rose, I set off for Holland House. We had a small party, but a very distinguished one. – Lord Grey, the Chancellor, Lord Palmerston, Luttrell and myself were the only guests.[2] Allen was of course at the end of the table, carving the dinner and sparring with my Lady. The dinner was not so good as usual – for the French Cook was ill; and her Ladyship kept up a continued lamentation during the whole repast. I should never have found out that everything was not as good as usual but for her criticisms. The soup was too salt; the cutlets were not exactly comme il faut; and the pudding was hardly enough boiled. I was amused to hear from the splendid mistress of such a house the same sort of apologies which Mary Parker made when her cook forgot the joint and sent up too small a dinner to table. I told Luttrell that it was a comfort to me to find that no rank was exempted from these afflictions.

[1] Luke 14: 20. Howick married Maria Copley (1803–79) on 9 August.
[2] Greville was there too; he writes that 'Macaulay and Allen disputed history, particularly the character of the Emperor Henry VI, and Allen declared himself a Guelph and Macaulay a Ghibelline. Macaulay is a most extraordinary man...but (as far as I have yet seen of him, which is not sufficient to judge) he is not *agreeable*' (*Memoirs*, II, 317).

I learned two things at this dinner which I repeat to all my unfashionable friends for their guidance, and which you will do well to teach to friends at Liverpool. The time for eating melon is at the beginning of dinner – before the soup. It is handed round with ginger, pepper, and salt. The time for eating maccaroni is between the fish and the meat, – just as you would eat patties. Treasure up these instructions, my darlings, that, if you ever preside over banquets, you may do the genteel thing.

They talked about Lord Abercorn's approaching marriage.[1] He is to be married to Lady Louisa Russell. All the noble persons present are very intimate friends of the Bedford family. They, however, treated the whole thing as a take-in, and laughed at the Duchess for pouncing on so rich a youth before he knew what he was about. Lady Holland vehemently defended the match; and when Allen said that Lord Abercorn had caught a Tartar, she quite went off into one of her tantrums – "Lady Louisa a Tartar! – such a charming girl a Tartar! – He is a very happy man, and your language is insufferable – insufferable, Mr. Allen." Lord Grey had all the trouble in the world to appease her. His influence however is very great. He prevailed on her to receive Allen again into favour, and to let Lord Holland have a slice of melon, for which he had been petitioning most piteously, but which she had steadily refused on account of his gout. Lord Holland thanked Lord Grey for his intercession. "Ah, Lord Grey, I wish you were always here. It is a fine thing to be prime minister." This tattle is worth nothing – absolutely nothing, except to shew how much the people whose names will fill the history of our times resemble in all essential matters the quiet folks who live in Mecklenburgh Square and Brunswick Square.

I slept in the room which was poor Mackintosh's. The next day – Sunday, – I walked over to James Stephen's, and sate there two hours. Fanny was well and seemed very comfortable. In the afternoon I walked back to Holland House and found her ladyship in her poney cart, being wheeled up and down the pretty lawn behind the house. I walked beside her for half-an-hour. She shewed me the beauties of the gardens, and read me some letters which Lord Grey had just sent to Lord Holland, giving a more favourable account of the state of things in Portugal than I had at all expected. Henry Fox,[2] Miss Fox, Lord Holland's sister, and Tom Duncombe, came to dinner. Henry Fox I had before seen – but

---

[1] James Hamilton (1811–85: *DNB*), second Marquess and later first Duke of Abercorn, married Lady Louisa Jane Russell (1812–1905), second daughter of the sixth Duke of Bedford, on 25 October 1832. In 1840 Lady Holland, after entertaining Lord and Lady Abercorn, wrote to her son that "it is pleasant to see people so happy and so handsome" (Lord Ilchester, *Lady Holland to Her Son*, p. 187).

[2] Henry Fox (1802–59), second son and heir of Lord Holland. He was in the diplomatic service, 1831–46, had lived much abroad since leaving college, and had just returned for a brief stay with his parents.

I had never heard his voice. He scarcely ever speaks in the society of Holland House. Rogers, who is the bitterest and most cynical observer of little traits of character that ever I knew, once said to me of him, "Observe that man. He never talks to men. He never talks to girls. But, when he can get into a circle of old tabbies, he is just in his element. He will sit clacking with an old woman for h[ours][1] together. That always settles my opinion of a young fellow." This description is quite correct. Yet Fox's address is extremely polished, his person agreable, and his mind, I believe, not uncultivated. He was, on this occasion, very courteous to me. But I despise his shallowness and instability; and I hate him for his conduct to Mrs. Lister.[2] Labouchere told me some circumstances about that affair which made me think much worse of it than I had ever before thought. But my paper is nearly full; and this letter will weigh an ounce or very nearly so. I therefore must stop for the present.

Ever yours, dear girls

T B M

TO HANNAH AND MARGARET MACAULAY, 17 AUGUST 1832

MS: Trinity College. *Address:* Miss Macaulay / J Cropper's Esq / Dingle Bank / Liverpool. *Frank:* London August seventeen 1832 / T B Macaulay. *Mostly published:* Trevelyan, 1, 270–2.

London August 17. 1832

Dearest girls,

I do not know what Nancy means by saying in her letter written on Wednesday that she had not heard from me touching Holland House. I wrote, if I remember rightly, on Monday:[3] and brought down my story to dinner time on Sunday evening. I have since been too busy to write to any body. All the morning I have been transacting political affairs, and all the evening feasting and revelling. To resume my narrative, I slept on Sunday night at Holland House. On Monday morning, after breakfast, I walked to town with Luttrell, whom I found a delightful companion. Before we went we sate and chatted with Lord Holland in the library for a quarter of an hour. He was very entertaining. He gave us an account of a visit which he paid long ago to the Court of Denmark, and of King Christian,[4] the madman, who was at last deprived of all real

---

[1] Paper torn away with seal.

[2] The affair between Theresa Villiers and Henry Fox dated from around 1824, when he was sent abroad by his parents in order to break it off: see Lord Ilchester, *Lady Holland to Her Son*, pp. 24; 41.

[3] TBM's last letter to Hannah and Margaret was Tuesday, 14 August.

[4] Christian VII (1749–1808). Lord Holland was in Denmark in 1792.

share in the government on account of his infirmity. "Such a Tom of Bedlam I never saw," said Lord Holland. One day the Neapolitan Ambassador came to the levee, and made a profound bow to his majesty. His majesty bowed still lower. The Neapolitan bowed down his head almost to the ground; – when behold! – The King clapped his hands on his excellency's shoulders and jumped over him like a boy playing at leap-frog. – Another day the English Ambassador was sitting opposite the King at dinner. His Majesty asked him to take wine. The glasses were filled. The Ambassador bowed and put the wine to his lips. The King grinned hideously and threw his wine into the face of one of the footmen. The other guests kept the most profound gravity. But the Englishman who had but lately come to Copenhagen, though a practiced diplomatist, could not help giving some signs of astonishment. The King immediately addressed him in French, "Eh – mais, Monsieur L'Envoyé d'Angleterre, qu'avez vous donc? Pourquoi riez vous? Est-ce qu'il y ait quelque chose qui vous ait diverti. Faites moi le plaisir de me l'indiquer. J'aime beaucoup les ridicules."

Parliament is up at last. We official men are now left alone at the West End of London, and are making up for our long confinement in the mornings by feasting together at night. On Wednesday I dined with Labouchere at his official residence in Somerset House.[1] It is well that he is a bachelor. For he tells me that the ladies his neighbours make bitter complaints of the unfashionable situation in which they are cruelly obliged to reside gratis. Yesterday I dined with Will Brougham[2] and an official party in Mount Street. We are going to establish a club to be confined to members of the house of Commons in place under the present government. [We][3] are to dine together weekly at Grill[on's][3] Hotel and to settle the affairs of the state better, I hope, than our masters at their Cabinet Dinners.

When do you positively mean to leave Liverpool. The Philipses have been very urgent with me to pay them a visit in Warwickshire.[4] I should like to pass a day or two with them, – then to go on to you, and to escort you to the Temple, – thence to proceed to Leeds, and again shew myself to the people there. But I can not positively determine any thing. Let me know whether your plans are arranged.

Ever yours dear girls
T B M

---

[1] Labouchere, appointed a Commissioner of the Admiralty in June 1832, had an official residence at 8 Somerset House.
[2] Brougham was M.P. for Southwark, 1831–4.
[3] Paper torn away with seal.
[4] Philips, about 1830, left Manchester for Weston House, near Shipston on Stour.

TO MARGARET MACAULAY, 18 AUGUST 1832

MS: Mrs Lancelot Errington. *Address:* Miss M Macaulay / J Cropper's Esq / Dingle Bank / Liverpool. *Frank:* London August eighteen 1832 / T B Macaulay.

[London]

How could you think, my darling Margaret, that any event could diminish the tender love which I feel for you?[1] – It is true that I shall grieve to lose you. It is true that I could not learn, without a flood of very bitter tears, that we are to be separated. But my love for you is not so selfish that I should repine at your decision. In a pecuniary point of view the connection is highly advantageous. It is no disrespect to Edward to say that in other things I do not consider him worthy of my Margaret. For I know very few people in any rank of life who are worthy of her. I believe him to be in all essential things a good man. I do not wonder that, situated as you were with respect to him and to his late wife, you should have become attached to him. I rather expected, before you went down to Liverpool, that this would happen, – not from any particular information which I had received, – but from my general knowledge of men and women. You were near each other. You had with each other sympathies of a very peculiar kind. The result was quite natural and in the common order of things.

You have nothing, my own dearest girl, of censure or of coldness to fear from me. Let Edward make you happy, and he shall be as a brother and more than a brother to me in affection. Of this I am sure, that, love you as he may, he will never love you more dearly than I have done.

God bless you, my own dear Margaret – and make you as happy as I wish you to be. I had much more to say – but I can scarcely see the paper for weeping.

Farewell, dearest,

T B M

---

[1] Margaret had just informed TBM of her engagement to Edward Cropper. Cropper (1799–1877), second son of James Cropper, was a partner in his father's house of Cropper, Benson and Co. and a director of the Liverpool and Manchester Railway. He was a Quaker, but left the society to marry Margaret (Hannah to Fanny Macaulay [21? August 1832]: MS, Huntington). Cropper's first wife had died in 1830 (see 26 August 1830), nursed by Margaret Macaulay. In 1848 he married a second Margaret Macaulay, the widow of TBM's brother Henry.

TO HANNAH AND MARGARET MACAULAY, 20 AUGUST 1832

MS: Trinity College. *Address:* Miss Macaulay / Messrs. Croppers Benson and Co / Liverpool. *Frank:* London August twenty 1832 / T B Macaulay.

London August 20. 1832

My dearest girls,

I had a heavy day of it on Saturday, and not a very light one yesterday. But to day I am in tolerable spirits again. I do not think that I ever felt any event so sharply as this separation, though accompanied with many pleasing circumstances; not that I am at all of the mind of Mr. Woodhouse, or in the least disposed to talk about "poor Margaret."[1] It has always been my wish to see my dearest girls honorably and happily married. But still it is impossible not to feel keenly the pain of parting from one whom I have loved so dearly, and of resigning to new claims that place which I had gained for myself in her affection. Time, however, which heals all wounds will heal this also: and we shall still be happy – as happy as ever, I hope. My father, from whom I have heard this morning, speaks very favourably, not only of Edward's principles and temper, but of his good sense. My dear girl will therefore have every chance for happiness. But I can tell her that she will be fortunate indeed if she finds in any husband or in any children a love so tender and constant, so little subject to interruptions and overcloudings, so thoroughly proof to all changes which time and fortune can produce as mine has been and will be.

My father is the oddest manager of a secret in the world. He told you to keep this affair quite close. He then wrote to George saying that he supposed that I should tell them all the great news about the girls at Liverpool. Accordingly, as you may suppose, when I reached Kensington yesterday afternoon, I had George, Fanny, Sarah Anne, and Charles upon me, catechising and cross questioning in all directions. Fanny indeed had given a shrewd guess at the matter; and asked me plainly whether Edward had not been proposing to Margaret. I thought it best, on the whole, to tell them and to enjoin secrecy on all of them except Sarah Anne. For I knew her disposition to be like that of the cleansed leper;[2] and that the more I charged her to keep it secret, so much the more she would publish it. They all, and George particularly, seemed thoroughly delighted. They had none of them to go through a struggle like mine. I told them not to write to Selina about it.

To day I have heard from my father. He tells me the whole story, because, he says, I am not a person given to gossiping, and solemnly charges me to keep this secret which every body knows. I have no doubt

---

[1] Cf. Jane Austen, *Emma*, e.g., ch. 1.   [2] Mark 1: 40–5.

that he has already written a full account of it to Selina. That, however, is his own affair.

The next time that I write I will let you know my plans. I hope to be able to leave London at the beginning of September. If I should then go to Liverpool, shall you be able to accompany me on a short tour of four or five days, and so to the Temple? Let me know, my darlings, as soon as possible. For I shall have many arrangements to make both with respect to our board and to the people of Leeds.

Apropos of Leeds, I have fought a very hard battle there, and have come off quite triumphant.[1] I have sent the paper which contains a full account of the affair to my father, and have told him to forward it to you. If I had sent it to you first, you would not have known whether to send it to him, as he is wandering among places with unutterable names in Wales. Ever yours, my two sweet sisters. I am most impatient to see you again.

TBM

TO HANNAH AND MARGARET MACAULAY, 22 AUGUST 1832

MS: Trinity College.

London August 22 / 1832

My darlings,

I need not tell you how much your sweet letters have affected me. God bless you both! I have hardly a minute to write. But, as you seem desirous to leave Liverpool, I send you a plan. Let me know, by return of post, what you think of it, and whether you have any change to propose. I will leave London by the mail on Tuesday night. I shall reach Liverpool on Wednesday night. Late on Thursday or early on Friday we will go to Manchester by the rail-road. On Friday we will go, in a post-chaise, to Lichfield, sleep there, and see the cathedral, which I never saw, and which is, I believe, next to those of York and Lincoln, the finest in England. On Saturday we will go on to Oxford, and stay there Sunday, Monday, and Tuesday. On Wednesday we will go to the Temple.

If you like this plan we had better send across from Manchester to Leicester whatever baggage we are not likely to want: for the cargo

---

[1] The meeting of the Leeds Political Union, 14 August, held to determine which of the three candidates the Union would support and at which TBM's letters of [2], 10, and 11 August were read. TBM's refusal to give pledges created a difficulty, but the resolution that TBM was 'a fit and proper person to represent the borough of Leeds in the ensuing parliament' was passed 'unanimously' (Leeds *Mercury*, 18 August) or 'with one dissenting voice' (Leeds *Intelligencer*, 16 August).

which I remember to have seen stowed at the Inn in Wood Street Cheapside would hardly suit a post-chaise.

Farewell, dearest, sweetest sisters, and let me have your answer directly.

T B M

By the bye, is it settled that you are to go to the Temple? We cannot go thither without notice. If you like my scheme, write immediately to Selina, and learn whether they can conveniently receive us.

TO HANNAH AND MARGARET MACAULAY, [23 AUGUST 1832][1]

MS: Trinity College.

London Thursday

Dearest girls,

I shall be in Liverpool on Sunday evening and ready to start with you on Monday morning. A night's rest is as good as a month's. The plan of our journey may stand, if you see no objection, exactly as I proposed it in my letter of yesterday, changing only the days. You had better therefore only take places by the rail-road to Manchester for Monday morning. I have never seen that great work, and should like much to see it in your company. But perhaps you may have particular reasons for wishing to go directly to the Temple. Please yourselves in your arrangements, my darlings, and you will be sure to please me.[2] I shall sleep at the inn where the mail stops, and eat a beef-steak there. So do not let any body be put out of the way to show me hospitality.

Ever yours, my loves,

T B M

[1] Endorsed 21 August 1832, but Thursday was 23 August and the letter was evidently written the day after that of 22 August.
[2] The tour was apparently made: TBM's letter of 29 September refers to their visit to Oxford, and, revisiting Lichfield Cathedral in 1849, he recalls his visit there in 1832 with Margaret (Trevelyan, I, 568n).

TO HANNAH MACAULAY, 4 SEPTEMBER 1832

MS: Trinity College. *Address:* Miss H M Macaulay / Rothley Temple / Leicester. *Frank:*
Leeds September four 1832 / T B Macaulay. *Extract published:* Trevelyan, 1, 272.

Leeds September 4. 1832

My own Nancy,

I arrived at this place yesterday evening,[1] and this morning we had
a great meeting, and a complete victory.[2] Every thing is going on as well
as possible hitherto; and I, as well as most of our friends here, feel
sanguine as to the result. Particulars I will tell you or bring you in print.
I am to pass the next three days in haranguing the different out-townships
as they are called which lie round the town of Leeds.[3] On Friday night
I hope to be able to set off, and to be at the Temple on Saturday morning.
But, as unforseen circumstances may render it necessary for me to stay
here longer, you must not be frightened if I do not appear at that time.

About half of my day here is spent in speaking and hearing other
people speak, in squeezing and being squeezed, in shaking hands with
people whom I never saw before and whose faces and names I forget
within a minute after being introduced to them. The rest is passed in
conversation with my leading friends, who, whatever you may think of
their refinement, are very honest substantial manufacturers. They feed
me on roast-beef and Yorkshire pudding. I ask for beer and they give
me porter – yea they bring forth hock in a lordly bottle.[4] At night they
put me into capital bed rooms: and the only plague which they give me
is that they are always begging me to mention some food or wine for

[1] TBM was in Leeds to support the canvass being made in his favor. If he did not personally
ask for a single vote (see 15 October 1832), still he and Marshall 'deemed it right...', as
they declined to avail themselves of the advantages of personal application and entreaty,
to address the electors in all the great divisions of the borough' ('Preliminary Proceedings
Relative to the First Election of Representatives for the Borough of Leeds,' Leeds [1832],
p. 4). If TBM adhered to the schedule given in [23 August 1832] he had arrived with his
sisters at Rothley Temple from Oxford on Sunday, 2 September. The Leeds *Mercury*, 8
September, reports that he reached Leeds on Monday evening, met his committee, and
was put up at the house of George Rawson, co-chairman of the committee.
[2] After a public breakfast for Marshall and TBM, all three candidates spoke from the hustings
in the yard of the Coloured Cloth Hall before a crowd that the *Intelligencer*, 6 September,
put at 15,000; this was the first time that the three candidates had appeared together. TBM
had to appeal to the crowd for a fair hearing for Sadler, who was much heckled.
[3] TBM spoke on 5 September at Hunslet and Holbeck; on 6 September at Bramley, Wortley,
and Armley; on 7 September at Kirkstall, at the Free Market, Leeds, and at a public dinner
in the Commercial Buildings, Leeds. Full reports of these speeches are given in a pamphlet
published by the *Mercury*, 'The Preliminary Proceedings Relative to the First Election of
Representatives for the Borough of Leeds'; the *Mercury*, 15 September, explained that 'our
chief motive in issuing this publication...has been to place the instructive and admirable
speeches of Mr. MACAULAY on record; they are worthy of being preserved, and of being
read again and again, and they will ever yield new instruction and delight.'
[4] Cf. Judges 5: 25.

which I have a fancy, or some article of convenience which I wish them to procure.

My prospects here are very good. But, thank heaven, my happiness does not depend on the electors of Leeds or of any other place. Do you remember the old French song which the misanthrope quotes in Molière and extols as better than all the smart sonnets of Louis the Fourteenth's time?

> Si le roi m'avoit donné
> Paris sa grande ville,
> Et me faudroit quitter
> L'amour de ma mie,
> Je dirois au Roi Henri
> Reprenez votre Paris
> J'aime mieux ma mie, [oh?][1] gai,
> J'aime mieux ma mie.[2]

I think those are the lines: but I may be out as to some words. I would translate them into language as simple as their own.

> If our good King would give me
> His London town this day,
> All for to leave my Nancy,
> I know what I would say.
> Keep, – keep, – an't please your Majesty
> Your London east and west;
> And I'll keep my little Nancy.
> I love my Nancy best.

But I must have done. Kindest love to all at the Temple. I have fallen among several Quakers here – tell Margaret – according as it is written "A certain traveller fell among thieves."[3] The friends are my warm supporters. If they knew all – if they knew that, on account of a sister of mine a member of the society is even now being dealt with,[4] what would they say? But I positively must stop. Love me, dearest, as I love you.

T B M

[1] Words illegible: the phrase in Molière is 'au gué!'
[2] *Le Misanthrope*, I, ii.
[3] Luke 10: 30.
[4] I.e., Edward Cropper's leaving the Society of Friends in order to marry Margaret.

TO MACVEY NAPIER, 5 SEPTEMBER 1832

MS: British Museum. *Address:* Macvey Napier Esq / Castle Street / Edinburgh. *Frank:* Leeds September five 1832 / T B Macaulay. *Mostly published:* Napier, *Correspondence,* pp. 130–1.

Leeds September 5. 1832

Dear Napier,

I have just received your letter with the inclosed draft.[1] I am in the midst of a storm, – making four or five speeches a day, riding in procession, shaking the hands of thousands. My success here is, I believe, out of all doubt. On Saturday I hope to make my escape, and to pass ten days at Mr. Babington's – Rothley Temple – Leicester.

If the next Number is to come out on the 1st of Octr. I fear that I can do nothing for you. I thought of reviewing Lord Mahon's book on the war of the Spanish Succession,[2] that is if it should be good enough to deserve a sentence of commendation; for I have a kindness for his lordship, and should not like to cut up his work. The nature of that war, – the policy of Louis – his character and that of Philip V – the state of parties in England during the reign of Anne – the chief public men, – Marlborough – Godolphin – Sunderland – Harley – St John – Swift, – Addison – would be capital subjects. If you h[ave][3] no objection I will at all even[ts][3] take the subject for the Jany. Number. Will you desire Longman to send the book to my chambers?

Ever yours truly
T B M

I know nothing of Empson.

TO LADY HOLLAND, 9 SEPTEMBER 1832

MS: British Museum.

Rothley Temple[4] – Leicester – / Septr. 9 – 1832

My dear Lady Holland,

Your letter followed me into the country. I have been at Leeds speaking, eating, drinking, shaking hands with thousands of people, riding in

---

[1] In payment for 'Mirabeau' and probably for 'Burghley' too: see 18 July 1832.

[2] *History of the War of the Succession in Spain,* published 20 June 1832. TBM's review of it is 'Lord Mahon's *War of the Succession*,' *ER,* LVI (January 1833), 499–542.

[3] Paper torn away with seal.

[4] TBM left Leeds on 8 September for Rothley Temple, though the Leeds *Mercury* reported on that day that he was going to London, 'to resume his important duties at the Board of Control, on the affairs of India.' In the contest at Leeds TBM's office had been attacked as a sinecure, which no doubt explains the *Mercury*'s language.

procession surrounded by banners and music, and performing the part of a candidate to admiration. From your constant kindness to me you will, I am sure, be glad to learn that my success is beyond all doubt.

I have sent your letters to the India Board, and they will, of course, be forwarded to Lord W Bentinck and Sir Frederick Adam[1] by the first conveyance. – Next week I hope to be in London; – and I shall be quite consoled for the emptiness of that great city, if Holland House is still inhabited. / Believe me ever, / Dear Lady Holland,

> Your Ladyship's faithful Servant
> T B Macaulay

TO HANNAH MACAULAY, 18 SEPTEMBER 1832

MS: Trinity College. *Partly published:* Trevelyan, I, 272–3.

London Septr. 18. 1832

My darling,

I have but a moment; and I sit down to employ it in telling you that I have nothing to tell. There is no news from Leeds. But in such a case no news is good news. I have found abundance of work, and great scarcity of company. I travelled with a family of children who ate without intermission from Market Harborough where they got into the coach to the Peacock at Islington where they got out of it. They breakfasted as if they had fasted all the preceding day. They dined as if they had never breakfasted. They lunched like – you know whom. They ate on the road one large basket of sandwiches, – another of fruit, – and a boiled fowl – besides which, there was not an orange-girl, – an old man with cakes, – or a boy with filberts who came to the coach side when we stopped to change horses of whom they did not buy something. I had as great a mind to quarrel with them as of old with Selina when she ate sugar and called it currant pudding. But I must stop. Kindest love to all – sisters and cousins. I have had a glimpse and but a glimpse of Fanny. She seems to be hurt by something that you have said to her. Set it right – for she is really very kind, and takes a warm interest in all Margaret's affairs.

I suppose my uncle and aunt are at Yoxall.[2] Farewell, dearest, and write soon.

> Ever yours
> T B M

---

[1] Governor of Madras: see 15 June 1834.
[2] Babington's brother-in-law Thomas Gisborne lived at Yoxall Lodge, Staffordshire.

TO HANNAH MACAULAY, 20 SEPTEMBER 1832

MS: Trinity College. *Address:* Miss H M Macaulay / Rothley Temple / Leicester. *Frank:* London September twenty 1832 / T B Macaulay. *Partly published:* Trevelyan, I, 273.

London Sept 20. 1832

My love,

I am living here by myself – with no society or scarcely any except my books. I read a play of Calderon before I breakfast – then look over the newspaper – frank letters – scrawl a line or two to a foolish girl in Leicestershire, – and walk to my office, calling in Golden Square[1] by the way. At my office I stay till near five, examining claims of money-lenders on the native sovereigns of India, and reading Parliamentary papers. I am beginning to understand something about the Bank,[2] and hope, when I next go to the Temple, to be a match for the whole firm of Mansfield and Babington[3] on questions relating to their own business. When I leave the Board I walk for two hours, – then I dine, – and I end the day quietly over a bason of tea and a novel.

What a happy life! How strange that a man who can lead it should ever trouble his head about sisters! Yet I have not forgotten mine, though absent. My affection for them is like to cost me six or seven pounds. For firstly I have discarded the torn black stock which did not find favour in their sight, and have bought another which, I hope, will please them better. Secondly I have put my watch into the hands of Mr. Ganthony[4] that it may be taught its duty. Thirdly I have bought a seal, and ordered an engraver to engrave thereon the arms of the house of Macaulay.[5] And when my watch and seal are finished, I shall buy a watch-ribband of the latest pattern and liveliest colour. Encourage me, dearest, in this good and brotherly line of conduct.

On Saturday I shall go to Holland House and stay there till Monday. Her ladyship wants me to take up my quarters almost entirely there: but I love my own chambers and independence; and am neither qualified nor inclined to succeed Allen in his post. On Friday week – that is to-morrow week – I shall go for three days to Sir George Philips's. He has written again in terms half complaining. And, though I do not anticipate much

---

[1] George and Sarah Anne Babington and Fanny Macaulay had evidently returned from Kensington to Babington's residence, 26 Golden Square.

[2] The report of the committee 'appointed to inquire into the expediency of renewing the Charter of the Bank of England,' dated 11 August 1832, is in *Parliamentary Papers*, 1831–2, VI, 1–677.

[3] The Leicester Bank of Matthew Babington.

[4] Richard Ganthony, watch-maker, 83 Cheapside (*Post Office London Directory*, 1830).

[5] TBM's seal is the Macaulay crest: a boot and spur with the motto 'Dulce Periculum.' It is reproduced on the title pages of the volumes in this edition.

pleasure from the visit, yet, as he was very kind to me when his kindness was of some consequence to me, I cannot refuse. A great favourite of of mine, Mrs. N Hibbert, Sydney's eldest daughter,[1] as beautiful, – at least formerly, – as an angel, and as black as the opposite of an angel, saving your presence, is to be there.

I have not the least notion what my father's plans may be. He is going to the Temple, but he means to visit several people on the way; and how long he means to stay at each resting-place I cannot guess. You must have seen in the papers an extravagantly absurd story about a petition said to be signed by him, Buxton, and Lushington, and presented to the Congress of the United States.[2] I was quite sure that the whole was a lye, and I am glad that it has been publicly contradicted. If it had been true, it would, I am sure, have brought more discredit on the party opposed to colonial slavery than all the blunders that they ever committed or than all the slanders of all their enemies put together.

Kindest love to Selina and Margaret, or rather Chitapet – for, change her name as she will, she will always be Chitapet with me. Love also to Jane, and, in short, to your whole party. Sarah Anne is getting well fast, and George, I hope, is getting rich fast. For I never can find him at liberty.

Ever yours, my love,

T B M

TO MARGARET MACAULAY, 21 SEPTEMBER 1832

MS: Morgan Library. *Address:* Miss M Macaulay / Rothley Temple / Leicester. *Frank:* London September twenty one 1832 / T B Macaulay.

London Sept 21 – 1832

Dearest Margaret,

I have only time to inclose these two letters, and to say that the result of the canvass at Leeds as far as it has proceeded is favourable even beyond the expectations which I entertained when I was with you. About three thousand voters out of four th[ousand][3] five hundred have been canvassed. About four hundred are doubtful. Sadler has six hundred and twenty, Marshall has 1950, and I have 1976.

I wish that, as soon as you learn from the enclosed letter to Selina, what is my father's address, you would let me know. Kindest love to all.

T B M

---

[1] Emily Hibbert was Sydney Smith's younger daughter.

[2] *The Times,* 17 September, reported that a petition signed by Zachary Macaulay, Buxton, and Lushington 'praying an immediate abolition of slavery' had been presented to the Congress of the United States; Zachary Macaulay's denial that he signed 'or had any thing to do with the memorial' appeared in *The Times,* 20 September.

[3] Paper torn away with seal.

TO HANNAH MACAULAY, 22 SEPTEMBER 1832

MS: Trinity College.

London September 22 – 1832

My darling,

What do you think of my new seal? But you did not smoke it, you gipsey; – and now it is broken to pieces and you cannot judge of its beauties. Very hard! I must buy seals to please you; and you take no notice of them. I might just as well have put a wafer. What think you the seal and the engraving cost? An ounce of gold. You who have studied the Bank question so deeply must know how much that is. If not my uncle will tell you. I have a smaller seal in progress with my initials; and I think that when my salary comes in I shall, like Lord Glenthorn,[1] visit the jewellers day by day, and ruin myself between Mr. Ganthony and Mr. Strong i'th'arm.[2]

But I must stop. I will, if possible, take you to Cambridge. Keep me informed accurately of your plans that I may make my arrangements when the time approaches. Charles Grant is still in Scotland – Villiers is at Windsor – Gordon is in Dorsetshire. I have the board all to myself. I must go forthwith and write a memorandum touching the debts due by Asoph ul Dowla Vizier of Oude to Monhur Doss the Banker. Kindest love to all.

Ever yours, dearest
T B M

TO HANNAH MACAULAY, 25 SEPTEMBER 1832

MS: Trinity College. *Address:* Miss H M Macaulay / Rothley Temple / Leicester. *Frank:* September twenty five 1832 / T B Macaulay. *Mostly published:* Trevelyan, 1, 274–5.

London Sept 25 – 1832

My sweet Nancy,

I went on Saturday to Holland House and staid there Sunday. It was legitimate Sabbath employment, – visiting the sick, – which, as you well know, always stands first among the works of mercy enumerated in good books. My Lord was ill, and my Lady thought herself so. He was, during the greater part of the day, in bed. For a few hours he lay on his sofa, wrapped in flannels. I sate by him about twenty minutes, and was then ordered away. He was very weak and languid; and, though the torture

---

[1] The hero of Maria Edgeworth's *Ennui.*
[2] John Strongitharm, engraver, 1 Waterloo Place, Pall Mall (*Post Office London Directory,* 1832).

of the gout was over, was still in pain. But he retained all his courage, and all his sweetness of temper. I told his sister that I did not think that he was suffering much. "I hope not," said she: "but it is impossible to judge by what he says. For through the sharpest part of the attack, he never complained." I admire him more, I think, than any man whom I know. He is only fifty seven or fifty eight.[1] He has strong passions and appetites. He is precisely the man to whom health would be particularly valuable: for he has the keenest zest for those pleasures which health would enable him to enjoy. He is, however, an invalid and a cripple. He passes some weeks of every year in extreme torment. When he is in his best health he can only limp a hundred yards in a day. Yet he never says a cross word. The sight of him spreads good humour over the face of every body who comes near him. His sister, – an excellent old maid as ever lived, and the favourite of all the young people of her acquaintance, – says that it is quite a pleasure to nurse him. She was reading the Inheritance[2] to him as he lay in bed: and he enjoyed it amazingly. She is a famous reader, more quiet and less theatrical than most famous readers, and therefore the fitter for the bedside of a sick man.

Her ladyship had fretted herself into being ill, – could eat nothing but the breast of a partridge, – and was frightened out of her wits by hearing a dog howl. She was sure that this noise portended her death or my Lord's. Towards the evening however she brightened up, and was in very good spirits. My visit was not very lively. They dined at four, and the company was, as you may suppose at this season, but scanty. Charles Greville,[3] commonly called, Heaven knows why, Punch Greville, came on the Saturday. Byng,[4] named from his hair Poodle Byng came on the Sunday. Allen, like the poor, of whom he is one, we had with us always.[5] I was grateful, however, for many pleasant evenings passed there when London was full and Lord Holland out of bed. I therefore did my best to keep the house alive. I had the library and the delightful gardens to myself during most of the day; and I got through my visit very well.

Sir James Graham came over on the Sunday for an hour. He and I had a little confidential talk about politics with which I will not trouble you at present.

---

[1] Lord Holland was in his fifty-eighth year.

[2] Susan Ferrier, *The Inheritance*, 1824.

[3] Charles Greville (1794–1865: *DNB*), Clerk of the Privy Council, 1821–59, patron of the turf, and diarist.

[4] Frederick Gerald Byng (1784–1871: *Boase*), youngest son of the fifth Lord Torrington; clerk in the Foreign Office, 1801–39; Gentleman Usher of the Privy Chamber, 1831–71; a well-known man about town. He was called Poodle on account of his curly hair, according to one explanation; but Henry Reeve says he was called '"The Poodle" probably because he once kept a fine animal of that breed' (*Greville Memoirs*, ed. Reeve, Part 1, 1874, 1, 241n).   [5] Mark 14: 7.

Now for my plans. I go on Friday to Sir G Philips's. There I shall stay till the following Tuesday. Suppose that on Wednesday the 3d of September[1] I should reach the Temple, could you and Meg be ready to set off with me on Friday the 5th. We would pass Saturday and Sunday at Cambridge, and we should be in London on the Monday.[2] The Cabinet ministers are to assemble in town on the 10th; and from that time I must be constantly on duty. A committee of the cabinet will probably be appointed to sit on Indian affairs; and my attendance will be required. Unless therefore we see Cambridge before the 10th, we shall not, I fear, see it at all. Let me have your answer by return of post.

After to morrow direct to me at Sir G Philips's Ba[rt][3] Weston House, near Chipping-Norton.

News you have in the papers. Poor Scott is gone;[4] – and I am not sorry for it. A powerful mind in ruins is the most heart-breaking thing which it is possible to conceive. Ferdinand of Spain is gone too:[5] and, I fear, old Mr. Stephen is going fast.[6] I am safe at Leeds. Poor Hyde Villiers is very ill. I am seriously alarmed about him. Kindest love to all.

Ever yours darling,
T B M

I have a very nice black stock indeed. You will be charmed with it.

---

[1] Thus in MS, for October.

[2] The visit was made, and is recorded by a Fellow of Trinity thus: ' *Sat. 6* . . . . We dined with [Thomas] Thorp to meet Macaulay (whose fellowship we filled up on Monday) & his 2 agreeable sisters, Thirlwall, & Whewell. – Much brilliant convers[n] from Macaulay, & Whewell: no politics at all: – Macaulay's manners amazingly improved: he was very agreeable & full of anecdote & quot[n] – He says Mac[k]intosh's best work is an unpublish[d] char[acte][r] of Burke, his next the preface to the Encyc[lopaedia] Metrop[olitana]. *Sun. 7* . . . . Breakfast to Macaulay & his 2 sisters (agreeable girls with sweet voices: not pretty but clever and conversible & very young), Whewell, Thirlwall, Thorp & Lodge –Walk with Lodge who dined in hall with me to meet Macaulay:. . . then tea at Thorps to meet the Macaulays &c' (J. P. T. Bury, ed., *Romilly's Cambridge Diary, 1832–1842*, Cambridge, 1967, p. 20).

[3] Part of word cut off by mounting of MS.

[4] Scott died on 21 September.

[5] Ferdinand VII did not die until 29 September 1833. Reports of his death reached London on 23 September which *The Times*, 25 September, saw 'no reason to doubt.'

[6] The elder James Stephen died on 10 October.

TO HANNAH MACAULAY, 29 SEPTEMBER 1832

MS: Trinity College: *Address:* Miss H M Macaulay / Rothley Temple / Leicester. *Frank:* Chipping Norton September twenty / nine 1832 / T B Macaulay. *Mostly published:* Trevelyan, I, 275–7.

Weston House Septr. 29. 1832

My own Nancy,

I came hither yesterday, and found a handsome house, pretty grounds, and a very kind host and hostess. The house is really very well planned. I do not know that I have ever seen so happy an imitation of the domestic architecture of Elizabeth's reign. The oriels, towers, terraces, and battlements are in the most perfect keeping; and the building is as convenient within as it is picturesque without. A few weather-stains, or a few American creepers, and a little ivy would make it perfect: and all that will come, I suppose, with time. The terrace is my favourite spot. Indeed I always liked the "trim gardens"[1] of which Milton speaks, and always thought that Brown[2] and his imitators went too far in bringing forests and sheep walks up to the very windows of drawing rooms. The terrace here consists of three stages, – all turf and flowers, with here and there a fountain playing. You descend from stage to stage by stone steps adorned with vases. At one end the terrace ends in a very beautiful conservatory, the only Gothic conservatory that I ever liked.

I came through Oxford. It was as beautiful a day as the second day of our visit;[3] and the High Street was in all its glory. But it made me quite sad to find myself there without my dear girls. All my old Oxford associations are gone. Oxford, instead of being, as it used to be, the magnificent old city of the seventeenth century still preserving its antique character among the improvements of modern times, and exhibiting in the midst of upstart Birminghams and Manchesters the same aspect which it wore when Charles held his court at Christchurch, and Rupert led his cavalry over Magdalene Bridge, is now to me only the place where I was so happy with my little Nancy and my little Chitapet. I assure you that it made me quite dull to miss you. But I was restored to mirth and even to indecorous mirth by what happened after we had left the fine old place behind us. There was a young fellows of about five and twenty, mustachioed and smartly dressed, in the coach with me. He was not absolutely uneducated: for he was reading a Novel – the Hungarian Brothers[4] – the whole way. We rode, as I told you, through the High Street. The Coach stopped to dine; and this youth passed half an hour in the midst of that city of palaces. He looked about him with his mouth open, as he re-entered

---

[1] 'Il Penseroso,' line 50.
[2] Lancelot ('Capability') Brown (1715–83: *DNB*), landscape architect.
[3] 31 August: see [23 August 1832].   [4] By Anna Maria Porter, 1807.

the coach and as we drove away passing by the Ratcliffe Library – the great Court of All Souls – Exeter – Lincoln – Trinity – Baliol, and St John's. When we were about a mile on the road he spoke the first words that I had heard him utter. "That was a pretty town enough. Pray, Sir, what is it called?" I could not answer him for laughing. But he seemed quite unsuspicious of his own absurdity.

I shall be at the Temple on Wednesday, my darling; and I am glad to hear that I shall find my Uncle and Aunt there. Mr. Stephen is alive, though very ill. Fanny wrote under a mistake which I will explain when I see you. It is not worth writing. Kindest love to all.

Ever yours, my love,

T B M

TO THE ELECTORS OF LEEDS, 15 OCTOBER 1832

Text: Leeds *Mercury*, 20 October 1832.

Gentlemen,

The canvass of the Borough is now nearly completed: and the examination of the disputed votes is about to begin. I cannot refrain, at this juncture, from expressing to you the feelings of gratitude and pride with which I have learned the extent of your kindness towards me.[1]

I have not, as you are aware, asked for a single vote. I conceived that, by the Reform Bill, a high and solemn trust had been reposed in you, – not for your benefit solely, still less for mine, – but for the benefit of this great Empire. I conceived that it would be insulting to suppose that caresses and supplications would induce you to betray the trust. To vote for the fittest Candidate is the plain duty of an Elector. To entreat a man to perform a plain duty is no high compliment. To entreat a man to violate a plain duty is the grossest of outrages.

I have heard many among you speak with just indignation of those Members of Parliament who, to oblige a friend, run down to a Committee, and vote for or against a Bill without hearing the evidence or understanding the case. We can all see distinctly that a Legislator who barters away in a commerce of private civilities the powers which have been entrusted to him for the general good, is unworthy of the esteem and confidence of his countrymen. But surely, if this easiness of temper, – this inability to resist solicitation, – this disposition to gratify individuals at the expense of the community, – be scandalous in the Legislator, it is no less scandalous

---

[1] No report of the results of the canvass appears in either the *Mercury* or the *Intelligencer*. TBM was later reported to have 2,300 votes in prospect: see 1 December.

in the Elector. If Constituents give their votes in exchange for the personal attention of a Candidate, with what face can they afterwards blame the man of their choice for giving his vote concerning a rail-road or a canal, in exchange for the personal attentions of an interested party? What right have they to expect that their Member shall be more honest than themselves – that he shall be proof to that same coaxing and begging which they have themselves been unable to resist? How can they complain, if he sells them for the same wretched consideration for which he bought them? It is in vain to expect that there will be a high standard of political morality in the representative body, when there is a low standard in the constituent body.

But I need not press this argument. All that I saw during my last visit to Leeds, – all that I have since learned, – has convinced me that my resolution not to solicit you in person, is decidedly approved by you. I was received by you with a cordiality, the remembrance of which will never be effaced from my mind. The result of the canvass, which has since been carried on by my friends, is such as, in my most sanguine moments, I had never ventured to anticipate. I rejoice in our success, and I glory in it: for it has been gained by no unworthy arts. If I had stooped to one act of meanness, if I had breathed one secret calumny against an opponent, if I had sacrificed one principle, if I had skulked away from one questioner, if I had returned one insincere or evasive answer, if I had owed one advantage to fawning, to corruption, or to intimidation, if I knew that there was in all the long list of those who have promised me their support, the name of one Elector whose promise had been extorted by the menace of a customer, a landlord, or a revenue officer, I should be, not elated, but humbled by the intelligence which I have received. You will bear me witness that I have, on every occasion, spoken to you with the freedom which becomes the man who aspires to represent a free people. You will bear me witness, that I have never, by any disingenuous artifice, attempted to keep out of sight those parts of my political creed which were likely to make me unpopular. If I should be returned, as I confidently expect to be returned, to the next Parliament by the people of Leeds, I shall be returned in a manner honourable to them and to me, without having spent one shilling, without having begged one vote, without having flinched from one question, without having concealed or softened down one opinion, without deception, without corruption, and without intimidation.

From what I have seen of your vigour, your activity, and your public spirit, I am certain that it is unnecessary for me to exhort you to persevere. You know the magnitude of the objects which are at stake. You know by how much power and by how much artifice we are opposed. I entertain not the slightest doubt that your energy will hold out unabated to the end; and that the good cause in which we are engaged, – the cause of liberty and order, – will signally triumph over the monstrous coalition which has been formed between those who hate all order and those who hate all liberty. / I am, Gentlemen,

Yours most faithfully,
T. B. Macaulay.

London, October 15, 1832.

TO MACVEY NAPIER, 31 OCTOBER [1832]

MS: British Museum.

London Oct 31

My dear Napier,

I hope to send you before New Year's Day at latest my promised article.[1] But I am very busy, – and, when parliament is dissolved, shall be more busy still.

I send you by this day's post under a government frank an article which Buxton has put into my hands.[2] He has not told me the name of the writer: nor have I the least guess whose it is. I know only that it is not his own. He made me promise to submit it to you. I have not read it through. But what I saw of it did not appear to me to be bad. If it does not suit you, write a few lines such as I can shew to him. For he seems particularly interested about the matter: and he is a man whom, both on public and private grounds, I am inclined, – and whom you, I am sure, would be inclined, – to treat with the greatest civility.

Ever yours
T B Macaulay

A little Edinburgh election news,[3] more to be trusted than what we learn here from your lying papers, will be acceptable.

1 'Lord Mahon's *War of the Succession in Spain.*'
2 The letter is endorsed by Napier: 'With art. sent by Mr Buxton on South Sea Missions.' The article, 'Montgomery's *Missionary Voyages and Travels,*' *ER*, LVII (April 1833), 80–95, was by Buxton's daughter Priscilla (1808–52). George Stephen says that she was her father's 'guardian angel. . . . She acted as his secretary, his librarian, his comforter, and often as his adviser and guide' (*Anti-Slavery Recollections*, p. 197). She married Andrew Johnston in 1834.
3 Jeffrey and James Abercromby were returned for Edinburgh to the first reformed Parliament.

TO MACVEY NAPIER, 12 NOVEMBER 1832

MS: British Museum. *Address:* Macvey Napier Esq / Edinburgh. *Frank:* London November twelve / 1832 / T B Macaulay.

London Nov 12. 1832

Dear Napier,

I will do my best. But my mornings are occupied by Indian politics; – and I shall be forced to pass a fortnight or more before long in electioneering at Leeds. In fact my only time for writing is before breakfast: and as the subject which I have taken requires reading as well as writing I get on but slowly. I wish you would tell Longman to send me Captain Carleton's memoirs of the Spanish war.[1] It is a curious and interesting book published from the original manuscript a few years ago, in one octavo volume. I have asked for it at two or three shops; and have not been as yet able to procure it.

I asked Buxton who was the author of the article which I sent to you. He would not tell me, till I assured him that you made it a sine qua non that he should be open on that subject. He then, to my great amazement, confessed that it was the work of his daughter, – a young lady whom I have sometimes met, and whom I should as soon have suspected of being concerned in a gang of Burkers as of writing reviews. I thanked Heaven that I had not shewn him your letter, which, civil as it was, scarcely came up to what fatherly partiality might expect.

The young lady has golden hair. She may therefore be properly nicknamed Blue and Yellow,[2] on more accounts than one. Malkin's article[3] is not by any means striking. Your insertion[4] was the part of it which I liked best.

Ever yours
T B Macaulay

[1] *Memoirs of Captain Carleton*, 1743; originally published as *The Memoirs of an English Officer*, 1728, this is in fact by Defoe, though Lord Mahon treats the book as authentic, as did Sir Walter Scott, who published an edition in 1809. In his Journal for 5 February 1856 TBM wrote: 'As to Carleton's Memoirs I see no proof that DeFoe wrote them; nor do I believe it' (IX, 70–1).
[2] The Whig colors, used on the cover of the *ER*.
[3] 'Brewster's *Life of Sir Isaac Newton*,' *ER*, LVI (October 1833), 1–37.
[4] There is no evidence in the published text to show what this is.

TO [EDWARD BAINES],[1] 14 NOVEMBER 1832

MS: Duke University.

E[ast] I[ndia] Board Nov 14 / 1832

Dear Sir,

I snatch a single moment to tell you how much I feel obliged by your very kind and very able defence[2] of my character and interests.

In a fortnight, I suppose, I shall have an opportunity of thanking you and of defending myself in person. We expect the dissolution on the 3d of next month. By that time, I hope, this stubborn sulky Dutchman[3] will be brought to reason. / Ever, my dear Sir,

Yours most truly
T B Macaulay

TO EDWARD BAINES, JR, 21 NOVEMBER 1832

MS: Duke University. *Address:* E Baines Esq Jun / Mercury Office / Leeds. *Frank:* London November twenty one 1832 / T B Macaulay.

[London]

This is, as you will perceive, a very hasty statement.[4] I have not time to read it over. I shall be in Leeds next Tuesday evening.[5]

Ever yours
T B M

1 The letter is among the papers of Sir Edward Baines. TBM wrote to both father and son about his Leeds affairs; in the absence of external evidence it is impossible to be certain which Baines is the recipient, but the elder Baines seems more likely.
2 A letter signed 'Common Sense,' enumerating all the places held by the Macaulay family, appeared in the *Intelligencer*, 18 October; this was replied to in a pamphlet, presumably by Baines, entitled 'The Tables Turned' (copy dated 9 November in Thoresby Society, Leeds). The *Mercury* notices the pamphlet, 10 November, and prints extracts from it, 17 November. Since TBM, his father, and his brother Henry did in fact all have government places (and John a church living in the gift of the Chancellor), the attack could hardly be ignored.
3 England and France were acting together to compel the Netherlands to accept the independence of Belgium. A French army entered Belgium on 15 November to drive the Dutch from Antwerp; the Dutch, however, did not finally accept the French and English terms until 1839.
4 Not identified; evidently an enclosure accompanying this note.
5 He arrived on Wednesday, 28 November.

TO MARGARET MACAULAY, 26 NOVEMBER 1832

MS: Mrs Lancelot Errington. *Extracts published:* Trevelyan, I, 286–7.

London Nov 26. 1832

My dearest Margaret,

When you receive this letter, I shall be on the road to Leeds; and I shall not see you again till the separation of which I cannot think without losing all my firmness shall have taken place. I have not taken leave of you. For I wished to spare you the pain of witnessing distress which you would, I know, feel acutely, but which you would not be able to relieve. I purpose to bear my affliction, as I have borne it hitherto, that is to say, alone. Mine is no case for sympathy or consolation. The heart knows its own bitterness.[1]

My sufferings, like the sufferings of most other men, are the natural consequences of my own weakness. The attachment between brothers and sisters, blameless, amiable, and delightful as it is, is so liable to be superseded by other attachments that no wise man ought to suffer it to become indispensable to his happiness. Very few, even of those who are called good brothers, do suffer it to become indispensable. But to me it has been in the place of a first love. During the years when the imagination is most vivid and the heart most susceptible, my affection for my sisters has prevented me from forming any serious attachment. But for them I should be quite alone in the world. I have nothing else to love. Yet I knew, or ought to have known, that what was every day becoming more and more necessary to me might be withdrawn in a moment. That women shall leave the home of their birth and contract ties dearer than those of consanguinity is a law as ancient as the first records of the history of our race, and as unchangeable as the constitution of the human body and mind. To repine against the nature of things, – against the great fundamental law of all society, because, in consequence of my own want of foresight, it happens to bear heavily on me, would be the basest and most absurd selfishness. And I do not repine. You can bear me witness that I have suffered with fortitude; and, if I now break silence for the first and last time, it is only that you may not attribute my sudden departure to any want of affection for you.

I have still one more stake to lose. There remains one event for which, when it arrives, I shall, I hope, be prepared. I have another sister, no less dear to me than my Margaret, from whom I may be separated in the same manner. From that moment, with a heart formed, if ever any man's heart was formed for domestic happiness, I shall have nothing left in this world but ambition.

[1] Proverbs 14: 10.

There is no wound, however, which time and necessity do not render endurable. And, after all, what am I more than my fathers, – than the millions and tens of millions who have been weak enough to pay double price for some favourite number in the lottery of life, and who have suffered double disappointment when their ticket came up a blank? All life is a system of compensations. My reason tells me that, but for the strong attachment which is at this moment a cause of pain to me, I might, like my friend Charles Grant, have been crossed in love,[1] or, what is much worse, might, like his brother, have married a fool. I am glad too, in the midst of my sorrow, that I shall not be at the wedding, that I shall pass the next fortnight in a constant storm, that I shall have no time to be sad, and that, at the worst, I shall be able to wreak all the bitterness of my heart on Michael Sadler.

When we meet I shall, I hope, be reconciled to what is inevitable. But I cannot think, without a flood of tears, of that meeting. Once so much to each other – and henceforth to be so little.

Farewell, dearest. From my soul I thank you for the many happy days which I have owed to you, and for the innumerable proofs which I have received of your affection. May he to whom you are about to entrust the care of your happiness love you as much as you deserve, – as much as I have loved you. And, at this parting, – for it is a parting scarcely less solemn than that of a death bed, – forgive me, my own Margaret, if I have ever neglected you, if I have ever, from thoughtlessness or in a moment of irritation, wounded your feelings. God knows that it must have been by inadvertence, and that I never in my life did or said anything intended to give you pain.

Lastly, shew this letter to no person, – not even to my dear Nancy. I do not wish her to know how deeply this separation has affected me, lest, on some future occasion, she should take my feelings into the account in forming a decision which she ought to form with a view to her own happiness alone.

Again and again, dearest, farewell.
T B Macaulay.

---

1 'Tom always laughs at me for assigning as a cause of [Charles Grant's] worn countenance, full of deep feeling and composed melancholy, that he had been crossed in love. He is very much diverted at such a young-lady-like reason for the grave looks of an old statesman' (Margaret Macaulay, *Recollections*, 21 February [1832], p. 235).

TO HANNAH MACAULAY, 28 NOVEMBER 1832

MS: Trinity College.

Leeds.[1] Nov. 28 – 1832

My dearest Nancy,

I am here – very pleasantly lodged[2] – in a large airy bedroom with a bow window, a fine prospect without, and a blazing fire within. I shall, I find, have most of my mornings here to my self, and I shall, therefore, I hope, be able to finish my article for Napier in time. Our electioneering business is reserved for the evenings.

Every thing, as far as I have yet learned, is going on satisfactorily. But I shall obtain fuller information at the meeting of our Committee to night. Kindest love to all.

Ever yours
T B M

TO MARGARET MACAULAY, 29 NOVEMBER [1832]

MS: Mrs Lancelot Errington.

Leeds Nov 29 –

My dearest Margaret, –

I am, as you may suppose, very much pressed for time. But I cannot let a day pass without answering your sweet letter. I will not tell you, I cannot tell you, how much it has affected me. I will hope that your predictions may be accomplished, and that as our love has been such as the love of brothers and sisters has seldom been, it may survive even that separation by which the love of brothers and sisters is generally almost extinguished.

But I must stop, dearest, for two reasons. The first is want of time. The second is that, if I go on, I shall have red eyes: and a man is coming to take my face in a few minutes.[3] My host is disposing the curtains and shutters that my face may be seen in a favourable light; and it would be ungrateful in me to spoil my beauty with crying at such a moment.

Ever yours, my own darling,
T B M

---

[1] The Leeds *Intelligencer*, 29 November, reported that TBM 'arrived in Leeds yesterday.... Last night he attended a meeting of the canvassers of the Orange Committee, to hear their reports as to the probability of his success.'

[2] Probably he stayed with George Rawson, as he had done on his two previous visits to Leeds in June and September.

[3] See next letter.

TO HANNAH MACAULAY, 29 NOVEMBER [1832]

MS: Trinity College.

Leeds Nov 29

Dearest Nancy,

I shall be very concise to day, and indeed generally during my stay here. I have been to see Marshall's factory[1] this morning. This evening we are to have a great meeting of electors at the music-room, whom I am to harangue.[2] The ladies are to be admitted to the gallery so that I shall doubtless leave many broken hearts behind me, – particularly as I shall speak in a new black stock. I am afraid that my succession of stocks will remind you of Benbowie's long series of waistcoats, every one uglier than its predecessor.

But I must stop. Here is a man come to take my face[3] which is to be lithographed by the day of chairing. The former picture, I find, was thought a failure. This artist is expected to succeed better. I must give him a sitting till dinner time; and then I must eat, drink and spout till bed-time.

I dare say that you had to pay for my letter of yesterday. Ten to one I wrote London instead of Leeds yesterday.[4] You were even with me at any rate – for you sent me a letter above weight. As Sir Charles Grandison says, "Let us bear each other's imperfections, Charlotte."[5]

But the artist is clamorous.

Ever yours
T B M

[1] Marshall's flax-spinning mills in Water Lane, the largest such establishment in England, employed about 1,200 hands in 1832.

[2] TBM gave a series of four speeches, or 'lectures,' in the Music Hall, Leeds, 29, 30 November; 3, 4 December; they are reported in the Leeds *Mercury*, 1 and 8 December, and in the Leeds *Intelligencer*, 6 December. Admission was by ticket, and the electors belonging to different divisions of the city were invited on successive nights.

[3] From the evidence of this letter and that of 1 December, there were three portraits made at Leeds of TBM: the 'former picture' mentioned in this paragraph; the portrait made on 29 November, and that made on 30 November (see 1 December). One of these – probably the first, which is called a 'failure' – is the wretched lithograph of which a copy is at Trinity, captioned: 'I. Atkinson. Del: Inchbold Litho: / T. B. Macaulay Esqr. M.P. / Published by W. Parson, Directory Office Leeds. 1832.' It was perhaps of this that Fanny Macaulay wrote to Margaret [18 December 1832] that it was 'intended for a ruffian' (MS, Huntington). Two undated lithographs of TBM in the British Museum, one by the Leeds artist John N. Rhodes and the other unattributed but probably also by Rhodes, are very likely the drawings that TBM refers to in this letter and the next. Neither these nor the Atkinson lithograph have any merit as likenesses.

[4] In the frank on the cover, which has not survived. The error would invalidate the frank.

[5] 3rd edn, III, 129, letter 16: 'But he said, let us forget each other's failings, Charlotte.'

TO HANNAH MACAULAY, 1 DECEMBER 1832

MS: Trinity College. *Address:* Miss H M Macaulay / 44 Bernard Street / London. *Frank:* Leeds December one 1832 / T B Macaulay.

Leeds December 1. 1832

My darling,

You never in your life were more mistaken than in supposing that I have much time on my hands. I am overwhelmed with hospitality, and occupied every night in feasting and haranguing. I have moreover to get on, as fast as I can, which is very slow, with an article for the Blue and Yellow. And Charles Grant has sent me the Cabinet plan about India, which he wishes me to study, and to report upon as soon as possible. We think that we are perfectly safe. The audiences which we address every night, though not packed, are very enthusiastic in their applause. Our canvassers have made their final return giving us 2300 votes each or thereabouts, and Sadler little more than half that number. The returning officer, though of the party opposed to us, seems inclined to act with strict impartiality. Some of our people think that the other party will not venture to go to a poll. They are, I think, too sanguine.

I send you a Mercury of this day.[1] The reports are but poorly executed. You will however be able to form a general notion of what is going on. During the two days of the election I shall make arrangements for letting you know the state of the poll earlier than by course of post you could learn it.

I have been pestered out of my life by the artist of whom I told you. He made me sit for two hours; and produced a picture which the Chairman of our Committee, the Secretary of the Political Union, as well as my good hostess and her daughters pronounced to be a failure. It did not give the expression. It made me too contemplative etc. etc. The next day, accordingly, my man of pencils and paste board came again. He made me stand half the morning in an oratorical attitude; and at last produced something which he and the Secretary of the Union thought very like. Nobody else has seen it; so that I cannot tell whether I am to take my idea of my own face from it or no. I can truly say, as Charles the Second said on a similar occasion – "Odd's fish – if this is like me, I am a very ugly fellow." It is to be lithographed against the chairing day. I shall procure several copies for you.

I am glad for your lungs, dearest, and sorry for your liver. Nurse yourself thoroughly; and be in excellent health against my re[turn.][2] Kindest love to all – especially to dearest, dearest, Margaret. I can hardly

[1] TBM's speeches of 29 and 30 November at the Music Hall, Leeds, are reported in the *Mercury*, 1 December.
[2] Paper torn away with seal.

command my feelings about her even in the midst of all these distractions. Yet how remarkable it is that even the sorrows which arise from our good and kind affections are more pleasing to us than the pleasures which arise from our angry and vindictive passions.

Farewell, dearest Nancy,

T B M

TO HANNAH MACAULAY, 3 DECEMBER 1832

MS: Trinity College.

Leeds Dec 3 – 1832

My love,

To day, I have reason to believe, the parliament will be dissolved; and my privilege of franking will expire to morrow. I write, therefore, though I have absolutely only a single moment, to say that my correspondence with you will not during the next week be very animated. I shall be too busy to write long letters, and I shall not chuse to make you pay for short ones. Write to me, however, without scruple, – double or triple letters daily, if you will. The more postage I pay the more I shall be obliged to you.

I hope that all will go right. But it is well to be prepared for the worst. I am astonished at my own philosophy. I think a great deal more of Margaret than of the election. But I must not be sad. Give her my love. She knows what my love sent to her means. Love to all.

Ever, my own sweet sister, yours

T B M

TO MARGARET MACAULAY, 8 DECEMBER 1832

MS: Morgan Library. *Address:* Miss M Macaulay / 44 Bernard Street / Russell Square / London.

Leeds Decr. 8 – 1832

My dearest Girl,

I write from our Committee room in the midst of noise and interruption to tell you that my heart is always with you. But I must come to news and business, or I shall not be able to refrain from tears. I was shocked and deeply grieved, as you may well imagine, to hear the sad news of Villiers's death.[1] Poor fellow! He was very kind to me, and I was truly attached to him. I have heard from C Grant. The government press me earnestly

---

[1] Villiers died on 3 December.

to take the vacant office; and I have consented to do so.[1] The salary is 1500 £ a year; and I shall have, what you will like, but what I could very well dispense with, the privilege of unlimited franking. For mercy's sake let not the Macaulays know this. I shall have also very hard work. But this I am quite willing to undertake, and, I hope, quite able to perform.

I will send you the Leeds Mercury by to day's post.[2] It comes out only on Saturdays. But we mean to have an extraordinary Mercury on Tuesday[3] with the proceedings of the day of nomination. On Wednesday and Thursday the poll will take place. On Friday we shall be chaired, if, as we hope, we are successful. And on Saturday I shall return to that home which is no longer to be the home of my dearest Margaret. I cannot go on. Give my love to all. Thank Selina for her kind letter, and Nancy for several notes which I have not had time to answer. And farewell, dearest, dearest, dearest. What are the anxieties of elections and of office. What is even the death of common friends to the bitterness of this parting.

T B M

TO HANNAH MACAULAY, 10 DECEMBER 1832

MS: Trinity College. *Address:* Miss H M Macaulay / 44 Bernard Street / Russell Square / London.

Leeds Decr. 10 – 1832

Dearest Nancy,

I have only a minute to say that we have had a most stormy meeting for the nomination, – twenty thousand at least, – a tremendous clamour, – a bloody fight, – half a dozen fellows lodged in prison and half a dozen more in the Infirmary.[4] Sadler brought in bludgeon men from the

---

1. TBM's patent of appointment as Secretary of the Board of Control is dated 19 December, but the notice of the appointment is recorded in the Minute Book of the Board of Control on 10 December (India Office Library).
2. The *Mercury*, 8 December, reports TBM's speeches at the Music Hall, 3 and 4 December; at a county meeting for the Whig candidates, Lord Morpeth and George Strickland, 4 December; at Hunslet, 6 December; and at Holbeck, 7 December.
3. The 'extraordinary' number of the *Mercury* appeared on 11 December; for the events that it reports, see next letter.
4. The events of the nomination day began with a public breakfast to TBM and Marshall, after which the candidates went to the hustings in the Mixed Cloth Hall Yard, where a crowd of 20,000 had assembled. When John Marshall, Senior, rose to nominate TBM a banner depicting half-naked children going to work in Marshall's mill on a winter day, inscribed 'A scene in Water Lane at five o'clock in the morning,' was raised and fighting broke out. 'During these struggles the scene became quite alarming; many desperadoes among Mr. Sadler's party pulled out thick staves which had been concealed about them, and struck right and left in the most brutal manner.' Nine persons were taken to the infirmary, and though special constables succeeded in putting an end to the fighting the tumult continued too great to allow TBM to speak from the hustings. On the show of hands the Mayor

surrounding places: but all to no purpose. We had a majority of two to one on the shew of hands. Sadler demanded a poll which will take place on Wednesday and Thursday. We think ourselves quite safe. Love – kindest, tenderest, love, and all best wishes to our sweet Margaret. Love to all – not forgetting him who on the day on which you receive this will become our brother.

Ever yours, dearest,

T B Macaulay

TO HANNAH MACAULAY, 12 DECEMBER 1832

MS: Trinity College. *Address:* Miss H M Macaulay / 44 Bernard Street / Russell Square / London. *Partly published:* Trevelyan, 1, 287–8.

Leeds Decr. – 12 – 1832

My darling,

The election here is going on as well as possible. To day the poll stands thus

Marshall	Macaulay	Sadler
1804	1792	1353

The probability is that Sadler will give up the contest. If he persists he will be completely beaten. The voters are under 4000 in number. Those who have already polled are 3100, and about five hundred will not poll at all. If we were not to bring up another man, the probability is that we should win.[1]

On Sunday morning early I hope to be in London; and I shall see you in the course of that day.

I had written thus far when your letter was delivered to me.[2] I am sitting in the midst of two hundred friends, all mad with exultation and party-spirit, all glorying over the Tories, and thinking me the happiest man in the world. And it is all that I can do to hide my tears and to command my voice when it is necessary for me to reply to their congratulations. Dearest, dearest, girl, you alone are now left to me. – Whom have I on *earth* but thee – and what is there in *heaven* that I desire in comparison of

---

declared TBM and Marshall elected; the Tories thereupon demanded a poll, which was appointed for 12 and 13 December. After leaving the hustings TBM addressed a crowd 'from the windows of Messrs. Stansfeld's warehouse' (*Mercury*, 11 December). A rather summary description of the scene on nomination day (misdated 12 December) appears in Mrs G. L. Banks (Isabella Varley), *Wooers and Winners*, 1880, II, ch. 14.

[1] At the close of the poll the numbers were Marshall, 2,012; TBM, 1,984; Sadler, 1,596.

[2] Margaret's wedding was 11 December, at St George's, Bloomsbury; the Rev. John Macaulay performed the service. But it is doubtful that Hannah's account of it could reach TBM in Leeds by the twelfth. Perhaps her letter describes the final preparations.

thee? But for you, in the midst of all these successes, I should wish that I were lying by poor Hyde Villiers. But I cannot go on. I am wanted to write an address to the electors: and I shall lay it on Sadler pretty heavily. By what strange fascination is it that ambition and resentment exercise such power over minds which ought to be superior to them? – I despise myself for feeling so bitterly towards this fellow as I do. Yet I must own to you dearest, to whom I own almost every thing, that I enjoy my victory over him and his impotent, envious, fury, more than any thing else in this contest. But this separation from dear Margaret has jarred my whole temper. I am cried up here to the skies as the most affable and kind hearted of men, while I feel a fierceness and restlessness within me quite new and almost inexplicable. When shall I be with you, my darling, and be soothed by your sweet tenderness, and amused by your kind womanly vivacity. I see some pleasing women here, some who have pretty faces, and some who wear my orange ribbands, and some who quote Latin to me; – but none who is worthy to tie the shoe-latchet of my two darling sisters.

I shall send you a second Edition of the Leeds Mercury Extraordinary to night. It will contain my address.[1] Kindest love to all. Thank my father for his letter and for his congratulations.

Ever yours, dear, dear, girl,
T B M

TO THE ELECTORS OF LEEDS, 12 DECEMBER 1832

Text: Leeds *Mercury*, 15 December 1832.[2]

Gentlemen,

With feelings of the warmest pleasure I congratulate you on the result of this day's poll. An attempt has been made to introduce into Leeds all the corruption and intimidation which disgraced the elections of Newark:[3] and an ingenious malevolence has employed against us arts such as even Newark never witnessed. Slander and hypocrisy, threats and caresses, bludgeons and gin, have done their worst: and the result is that the cause of Reform has triumphed in this great community by means worthy of such a community and of such a cause.

I have but one word to add. Let not the advantage which you have obtained induce you to relax in your exertions. Persist. Be firm. Be

---

[1] See next letter.

[2] TBM says (to Hannah Macaulay, 12 December) that this address was to appear in a second edition of the Leeds *Mercury* 'extraordinary,' 12 December; I have not seen a copy of that number. The address appeared also as a placard (copy in Thoresby Society, Leeds).

[3] By which Sadler had been returned, 1829 and 1830.

vigilant. Remember how desirable it is that your success should be complete and decisive. Be content with nothing short of a final victory over those who, having long misgoverned you by means of a vicious representative system, are now attempting to misgovern you by means of that franchise, which you have at length acquired in despite of them.

I am, Gentlemen, your faithful, humble Servant,

T. B. Macaulay.

Dec. 12, 1832.

TO THE ELECTORS OF LEEDS, 14 DECEMBER 1832

Text: Leeds *Mercury*, 15 December 1832.

Gentlemen,

I have now the honour of being your Representative in the First Reformed Parliament.[1] It is, I hope, unnecessary for me to assure you that the power which I owe to your choice shall be industriously and honestly employed for your benefit.

To those who, with a firmness and public spirit almost unparalleled in the History of Elections, have supported my Cause, I owe the warmest personal gratitude. To all of you diligent and faithful service. The victorious and the vanquished party are now equally my constituents; and I pledge to you my word, that no inhabitant of Leeds, who has occasion for my assistance, shall ever discover from my conduct towards him that I know whether he voted for me or against me. / I am, Gentlemen,

Your faithful and obliged Servant,

T. B. Macaulay.

Dec. 14, 1832.

TO MACVEY NAPIER, 17 DECEMBER 1832

MS: British Museum. *Address:* Macvey Napier Esq / Castle Street / Edinburgh. *Frank:* London December seventeen 1832 / T B Macaulay. *Published:* Napier, *Correspondence*, p. 131.

London Decr. 17. 1832

Dear Napier,

I am in London again after three weeks spent in electioneering. I find abundance of official business awaiting me here. In consequence of poor

---

[1] The significance of the Leeds election as a test of the Reform Bill has made it the subject of several studies, the fullest of which is A. S. Turberville and Frank Beckwith, 'Leeds and Parliamentary Reform, 1820–1832,' in *Thoresby Society Publications*, 41 (November 1946), 1–88.

Hyde Villiers's death I have been removed to an office far more laborious than that which I lately held, and never more laborious than at the present juncture. I will, however, do what I can for you. That is I will rise at five every morning and work for you till breakfast. I have refused an invitation to pass the Christmas week at Bowood solely that I may not disappoint you. I mention this to shew that, if I should delay the appearance of your next Number, it will not be from want of good will. I will try to be ready by New Year's day. But I cannot promise. You shall have the article as soon as it is finished, and it shall be finished as soon as I can finish it. This is all for which I can engage.

You will of course see the poll at Leeds in the newspapers. Sadler is mad with rage: and I cannot help pitying him though he does not deserve it. There is no baseness to which he has not stooped, no malicious art to which he has not had recourse. But enough and too much of him. His public life is, I think, over.

You will hear scarcely any thing but good news from England. I hope that you will send us back news as good from Scotland.

Ever yours most truly

T B Macaulay

TO HENRY MACAULAY, 20 DECEMBER 1832

MS: University of Texas.

London December 20 – 1832

My dear Henry,

I was truly glad to receive your letters, and such letters, proving at once your intelligence, your spirit, your humanity, and your regard for me. If I am a bad correspondent, attribute my remissness to any cause rather than to want of brotherly affection.

As to Maxwell[1] I have not had time to do much. I have spoken, however, to Rice,[2] and also to Robert Grant[3] who has the case now before him, and who assures me that he will give his best attention to it before he forwards it to the Horse Guards.

As to yourself it is my earnest wish that you would come to England during the rains.[4] Your health is the first object: and such an excursion

---

[1] A Cole Maxwell, ordnance storekeeper at Sierra Leone, had been court martialed, on 31 July 1832, for neglect of duty, insolence, and drunkenness. The proceedings in his case are in the Public Record Office, W.O. 71/280.

[2] Spring Rice was then one of the Secretaries to the Treasury.

[3] Judge Advocate General.

[4] Henry had been away since January 1831, and seems to have remained in Africa until 1836, when he was home on leave.

would certainly be of use to you in that respect. Whether it may be in my power to serve you in any other way is very doubtful. If it is in my power, you may depend on my inclination.

You will find us greatly changed – our dear mother gone – Margaret married – and possibly John married too,[1] – our father, I very much fear, breaking fast, – me member of parliament for the new borough of Leeds and Secretary of the Board of Controul, – Charles cutting up dead bodies,[2] – every thing in short turned topsy-turvy. But we shall be as glad as ever to see you, and nobody more glad than I.

I must stop. If I do not write to day I am told that I may lose a ship – and I have two large boxes full of dispatches to read before dinner. / Ever, my dear brother,

Yours, with true affection,

T B Macaulay

TO MRS EDWARD CROPPER, 22 DECEMBER 1832

MS: Morgan Library. *Address:* Mrs. Cropper / York Hotel / Brighton.[3] *Frank:* London December twenty two / 1832 / T B Macaulay.

London Decr. 22 1832

Dearest Margaret,

Thanks for your pun. It is detestable beyond any thing that I have heard this long time. But small thanks to you for finding any resemblance in my face to the hideous hangman-like fellow whom the Vandyke of the Leeds Political Union has drawn.[4] Take care of dearest Nancy, and bring her back well and strong. I mean to read the Busy Bodies[5] and to enrich my colloquial style from the mines of idiomatic eloquence which, as I am assured, it contains.

I dine to day with Lord Essex[6] – the most famous bon-vivant of our day – the true Lord Guloseton. He never, I am told, entertains a party of more than eight – seldom more than six. His cook stands him in what would keep five curates and their families. People have been known to swoon with rapture at the first mouthful of his *epigrammes d'agneau*; and

---

[1] John had been engaged since 1831 to Emma Jane Large, whom he married in December 1834.

[2] Charles was the first student entered in the medical classes of the London University on their opening in 1828; he began his surgical studies in July 1831.

[3] The Croppers spent the first part of their honeymoon at St Leonards and then went on to Brighton, where Hannah joined them.

[4] The portrait by Rhodes? See *to* Hannah, 29 November [1832].

[5] [The Misses Corbett], *The Busy-Bodies*, 3 vols., 1827.

[6] George Capel-Coningsby (1757–1839), fifth Earl of Essex.

some pillars of the Church have been seen to reel after partaking of his Burgundy. I shall write to Nancy a full and true account of the regale.

Admire my charity, temperance, in short all my cardinal virtues. Rice asked me to a luxurious official dinner which he gives in Mansfield street to morrow. Ellis sent to complain that he was lonely, (you know he is just recovering from the small-pox which he has had a second time) – and begged me to partake of his chicken and soupe maigre; and, like a good friend and a good Christian, I prefer visiting the sick to feasting with privy councillors. I shall soon, you perceive, be a perfect Sir Charles Grandison. In the meantime you, I hope, will not be a Lady G. Has Edward yet mashed a piano forte? Have you returned his hat and called him a violent wretch? Have you pinned his coat to your apron? Do you enrage him by calling him "honest man," and quiet him by crying Soh! Soh! as Beauchamp cried to his restive horse?[1] [If][2] you do such things, I shall, like Sir Charles, be apt to forget that I have more than one sister.[3] And then what will become of you – your brother gone – your man excessive unruly. But I must leave off trifling and read a wheel barrowfull of East India dispatches. Kindest love to Nancy and Edward. Tell my darling little girl that I will write to her on Monday, if possible.

Ever yours dearest

T B M

TO HANNAH MACAULAY, 24 DECEMBER 1832

MS: Trinity College. *Address:* Miss H M Macaulay / York Hotel / Brighton. *Frank:* London December twenty four / 1832 / T B Macaulay. *Mostly published:* Trevelyan, I, 288–9.

London Decr. 24. 1832

My darling, –

I am much obliged to you for your letter, and much gratified by all its contents, except what you say about your own cough. As soon as you come back, you shall see Dr. Chambers, if you are not quite well. Do not oppose me in this: for I have set my heart on it.

I dined on Saturday at Lord Essex's in Belgrave Square. But never was there such a take-in. I had been given to understand that his Lordship's cuisine was superintended by the first French artists, and that I should find there all the luxuries of the Almanach des Gourmands,[4] – the Dindon-

---

[1] *Sir Charles Grandison*, 3rd edn, v, 51; IV, 255; IV, 258; v, 47.
[2] Paper torn away with seal.   [3] *Sir Charles Grandison*, 3rd edn, III, 166.
[4] [Alexandre Grimod de la Reynière], *Almanach des Gourmands*, 8 vols., Paris, 1803–12. Trevelyan says that TBM 'had by heart the choice morsels of humour and extravagance that are so freely scattered through the eight fat little volumes' (II, 401). A copy of the second edition is in the library at Wallington, though not identified as TBM's.

aux-truffes, the marinades, capillotades, and all the other luxuries of a Parisian bon-vivant. What a mistake. His Lordship is luxurious indeed – but in quite a different way. He is a true English gourmand. Not a dish on his table but what Sir Roger de Coverley or Sir Hugh Tyrold[1] might have set before his guests. A huge haunch of venison on the sideboard; – a magnificent piece of beef at the bottom of the table; and before my Lord himself smoked – what for a kiss? – not a fricandeau – nor a ragout – but a fat roasted goose stuffed with sage and onions. I was disappointed; but very agreably. For my tastes are, I fear, incurably vulgar, as you may perceive by my fondness for Mrs. Meeke's novels. So I devoured two great slices of venison, and half the breast of the goose with a due proportion of potatoes which, to Lord Essex's honour be it said, he allows to his guests in great abundance.

Our party consisted of Sharp – Lubbock[2] – Watson[3] M P for Canterbury – Rich[4] who wished to be M P for Knaresborough, the author of " What will the Lords do?" and some other political tracts – and another man whose name I did not catch, but whose business it was to carve at the bottom of the table. Rogers was to have been of the party: but his brother[5] chose that very day to die upon, so that poor Sam had to absent himself. The Chancellor was also invited but he had scampered off to pass his Christmas with his old mother in Westmoreland. We had some good talk – particularly about Junius's letters. I learned some new facts which I will tell you when we meet. I am more and more inclined to believe that Francis[6] was one of the people principally concerned.

What a world we live in! Edward and Margaret going to see Matthews![7] I shall read them a lecture like that which the elders thundered in the ears of John Dighton. I must stop for the present. To morrow I will write again. Kindest love to the two sinners who have committed this dreadful act of apostasy.

Ever yours my own love

T B M

---

1 In Fanny Burney, *Camilla*, 1796.
2 John Lubbock (1803–65: *DNB*), later third Baronet; banker, mathematician, and astronomer. He was at Trinity College, 1821–5, and was a member of the committee of the SDUK.
3 Richard Watson (1800–52: *Boase*), M.P., Canterbury, 1830–4.
4 Henry Rich (1803–69: *Boase*), Whig M.P. for Knaresborough, 1837–41; for Richmond, 1846–61; created Baronet, 1863. He wrote on political subjects for the *ER*, 1831–42.
5 Henry Rogers (1774–1832), younger brother of Samuel, a partner in the family bank.
6 Sir Philip Francis (1740–1818: *DNB*), politician and political writer; reputed author of the 'Junius' letters (1768–72). The identification of Junius with Francis was first made in 1813; the summary of the arguments for Francis's authorship that TBM presented in the essay on Warren Hastings makes him, according to the latest writer on the subject, 'the most effective advocate of Francis' claims' (Alvar Ellegård, *Who Was Junius?*, Stockholm, 1962, p. 150).
7 Charles Mathews (1776–1835: *DNB*), comedian. TBM called him 'certainly the greatest actor that I ever saw' (Trevelyan, II, 289).

TO HANNAH MACAULAY, 26 DECEMBER 1832

MS: Trinity College. *Address:* Miss H M Macaulay / York Hotel / Brighton. *Frank:* London December twenty six 1832 / T B Macaulay.

London Decr. 26 1832

My love,

I have only time to write a line or two. I am delighted to hear that your cough is better. George assures me that, with proper care on your part, it will soon be removed.

I have no news for you. The papers will tell you that the citadel of Antwerp has fallen,[1] that the elections are going as much against the Tories as ever, and that a most horrible murder has been committed at Enfield.[2] I can give you no private information that you will care to hear. I dined in Bernard Street yesterday, though my Lord Essex begged me to feast with him again. In the evening I went to see Ellis, and found the family keeping their Christmas after the fashion of the old time. They were playing Pope Joan with a pack of cards which, I hear, is produced only once a year, and which, to judge by its appearance, must have been used to celebrate every Christmas day since the time of Queen Anne. Ellis's beauty is now beyond all description. He can be compared only to the starry heavens. His wife however seems quite content with her speckledy husband. I, however, say with the judicious poet.

> "I never thought, in all my life,
> That good could come, I wow,
> Of giving to a Christian
> The diseases of a cow.
> Ellis was waccinated:
> Yet now you see he's peppered,
> And comes out of his bed-room
> As spotty as a leopard."

Perhaps this small-pox is a judgment upon him for allowing card-playing in his house on Christmas day. If so, you will, I hope, take warning and not go to see Matthews. The great Dr. Styles[3] of Brighton, in his book on the stage, pronounces acting to be a far more heinous sin than even card-playing. And you, who are so happy as to be near to that illustrious man, will surely not neglect his admonitions. Remember that beautiful epigram of a Christian poet.

[1] On 23 December, to the French troops assisting the Belgians against the Dutch.
[2] A Mr Danby had been stabbed to death: see *The Times*, 24 and 26 December.
[3] Dr John Styles, *An Essay on the Character, Immoral and Antichristian Tendency of the Stage*, Newport, 1806; this reached a fourth edition, 1838.

"Ye fools, no longer after Matthews roam.
Take his example. Be, like him, *at home.*"[1]

So now I have made a letter out of nothing at all. Farewell, dearest.
Kindest love to Margaret and to our brothers. Is it true that Faithful[2] the
member for Brighton is dead. If it is we shall, I trust, be able to find
a Hopeful to succeed him. There is a better pun than either of Margaret's.

Ever yours, dearest,

T B M

[1] Mathews' 'At Homes' were a series of entertainments, including songs, imitations, recita-
tions, and the like, which began in 1808.
[2] George Faithfull (1790–1863: *Boase*), solicitor, M.P. for Brighton, 1832–4. Greville puts
him among the 'very bad characters' (a class including Cobbett and Gully, the prize-
fighter) returned to the reformed Parliament (*Memoirs*, II, 334).

REFORM PARLIAMENT AND
THE ANTI-SLAVERY CRISIS, 1 JANUARY–
15 AUGUST 1833

1833 January 9
  Finishes 'Lord Mahon's *War of the Succession*' (*ER*, January)

– February 6
  Speech on Irish union

– February 28
  Speech on Irish Coercion Bill

– April 17
  Second speech on Jewish disabilities

– Early May
  Offers to resign his office over Anti-Slavery Bill

– Early July
  Again offers resignation

– July 10
  Speech on India Bill

– July 24
  Speech on Anti-Slavery Bill

TO UNIDENTIFIED RECIPIENT, 1 JANUARY 183[3]

Text: Leeds *Mercury*, 5 January 1833.

London, Jan. 1st, 1832.

My Dear Sir,

On receiving your letter I went to a Coffee-House, got a sight of the *Leeds Intelligencer*, transcribed the absurd slander about which you wrote to me, and sent it off to Mr. Buxton.[1] I inclose his answer,[2] which will neither surprise you, nor shame the Author of the lie.

You advise me to call on the Editor[3] of the *Intelligencer* to give up his authority. The call would be quite useless. He has no authority to give up. The story is, on the face of it, an impudent invention. It is not, as you are aware, the first, or the second, or the third, or the fourth calumny, in which I have detected him; and I have no doubt that he will, on this occasion, as on former occasions, give himself all the airs of the injured party.

I earnestly hope that my friends at Leeds do not expect me to take the trouble of refuting every lie which this writer may think fit to publish. To do so would be the business of a life: and as Member for a great town, and Secretary to an important department, I have other and better employments. / Believe me ever, my dear Sir,

Your faithful Servant,
T. B. Macaulay.

---

[1] The Leeds *Intelligencer*, 27 December, giving as its authority 'a Gentleman to whom Mr. Buxton stated it,' said that when Buxton 'requested Mr. Macaulay's support to one of his propositions in a more marked manner than as a mere member of the Commons,' TBM replied '"I am a young man rising in the world of politics, and would you have me ruin my prospects for the sake of the Slave Question?"'

[2] 'My Dear Macaulay, – The extract from the Leeds newspaper surprises me as much as yourself. / If you take the trouble to notice it, I must beg that you will state that you have my authority for saying "that I not only disclaim the conversation, but that I never heard you express a sentiment which could be tortured into a willingness to sacrifice the Slave question, in exchange for official preferment." Your vote, last May, for my resolution, and against the amendment proposed by Government, at the time when you held office, might, I should have thought, have saved you from the possibility of such an imputation' (Leeds *Mercury*, 5 January 1833). Buxton refers to TBM's speech of 24 May 1832 (*Hansard*, 3rd Series, XIII, 52–5), in which he supported against the government Buxton's motion for a select committee on slavery.

[3] Robert Perring (1787?–1869) edited the *Intelligencer*, 1829–42.

TO MRS EDWARD CROPPER, 7 JANUARY 1833

MS: Morgan Library.

London Jan 7. 1833

Dearest Margaret,

I have been writing all day to finish my article for Napier – and I have still something more to do. But I cannot let another post go without a line – it must be only a line – to tell you, my darling, how often I think of you, and how much I love you. When my work is over I will try to be a more regular correspondent than I have been hitherto. Kindest love to Edward. Ever, my dearest love,

Yours
T B M

TO MACVEY NAPIER, 9 JANUARY 1833

MS: British Museum. *Address:* Macvey Napier Esq / Castle Street / Edinburgh. *Frank:* London January nine 1833 / T B Macaulay. *Published:* Napier, *Correspondence*, p. 132.

London Jan 9. 1833

Dear Napier,

I send off an article written in so much hurry and amidst so many distractions that I hardly know what it contains – many blunders no doubt. I hope that you will keep a vigilant eye both on the style and on the typography. There are several sheets which I have not been able to read since I wrote them.

Ever yours
T B M

TO MRS EDWARD CROPPER, 11 JANUARY 1833

MS: Morgan Library. *Address:* Mrs. E Cropper / Dingle Bank / Liverpool. *Frank:* London January eleven 1833 / T B Macaulay.

London Jany. 11. 1833

My darling Margaret,

I have about ten minutes of perfect leisure – and I do not know how I can use them better than in writing to my sweet friend and sister. But what have I to say? There is no scandal stirring as far as I am aware. The political news is in the papers: and London is so empty that there are few dinners. Shall I tell you of my superb official garb, just ordered from a topping tailor in Bond Street who makes uniforms for His Majesty's Guards, – a blue coat, with collar and cuffs blazing with gold lace, – blue trowsers with a lovely delicate stripe of gold running down them, – a hat enough of itself to break all the hearts in sixteen boarding-schools, a sword – such a sword –

> "A better never did sustain itself
> Upon a soldier's thigh."[1]

Or shall I tell you how my villains at Leeds have used me? Will you believe it? After all their fine speeches they have left me the hustings and polling-booths to pay for – near a hundred and twenty pounds.[2] It is well I am in office. But I will be wiser another time.

Or shall I tell you that I have been applied to by Walker[3] – the man who engraved that very fine print of Lord Brougham from Lawrence's picture[4] to sit to a friend of his in order to have an engraving of me taken? To morrow is to be the first sitting. Nancy is to go with me at two o'clock to an artist in Margaret Street Cavendish Square. And Walker hopes to make something by the engraving. I told him that he was very much mistaken; and that he would not sell twenty. But, as he chose to run the risk, I have no objection to contributing my share. I will send you a proof impression.

I have at last sent off a long and, I fear, a very dull article to Edinburgh. It is on Lord Mahon's History of the War of the Spanish Succession.

But here comes a bore; – a regular bilious East Indian bore. I must attend to him. Give my love to Edward.

Ever yours, dearest

T B M

[1] *Othello*, v, ii, 260–1.

[2] The official return of election expenses shows a total of £335 9s. 0d., of which TBM's share was apparently £102 3s. 0d., Sadler paying a larger proportion than either Marshall or TBM (*Parliamentary Papers*, 1833, XXVII, 147–8).

[3] William Walker (1791–1867: *DNB*), engraver, collaborated with his father-in-law Samuel William Reynolds (1773–1835: *DNB*) and Samuel William Reynolds, Jr (1794–1872: *DNB*), at 64 Margaret Street, Cavendish Square. Walker's 'friend' was the younger Reynolds, whose portrait of TBM was finished c. July and the engraving of it by the elder Reynolds published 24 July (examples in the British Museum and the National Portrait Gallery). The portrait is now in the possession of Mrs Lancelot Errington, who also owns a copy of the engraving whose caption attributes the engraving as well as the painting to the younger Reynolds. The portrait is reproduced as the frontispiece of vol. I of this edition.

[4] Published in 1828, from a portrait commissioned by Walker.

TO MRS EDWARD CROPPER, 16 JANUARY 1833

MS: Morgan Library.

London Jany. 16. 1833

My love,

I snatch a minute to write to you. It is only a minute. I have but just escaped from the painter to whom I am sitting. I have to meet the President of the Board of Trade[1] in a quarter of an hour, and, in the meantime, I am liable to be broken in upon by half London. The hard part of my duty is the necessity under which I lie of seeing and hearing all the bores who chuse to bestow their tediousness on me. It is all that I can do to be civil to them. I improve however; and in time I shall lie like a true courtier.

I picked up a good story from one of my visitors the other day. You have heard of Sir David Baird,[2] – a brave officer, but a rough, imperious, and intractable man. He went to India young, and was taken prisoner by the Hyder Ali, about the time at which our uncle was taken.[3] It was for a time believed that Baird had been killed. At last however news came to England that he was alive, but alive in a situation more horrible than death. He was treated with the utmost cruelty by Tippoo Saib, immured in a dungeon and almost starved. It was also discovered that the prisoners were chained together two and two in order to prevent their escape. The friends of old Mrs. Baird, the mother of the officer, hardly knew how to break this frightful intelligence to her. At last, with due preparation, they told her of the state in which her poor son was. The good old Lady turned up her eyes devoutly and ejaculated only – "God help the puir lad that's chained to my Davie." A beautiful sample of maternal tenderness is it not?

But here comes – just as I predicted – a bore – a yellow bore from Madras with a long story and a bad liver. Farewell, dearest. Give my love to the "puir mon that's chained to my Maggie."

Ever yours, darling,

T B M

---

[1] George Eden (1784–1849: *DNB*), second Baron Auckland, afterwards first Earl of Auckland; Whig statesman; succeeded Lord William Bentinck as Governor-General of India, 1835; First Lord of the Admiralty in Lord John Russell's cabinet, 1846–9.

[2] Baird (1757–1829: *DNB*) was the captive of Haider Ali and of his son Tipu Sultan, 1780–4; in 1799 he led the assault on Seringapatam in which Tipu was defeated and killed. The same anecdote is told in Edgar Johnson, *Sir Walter Scott*, I, 734.

[3] Colin Macaulay was imprisoned for four years at Seringapatam by Haider Ali and Tipu Sultan during the second Mysore war.

TO MRS EDWARD CROPPER, 21 JANUARY 1833

MS: Morgan Library. *Address:* Mrs. E Cropper / Dingle Bank / Liverpool. *Frank:* London January twenty one / 1833 / T B Macaulay.

London Jan 21. 1833

My darling,

I am delighted to see your handwriting again, and to hear that you are well, and that you liked my story about Sir David Baird. But I am not at all delighted to find that you take the part of those villains at Leeds.[1] Do not defend them. I told them that I would not pay a shilling. They declared that I should never be asked for a shilling: and after all they send me in a bill for a hundred and twenty pounds. If I had not been in office I could not have paid it. If I had been beaten at the election I would not have paid it. Do not proclaim, however, how angry it has made me. Above all do not let it come to Rawson's ears.[2] The money is paid: and I may as well have the credit of paying it graciously. If I had known, when first I agreed to stand, that they would have played me such a trick I would not have consented to stand. For when I consented I had no reason to hope that I should be able to pay the money. But every body comes without remorse on a man who has a salary from the public. Here is a ragamuffin of a Duncan Macaulay at Aberdeen – whom I never saw and whose connection with us is so remote that he does not attempt to explain it, who has written to me to ask for thirty pounds to take him to preach the Gospel, as he calls it, in Canada. One man calls on me to subscribe to Mr. Banim[3] the novellist. Another wants me to give my name and five guineas for a new translation of the Book of Jasher[4] from the Hebrew. Yet I can excuse those who beg for money better than those who dun me for places. "Make me a Cadet" – cries one man from Leeds. "Make me a writer" says another. "I have a friend," says Mr. Stephenson, "thirty years old who will be satisfied if you can give him a situation of only a hundred and fifty pounds a year." "I want to be an exciseman" – "I will be content to be a porter" – "I must be a clerk." Such are the letters I receive every day. And, what put me in the greatest rage, Charles must send me a servant who had been turned off from St George's Hospital w[ith a][5] note begging me to make him a tide-waiter. I gave

[1] '. . . it seems to me only right and fair that the member should pay all the expenses that are legal under the new act – you think so to my belief though you do not own it' (Margaret Cropper to TBM, 18 January: MS, Huntington).

[2] George Rawson was co-chairman of the committee for Marshall and Macaulay.

[3] John Banim (1798–1842: *DNB*), Irish novelist, dramatist, and poet. He was ill and in poverty in 1833 when a public appeal was made for him.

[4] No new translation of the Book of Jashar – presumably one of the medieval imitations of this lost document is meant – seems to have appeared at this time.

[5] Paper torn away with seal.

Charles a good lecture which my father overhearing broke forth "No, Charles; you must not ask Tom for places for people. I want all that he has to give. I want a clerkship for Mr. Stokes,[1] a place in the excise for Mr. Baines –" and he was going on to demand, I suppose, a portership for the black man, when I stopped him by saying I had nothing to give. "What – not a cadetship for Pate!"[2] – But my paper is full – and so, as you will believe, is my heart, at this recital of my wrongs. Love to Edward, and farewell, dearest.

T B M

TO MRS EDWARD CROPPER, 26 JANUARY 1833

MS: Mrs Lancelot Errington.

London Jan 26 1833

My dearest Margaret,

I have but a short time to write and little to say. My picture is nearly finished. Hannah and Fanny extol it to the skies; and I have told the painter that I shall buy it of him. I gave you nothing at the time of your wedding. I was not in a mood to be thinking about matters of ceremony. But if you care to accept this picture when it is finished – not as a wedding present but as a funeral relique – as a memorial of one who, though still living, is separated from you by a gulph like that which parts the living and the dead – as a memorial of ties so close and dear that, though severed, they can never be forgotten, it shall be yours.[3] But I must stop. It will not have a good look for an official man to be found crying in the middle of green boxes and dispatches tied with red tape. The Clerks will

---

[1] With the abolition of slavery in prospect, Zachary Macaulay was thinking of winding up the Anti-Slavery Society and of providing for its employees. Stokes was his clerk; Baines (probably the William Baines of 31 May 1826) and the black man are unidentified but presumably were employed by the Society.

[2] Patrick Robertson, one of the children of Zachary Macaulay's cousin Roderick Robertson, a Calcutta merchant, who sent his children to England to be educated under Zachary Macaulay's care. Pate obtained a place in the East India Company's military seminary at Addiscombe in 1834, went to India in 1836, and died there in 1844.

[3] After receiving this letter, Margaret wrote to Hannah that it had 'affected me very much and I cannot yet get quite over it. Some sentences of it constantly run in my mind and call up unbidden tears. You will not know dear Hannah till you are parted from him as I am how much you love him. Then if ever you are tempted to leave him, be sure first that you know well what you are going to, and for whom you exchange him. . . . Dearest, dearest Tom! You remember those notes about him of which I read you part [Margaret's *Recollections*]. I have never opened that book till a day or two since, from the time of my engagement, and sometimes could not bear to look to that side of the room where it lay. The other day I read some of it to Edward who was extremely interested in it but I began some passages I could not get through, and I felt almost as if I had broken faith, as if I were reading my love-letters to my first love' (28 January 1833: MS, Huntington).

think that we are going to be turned out, and that the Tories are coming in.

How do you like my article in the Edinburgh Review. Lady Holland magnifies it to the skies. Love to Edward.

Ever yours, dearest,

T B M

TO MACVEY NAPIER, 26 JANUARY 1833

MS: British Museum. *Mostly published:* Napier, *Correspondence*, pp. 132–3.

London Jany. 26. 1833

Dear Napier,

I am glad that you like my article. I do not dislike it as it appears in print. I have heard no opinion yet except from Holland House, where they are loud in praise: and I set some value on that praise. For there is no house in England where Spain and Spanish literature are better known.

I think that I could contrive, even in the midst of our parliamentary squabbles,[1] to write something about Madame D'Arblay's Book.[2] I have not read it; but I hear that it is an amusing sketch of her early life, and that it contains some curious anecdotes about Goldsmith, Garrick, and the other members of that circle. If I cannot finish an article on it for the next number you shall have one for the number following.

Ever yours truly

T B Macaulay

If you like the scheme tell Longman to send me the Book.

TO MRS EDWARD CROPPER, 8 FEBRUARY 1833

MS: Morgan Library.

House of Commons Feby. 8. 1833

Dearest Margaret,

You will think that I write to you seldom. Think so, if you will; but attribute it to any thing but want of affection for you. Indeed, my dear

---

[1] TBM means the squabbles that will come: the first reformed Parliament was opened on 29 January.

[2] *Memoirs of Doctor Burney*, 3 vols., 1832. No more is heard of this proposed review. Ten years later, in his review of Mme D'Arblay's *Diary and Letters*, TBM observes of the *Memoirs of Doctor Burney* that it was 'received with a cry of disgust, and was speedily consigned to oblivion,' for it was 'written in Madame D'Arblay's later style – the worst style that has ever been known among men' (*ER*, LXXVI [January 1843], 524).

girl, I love you very much. I am sitting in our library, crowded by
Members of parliament. A fierce debate is going on. Yet I cannot begin
a letter to you without being quite blinded with tears. We are engaged
in most agitating discussions.[1] We are on the verge of great events. I do
not know what a week may bring forth. But my fears are stronger than
my hopes. Yet of this I am sure, that if the worst come I shall meet the
worst with unalterable philosophy. To be in or out – popular or unpopular – is a small matter. I shall bear the most adverse turn of political
fortune in a manner very different from that in which I bore the loss of
you.

But why should a man be sad in a world so full of things to laugh at?
To day your Quaker – Mr. Joseph Pease[2] – tried to take his seat. The
matter is not decided. We have appointed a Committee to examine the
Journals and the Statute Book. I have very little doubt that he has a right
to sit: and I have no doubt at all that, if he has not a right, a law must be
made to admit him. But how I was astonished! He called on me at the
India Board a day or two ago to solicit my assistance. The porter brought
in his name on a card – "Joseph Pease." "Shew him in." The card ought
to have awakened my suspicions. For would a truly simple Christian
have had his name engraved in copperplate on paste board? I am sure you
will feel with me how inconsistent such a luxury was with such a profession. This, however, escaped me. I imaged Joseph to my self as a tall,
stiff, elder, – a public friend, – with grey hair hanging down his shoulders,
a hat like an umbrella, and a vocabulary full of third days and twelfth
months. Alas! Alas! [   ][3] male friends abstained from worldly dress,
manners, and conversation? I know of one sad exception. In came a smart,
slender, dapper, grinning young gentleman, or rather gemman, with a sort
of overstrained civility and alacrity in his manner, – bowing, skipping,
smirking, – and flourishing his hands, instead of contenting himself with
the Christian pastime of twirling his thumbs. Nothing was wanting to
make a very good third rate dandy of him but to have taken away two
inches from the brim of his hat and added them to the collar of his coat.[4]
Then his talk. Not – as it should have been – "Behold, Thomas, hum!

---

1 The debate on the address continued for four days over the question of Ireland. O'Connell
   attacked the government's announced intention to ask for extraordinary coercive powers
   in Ireland; TBM spoke in reply to him, 6 February (*Hansard*, 3rd Series, xv, 250–64). The
   issue was one which divided Whigs and Radicals and on which even the Ministry was
   disagreed, so that TBM's anxiety was justified.
2 Joseph Pease (1799–1872: *DNB*), of Darlington, the first Quaker M.P.; he refused to take
   the usual oath, but on 14 February he was, by decision of a select committee, allowed to
   make solemn affirmation as a Quaker and to take his seat.
3 An illegible word of what seem to be three letters here.
4 Pease was called 'the best dressed man in St. Stephen's' (*Notes and Queries*, 24 February
   1866, p. 153).

I pray thee to be good unto our people, hum! that they may sit among the elders without swearing, hum! and be judges in the gate without kissing the skin of calves – hum! hum!" Instead of that he talked as the carnal man talketh. But this is not the worst. To day he did hat-worship to the Speaker. He stood bare headed – bowed over and over again. I grieve to write these. One of our Irish members has also written a beautiful stanza on the subject, if you can allow for the Hibernian brogue in the last line.

> "There was a sturdy quaker –
> His hat-brim measured an acre
> But he took it off
> While the Churchmen did scoff,
> In honour of Sutton our *Spaker*.

But I must have done with this rambling nonsense.

Ever yours, my darling

T B M

TO MRS EDWARD CROPPER, 23 FEBRUARY 1833

MS: University of London. *Address:* Mrs. E Cropper / Dingle Bank / Liverpool. *Frank:* London February twenty three / 1833 / T B Macaulay.

London Feby. 23. 1833.

Dearest Margaret,

You say that you do not attribute my silence to want of affection. Indeed, dearest, you have no reason. Time, absence, business, and those storms of faction amidst which I am, as it seems, fated to live, have as yet failed to do for me what, I suppose, they will do at last. If I write sparingly it is because I cannot yet write cheerfully. But everything has its day, – sorrow as well as joy. A time will come when I shall be able to prattle with you on paper without discomposing myself for a morning, and making my brother commissioners, and all the clerks and porters of our office, wonder at my red eyes.

We are very hard worked; and, if ever we can steal an evening from the House some great man forces me to dine with him, and some great lady summons me to her rout, drum, conversazione, or whatever she calls her midnight squeeze. This afternoon I meditate a walk with Nancy. I dine with Sir George Philips – thence to Mrs. Stanley's[1] in the evening; – to morrow I dine with Lord J Russell. On Monday the House does not sit on account of the Queen's Birthday. But Lord Goderich has asked

---

[1] Emma Caroline Wilbraham (1805–76), married Edward Stanley, afterwards fourteenth Earl of Derby, in 1825.

me to dinner – such instances of elegant breeding not being uncommon, as Sir William Lucas well observed,¹ about the court; and I must go in all my official finery. I must adjourn thence at eleven to the Marchioness of Lansdowne's birthday rout. What will your Quaker friends say to this? How will friend Obadiah stare! How sad will friend Ephraim look! How deep will be the groan of friend Maher shalal hashbaz, and how quickly will revolve the thumbs of friend Kerenhappuch.²

Truly Pease hath not borne a good testimony. He leaveth his hat below stairs, that when he walks about the house he may not be called to order. He also standeth up to speak. This however may be excused, as it is not so much a posture of reverence as of convenience. Yet I think that he had better be at meeting, gathering home to his own gift, than holding forth among us.

I judge by your letters that you are turning O'Connelite. I have not time to argue the question. I think the Ministers quite right as to essentials, – but mistaken as to some details, and not very judicious in their parliamentary tactics.³ The breaking up of this government would be the signal for universal confusion. I shall therefore stand by them as long as I can do so with honor; and I think that I see my way pretty clear at least to the [end]⁴ of the present Session. All this is quite confidential.

I am sorry to tell you that your member Ewart⁵ is turning out one of the most hot headed and unreasonable persons that I ever saw. But I must stop. When we meet I will let you into all the mysteries of the present state of parties.

Love to Edward. I wish he would come into Parliament and take a house in Westminster. Then I would drop in every evening while the Irishmen were *spaking* about the *repail*.

Ever yours dearest
T B M

---

¹ *Pride and Prejudice*, ch. 29.
² See Isaiah 8: 1, 3; and Job 42: 14. The imaginary puritan in TBM's essay on Leigh Hunt names his child Maher-shalal-hash-baz, and Ellis, according to the census of 1841, actually had a servant named Kerenhappuch. TBM had joked with this name before in connection with the Quakers: see 21 June 1832.
³ The ministers had introduced a severe Irish Coercion Bill and a conciliatory Irish Church Bill, a combination described as 'a quick alternation of kicks and kindness...to satisfy and subdue the Irish' (Walpole, *History of England*, III [1880], 146). Althorp had threatened to resign over the Coercion Bill, and there was much dissatisfaction in the Cabinet over the arrangement of the measures. TBM spoke in defense of the Coercion Bill on 28 February (*Hansard*, 3rd Series, xv, 1326–37) but without conviction; there was general agreement, as Fanny wrote to Margaret, that the speech was 'the least successful he has yet made' ([1 March]: MS, Huntington). TBM also spoke on the Church Bill, 1 April (*Hansard*, 3rd Series, xvi, 1383–93).   ⁴ Paper torn.
⁵ William Ewart (1798–1869: *DNB*), liberal M.P. almost continuously, 1827–68; sat for Liverpool, 1830–7. Nothing hot-headed appears in the brief speeches he had so far made in the Parliament. He had been on the Committee on the Commercial State of the West Indies with TBM in 1832.

TO UNIDENTIFIED RECIPIENT, 25 FEBRUARY 1833

MS: Trinity College.

East India Board / Feby 25. 1833

My dear Sir,

I am truly sorry to say that I am engaged to dinner on Saturday 9 March. I have been resolving to call on you every day since the commencement of the Session. But what with Nabobs in the morning and Repealers in the evening, I have never been able to accomplish my purpose. / Ever, my dear Sir,

Yours most truly
T B Macaulay

TO MRS EDWARD CROPPER, 7 MARCH 1833

MS: Morgan Library.

London March 7. 1833

Dearest Margaret,

One line of congratulation.[1] You will imagine all that we have felt. Love to Edward.

Ever yours dearest
T B M

TO MRS EDWARD CROPPER, 11 MARCH 1833

MS: Morgan Library. *Address:* Mrs. E Cropper / Dingle Bank / Liverpool. *Frank:* London March eleven 1833 / T B Macaulay.

London March 11. 1833

Dearest Margaret,

One line to say that you need be in no apprehension about the composition of your Liverpool committee.[2] The ballots are always well attended, and the Conservatives are so few that there is no chance of their having a majority.

As to Rice's speech[3] which astonished you so much the explanation is quite simple. He had been dining with the Lord Mayor, and was as

---

[1] Some time near this date Margaret had escaped injury when the horses ran away with her carriage. Perhaps TBM refers to that: see Margaret Cropper to Hannah Macaulay [14 March 1833]: MS, Huntington.

[2] A motion for a select committee of inquiry into charges of corruption in the Liverpool elections had been passed on 6 March. Thirteen of the fifteen committee members were to be chosen by ballot on 12 March.

[3] Spring Rice, then Secretary to the Treasury, on 7 March made an incoherent reply to some remarks by Cobbett on the stamp duties: *Hansard*, 3rd Series, XVI, 385–6.

drunk as a fiddler. Lord Althorp called out to some of those who were sitting on the Treasury Bench to pull the poor Secretary down by his coat-tail. We are a very joyous assembly. The other day Colonel Torrens[1] made a tipsy speech about rent and profits, and then staggered away, tumbled down a staircase, and was as sick as a dog in the Long Gallery.

I am impatient for the time of your visit to London. I hope that it will include the Easter Holidays, when I shall have plenty of leisure. Tell me when you mean to come. Love [to][2] Edward.

Ever yours, my darling,
T B Macaulay

TO [ISAAC GOLDSMID?],[3] 19 MARCH [1833]

MS: University College, London.

East India Board / March 19

My dear Sir,

I am truly sorry that a previous engagement renders it impossible for me to dine with you on Sunday next. It has occurred to me that our Easter vacation may by possibility extend over the 17th of April.[4] Robert Grant can learn from Lord Althorp, I should suppose, whether this is likely to be the case. If there is the least risk, another day ought to be instantly appointed. If we delay every notice-day to the end of the Session will be occupied.

Ever yours truly
T B Macaulay

TO EDWARD BAINES, 25 MARCH 1833

MS: Duke University. *Address:* E Baines Esq / Mercury Office / Leeds. *Frank:* London March twenty five / 1833 / T B Macaulay.

PRIVATE

London March 25. 1833

My dear Sir,

Till this day I should not have been justified in divulging the plan which the government has it in view to propose respecting the East India

---

[1] Robert Torrens (1780–1864: *DNB*), economist; M.P. 1826–7; 1831–4; TBM refers to Torrens's speech of 19 February: *Hansard*, 3rd Series, XV, 970.
[2] Paper torn away with seal.
[3] The letter is among the Goldsmid family papers.
[4] On 17 April Robert Grant's resolution in favour of Jewish emancipation was carried after TBM had spoken in support of it: *Hansard*, 3rd Series, XVII, 227–38.

Company. The secret is now no longer a secret.[1] We intend to throw the China Trade open, and to make India bear its own expenses. We have reason to expect strong opposition from the Company backed by the Tories. Our hope is in the press throughout the country and in the public feeling. Leeds ought to petition.

The plan – the first principles of it at least – will in a few hours be made public. You will see that the government has not had in view any increase of its own patronage. If we have erred, it has been in too scrupulously avoiding whatever might bear such a semblance.

Remember me kindly to all friends.

Ever yours truly
T B Macaulay

TO MRS EDWARD CROPPER, 29 MARCH 1833

MS: Morgan Library.

London March 29. 1833

Dearest Margaret,

One line to say that I do not think Hannah's indisposition serious.[2] I have been very anxious about her now and then. But George seems to understand the case thoroughly. He says that her lungs are not in the least affected; and that the complaint is one over which medical treatment is sure in the long run to achieve a victory, but that the cure will be slow. She declares that she is steadily, though slowly, getting better.

I have sent your letter to George. I hope that what he writes will agree with what I tell you.

Kindest love to Edward. I am impatient – I cannot tell you how impatient – to see you again. Your Liverpool witnesses seem to be very trumpery people; and, by all that I can learn, you have very little chance of being able to disfranchise the rascally freemen.[3]

What do you say to the India plan? And why are your Associators

---

[1] The government's plan is reported in *The Times*, 26 March. Its main provisions were that the Company's trading monopoly to China should cease, that the Company's assets should go to the Crown in return for a subsidy, but that the Company should retain its political functions and its patronage.

[2] Hannah had caught a cold soon after Margaret's marriage and, she says, 'became quite ill caused partly no doubt by the misery of losing Margaret' (Hannah Trevelyan, Memoir of TBM). In May she went with the Croppers to Liverpool for the sake of her health.

[3] The committee of inquiry into Liverpool elections recommended in its report, 29 July, that the freemen of the city, who were accustomed to be systematically bribed, should be disfranchised. The bill introduced for that purpose was ultimately dropped in prospect of the Municipal Reform Bill of 1835.

always taking fright about nothing at all? I hear every day that all Liverpool is in an uproar about some monstrous restriction on the China trade of which I am perfectly ignorant.

Ever yours dearest,
T B M

TO MRS EDWARD CROPPER, 6 APRIL 1833

MS: Morgan Library. *Address:* Mrs. E Cropper / Dingle Bank / Liverpool. *Frank:* London April six 1833 / T B Macaulay.

London April 6. 1833

Dearest Margaret,

Every body has been ill – Hannah, and George, and Sir Robert Inglis, and Halcomb[1] the Member for Dover, and our Servant, and Lord Althorp, and Lord Durham, and the Under-Doorkeeper of the House of Commons. There has been a sort of influenza which scarcely any person has wholly escaped. I have passed two or three days in bed; and am now up, and all but quite well.

Hannah must leave London. George has been for some time considering the matter, and has made up his mind. He says, and I feel convinced, that her lungs are not affected. But the state of her health is far from satisfactory. She has never quite recovered from the excitement of last autumn. Change of air, change of scene, and an easy way of living, amusement without excitement, is what she requires. I had thought of taking her for a week to Brighton or Ramsgate during our short Easter Holiday. But George has, after much deliberation, decided for Liverpool. If less than her health and comfort were at stake, this would be a most unpleasant occurrence to me, – both because it takes her away, and keeps you away. Even if her strength should be completely restored by six weeks of the Dingle you would scarcely, I fear, chuse to come to London at the end of that time, and forego the glories of a country June for religious meetings and new Panoramas.

However the thing must be done: and a great comfort it is that she has such a home and such a sister to go to. My present plan is to take her as far as the Temple, and then to return instantly to London, sleeping at my Uncle's one night only. I think that we shall set out from London on Wednesday. I would gladly escort her the whole way, – and pass a few hours at least with you. But, as I have lost one week by sickness, I must not, at such a crisis, lose another by idling. When shall we meet, my dear, dear, girl? But I shall be foolish if I go on. So I will only send kindest love to Edward and sign myself, dearest,

Yours most tenderly
T B M

[1] John Halcomb (1790–1852: *DNB*), Tory M.P. for Dover, 1831–5.

TO [GEORGE RAWSON], 6 APRIL 1833

MS: John Rylands Library.

London April 6. 1833

My dear Sir,

I should be most truly glad to comply with any request of yours. But I really am so much occupied, or rather overwhelmed by business of different kinds, that it will, I fear, be quite out of my power to write any thing for your friend's collection. I have no fragment by me which would be of the least use to her.

I am truly glad to hear that your cough has departed, and that you have had so long and so quiet a holiday. What do you think of Sir Andrew Agnew's Lord's Day Bill?[1] And what does Mrs. Rawson think of it? We had an argument on the subject, I remember, at Hanover Square.[2] I am favorable to temperate legislation on the subject. But this measure seems to have been framed by persons very much of the temper of those who forbade the disciples to rub the ears of corn in their hands.

Remember me kindly to all your family, and believe me ever, / My dear Sir,

Yours most truly
T B Macaulay

TO [THOMAS TENNANT],[3] 11 APRIL 1833

Text: Leeds *Mercury*, 27 April 1833.

London, 11th April, 1833.

Dear Sir,

I shall have great pleasure in presenting the petition[4] as early as possible. I quite agree with the petitioners in wishing for a Bill on the subject. As to the particular Bill introduced by Sir Andrew Agnew, it seems to me to be absurd and tyrannical in the highest degree. I am truly glad to find that the large and respectable body whose Petition you have transmitted to me expresses no desire that their Representatives should support that measure. / Believe me ever, my dear Sir,

Your faithful Servant,
T. B. Macaulay.

The Mayor of Leeds.

[1] Sir Andrew Agnew (1793–1849: *DNB*), M.P. for Wigtownshire, brought in a 'Lord's Day Observance Bill' on 20 March. The bill, prohibiting virtually all labor on Sunday, was defeated on its second reading, 16 May.

[2] On his visits to Leeds in June and September 1832, TBM had stayed with Rawson at his house in Hanover Square.

[3] Tennant (1764–1833), a cloth merchant, was Mayor of Leeds.

[4] Praying for the 'better Observance of the Sabbath' (Leeds *Mercury*, 27 April), the petition had 8,545 signatures. TBM presented it on 17 April.

TO MRS EDWARD CROPPER, 13 APRIL 1833

MS: Morgan Library. *Address:* Mrs. E Cropper / Dingle Bank / Liverpool. *Frank:* London
April thirteen 1833 / T B Macaulay.

London April 13. 1833

Dearest Margaret,

I do not quite understand the course which has been pursued about
Hannah. She suspects, and so does Selina, that there has been some under-
plot between George and my father. I have not a very quick eye for
mysteries of this kind: but I must say that my father's reluctance to let
Hannah go at present to the Dingle is to me quite unintelligible, that
George's conduct has been irresolute, and that his answers to questions
have been unusually short and odd. His medical opinion is very cheering.
He says that his patient is very much better than she was a few weeks ago,
although the weakness and distress produced by the influenza prevent us
from seeing the real progress which she has made. She is much vexed by
thinking that you have been kept in suspense and your visit to London
prevented by conduct for which she is not answerable, and which, to me
at least, is quite incomprehensible. At present he says that she may go to
you at the end of this month, but not earlier. My father comes to London
to day, and we shall probably soon know more. In the mean time, dearest
Margaret, do not be uneasy. If I thought that there was any reason for
uneasiness I should be miserable beyond expression, incapable of business,
and unable to sleep or eat. But I am quite sure that the complaint is one
which quiet, ease of mind, and change of air and scene, will soon remove.

I begin to despair of seeing you, my darling, till the prorogation – that
is, till July. Be assured that on the very first day on which it is in my power
to join you, I will join you. How much we shall have to hear and to tell.
Love to Edward.

Ever yours, dearest,
T B M

TO JOHN BUTTREY,[1] 16 APRIL 1833

Text: Leeds *Mercury*, 20 April 1833.

London, April 16th, 1833.

Sir,

I have received the important petition which you have forwarded to
me, and I will take the earliest opportunity of presenting it.[2] You would

---

[1] Buttrey, a woolstapler of Leeds, was chairman of the committee superintending a petition
for corporation reform.　　　[2] TBM presented it on 17 April.

probably wish me to move that it be referred to the Committee on Corporations. / I have the honor to be,

Sir, your most faithful Servant,

T. B. Macaulay.

TO MRS EDWARD CROPPER, 17 APRIL 1833

MS: Morgan Library.

London April 17. 1833

Dearest Margaret,

I cannot tell you how much I am delighted to learn that you are coming up to London. You will find Nancy very much better indeed. I really scarcely ever saw such a change in a few days. The influenza has left her, and her old complaint seems to be much mitigated. She will, I hope, return to the Dingle with you.

I have absolutely not another moment. Love to Edward.

Ever, my darling, yours

T B M

TO UNIDENTIFIED RECIPIENT, 20 APRIL 1833

MS: Huntington Library.

London April 20. 1833

Sir,

I have presented the petitions which you sent up to me, and have expressed in the strongest terms which I could employ my full concurrence in their prayer.[1] I hope and believe that, before many weeks have passed, a decisive and satisfactory measure will be brought forward by the Government. / I have the honour to be, / Sir,

Your faithful Servant

T B Macaulay

[1] Probably the petitions from Leeds for the abolition of slavery that TBM presented on 17 April, when he 'took the opportunity of expressing his opinion that the public feeling in favour of emancipation could not be resisted, and his hope that the plan of Ministers would include "a safe and immediate extinction of Slavery"' (Leeds *Mercury,* 20 April).

TO LORD MAHON, 3 MAY 1833

MS: Stanhope Papers, Chevening.

East India Board / May 3. 1833

Dear Lord Mahon,

I should be glad to join in paying a tribute of respect to the memory of so great a writer and so amiable a man as Scott.[1] But I cannot engage, pressed for time as I just now am, to be at the Egyptian Hall on Saturday week.

I will tell you fairly that I have some doubts about this Abbotsford business. I have not leisure to explain them fully: but we will talk them over the next time that I have the pleasure of seeing you. / Ever, dear Lord Mahon,

Yours most truly

T B Macaulay

TO [GEORGE RAWSON?], 6 MAY 1833

MS: John Rylands Library. *Extract published:* A. Aspinall, *Lord Brougham and the Whig Party*, Manchester, 1927, p. 193.

London May 6. 1833

Dear Sir,

I send you my authority to vote for Mr. Teale.[2] I am truly glad to find that you are not, like some of my friends at Leeds, inclined to blame my recent conduct.[3] I am fully convinced that it is the duty of public men to make a firm stand at this conjuncture in defence of order, property, and public credit. I wish from the bottom of my soul that the ministers would move quicker in the work of reforming abuses. But after all we are moving in the right direction, though not, I think, at the right pace.

As to the question of slavery, I know no more than you what the government intends to do.[4] I have fully made up my mind as to what I shall do.

Ever yours truly

T B Macaulay

P S. Kind remembrances to your son.[5]

---

[1] Mahon was active in the campaign to raise £17,000 for the purchase of Abbotsford as a present to Scott's family; a public meeting on the subject was held at the Egyptian Hall, 18 May. The subscription fell short of its goal, but the sum raised paid off the debt on the library and museum at Abbotsford (J. G. Lockhart, *Life of Scott*, new edn, 1845, ch. 84).

[2] Perhaps Thomas Pridgin Teale (1800–67: *Boase*), surgeon at the Leeds Public Dispensary and afterwards at the Leeds General Infirmary.

[3] The reference is probably to TBM's support of the government's Irish Coercion Bill.

[4] The government's plan of abolition was laid before the West India Committee on 10 May. Its main provisions, reported in *The Times* on 11 and 13 May and afterwards changed, were for an apprenticeship of twelve years and a loan of £15,000,000 towards the compensation of the slave-owners.

[5] If the recipient of this letter is George Rawson then TBM means the younger George Rawson (1807–89: *Boase*), a solicitor at Leeds.

TO ZACHARY MACAULAY, [13? MAY 1833]

Text: From MS in possession of Mr C. S. Menell, who furnished transcript.

Bernard Street / Monday

My dear Father,

Things look a little better. I saw Graham and heard from Lord Althorp yesterday evening. They have agreed to frame their resolutions in such a way as not to raise the question whether the slave shall have to pay any thing for his liberty or not.[1] They intend to have the resolutions printed tomorrow night, but not to take a vote on them for a fortnight; and, during the interval, they will, if possible, alter the plan in such a way as to meet my wishes.[2] They say that much will depend on the feeling of the country and on the conduct of the abolitionists.

If the abolitionists will stand by them as to the 15,000,000 they hope to be able to meet the views of the abolitionists as to the point which we hold to be vital.

Under these circumstances I have consented to remain in office till the cabinet has formed its final decision. It is very desirable that Buxton and Lushington should understand that the most objectionable part of the plan may probably be altered, and that they should not altogether break with the government.

Ever yours affectionately,

T B M

TO HANNAH MACAULAY, 17 MAY 1833

MS: Trinity College. *Address:* Miss Macaulay / E Cropper's Esq / Dingle Bank / Liverpool. *Frank:* London May seventeen 1833 / T B Macaulay.

London May 17. 1833

Dearest Nancy,

Great news for you. I have to inform you that on Thursday morning[3] Mr. and Mrs. Edward Cropper with their sister, a very agreable young

---

[1] The government plan of abolition as first framed by Stanley was explained to Whig M.P.s at a meeting at Lord Althorp's, 11 May; the provision that freed slaves' earnings should be applied to the compensation of the masters was rejected by the Anti-Slavery party, which accepted only with great reluctance the principle of compensation for the owners in any form. When the plan was explained in the House of Commons nothing was said of the slave's paying for his freedom. In deference to his father's objections to the original plan, TBM had offered his resignation to the ministers – precisely when is not recorded, but probably on 12 May: see A. Aspinall, ed., *Three Early Nineteenth Century Diaries*, p. 330. This was the second occasion on which he had offered to resign either his seat or his office over the slavery question: see 11 May 1831.

[2] Stanley moved the government's resolutions in the House of Commons on 14 May; no vote was taken, the debate being adjourned to 30 May.   [3] 16 May.

lady, left London for Liverpool. They had a very fine day. But the Sun was hot and the roads dusty. They got in to tea at Leicester; and slept there. This day – Friday – they were off in the cool of the morning. They had a delightful ride by Matlock and through the valley of the Dove close under the walls of Haddon House to Buxton. They are at this moment dining at that celebrated watering place. Nancy, I am truly glad to say, has borne the journey well, and is in excellent health considering the heat. But she exposes her face too much to this hot sun, and will be dreadfully tanned if she does not take more care. Tell me when you write if every word of this is not true. If it is will you not allow me to possess the gift of presentiment in as large measure as yourself.

And now that I have told you the news of our travellers, which of course you were anxious to hear in the first place, let [me] see whether I have any London news for you, – that is news which is not secret. For I shall not be so shallow a politician as to tell you my nixams of state. What says the poet?

> If folks can't keep a nixam
> I beats 'em and I kicks 'em.

The news then which it is fit for you to know is that my father has left London for a fortnight; that Cobbett[1] made a beast of himself yesterday night, and that Sir Robert Peel rather forgot his dignity in replying to the old ruffian, – that Praise God Barebones has been defeated on his Sabbath-day Bill by a small – a shamefully small – majority[2] – that Charles Grant has a toothache, – that George Stephen is as mad as any Tom of Bedlam that ever roared in a dark cell,[3] – that I gave audience to day to a deputation of long-ell-manufacturers from Devonshire who came to complain that the Company had given over buying their goods to send to China, and that the private traders had not yet begun. I told them that I had a brother in law who would do wonders in the China trade, and that I had no doubt that he would buy up all their long ells before many days are passed.

---

[1] Cobbett had been elected M.P. for Oldham to the reformed House of Commons; his career there was tumultuous and unsuccessful. On 16 May he moved to dismiss Peel from the Privy Council in consequence of Peel's monetary policies of 1819. The attack stirred up noisy derision. In 1851, after re-reading the volumes of Cobbett's *Political Register* for 1832 and 1833, TBM wrote in his journal that 'My own name often appears in these volumes. Many people thought that he had a peculiar animosity to me; but I doubt it. He abuses me; but less than he abused almost every other public man whom he mentioned' (Trevelyan, II, 295).

[2] Agnew's Sabbatarian bill lost by six votes.

[3] Stephen's Anti-Slavery Agency Committee, the radical wing of the Anti-Slavery party, was pledged to the proposition that 'to uphold slavery is a crime before God, and the condition must therefore be immediately abolished' (Stephen, *Anti-Slavery Recollections*, pp. 134–5). The Committee had undertaken violent agitation against what it regarded as the temporizings of the proposed abolition measure, creating some risk of a split in the Anti-Slavery ranks. As Stephen remarks, Zachary Macaulay 'distrusted [the Committee's] policy almost to the last' (*ibid.*, p. 169).

This is a very poor letter. I shall write much better letters when my hand gets in again, and when the thermometer falls to 150° in the shade. As Shakespear says

> "None of you will bid the winter come
> And thrust his icy fingers in my maw" —[1]

Or as Fletcher says in his Wife for a Month

> "Oh for a cake of ice
> To clap unto my heart to comfort me."[2]

Or as Lord Holland says

> "Oh where are all the winds? Oh who will seize
> And bear me gasping to some northern breeze."

Or as a still greater poet than any of the three says.

> "This heat does make me cross and giddy.
> I'm broiling like an Indian viddy,
> Or like Bishop Ridley in Baliol ditch
> In the middle of faggots and of pitch.
> Even our father would not call his meat underdone,
> If 'twere half as well roasted as his son.
> When I want my kettle to boil in a minute
> I only just dip my finger in it.
> The most skilful cook would to me be a dunce:
> For I dress my beef steak and eat it at once.
> I beat all jugglers that ever you saw.
> For I take up a piece of meat blood-raw.
> I chew it; and see what wonders follow,
> It's overcharked by the time that I swallow.
> Poor Fanny cries out when I kiss her or stroke her
> As if she were touched with a red hot poker.
> Alack how I burn! alack how I fry,
> I'm always drinking yet always dry.
>   My clothes are tinder
>   My pen's a cinder
> Farewell dearest Nancy. I faint. I [die.][3]

Love to Meg and Edward. [I][3] hope to hear from you and them very soon.

Ever, my darling, yours

T B M

---

[1] *King John*, v, vii, 37.   [2] Beaumont and Fletcher, *A Wife for a Month*, iv, i.
[3] Paper torn away with seal.

TO HANNAH MACAULAY, 21 MAY 1833

MS: Trinity College.

London May 21. 1833

My darling,

I write to you again though I have not had a word from you, and though I am plagued out of my life between the Mogul and the methodists, Ramohun Roy and the Antislavery Agency Society. Often do I murmur to myself those sweet and affecting lines in which a judicious poet beautifully reprehends the ambition of public men.

> " Oh the charming month of May
> When I was in opposition,
> I walked ten miles a day,
> And lounged at the Exhibition.
>
> Oh the hateful month of May
> Now that I am in power
> No longer can I ramble
> In the streets to the East of the Tower.
>
> The Niggers in one hemisphere
> The Brahmins in the other
> Disturb my dinner and my sleep
> With "An't I a man and a brother?" " [1]
>
> And May for the first time goes by
> And brings me no delight:
> I am stewed at the Board all day:
> I am stewed in the House all night."

While I was stewing here yesterday, who should make his appearance but Napier – just arrived from Edinburgh? He sate with me an hour or so. We had a hearty laugh at Miss Priscilla Buxton. I call her Miss Priscilla Buxton; because Lady Holland read me, her son and Labouchere a long lecture last Sunday night on the indecorum of talking about young ladies without adding the *Miss*. "It is quite a scandal – quite a cruelty. It always gives the idea of great levity of behaviour on a young woman's part. I hate to hear of Emily Littleton[2] or Theresa Villiers."[3] Therefore in

---

[1] The seal of the Anti-Slavery Society derived from a Wedgwood cameo, modelled in 1786, 'showing, on a white background, a Negro kneeling in supplication, while he utters the plea to become so famous, "Am I not a man and a brother?"' (Howse, *Saints in Politics*, p. 40). The question had been used as the title of a pamphlet published anonymously in 1778 by Peter Peckard.

[2] Second daughter of E. J. Littleton, Emily (1816–52) married Lord Newark in 1832.

[3] I.e., Mrs Thomas Lister.

compliance with My Lady's directions I say Miss Priscilla Buxton. An eminent writer has made a beautiful epigram on the damsel:

> "No wonder that the Edinburgh Review
> In blue and yellow bound, has charms for you.
> For you are blue and yellow too, my fair.
> Blue are your stockings, yellow is your hair."

And now I must be off to the House of Commons. Farewell and again and again farewell dearest. And do not forget me, Miss my darling. Love to Margaret and Edward. I am dying to be with you all at the Dingle. But at present I must be content with such mouthfuls of fresh air as I can catch in Solomon's Porch.

Farewell dearest
T B M

TO HANNAH MACAULAY, 23 MAY 1833

MS: Trinity College.

London May 23. 1833

My darling,

At last I have had a letter from my dear little girl in which she says nothing about what I most want to know – that is her own health. Margaret must write me a line on that subject. All my letters you and she have in common, I suppose. Yet it will hardly be safe for me to write nixams in that case. For what you shew her she tells Edward, and he tells John, and he tells Anne, and she tells Mary Wakefield,[1] and she tells Josiah, and Ebenezer, and Habakkuk and Maher-shalal-hashbaz, and all other friends.

Yesterday I stepped into the Board Room. There was a person in conference with Grant. Who should it be but David – even David Hodgson – come of course on a vile money-getting errand. Indeed, as Mrs. Bennet would say, I observe that the Liverpool people – at least those who come to our Board – are all for what they can get.[2] Well and truly does a great poet say

> "The Liverpool merchants are so stingy
> They only want to make money from Ingee."

David was here about salt. He wants to do the Indian government out of its salt revenue for his own filthy lucre. A villain! See whether we are not up to him.

---

[1] Mary Wakefield lived at Dingle Bank with her sister Anne and her brothers-in-law, John and Edward Cropper.   [2] *Pride and Prejudice*, ch. 25.

Yesterday we read the Jew Bill a second time. Inglis divided the house. We were 189 to 52. It was a dull debate as ever I heard; on one side the merest Praise-God Barebones cant that has been obtruded on the House of Commons since the Restoration; on the other, – though I say it that should not say it – nothing so good as a speech that was made in the former debate[1] by a young gentleman who shall be nameless. We coughed Robert Grant down, and he richly deserved it. But I felt for his grey hairs. Tediousness is the privilege of old age.

By the bye I have received from those unbelieving dogs – that is to say the Jews – several copies of my speech which the stiffnecked generation have reprinted from the Mirror of Parliament.[2] I send it to you under this cover. It is middling – the report I mean: for the speech was capital. It is however the best report that there is of what I said. The ungrateful wretches do not spell my name right.

I have nothing more to tell you. This is the Derby. Why did you not stay for the Derby? What a dashing figure you would have made in Meg's Britchska on the race ground! All the ministers are gone except Grant who thinks it a sin and myself who think it a bore. What a height of human virture have I attained to take no pleasure in such vanities. It is expected that the prophets will be on the ground to give the wicked spectators a screed of doctrine. Those fellows will get themselves into trouble. As the hymn says

> "Henry Drummond
> Will be summoned
> Unto Bow Street without fail.
>
> Edward Irving
> Is deserving
> To be whipped at the cart's tail."

What a foolish letter this is. Just like the nonsense that I talk in the sofa; and then you and Meg come and kiss me and say "My dear foolish boy" – and "What a foolish brother I have," – and other such complimentary and endearing expressions. Farewell – dearest dearest girl – and give my love to Margaret and Edward and all friends, specially Adonibezek and Zephaniah, not forgetting that excellent man who gathers to his own gift so efficiently, – I mean the worthy Jehoiakim. Love again to you and Margaret.

Goodbye, my darlings
T B M

[1] 17 April 1833.

[2] *Mirror of Parliament*, 1833, II, 1271–4, where TBM's name is spelled 'Macauley.' A reprint of the speech, without title page or other identification, is at Trinity. Goldsmid's committee reprinted the debates in a pamphlet entitled 'Speeches of the Right Hon. Robert Grant, the Right Hon. T. B. Macaulay, Joseph Hume, esq. and D. O'Connell in the House of Commons...on Mr. Grant's Moving a Resolution Relative to the Civil Disabilities of the Jews,' 1833.

TO HANNAH MACAULAY, 28 MAY 1833

MS: Trinity College. *Extract published:* Trevelyan, I, 296.

London May 28. 1833

My darling, why am I such a fool, as to write to a gypsey at Liverpool, who fancies that none is so good as she, if she sends one letter for my three, a lazy chit whose fingers tire with penning a page in reply to a quire? – There, Miss, – Pecks – Pecks – Bushels of Pecks – Volumes of Pecks. You read all the first sentence of my epistle and never fancied that you were reading verse. I have no time to write, and yet here I am idling with unread dispatches and the proof sheets of our India Bill lying before me writing to a foolish girl who will never do any good in her generation. Who is to atone to the people of Bombay and Trichinopoly, not to mention those of Furruckabad and Moorshedabad, for the invaluable time which you make me lose – I should like to know that, mistress. –

> The people of Calcutta
> They grumble and they mutter: –
> The people of Bombay
> Think my wits are gone astray:
> The people of Madras
> Stare like Nancy at her glass.
> The people of Allahabad
> Think the Sec is going mad.
> Not one of the Directors
> But reads me daily lectures:
> And as to the poor chairs
> They weep and rend their hairs.
> Grant says with a sigh
> "You're as lazy as I."
> Says Rice "You must be tipsy
> As I have known your betters" –
> No – I'm writing to a gypsey
> Who papers her hair with my letters.

My dearest little girl, I am so glad to learn from Margaret that you are better. Go on, and get better and better every day. You cannot have kinder people to look after you. I dare say that if, like Miss Smith, you are partial to one of their cows they will call it your cow?[1] I hope you drink milk like a sucking calf. – I hope you are up by six and in bed by nine. I hope you milk the huge beasts yourself.

[1] Jane Austen, *Emma*, ch. 4.

"I almost fancy
I see my Nancy
With a little straw bonnet
And a pail balanced on it."

You are ashamed by this time of your Smithfield terrors. You often sing, I am sure

"Without the cows what should we do?"

I hope you will be able to make me a capital syllabub by the time that I come to the Dingle. When will that be? Early in August, I hope. Within twenty four hours after the prorogation, I am determined. I long to be with my dear little girls.

From repealers and Tories I then shall be free –
Neither planters nor canters will make my ears tingle
And West Indian sugar, and East Indian tea
Will both be forgot as I ride to the Dingle
Derry Down.

That is so capital a verse that I shall hardly mend it. I will leave off while I am well. I have some Edinburgh Review gossip for you – and other things. But they will keep. What nonsense I have been writing. Kindest love to Margaret and Edward.

Ever yours my little girl
T B M

TO HANNAH MACAULAY, 1 JUNE 1833

MS: Trinity College. *Address:* Miss Macaulay / E Cropper's Esq / Dingle Bank / Liverpool. *Frank:* London June one 1833 / T B Macaulay. *Partly published:* Trevelyan, I, 294–5; 296.

London June 1. 1833

My love,

You have public news of course. What say the Liverpool abolitionists, specially they of the drab coat and the broad brim, to the modifications introduced into Stanley's bill.[1] I am very nearly satisfied; and so Buxton seems to be. The papers will scarcely contain any account of what passed yesterday in the House of Commons at 12 o'clock in the middle of the day. Grant and I fought a battle with Fool Briscoe[2] and Rogue O'Conel

---

[1] The government now proposed to make the £15 million a gift and to allow the slaves to reduce by their labor the twelve-year period of apprenticeship: see Stanley's speech, 30 May, *Hansard*, 3rd Series, XVIII, 138–40.
[2] John Ivatt Briscoe (1791–1870: *Boase*), M.P. for various constituencies from 1830.

in defence of the Indian people, and won it by 38 to 6. It was a rascally claim of a dishonest agent of the Company against the employers whom he had cheated and sold to their own tributaries.[1] The nephew of the original claimant has been pressing his case on the Board most vehemently. He is an attorney living in Russell Square and very likely hears the word at St John's Chapel.[2] He hears it however to very little purpose: for he lies as much as if he went to hear a "cauld clatter of morality"[3] at the parish Church. He wanted 50000 £ or thereabouts out of the Indian revenues, and thought himself sure of pouching that sum. Indeed he would have succeeded but for me: for Grant at one time wavered much. It was by our uncle when he was Resident at Travancore that the rascality of the trans-action was originally exposed twenty five or twenty six years ago. It was by me that the coup-de-grace was given. Mr. Hutchinson must love the name of Macaulay. Do you know him? Is he a Johnian?

Apropos of Johnians – what differences of taste and feeling there are in this world! The day before yesterday I found Selina and Fanny in ecstasies over a note which they had received from Baptist Noel – the sweetest note – oh such a sweet note – they must shew it me – and they shewed it me. This sweet note set forth that Baptist had seen his sister Augusta[4] – but that, as other people were by, he had not had an oppor-tunity of talking with her and ascertaining the state of her mind; but that he very much feared that she was – and then came the usual cant. How sweet that a brother should write to all his acquaintance the glad tidings that his sister is dying in a state of reprobation. I stormed till I think I made both Selina and Fanny a little ashamed of themselves and of their spiritual pastor and master.[5] I hope that your confidential communications to Noel are not of this kind. I always hated confessors – protestant or Catholic. But this is enough of theology for one letter. I have written these edifying remarks because you may possibly receive my letter on Sunday evening and I wish you to employ your Sunday more Agnewishly than you did when you read my speech about the Jews.

I remember that when you were at Leamington two years ago I used to fill my letters with accounts of the people with whom I dined. High life

---

[1] *Mirror of Parliament*, 1833, II, 2016–17; the debate is not reported in *Hansard*.

[2] His name was Hutchinson. St John's Chapel was Baptist Noel's church.

[3] Scott, *Old Mortality*, ch. 42: 'a dry clatter o' morality.'

[4] Mrs Thomas Gisborne Babington, then dying of tuberculosis.

[5] Noel, however, continued to be a favorite of TBM's sisters. In 1838 he wrote to Fanny to urge the 'importance of endeavouring to draw your Brothers mind to God. . . . Within the last few days two gentlemen with whom I am acquainted said bitterly that they knew him to be an infidel. One of them from Calcutta stated that in India except on state occasions, he was believed never to attend public worship. . . . Having great admiration for his talent and for the high feeling which often appears in his writings, I am the more grieved to hear him spoken of with a feeling approaching to enmity as a man whose talents are very likely to do mischief; and not to be able to defend him' ([8 July 1838]: MS, Trinity).

was new to me then; and now it is so familiar to me that I should not, I fear, be able, as I formerly was, to select the striking circumstances. I have dined with sundry great folks since you left London. Yesterday night I went to a very splendid rout at Lord Grey's – the last party which he or more properly speaking my Lady gives this season. I stole thither at about eleven from the House of Commons with Stewart Mackenzie. I do not mean to describe the beauty of the ladies – who, excepting always Lady Seymour,[1] were all of them as ugly as sin – nor the brilliancy of stars and uniforms. I mean only to tell you one circumstance which struck and even affected me. I was talking to Lady Charlotte Lindsay,[2] a great favourite of mine, about the apartments and the furniture, when she said with a good deal of emotion, "This is an interesting visit to me. I have never been in this House for fifty years. It was here that I was born. I left it a child when my father fell from power in 1782, and I have never crossed the threshold since." Then she told me how the rooms seemed dwindled to her – how the stair case which seemed to her in recollection to be the most spacious and magnificent that she had ever seen had disappointed her. She longed, she said, to go over the garrets and rummage her old nursery. She told me how in the riots of 1780 – the No Popery riots – she was taken out of bed at two o'clock in the morning. The mob threatened Lord North's house. There were soldiers at the windows, and an immense and furious crowd in Downing Street. She saw, she said, from her nursery the fires in different parts of London. But she did not understand the danger; and only exulted in being up at midnight. Then she was conveyed through the Park to the Horseguards as the safest place; and was laid, wrapped up in blankets, on the table of the guard-room in the midst of the officers. "And it was such fun," she said, "that I have ever since had rather a liking for insurrections."[3]

I must stop here. I dine to day with Ellis – and Napier is to be of the party. His name reminds me that I have some gossip for you about the Edinburgh Review but that must wait for another day. I am delighted to learn, dearest, that you are better and that you are comfortable, though I never doubted that with country air you would soon be better and that with Margaret and Edward you would be perfectly comfortable. Dear Margaret! I love her as much as ever. But I shall not write to her for the same reason for which Frank gave the extra piece of cake to poor James

---

[1] Jane (1809–84), youngest of the three daughters of Richard Brinsley Sheridan's son Thomas, celebrated for their beauty; married, in 1830, Lord Edward Adolphus Seymour, later twelfth Duke of Somerset.

[2] Lady Charlotte (1771–1849), was Lord North's youngest child and the widow of Col. John Lindsay.

[3] TBM uses this anecdote in his speech on education, 19 April 1847: *Hansard*, 3rd Series, XCI, 1008.

who had no pudding at dinner.[1] She has a husband to look after her; and you have only a brother; so I shall continue to correspond with you. She has only herself to thank for my not writing to her. If she will only separate from Edward I will send her the most delightful letters that she ever read. In the meantime give her and Edward my love.

Ever yours dearest girl,

T B M

TO HANNAH MACAULAY, 3 JUNE 1833

MS: Trinity College. *Address:* Miss Macaulay / E Cropper's Esq / Dingle Bank / Liverpool. *Frank:* London June four 1833 / T B Macaulay. *Partly published:* Trevelyan, I, 295–6; 296–7.

House of Commons Monday night / 1/2 after 11.

My darling,

But oh – you naughty naughty girl – how could you break open the envelope of this letter so roughly? How could you destroy the most beautiful, exquisite, delicate, little love of a seal that ever was impressed with cornelian. You should have cut it out carefully with your scissars,[2] and treasured it in that box which the shopkeeper in Lamb's Conduit Street repaired and lined for you, and made bread seals from it. It was the loveliest thing, and you have broken it all to pieces. It is no use trying to piece it now. The mischief is done. – Well if you will be a good girl and write me a very long letter, perhaps I may seal another cover with the same signet. So now have done crying, and listen to me. For you know all the crying in the world will not mend a seal when once it is cracked.

I promised you some gossip about the Edinburgh Review. It is of no very great consequence; but it may amuse you. Napier is in London, and has called on me several times. He has been with the publishers who complain that the sale is falling off, and in many private parties, where he hears sad complaints, and the universal cry is that the long dull articles – particularly Empson's, – are the ruin of the review. As to my self he tells me that every body agrees that my articles are the only things which keep the work up at all. Longman and his partners correspond with about five hundred booksellers in different parts of the kingdom. All these booksellers, I find, tell them that the Review sells or does not sell according as there are or are not articles by Mr. Macaulay. So, you see, I, like Mr. Darcy, shall not care how proud I am.[3]

---

[1] 'I must give [the cake] to poor Edward, because he had no cherry-pie, to day, at dinner' (Maria Edgeworth, *Frank*, Part II [*Works*, Boston, 1825, XII, 42]).

[2] Hannah did: see 10 June.   [3] *Pride and Prejudice*, ch. 5.

But seriously this is an awkward state of things. It is most unpleasant to be forced to tell Empson all this: – for he, I find, is considered by every body as the evil genius of the Review. But, after all, it is more unpleasant that the Review should go to ruin. And this seems very probable. At all events I cannot but be pleased to learn that, if I should be forced to depend on my pen for subsistence, I can command what price I chuse.

I dined yesterday at Lady Davy's. In general her Ladyship has agreable parties. But her assemblage yesterday night was deplorably dull. The only amusement was that of laughing at her foolish insipid guests. The Lord Advocate[1] was there to be sure, and was pleasant enough when he could be heard. But that old ass in a lion's skin, Sir Edward Codrington,[2] had all the talk to himself, and it was all about himself. He did nothing but curse and swear and tell stories about his services, and his wrongs, and the honors paid him by foreign powers, and a certain cask of very fine Sherry which Louis Philippe had sent him as a present, and a correspondence of his with the Admiralty about Rotch's patent fid.[3] Malcolm is dead;[4] and therefore I do not hesitate to pronounce Codrington the greatest egotist now living in the world.

I write in the midst of a crowd. A debate on slavery is going on in the Commons, – a debate on Portugal in the Lords. The door is slamming behind me every moment, and people are constantly going out and in. Here comes Vernon Smith. "Well, Vernon, what are they doing." "Gladstone[5] has just made a very good speech and Howick is answering him." "Aye, but in the House of Lords?" "Brougham is firing into them." "Is there a chance of our being beaten in the Lords?" "They will beat us by twenty, they say." "Well, I do not think it matters much." "No – nobody out of the House of Lords cares either for Don Pedro or for Don Miguel."[6]

There is a conversation between two official men in the library of the House of Commons on the night of the 3d of June 1833 reported word for word. To the historian three centuries hence this letter will be invaluable. To you, ungrateful as you are, it will seem worthless. Never

---

[1] Jeffrey.

[2] Codrington (1770–1851: *DNB*), admiral; he commanded at Navarino and was afterwards recalled without explanation; Whig M.P., 1832–9.

[3] B. Rotch, of Furnival's Inn, was granted a patent on 29 April 1824 for 'an improved fidd for the upper masts of ships, and other vessels' (*Annual Register*, 1824, 271*). A fid is 'a square bar of wood or iron, with a shoulder at one end, used to support the weight of the topmast and also the topgallant mast' (*OED*).

[4] Sir John Malcolm died on 30 May.

[5] William Ewart Gladstone (1809–98: *DNB*), was in 1833 the newly-elected member for Newark; this was his maiden speech.

[6] See 6 June 1833.

mind: you are welcome to it just the same. So give my love to Margaret and Edward, and take shower baths, and milk the cows, and become quite healthy and strong, and love me, and farewell.

Ever yours dearest
T B M

TO HANNAH MACAULAY, 6 JUNE 1833

MS: Trinity College. *Address:* Miss Macaulay / E Cropper's Esq / Dingle Bank / Liverpool. *Frank:* London June seven 1833 / T B Macaulay. *Partly published:* Trevelyan, I, 297–8.

London June 6. 1833

My darling,

The House is sitting. Peel is just down. Lord Palmerston is speaking. The heat is tremendous, – the crowd stifling: so here I am in the smoking room – three filthy repealers making chimneys of their mouths under my very nose – writing to Nancy in the midst of stench and noise. I dare say my letter will bear to my Anna the exquisite scent of O'Connor's Havannah. Did you find out the rhyme?

Well but what news? – Public news you have. You know that the Lords have been foolish enough to pass a vote implying censure on the Ministers. The ministers do not seem inclined to take it of them. The King has snubbed their Lordships properly: and in about an hour as I guess (for it is near eleven,) we shall have come to a resolution in direct opposition to that agreed to by the Upper House.[1] Nobody seems to care one straw for what the Peers say about any public matter. A resolution of the Court of Common Council or of a meeting at Freemason's Hall has often made a greater sensation than this declaration of a branch of the legislature against the Executive Government. The institution of the peerage is evidently dying a natural death.

One of their Lordships has been taken away from the evil to come – and indeed he was one of whom their House was not worthy – poor Lord King.[2] Bless my soul! here are three more fellows with cigars. I shall smell like a tobacconist's foreman when I go out of this dusky atmosphere. That interruption has spoiled the funeral oration in which I was just about to celebrate my poor friend Lord King.

I dined yesterday – where and on what and for what I am ashamed to tell you. Such base scandalous gluttony and extravagance I will not commit to writing. I blush when I think of it. When we meet I will breathe my low confession in your ear; and receive absolution.

[1] On 3 June the Lords passed by a majority of six Wellington's resolution calling for English neutrality in the conflict between Don Miguel and Don Pedro of Portugal; the Commons responded by passing a resolution of confidence in government policy by a majority of 263.
[2] He died on 4 June.

You however are not wholly guiltless in this matter. My nameless offence was partly occasioned by Napier. And I have a very strong reason for wishing to keep Napier in good humour. He has promised to be at Edinburgh when I take a certain damsel thither, – to look out for very nice lodgings for us in Queen Street, to shew us every thing and every body, and to see us as far as Dunkeld on our way northward, if we do go northward. In general I abhor friends. But at Edinburgh we must see the people as well as the walls and windows; and Napier will be a capital guide.

I dine to morrow with the Duchess of Kent[1] and the Princess Victoria at Kensington Palace. – So I shall have something to tell you when I write next. What sad stuff my letters are! Kindest love to Margaret and Edward. London is swarming with quakers – there they are like troops of the shining ones, as Charles Lamb would say.[2] As the poet says

> "Come hither, my little foot page,
> And tell the truth to me –
> Look out into Bishopsgate Street
> And say what dost thou see."

> "Behold, Sir Knight, a cab
> With a brace of Quakers comes
> The wife in a bonnet of drab
> The husband a twirling his thumbs."

> "Come hither my little foot page
> I charge thee come hither to me
> Look forth into Grace Church Street
> And tell me what thou dost see."

> "I see a public friend, Sir Knight,
> Repeating an oration
> Which is to be given him half an hour hence
> By sudden inspiration."

Don't shew these atrocious lampoons to Edward, or he will perhaps slay me as he slew Canning's voter long ago.

Good bye my darling
T B M

[1] Victoria Mary Louisa, Duchess of Kent (1786–1861: *DNB*), mother of Queen Victoria.
[2] In the last sentence of 'A Quaker's Meeting,' *Essays of Elia*.

TO HANNAH MACAULAY, 10 JUNE 1833

MS: Trinity College. *Address:* Miss Macaulay / E Cropper's Esq / Dingle Bank / Liverpool. *Frank:* London June eleven 1833 / T B Macaulay. *Extract published:* Trevelyan, II, 193n.

London June 10. 1833

My darling,

You have certainly done me about the seal – I acknowledge it. Imagine my feelings when I saw on the letter inclosed to me my own impression. I felt like Othello when the story of the handkerchief was explained away. I saw at a glance that I had been wronging celestial innocence. Oh Nancy, can you forgive me? I feel that I never can forgive my self. How pathetic! Almost as pathetic as Miss Austin's Persuasion which I have just been reading. A charming novel. And Northanger Abbey too is excellent. A little less pure in manner than her later works. Yet much of the pleasantry on the romances of the Udolpho school is worthy of Addison himself, – and, I own, I think it a better, because a less unnatural satire on the appetite of young ladies for novel-reading than the Female Quixote[1] or Barrett's Heroine.[2] The publisher of the last volume of poor Miss Austin has succeeded in procuring two pictures decidedly worse than the worst that I ever saw before.[3] Get a sight of the Book next time you go to a circulating library at Liverpool; and tell me whether Henry Tilney be not the most offensive Varmint man that ever you saw. The artist must have read the book carelessly and must have confounded the adorable young parson with John Thorp. As to Miss Anne, sitting under a hedge, her appearance at once vindicates all Captain Wentworth's doubts as to her identity with the pretty girl whom he had known, and renders the final triumph of his constancy so admirable as to be almost incredible.

I dined at Holland House yesterday.

Dramatis Personæ

Men

| The Lord Holland / | a fine old gentleman very gouty and good-natured. |
| The Earl Grey / | Prime Minister, a proud, and majestic, yet polite and affable person. |

---

[1] Charlotte Ramsay Lennox, *The Female Quixote*, 1752.

[2] Eaton Stannard Barrett, *The Heroine, or Adventures of a Fair Romance Reader*, 1814. TBM writes on 22 May 1849 that he 'bought Barrett's Heroine. Trash – but Hannah wanted to see it. How tastes change. Once I thought it admirable' (Journal, II, 117).

[3] TBM is describing the frontispiece and the title-page vignette of *Northanger Abbey and Persuasion*, published on 1 June in the series of Bentley's Standard Novels. Both pictures were engraved by William Greatbach after Pickering.

The Revd. Sydney Smith / A holy and venerable Ecclesiastic, director of the consciences of the above named Lords.

Edward Ellice Esq M P / Brother in law to the Earl Grey, – a great jobber, liar, and rhodomontader.

Lord Russell / A meek God-fearing young gentleman.

John Allen Esq / Atheist in ordinary to the household of My Lady Holland.

T B Macaulay Esq M P / A virtuous and most accomplished man – the flower of the party.

Women

Lady Holland / A great lady – fanciful, hysterical, and hypochondriacal, ill-natured and good natured, sceptical and superstitious, afraid of ghosts and not of God, – would not for the world begin a journey on a Friday morning, and thought nothing of running away from her husband.

Lady Dover[1] / A charming woman, like all the Howards of Carlisle.

Lady Grey / A pattern wife and mother – has outlived her beauty if she ever had any.

Servants, Humble companions, My Lady's Page, Mr. Macaulay's Cabdriver etc. etc. etc.

I have occupied so much paper with the Dramatis Personæ that it will be impossible for me to give you the dialogue. Some parts of it however deserve to be remembered. But I may perhaps tell them to you when we meet. Lord Grey was very amusing. It was curious to see how he winced and kicked when Ellice tried to lead him by the nose.

As to your questions about the duties – I shall preserve the strict taciturnity which becomes a gentleman in office. A very few days will make all clear.

[Our?][2] India Bill comes on next Thursday. Till then I shall be very busy. So you must not be surprised if you should not hear from me till Sunday next. Kindest love to Margaret and Edward. Have you read the Parson's Daughter?[3] – I have. And very poor stuff it is.

> Ever yours, my own darling,
>
> T B M

---

[1] Georgiana (1804–60), second daughter of the sixth Earl of Carlisle, married George Agar-Ellis, afterwards first Baron Dover, in 1822. Greville calls her 'mild, gentle, and amiable' (*Memoirs*, II, 390).   [2] Paper torn away with seal.

[3] Theodore Hook, *The Parson's Daughter*, 3 vols., published on 2 May.

TO HANNAH MACAULAY, 14 JUNE 1833

MS: Trinity College. *Address:* Miss Macaulay / E Cropper's Esq / Dingle Bank / Liverpool. *Frank:* London June fourteen 1833 / T B Macaulay. *Mostly published:* Trevelyan, I, 298–300.

London June 14. 1833

My darling,

I do not know what Fanny may have told you. I may have grumbled, for aught I know, at not having more letters and longer letters from you: but as to being angry, you ought to know by this time what sort of anger mine is when you are its object. The more you write to me, dearest, the better I shall be pleased. But if you do not write I shall not be angry. We ought to know each other too well and to love each other too dearly to trouble ourselves about the ceremonies of correspondence.

You have seen the papers, I dare say, and you will perceive that I did not speak yesterday night.[1] The House was thin. The debate was languid. Grant's speech had done our work sufficiently for one night: and both he and Lord Althorp advised me to reserve myself for the second reading.

What have I to tell you. I will look at my engagement Book. Nancy will like to know where I am to dine.

Friday	June 14	Lord Grey
Saturday	June 15	Mr. Boddington
Sunday	June 16	Mr. S Rice
Saturday	June 22	Sir R Inglis
Thursday	June 27	The Earl of Ripon[2]
Saturday	June 29	Lord Morpeth.

Read, and envy, and pine, and die. What are Obadiah Smug, and Ebenezer Prim, and Hilkiah Pure, to such society as this. And yet I would give a large slice of my quarter's salary which is now nearly due to be at the Dingle. I am sick of Lords with no brains in their heads, and Ladies with paint and plaister on their cheeks, and politics and politicians, and that reeking furnace of a house. As the poet says

Oh rather would I see this day
My little Nancy well and merry
Than the blue ribband of Lord Grey
Or the blue stockings of Miss Berry.[3]

---

[1] Charles Grant moved the resolutions embodying the government plan for the East India Company's charter renewal on 13 June.

[2] Lord Goderich had been created Earl of Ripon on 13 April.

[3] Mary Berry (1763–1852: *DNB*), with her sister Agnes (1764–1852), presided over a *salon* which was a center for the best London society for more than half a century.

I hope you are well, dearest. – Margaret tells us that you are better, – and better. I want to hear that you are well. At all events our tour[1] will set you up, I am sure.

I hope for the sake of our tour that we shall keep our places. But I firmly believe that, before many days have passed, a desperate attempt will be made in the house of Lords to turn us out. If we stand the shock we shall be stronger than ever. I am not without anxiety as to the result. Yet I believe that Lord Grey understands the position in which he is placed, and, as for the King, he will not forget his last blunder,[2] I will answer for it, even if he should live to the age of his father.

But why plague ourselves about Miss Mary* Ticks when we have so much pleasanter things to talk about. The Parson's Daughter. Don't you like the Parson's Daughter? – What a sad wretch Harbottle was to make poor Hervey break his neck. And Lady Frances – what a sad worldly woman! But Mrs. Harbottle! Dear suffering angel! And Emma Lovel – all excellence! Dr. MacGopus you doubtless like; but you probably do not admire the Duchess and Lady Catharine.[3] There is a nice regular coze over a novel for you. But if you will have my opinion I think it Theodore Hook's worst performance – far inferior to the Surgeon's daughter[4] – a set of fools making themselves miserable by their own nonsensical fancies and suspicions. Let me hear your opinion; for I will be sworn that

> "In spite of all the serious world
> Of all the thumbs that ever twirled
> Of every broad-brim-shaded brow
> Of every tongue that e'er said "Thou"
> Of every Saint that e'er made shift
> To gather home to his own gift
> You still read books in marble covers
> About smart girls and dapper lovers."

There is beautiful extempore poetry for you. Really my facility approaches inspiration. But what folly I have been scrawling. I must go to work.

* Polly Ticks. Ah! ha! How witty [TBM's note].

[1] To Scotland: see 26 August.
[2] 'This "last blunder" was the refusal of the King to stand by his Ministers in May 1832. Macaulay proved a bad prophet; for, after an interval of only three years, William the Fourth repeated his blunder in an aggravated form' (Trevelyan, I, 299n).
[3] The true love of Captain George Sheringham, son of Lady Frances, for Emma Lovell, the parson's daughter, at last triumphs over all obstacles, with the help of a legacy from Mrs Harbottle.
[4] TBM means Hook's *Maxwell*, 3 vols., 1830, a story of the surgeon Maxwell, his son, and his daughter Kate; it was the novel of Hook's immediately preceding *The Parson's Daughter*.

> I cannot all day
> Be neglecting Madras
> And slighting Bombay
> For the sake of a lass.

So I must stop. Kindest love to Edward and the woman that owns him, as the Irish say in St Giles's.

Ever yours dearest
T B M.

TO HANNAH MACAULAY, 17 JUNE 1833

MS: Trinity College. *Address:* Miss Macaulay / E Cropper's Esq / Dingle Bank / Liverpool. *Frank:* London June eighteen 1833 / T B Macaulay. *Mostly published:* Trevelyan, 1, 300–3.

London June 17. 1833

Dearest Nancy,

All is still anxiety here. Whether the House of Lords will throw out the Irish Church Bill, – whether the King will consent to create new Peers, – whether the Tories will venture to form a ministry, – are matters about which we are all in complete doubt.[1] If the ministry should really be changed the Parliament will, I feel quite sure, be dissolved. Whether I shall have a seat in the next Parliament I neither know nor care. I shall regret nothing for myself but the loss of our Scotch tour. For the public I shall, if this Parliament is dissolved, entertain scarcely any hopes. I see nothing before us but a frantic conflict between extreme opinions, – a short period of oppression, then a convulsive reaction, and then a tremendous crash of the funds, the Church, the peerage, and the Throne. It is enough to make the most strenuous royalist lean a little to republicanism to think that the whole question between safety and general destruction may probably, at this most fearful conjuncture, depend on a single man whom the accident of his birth has placed in a situation to which certainly his own virtues or abilities would never have raised him.

The question must come to a decision, I think, within the fortnight. In the meantime the funds are going down. The newspapers are storming, – and the faces of men on both sides are growing day by day more gloomy and anxious. Even during the most violent part of the contest for the reform-bill I do not remember to have seen so much agitation in the political circles. I have some odd anecdotes for you which I will tell you when we meet.

[1] The Irish Church Bill had passed its second reading on 6 May and was now in committee. Its key provision, appropriating part of Church revenues to 'state purposes,' threatened to provoke revolt in the House of Lords and was for that reason withdrawn before the third reading in the Commons.

If the parliament should be dissolved the West Indian and East Indian Bills are of course dropped. What is to become of the slaves? What is to become of the Tea-trade? Will the negroes, after receiving the resolutions of the House of Commons promising them liberty, submit to the cart-whip? Will our merchants consent to have the Trade with China, which has just been offered to them, snatched away? The Bank Charter[1] too is suspended. But that is comparatively a trifle.

Smoke Presto writing politics to little M D.[2] After all what is it to me who is in or out, and whether those fools of Lords are resolved to perish and drag the King to perish with them in the ruin which they have themselves made? I begin to wonder what the fascination is which attracts men who could sit over their tea and their books in their own cool quiet room to breathe bad air, hear bad speeches, lounge up and down the long gallery and doze uneasily on the green benches till three in the morning. Thank God, these luxuries are not necessary to me. My pen is sufficient for my support, and my Nancy is sufficient for my happiness. Only let me see her well and cheerful; and let offices in government and seats in parliament go to those who care for them. Indeed, indeed, dearest, if I know my own heart, there is not the very smallest affectation or dis-guise in what I am now writing. If I were to leave public life to morrow, I declare that, except for the vexation which it might give you and one or two others, the event would not be in the slightest degree painful to me. As you boast of having a greater insight into character, you know, than I allow to you, let me know how you explain this philosophical disposition of mine, and how you reconcile it with my ambitious inclinations. That is a problem for a young lady who professes knowledge of human nature.

Did I tell you – I forget – that I dined at the Duchess of Kent's and sate next that loveliest of women – of women above forty, mind – Mrs. Littleton? She is the natural daughter of Lord Wellesley; and her husband, our new Secretary for Ireland,[3] told me this evening that Lord Wellesley, who sate near us at the Duchess's, asked Mrs. Littleton after-wards who it was that was talking to her. "Mr. Macaulay." "Oh," said the Marquess, "I am very sorry I did not know it. I have a most particular desire to be acquainted with that man." Accordingly Littleton has engaged me to dine with him, in order to introduce me to the Marquess. I am particularly curious, and always was, to know him. He has made a great and splendid figure in history, and his weaknesses and vices, though they make his character less respectable, make it more interesting as a study. Such a blooming old swain I never saw, – cheeks as brilliant as his

---

[1] The debate on the renewal of the Bank of England's charter began on 31 May.

[2] Cf. Swift, *Journal to Stella*, 1 January 1710–11: 'Smoak the politicks to M D.'

[3] Littleton had been appointed Chief Secretary for Ireland on 17 May.

handsome daughter's who has the highest colour of any beauty in London, – hair combed with exquisite nicety, – a waistcoat of driven snow, and a star and garter put on with rare skill.

To day we took up our resolutions about India to the House of Lords. The two houses had a conference on the subject in an old Gothic room called the painted chamber. The painting consists in an old mildewed daub of a woman in the niche of one of the windows. The Lords sate in little cocked hats along a table; and we stood uncovered on the other side, and delivered in our resolutions. I thought that before long it may be our turn to sit and theirs to stand. But I must stop. I write from the smoking room of the House of Commons. Halcomb is speaking, and every soul has gone out in order to avoid hearing him. I have not read Godolphin;[1] and I do not hear such an account of it as is likely to tempt me to read it. Kindest love to Margaret and Edward.

Ever yours my love
T B M

TO HANNAH MACAULAY, 21 JUNE 1833

MS: Trinity College. *Address:* Miss Macaulay / E Cropper's Esq / Dingle Bank / Liverpool. *Frank:* London June twenty one / 1833/ T B Macaulay. *Partly published:* Trevelyan, I, 303–4.

London June 21. 1833

Dearest Nancy,

I cannot tell you how delighted I was to learn from Fanny this morning that Margaret pronounces you to be as well as she could wish you to be. Only continue so, my dear, dear, love: – and all the changes of public life will be as indifferent to me as to Horatio. If I am only spared the misery of seeing my Nancy suffer, I shall be found, I hope, to be not undeserving of the character which Hamlet gives to his friend

> " A man that fortune's buffets and rewards
> Hast ta'en, with equal thanks."[2]

Whether we are to have buffets or rewards is known only to Heaven and to the Lords. Smoke the rhyme, little M D. I think that their Lordships are rather cowed. Indeed if they venture on the course on which they lately seemed bent I would not give sixpence for a coronet or a penny for a mitre.

As to the sugar duties your good abolitionists at Liverpool cannot eat their cake and have it too.[3] If the planters are to be compensated some

---

[1] Bulwer's *Godolphin*, 3 vols., was published anonymously in late April.

[2] *Hamlet*, III, ii, 72–3.

[3] The government proposed to raise money for compensating the slave-owners by increasing the duty on West Indian sugar.

additional tax must be imposed. If it is not imposed on sugar it must be imposed on some other article. No financier has yet, as far as I am aware, discovered a mode of paying debts without money or of raising money without incommoding somebody or other.

As to your strike I have heard much about it from Lord Sandon. I told him and I tell you to be easy. The evil must cure itself. Wait a little and see whether my prophecy be not accomplished.

I shall not read the Repealers;[1] and I think it very impudent in you to make such a request. Have I nothing to do but to be your novel-taster? It is rather your duty to be mine. What else have you to do? Nor do I mean to read, – at least unless I hear a better account of it, – the directions given to a large fish to depart.* I have read only one novel within the last week, and a most precious one it was – the Invisible Gentleman.[2] Have you ever read it? But I need not ask. No doubt it has formed part of your Sunday studies. A wretched trumpery imitation of Godwin's worst manner. I have sent it back to Lowe, and intend to take the taste out of my mouth by recurring to Langton Priory[3] or Stratagems Defeated.[4]

You do not answer my questions about the Parson's daughter? Is it not a trumpery performance? A knock! "Come in." That fool William Grant. The very sight of his face and tone of his voice make me sick. As Johnson said of some dunce of his time, "he helps forward the general disgrace of humanity."[5] Or as I would say in mellifluous rhyme

> "A greater fool than William Grant
> You may imagine; but I can't."

However, fool or no fool, I must attend to him. So farewell. To morrow I dine at Battersea Rise[6] – on Sunday with Ellice the Secretary at War, on Thursday next with Lord Ripon, and on Saturday week at Grillon's Hotel with Lord Morpeth. What a number of stories I shall have to tell you when we meet, which will be, as nearly as I can guess, about the 10th or 12th or August. I shall be as rich as a Jew by that time.

---

* Go dolphin. Hurrah! Hurrah! Hurrah! [TBM's note].

[1] Lady Blessington, *The Repealers*, 3 vols., published in early June.
[2] [James Dalton], *The Invisible Gentleman*, 3 vols., published in December 1832.
[3] Thus in MS. The novel is entered in the *London Catalogue 1800–1827* as *Langton Priory*, but is elsewhere always cited as *Laughton Priory*. I have found no copy of it.
[4] Gabrielli [Mrs Meeke], *Stratagems Defeated*, 4 vols., 1811.
[5] Mrs Piozzi's *Anecdotes*, in G. B. Hill, ed., *Johnsonian Miscellanies*, Oxford, 1897, 1, 294.
[6] The home of the Thornton family at the west side of Clapham Common, where Sir Robert Inglis now lived with his wards, the Thornton children.

> "Next Wednesday will be Quarter day
> And then, if I'm alive,
> Of sterling pounds I shall receive
> Three hundred seventy five.[1]
> "Already I possess in cash
>   Two hundred twenty four
> Besides what I have lent to John
>   Which makes up twenty more.
> "Also the man who editeth
>   The Yellow and the Blue
> Doth owe me ninety pounds at least
>   All for my last review.[2]
> "So if my debtors pay their debts,
>   You'll find, dear sister mine,
> That all my wealth together makes
>   Seven hundred pounds and nine.

There – that is the way to keep accounts. Don't you prefer my book keeping to any that you ever heard of. Ask Edward why he does not introduce this mode of registering mercantile transactions, and striking balances. Kindest love to him and dear, dear, Margaret.

                                                    Ever yours, my Nancy
                                                              T B M

TO HANNAH MACAULAY, 24 JUNE 1833

MS: Trinity College. *Address:* Miss Macaulay / E Cropper's Esq / Dingle Bank / Liverpool.
Frank: London June twenty five / 1833 / T B Macaulay.

                                                    London June 24. 1833
My darling,

    We are still in rather an awkward situation, though much better than it was. I think that we shall weather the storm which a few days ago I did not think. We had some very violent debating on Friday in which I took a small share:[3] and the result will, I hope, be that by sacrificing an idle and unmeaning clause in the Irish Church Bill we shall prevail on the Lords to give their assent to all its important provisions.

    I dined at Inglis's on Saturday. There I saw Henry Thornton and his destined bride.[4] Of course Fanny and Selina have fully informed you on

---

[1] The quarter of TBM's salary of £1,500 as Secretary to the Board of Control.
[2] 'Lord Mahon's *War of the Succession*.'
[3] TBM spoke in the debate on the Irish Church Bill, 21 June: *Hansard*, 3rd Series, XVIII, 1083–4.
[4] Thornton married on 31 August Harriet Dealtry (1816?–40), eldest daughter of William Dealtry, Rector of Clapham, 1813–30.

that subject. I am ashamed even to hint a doubt of the communicativeness of Lady correspondents happy in the possession of such a theme. The damsel is not very pretty, – a plump, red, butter-faced little dairymaid, and much more like her coarse aunt than her delicate mother. As to secrecy, Henry is quite a hero of an "old romance and glories in his chains."[1] Where is that? I will bet you three kisses and a pint of whiskey to be drunk on Loch Katrine that you do not guess. But be the passage where it may, it describes most justly the feeling of Henry Thornton who talks about nothing but his intention of being married, and indeed reminds me a little of the intended of Mrs. Waddell and "her situation." He intends to have the banns published according to the rubric, and to be married in the parish church with the doors wide open. A sermon is to be preached, as the prayer book directs, declaring the duties of husband and wife. The only reason which he can give for marrying the girl is that he is used to her and has known her all his life. He made her a present of some jewellery the other day, and among other things of a fine watch. The only specimen of his courtship that I have heard is what passed on this occasion. "Don't you remember Harriet that when you used to be naughty fifteen or sixteen years ago I held my watch to your ear, and made you laugh at its ticking." – And yet why should I ridicule his feelings when the dearest thing to me on the face of the earth is a gipsey whom I have fondled when she was less than a year old!

Sir Robert's party went off tolerably and no more. My lady,[2] who used to be very agreable in a small party, does not preside over a large dinner table like the ladies whom I have lately been used to see. –

Yesterday I dined with Edward Ellice, the Secretary at War, and the greatest liar and jobber that ever I knew in my life. But, whatever his political morality may be, he gave me a most glorious dinner. Indeed his dinner was better than his company. For, lest he should himself be the greatest rogue present, he had invited Tom Gisborne.[3] Ellice told me, as he tells me whenever we meet, many very curious anecdotes, all of which may be described in the pithy American phrase, "Important if true."

We shall be up, I hope and believe, by the 9th or 10th of August. I shall then take a holiday of two months or so, which I mean to spend at the Dingle, or in travelling with you, though I am honoured with invitations from many quarters.

So you do not put on mourning.[4] No more shall I. I have not even

[1] Jane Austen, *Mansfield Park*, ch. 36.
[2] Lady Inglis (d. 1873), called 'Milady,' is described by E. M. Forster as 'submissive, clinging, diffident' (*Marianne Thornton*, p. 74).
[3] Gisborne (1794–1852: *DNB*), son of Thomas Babington's brother-in-law, the Evangelical clergyman Thomas Gisborne, was Whig M.P. for various constituencies from 1830.
[4] Mrs Thomas Gisborne Babington died on 19 June.

written to Tom, though he wrote to me to beg my condolence on the fate of his poor suffering angel. I did not like to tell him a series of lies; and if I had told him the truth I should have said that he knew as well as I that the woman was a pest to every body connected with her, that he, I was sure, had long wished her dead, and that my only reason for not joining in the wish was that I wanted her to live in order to plague him. There is a sweet, cousinly, Christianlike, letter of condolence for you. I have not even put crape round my hat, though Fanny intreats me to proclaim by that token that I am connected with the Honourable Mrs T G Babington.

What stuff this is. But I have really nothing but political news to tell; and I write for the mere pleasure of writing to my dear little Nancy. Kindest love to Margaret and Edward.

Ever yours, darling
T B M

TO HANNAH MACAULAY, 28 JUNE 1833

MS: Trinity College.

London June 28. 1833

My darling,

I have but a moment for writing. We have been sitting in Board all day during this week, and giving the finishing touches to our Bill. Yesterday I was forced to leave Lord Ripon's table as soon as the Ladies retired and to come down to our office where I remained till twelve at night. I have therefore, you see, ample excuse, even if my letters were fewer and shorter than they are.

Lord Ripon has a delightful house – on one side a view towards the Abbey over St James's Park; – on the other, a view into the thick verdure of Marlborough Gardens. I saw his wife[1] for the first time. She is rather good looking. At the same time she appears to be, as she is, extremely susceptible and nervous. So indeed is he. You have heard, I dare say, from Fanny, who was present, how ludicrously he broke down in the House of Lords the other day.[2]

I have much to tell you – but I must stop. In a day or two I will write again. Kindest love to Meg and Edward. The picture is not yet ready. The artist begs for another sitting. But really I can hardly spare time for my meals.

Ever yours, dearest
T B M

[1] Sarah Louisa (1793–1867), daughter of the fourth Earl of Buckinghamshire.
[2] On 25 June 'Lord Goderich [i.e., Lord Ripon] brought forward the West India resolutions in the Lords. It was impossible to do it worse. He sat down several times wholly unable to continue his speech, whether from exhaustion of mind or body was not very evident' (Denis Le Marchant, Diary, in A. Aspinall, ed., *Three Early Nineteenth Century Diaries*, p. 341).

TO MACVEY NAPIER, 29 JUNE 1833

MS: British Museum. *Address:* Macvey Napier Esq / Edinburgh. *Frank:* London June twenty nine 1833 / T B Macaulay.

London June 29. 1833

Dear Napier,

I am really sorry to disappoint you. But it is absolutely out of my power to do any thing for this Number of the Review. We are working all day at the Board and all night in the House. Since I began this note I have been twice interrupted by pressing business; and I hardly know whether I shall find time to subscribe my name.

As soon as our Bill is through the House I will set to work for you with all my vigour.

Ever yours truly
T B Macaulay

TO HANNAH MACAULAY, 1 JULY 1833

MS: Trinity College. *Address:* Miss Macaulay / E Cropper's Esq / Dingle Bank / Liverpool. *Frank:* London July one 1833 / T B Macaulay.

London July 1. 1833

Dearest Nancy,

We have now finished our Bill and brought it in.[1] The second reading will not take place till next week. We shall have the Committee in the morning sittings of the House, so that the discussion will not interrupt the other government business. Every thing is at present going on well and quietly here.

Henry has written to us long and doleful accounts of his quarrels with the Governor[2] and with the Governor's creatures. He has sent to me some intelligence with which he has not thought it necessary to favour my father, – which is that within the last half year he has fought three duels.[3] By his own account he appears to have been in the right: and I love him for his spirit, and his disposition to stand by the oppressed at all hazards. At the same time three duels in half a year, in one of which at least he was the challenger, is decidedly too much of a good thing. I have written

---

[1] The first reading of the East India Company's Charter Bill was on 28 June.
[2] Lt. Colonel Alexander Findlay (d. 1851: *Boase*) was Governor of Sierra Leone until recalled in disgrace in July 1833.
[3] Henry 'led the opposition to Findlay; his family still preserve his duelling pistol. . . . Findlay left duelling to his two sons, contenting himself with pouring out in letters and despatches detailed libels on his enemies. Every trifle was included, even Macaulay's having played cricket in the street "with a parcel of dirty Black boys"' (Fyfe, *History of Sierra Leone*, p. 189). A brief and confused account of one of Henry's duels is in [Macaulay], *Memoirs of the Clan "Aulay,"* pp. 105–7.

strongly to him on the subject. Indeed by his letters to me he appeared sensible that he had been rather foolish; and he solemnly promises to keep out of such scrapes for the future. It will, I hope, be in his power to do so without difficulty; as the Governor, who was his personal enemy, and who, by all accounts, was as tyrannical and brutal a fellow as ever domineered over any society, has been recalled, and a successor of very different character has been appointed. My father does not know these circumstances; and I shall not mention them to Selina whose nervous state of mind and precise notions, as well as her peculiar affection for Henry, would make the intelligence extremely painful to her. You had better not take any notice of these transactions in any letter which you may write to Sierra Leone. My remonstrances on such a subject are likely to do more good than yours. No man will ever allow any weight to the judgment of a woman on points of this kind.

Above all keep these anecdotes from the knowledge of our friends the Quakers. What a scandal the poor fellow has brought on James Cropper's Counting-House. At all events however Henry has not yet killed a man, as one whom you wot of has done.

Àpropos of Quakers and peace – or rather of Quakers and Pease; I dined with Lord Morpeth at Grillon's on Saturday. We were a large party – all members of parliament. In the same way in which the Ladies of the Romp Club in the Spectator used once a month to demolish a prude,[1] Lord Morpeth had invited Pease to be our butt: and a precious one he was. "Did he observe strict temperance?" I fear there was a melancholy defect. He took, I suspect, too much of Mr. Grillon's excellent Champagne. For after dinner he began to preach against war with a strength of voice and a weakness of reason, a violence of gesticulation and an oddity of expression, which made us nearly die with laughing. I made up as grave a face as I could, and argued the matter with him for some time. I brought him into twenty gross contradictions. At one time he maintained that if people would only abstain from resistance God would always miraculously protect them from injury. "What proof have you of that?" "Why when William Penn went to Pensylvania, and settled among the Indians, they never did any harm to his colony, because the law of the settlement was not to resist." "Well," said I, "but we know that the very Quakers who went to Pensylvania had been driven by persecution from England, that Penn himself was twice imprisoned here and that some of the sect were treated with the utmost cruelty. How was it that providence, which watched so carefully over them on one side of the Atlantic, left them quite exposed to tyranny on the other?" Then he denied that resistance ever prospered. "Why," said I, "what do you say to the resistance of John

[1] *Spectator*, no. 217.

Knox and his presbyterian followers to Mary Queen of Scots?" "Ah," said he, "that resistance has produced its natural fruits. The Scotch have ever since been distinguished for their fierce, intolerant zeal." "Well," said I, "the Huguenots." "See there again," said this profound philosopher; "the French Protestants are the deadest and coldest Christian Church in the world. That comes of resistance." "Nay, my good Sir," I exclaimed, "surely you are blowing hot and cold. You say that in Scotland the effect of resistance is too great zeal, and that in France the effect of this same resistance is profound indifference." Not well knowing what to say he jumped up, slapped Vernon Smith on the back, clapped his hands and bawled out "Well, I won't resist. You may say what you will. I won't resist – and I won't pay tithes." Do not spread this scandal through the society. To say the truth the man is but a wet Quaker. He drank healths with shameful readiness. And he never used a single thou or thee through his whole conversation.

As to my plans, I think your scheme excellent. As soon as we rise, which, I fear will scarcely be till the middle of August, I shall go to Liverpool. If we are to go from Scotland to the Temple, it will be better to travel northward along the Eastern Coast, and to see the lakes on our way down. My scheme would be to visit Glasgow first, to make an excursion to Loch Lomond, then to go to Edinburgh, seeing Loch Katrine on the way, then to come by Melrose Abbey, Durham, York, and Lincoln to Leicestershire. I fear that it will be out of my power to go so far north as I had hoped.

Kindest love to Margaret and Edward.

Ever yours, my darling
T B M

TO HANNAH MACAULAY, 4 JULY 1833

MS: Trinity College. *Address:* Miss Macaulay / E Cropper's Esq / Dingle Bank / Liverpool. *Frank:* London July four 1833 / T B Macaulay.

London July 4. 1833

Dearest Nancy,

No end to my plagues! I am busy from morning to night with estimates and balance-sheets, preparing for the battle of next week. Gordon is a traitor in our camp; Robert Grant is a regular twaddle; and Charles, ever since he was, as you well know, crossed in love,[1] is but a languid politician – d'ailleurs le meilleur des hommes. Holt Mackenzie[2] is the only

[1] See 26 November 1832.
[2] Mackenzie (1787–1876: *Boase*), son of the novelist Henry Mackenzie, was in the service of the East India Company, 1807–31; Commissioner of the Board of Control, 1832–4.

one of our people who is up to the mark in energy and judgment, and he is not in parliament. Stuart Mackenzie – an excellent man and very sensible – is no speaker. So that a large portion of the battle will be left to me. I believe that we are safe enough. For if we know little about the matter, our opponents know far less; and on this occasion as on every other I am for shewing a bold front. " Be bold, be bold, and every where be bold," says Spenser,[1] – whom, I remember, you cannot bear. I quoted the line to Grant this morning when he looked rather dismal.

As if it was not plague enough to have to work all day at the India Board, we are to go at one o'clock to the House. The Ministers mean to fight their Irish Church Bill through in the mornings. I never was so worked in my life. But I eat and drink and sleep capitally; and never felt better. The only thing which I regret is that I have not time to write to my own darling Nancy so often or so copiously as formerly. Write to me, dearest, very soon, and tell me how you are, and all that you are doing. In six weeks at the latest, I hope and trust that we shall meet.

I must stop. And you must not be surprised, my darling, if, during the next week, my letters should be few and short. 1 have much to do; and I mean to do it well. Kindest love to Meg and Ned.

Ever yours, my dearest,

T B M

TO ZACHARY MACAULAY, 9 JULY 1833

Text: From MS in possession of Mr C. S. Menell, who furnished transcript.

London. / July 9, 1833.

My dear Father,

The West India Bill is put off for the present and the East India Bill is to have precedence. We shall not come to the question of slavery till next week.

I have told Lord Althorp that I shall both speak and vote against the apprenticeship, at least against the length of the term, and that my office is at the disposal of the government.[2] He was very kind, begged me not to resign, and said that the cabinet would consider whether they could or

---

[1] *The Faerie Queene*, III, xi, 54.

[2] This was TBM's third offer to resign over the question of the government's anti-slavery policy. He had made up his mind to support the objection of the Anti-Slavery Society and of Buxton to the apprenticeship provision of the bill, and spoke accordingly on 24 July 1833 (*Hansard*, 3rd Series, XIX, 1202–9). Trevelyan, following the recollections of one of TBM's cousins, reports him as saying on this occasion: 'I cannot go counter to my father. He has devoted his whole life to the question, and I cannot grieve him by giving way when he wishes me to stand firm' (Trevelyan, I, 306).

could not allow me to take my own course. I think it not improbable that they will. At all events my mind is immediately made up.

I should be truly glad to receive your comments on this part of the Bill before the debate.[1] As you may not have a copy I send you one.

Ever yours affectionately,

T B M.

TO HANNAH MACAULAY, 11 JULY 1833

MS: Mrs Humphry Trevelyan. *Address:* Miss Macaulay / E Cropper's Esq / Dingle Bank / Liverpool. *Frank:* London July eleven 1833 / T B Macaulay. *Mostly published:* Trevelyan, I, 310–11.

London July 11. 1833

Dearest Nancy,

I have been so completely overwhelmed with business for some days that I have not been able to find time for writing a line. Yesterday night we read the India Bill a second time. It was a Wednesday, and the reporters gave hardly any account of what passed. They always resent being forced to attend on that day, which is their holiday. I made the best speech, by general agreement, and in my own opinion, that I ever made in my life.[2] I was an hour and three quarters up. And such compliments as I had from Lord Althorp,[3] Lord Palmerston, Lord John Russell, Wynne, O'Connel, Grant, the Speaker, and twenty other people you never heard. As there is no report of the speech, I have been persuaded, rather against my will, to correct it for publication.

I will tell you one compliment that was paid me and which delighted me more than any other. An old member said to me "Sir, having heard that speech may console the young people for never having heard Mr. Burke."

The slavery bill is miserably bad. I am fully resolved not to be dragged through the mire, but to oppose, by speaking and voting, the clauses which I think objectionable. I have told Althorp this, and have again tendered my resignation. He hinted that he thought that the government would leave me at liberty to take my own line, but that he must consult his colleagues. I told him that I asked for no favour; that I knew what

[1] Zachary Macaulay had left town at the beginning of July; according to Knutsford, he left on account of illness and was thus absent 'when the great fulfilment of all his hopes and efforts arrived' (*Zachary Macaulay*, pp. 471–2). It is more likely that he was travelling on business as a Commissioner of Charities.

[2] *Hansard*, 3rd Series, XIX, 503–36.

[3] Althorp told Littleton that 'he thought it by far the finest speech he had ever heard in his parliamentary life' (Littleton's Diary, in A. Aspinall, ed., *Three Early Nineteenth Century Diaries*, p. 346).

inconvenience would result if official men were allowed to dissent from ministerial measures and yet to keep their places, and that I should not think myself in the smallest degree ill used if the cabinet accepted my resignation. This is the present posture of affairs. In the meantime the two houses are at daggers drawn. Whether the government will last to the end of the Session I neither know nor care. I am sick of boards and of the House of Commons, and pine for a few quiet days, a cool country breeze, and a little chatting and fondling with my own Nancy.

As to money matters, my love, I do intreat you to ask me for whatever you want without scruple. If we stay in place, I will try to arrange some plan for making you quite easy about your little expenses. Kindest love to Meg and Ned.

Ever yours

T B M

P S No news of the picture.

TO ZACHARY MACAULAY, 13 JULY 1833

MS: Trinity College. *Mostly published:* Knutsford, *Zachary Macaulay*, p. 471.

London July 13 – 1833

My dear Father,

I have been so completely occupied during the last three days that I have not been able to spare a single moment for writing. On Wednesday I spoke on our India Bill with more success, I think, than on any former occasion. But the house was thin, and the reporters, as usually happens on a Wednesday, would take nothing down. We are proceeding easily and speedily through the Committee.

The question of Slavery will not, I think, come on this year. The ministers fully expect to be out on Thursday;[1] and I believe that we shall have an immediate dissolution. The Lords seem resolved to throw out the Irish Church Bill. The King, I fear, will not create Peers: and the Tories trust, erroneously I am persuaded, that, by a new election, they shall obtain a manageable House of Commons. Every thing here is anxiety and confusion. / Ever, my dear Father,

Yours most affectionately

T B M

P S Selina went on Thursday to the Temple and I have been too busy to go to Bernard Street since.

---

[1] It was widely feared that the Lords would throw out the Irish Church Bill on the second reading; it passed on 19 July by a majority of fifty-nine.

TO HANNAH MACAULAY, 13 JULY 1833

MS: Trinity College.

London July 13. 1833

My darling Nancy,

We are working through the India Bill day and night. I am sorry to say, however, that it matters little what we do. The crisis has arrived at last: and I have very little hope that the ministers will be in office by this day week. If a change of administration takes place, it must, I think, be followed up by a dissolution: and whether I shall be in the next parliament or not I neither know nor care.

The Lords are out of their senses. What they want – unless they want revolution – I am at a loss to comprehend. And it seems odd that a revolution should be an agreable prospect to rich men and men of rank. But I will not plague you with forebodings of evil. Dark and sad as the aspect of things is, I keep my spirits, eat and drink as heartily, sleep as soundly, and laugh as much as ever; and, if I had but my little girl with me, should be as happy as ever I was in my life.

Lord Lansdowne sent for me to day; and we had a long talk about the aspect of political matters. He, though generally very sedate, seemed to be uneasy, and, though generally zealous for his order, owned that they were behaving most unreasonably and fatally.

But I am summoned to a Board. We are worked, as Mrs. Meeke says, to an oil. In office or out of office, in parliament or out of parliament, I will come to you on the first day on which I can come and will think myself rich enough and great enough while I keep your love, dearest dearest, Nancy [....][1]

TO HANNAH MACAULAY, 16 JULY 1833

MS: Trinity College. *Address:* Miss Macaulay / E Cropper's Esq / Dingle Bank / Liverpool. *Frank:* London July sixteen 1833 / T B Macaulay.

London July 16. 1833

Dearest Nancy,

I am very remiss as a correspondent. But in truth I never in my life found it so difficult to command a minute to my own uses. Yesterday I was at Grant's house in consultation from eleven to five, and at the House of Commons from five till one this morning. To day at noon I had to be again in the House of Commons and to remain there till three; nor

---

[1] The rest is missing; possibly TBM simply stopped here.

is this a mere idle attendance. I have to sit on the Treasury Bench the whole time, watching every word that is said, and ready to answer every objection to our India Bill.[1] I earnestly hope that to morrow we shall have finished the Committee.

As to the West Indian Bill, that is postponed till ours shall be concluded. It will not go through so quietly. But you are wrong, I am convinced, in thinking that the Government will be beaten on it. On some provisions they may be beaten. But if they stay in they will carry most of it through.

Their chance of staying in has greatly improved since I wrote last. The Lords are beginning to quail, as the crisis approaches. And the government is, I think, secure for this Session. Yet I am not altogether without anxiety. The Lords may recover their spirits, or may be shamming cowardice only in order to strike their blow with more effect. On the whole, however, I lean to the opinion that they are honestly frightened. For I am sure they have abundant reason to be frightened.

As to my self, even if the ministers stay in, it is not impossible that I may go out. Some parts of their West India Bill I cannot and will not support; and I am quite ignorant of the course which they may pursue with respect to me. I am not, however, more ignorant than careless. I have passed the whole of the last year in daily expectation of being turned out with disgrace; and, having kept up my spirits in such circumstances, I am not likely to be depressed, when the worst that can happen to me is to be turned out with honor.

And what after all does it matter. In parliament or out of parliament, in office or out of office, I have my own little Nancy. If my public life is to close, I shall have more of her society, and I am sure I shall not have less of her affection. Ambition has palled on me. The applauses of the House of Commons affect me less than those of the Union at Cambridge did eleven years ago. The only feeling which becomes stronger in my mind every day is my love for my dear sisters. How happy a law of our nature is it that our best and purest feelings should become more keen and exquisite from indulgence. But I have no time to moralize – or to send you an account of my Sunday dinner with a Jew, a Prince, four cabinet ministers, a Duke, and the Solicitor General.[2] Kindest love to Margaret and Edward.

T B M

---

[1] TBM's answers and remarks in the debates on the East India Charter Bill are reported in the *Mirror of Parliament* for 12, 15, 17, 19, 22 and 26 July and 24 August; almost none of this is in *Hansard*.

[2] John Campbell (1779–1861: *DNB*), afterwards first Baron Campbell, was Solicitor-General, 1832–4. Under the Whigs he was successively Attorney-General, Irish Chancellor, Chancellor of the Duchy of Lancaster, Lord Chief Justice, and Lord Chancellor. His *Lives of the Lord Chancellors*, 1845–69, is a standard work. After Campbell had been raised to the peerage Brougham said that 'Edinburgh is now

TO MRS EDWARD CROPPER, 17 JULY 1833

MS: Morgan Library. *Address:* Mrs. E Cropper / Dingle Bank / Liverpool. *Frank:* London July seventeen 1833 / T B Macaulay.

[London] Wednesday July 17. 1833

Dearest Margaret,

I steal a single moment from business to thank you for your affectionate letter, and to tell you how much I love you and how often I think of you. I am sitting in George Street, in Charles Grant's back drawing room with him, his brother Robert, Holt Mackenzie, Stewart Mackenzie, Pennington[1] the famous accountant, Coulson[2] our lawyer, and that beast Robert Gordon. We pass our mornings here in deliberating over our bill, and our nights in fighting it through the Committee. Our work is very quietly done, and the reporters take no notice of what is said on either side. Our discussions here are quite as warm, and our meetings very nearly as numerous as in the House. I can hardly comprehend the strange indifference of all classes of people, members of parliament, reporters, and the public to Indian politics. I do not however complain of it. It makes our labours much easier and has enabled us to effect some most valuable improvements with little or no opposition. The care with which our bill has been framed has rendered its passage smoother than it would otherwise have been. We have debated it among ourselves so warmly that our opponents can hardly raise any objection which has not been already considered by us.

I am sitting at a round table loaded with papers and red boxes and parcels tied up with red tape. Gordon is storming and talking nonsense, Holt Mackenzie demonstrating in his calm, clear manner, C Grant dosing, R Grant prosing, and I writing to my dear little sister.

As to politics their Lordships have, I believe, been fairly frightened. And I rather think that the Government is safe for the short remainder of the present Session. As to Stanley's Slavery Bill I dislike it more and more. I hardly know whether it will be possible for the ministers, in the present state of public business, to proceed further with that Bill during this year. The best thing which they can do is to withdraw it and frame another on different principles against next February.

celebrated for having given us the two greatest bores that have ever yet been known in London, for Jack Campbell in the House of Lords is just what Tom Macaulay is in private society' (*DNB*). Campbell, whose *Lives of the Lord Chancellors* was said to have added a new terror to death, did not outlive Brougham but wrote his life anyway and did not spare him.

[1] James Pennington (1777–1862: *DNB*) had been appointed in 1831 to investigate the accounts of the East India Company; he was regularly consulted by government on financial matters.

[2] Walter Coulson (1794?–1860: *DNB*), a protégé of Bentham, a friend of James Mill, and an associate of Brougham in the Society for the Diffusion of Useful Knowledge.

My picture is engraved[1] and, I think, very well engraved. It is about to be published. Those who have seen it think it very like. A few touches are still to be given to it; but I am assured that I shall have the picture in a week or two. My face will soon be every where. Poor Haydon[2] has been employed by Lord Grey to take portraits of the chief Whigs. He has already produced capital sketches of Stanley and Lord Melbourne. On Saturday he is to take me;[3] so that I shall appear in all the shop-windows very speedily.

I am pining for country-air, early hours, cool rooms, and, more than all, the society of my dear sisters. Within a month, I hope, this agitating and disastrous Session will come to a close; and, as soon as the King has prorogued us, I shall set off for the Dingle.

I have received a paper from Edward which, at present, I fear I shall not have time to read. Give him my kindest love – and love also to Nancy.

Ever, dearest, yours most affectionately

T B M

TO HANNAH MACAULAY, 19 JULY 1833

MS: Trinity College. *Address:* Miss Macaulay / E Cropper's Esq / Dingle Bank / Liverpool. *Frank:* London July nineteen 1833 / T B Macaulay. *Partly published:* Trevelyan, I, 311–12; 313.

London July 19. 1833

Dearest Nancy,

I snatch a few minutes to write a single line to you. We went into Committee on our Bill at 12 this morning, sate till three, and are just set at liberty for two hours. At five we recommence and shall be at work till midnight. In the interval between two and five I have to dispatch the current business of the office, which, at present, is fortunately not heavy, – to eat my dinner – which I shall do at Grant's, – and to write a short scrawl to my own dear little Nancy.

My work, though laborious, has been highly satisfactory. No bill, I believe, of such importance, – certainly no important bill in my time, –

---

[1] The engraving of the Reynolds portrait was published on 24 July.

[2] Benjamin Robert Haydon (1786–1846: *DNB*), historical painter and portraitist; 'poor' because he had long been harassed by debt and by the disappointment of his restless ambition. His painting of the Reform Banquet of 11 July 1832 was finished in 1834; it is now at Howick. The portrait sketches in chalk that Haydon made for his painting, including his sketch of TBM, are now in the possession of the Earl Spencer at Althorp.

[3] Haydon's diary for 21 July reports that 'On Saturday Macauley sat, and I never talked so powerfully. Macauley was excited & turned round and looked and well he might, for I was roused beyond example. Macauley is a clever fellow' (Willard Bissell Pope, ed., *The Diary of Benjamin Robert Haydon*, Cambridge, Mass., IV [1963], 117).

has been received with such general approbation. The very cause of the negligence of the reporters and of the thinness of the House is that we have framed our measure so carefully as to give little occasion for debate. Littleton, Denison, and many other members, assure me that they never remember to have seen a Bill better drawn or better conducted; and the contrast which it presents to the careless legislation of the other departments of government – particularly to the legislation with which Stanley has had any thing to do – is the subject of general remark.

On Monday night, I hope, my work will be over. Our Bill will have been discussed, I trust, for the last time in the House of Commons; – and, in all probability, I shall within forty eight hours after that time, be out of office. I am fully determined not to give way about the West India Bill; – and I can hardly expect – I am sure I do not wish – that the ministers should suffer me to keep my place and oppose their measure.

I had a good deal to tell you – not of much importance but mere gossip. Time flies however. The line which I meant to scrawl has expanded into a sheet. And Grant's dinner will be waiting. He keeps open house for us during this fight. His brother, Stewart Mackenzie, Holt Mackenzie, and I dine with him daily at four.

Farewell, dear, dear, Nancy. Give my kindest love to Margaret and Edward.

Ever yours
T B M

TO ZACHARY MACAULAY, 22 JULY 1833

MS: Trinity College. *Partly Published:* Trevelyan, I, 307.

London July 22. 1833

My dear Father,

I know nothing about the newspapers. Charles should have mentioned to me that he had sent them to my chambers. They must have been burned or swept away with other papers.

We are still very anxious here. The Lords, though they have passed the Church Bill through its first stage, will very probably mutilate it in Committee. It will then be for the Ministers to decide whether they can with honor keep their places. I believe that they will resign if any material alteration should be made: and then every thing is confusion.

These circumstances render it very difficult for me to shape my course aright with respect to the West India Bill, the second reading of which stands for this evening. I am fully resolved to oppose several of the clauses. But to declare my intention publicly, at a moment when the government is in danger, would have the appearance of ratting. I must be guided by circumstances. But my present intention is to say nothing on the second reading. By the time that we get into Committee the crisis will, I hope, be over. The fate of the Church Bill will be decided one way or the other; and I shall be able to take my own course on the slavery question without exposing my self to the charge of deserting my friends in a moment of peril.

Your old servant John Hudson has been here in great distress. I told him that I could not give him a character, and that you were out of London, but that I would mention his name to you. I remember his face; but what sort of servant he was I have utterly [. . . .][1]

to Hannah Macaulay, 22 July 1833

MS: Trinity College. *Address:* Miss Macaulay / Dingle Bank / Liverpool. *Frank:* London July twenty two / 1833 / T B Macaulay. *Extract published:* Trevelyan, I, 312.

London July 22. 1833

My darling,

Things are still as dark as ever. The Lords have read the Church Bill a second time. But we fear that they will mutilate it in the Committee, and that the ministers will be forced to resign before the end of his week. I am placed in a situation of peculiar embarrassment. The discussions on the West India Bill commence to day. I do not like to oppose the government at such a moment – both from fear of increasing their difficulties, and still more from fear that I may be suspected of ratting from them when their places are insecure. I have, however, fully made up my mind to vote and speak against some parts of the Bill. I shall do nothing however hastily. I shall defer taking part in the discussion as long as I can. And I hope that, before it becomes absolutely necessary for me to take part in it, the fate of the Irish Church Bill will be decided one way or the other. Which way it will be settled I do not know, and, in truth, do not very much care. I am much more desirous to come to an end of this interminable session and to see my dear girls again than to stay either in office or in parliament. The Tories are quite welcome to take every thing, if they will only leave me my pen and my books, a warm fire side, and my Nancy chattering beside it. This sort of philosophy, an odd kind of cross between Stoicism and Epicureanism, I have learned where most people unlearn all their philosophy, in crowded senates and fine drawing-rooms. I will say

---

[1] The rest is missing.

for myself that I am the only *parvenu* I ever heard of, who, after being courted into splendid circles, and after having succeeded beyond expectation in political life, acquired in a few months a profound contempt for rank, fashion, power, popularity, and money, – for all pleasures in short but those which arise from the exercise of the intellect and of the affections.

I have no dinner parties to tell you of. Lord Robert Grosvenor[1] and Lady Holland invited me for Saturday. Lord Palmerston and Strutt the Member for Derby invited me for yesterday. I was so tired that I refused all four, and had two quiet evenings over my tea and my books; – the first that I have had for a month.

I must stop here, my darling. Kindest love to Meg and Edward.

Ever yours, my love

T B M

TO HANNAH MACAULAY, 24 JULY 1833

MS: Trinity College. *Partly published:* Trevelyan, I, 313–14.

London July 24. 1833

My darling,

You will have seen by the papers that the West India debate on Monday went off very quietly in little more than an hour. To night we expect the great struggle, and I fear that, much against my inclination, I must bear a part in it. My resignation is in Lord Althorp's hands. He assures me that he will do his utmost to obtain for me liberty to act as I like on this question. But Lord Grey and Stanley are to be consulted; and I think it very improbable that they will consent to allow me so extraordinary a privilege. I know that if I were minister I would not allow such a privilege to any man in office; and so I told Lord Althorp. He answered in the kindest and most flattering manner, told me that in office I had surpassed their expectations, and that, much as they wished to bring me in last year, they wished much more to keep me in now. I told him in reply that the matter was one for the ministers to settle purely with a view to their own interest, – that I asked for no indulgence, – that I could make no terms, – and that what I would not do to serve them I certainly would not do to keep my place. Thus the matter stands. It will probably be finally settled within a few hours.

This detestable Session goes on lengthening and lengthening like a human hair in one's mouth – (do you know that delicious sensation?). Last month we expected to have been up before the middle of August.

---

[1] Lord Robert Grosvenor (1801–93: *DNB*), afterwards first Baron Ebury; third son of the Marquess of Westminster; Whig M.P. for Chester, 1826–47; for Middlesex, 1847–57.

Now we should be glad to be quite certain of being in the country by the first of September. One comfort I shall have in being turned out. I will not stay a day in London after the West India Bill is through the Committee, which I hope it will be before the end of next week.

My picture was brought to Gray's Inn to day. I am of course no judge of the likeness. But it seems to me to be a very fair painting. I do not know how to send it at present. Unless some good mode of conveyance should offer, it must stay here till the end of our Session, when you will have picture and original together.

The new Edinburgh Review is not much amiss. The best article, I think, is that on Mrs. Austin's Goethe.[1] It is written by some clever fellow. I shall write and ask Napier who he is. I do not recognize the hand of any old contributor. The first article – on the state of the Drama – is by Lister the author of Granby.[2] The article on Wright's[3] Translation of Dante is by Empson. I quite agree with the publishers, the editor, and the reading public generally, that the Number would have been much the better for an article of thirty or forty pages from the pen of a gentleman who shall be nameless.

Charles has been ill; but is getting well again. I scarcely ever see him, or indeed any body but clerks and members of parliament.

But I must have done. Give my kindest love to Margaret and Edward. If I have any news for you to morrow, I will write again.

Ever yours, my dearest,

T B M

TO HANNAH MACAULAY, 25 JULY 1833

MS: Trinity College. *Address:* Miss Macaulay / E Cropper's Esq / Dingle Bank / Liverpool. *Frank:* London July twenty five 1833 / T B Macaulay. *Mostly published:* Trevelyan, I, 314–15.

London July 25. 1833

My darling,

The plot is thickening. Yesterday Buxton moved an instruction to the Committee on the slavery Bill which the Government opposed and which

---

[1] The review of Sarah Austin's *Characteristics of Goethe*, *ER*, LVII (July 1833), 371–403, was by Herman Merivale (1806–74: *DNB*), then a fellow of Balliol and a barrister; succeeded Sir James Stephen at the Colonial Office, 1848; made permanent Under-Secretary for India, 1859. Merivale contributed over seventy articles to the *ER* between 1832 and 1874.

[2] Thomas Lister, 'Mr Sheridan Knowles's *Wife of Mantua* – State and Prospects of the Drama,' *ER*, LVII, 281–312.

[3] The first volume of Ichabod Charles Wright's translation of Dante (1833–40), dedicated to Brougham, was enthusiastically reviewed by Empson, *ER*, LVII, 412–24.

I supported.[1] It was extremely painful to me to speak against all my political friends, so painful that at times I could hardly go on.[2] I treated them as mildly as I could; and they all tell me that I performed my difficult task well. We divided at two this morning and were 151 to 158. The ministers found that, if they persisted, they would infallibly be beaten. Accordingly they came down to the House at twelve this day and agreed to reduce the apprenticeship to seven years for the agricultural labourers and to five years for the skilled labourers. What other people may do I cannot tell. But I am inclined to be satisfied with this concession; particularly as I believe that, if we press the thing further, they will resign, and we shall have no bill at all, – but instead of it a Tory ministry and a dissolution. Some people flatter me with the assurance that our large minority and the consequent change in the Bill have been owing to me. If this be so I have done one useful act at least in my life.

I shall now certainly remain in office; and if, as I expect, the Irish Church Bill passes the Lords, I may consider myself as safe till the next Session when Heaven knows what may happen.

It is still quite uncertain when we may rise. I pine for rest, air, and my sisters more than I can express. I see nothing but politicians, and talk about nothing but politics. My heart is growing as hard as a brick and my brain as dry as a sea-biscuit. It will take a week of laughing and talking and fondling with you to make me what I was when you left London.

I have not read Village Belles.[3] Tell me, as soon as you can get it, whether it is worth reading. As John Thorpe says – "Novels – Oh Lord! I never read novels. I have something else to do."[4]

Kindest love to Margaret and Edward. I am going to order a box for the picture, which is thought very like.

Farewell, dearest, dearest Nancy

T B M

[1] *Hansard*, 3rd Series, xix, 1202–9. Buxton's motion was to reduce the proposed twelve-year apprenticeship to the shortest possible time.
[2] Greville says that TBM's speech 'fell very flat' but allows that it influenced the vote (*Memoirs*, ii, 401).
[3] Anne Manning, *Village Belles*, 3 vols., published on 15 July.
[4] Jane Austen, *Northanger Abbey*, ch. 7.

TO ZACHARY MACAULAY, 27 JULY 1833

MS: Mrs Humphry Trevelyan. *Address:* Z Macaulay Esq / Bangor. *Frank:* London July twenty seven / 1833 / T B Macaulay. *Mostly published:* Trevelyan, I, 309–10.

London July 27. 1833

My dear Father,

The papers will have told you all that has happened as far as it is known to the public. The secret history you will have heard from Buxton. As to myself Lord Althorp told me yesterday night that the Cabinet had determined not to accept my resignation. I have therefore the singular good luck of having saved both my honor and my place, and of having given no just ground of offence either to the abolitionists or to my party-friends. I have more reason than ever to say that honesty is the best policy.

Yesterday we read our India Bill the third time. The Lords have pecked at trifling parts of the Church Bill, but are now quiet; and in three weeks, I hope, the Session will be over.

Ever yours affectionately

T B M

TO HANNAH MACAULAY, 27 JULY 1833

MS: Trinity College. *Address:* Miss Macaulay / E Cropper's Esq / Dingle Bank / Liverpool. *Frank:* London July twenty seven / 1833 / T B Macaulay. *Mostly published:* Trevelyan, I, 315–16.

London July 27. 1833

My darling,

Here I am safe and well at the end of one of the most stormy weeks that the oldest man remembers in parliamentary affairs. I have resigned my office, and my resignation has been refused. I have spoken and voted against the ministry under which I hold my place. The ministry has been so hard run in the Commons as to be forced to modify its plan, and has received a defeat in the Lords[1] – a slight one to be sure and on a slight matter – yet such that I and many others fully believed twenty four hours ago that they would have resigned.[2] In fact some of the cabinet – Grant, among the rest, to my certain knowledge, were for resigning. At last Saturday has arrived. The ministry is as strong as ever. I am as good friends with the ministers as ever. The East India Bill is carried through our House. The West India Bill is so far modified that, I believe, it will

[1] The government was defeated on an amendment to the Irish Church Bill, 25 July.
[2] See, e.g., Le Marchant's Diary in A. Aspinall, ed., *Three Early Nineteenth Century Diaries*, pp. 365–6; and Greville, *Memoirs*, II, 400.

be carried. The Irish Church Bill has got through the Committee in the Lords: and we are all beginning to look forward to a prorogation in about three weeks.

To day I went to Haydon's to be painted into his great picture of the Reform Banquet. Ellis was with me, and declares that Haydon has touched me off to a nicety. I am sick of pictures of my own face. I have seen within the last few days one drawing of it – one engraving – and three paintings.[1] They all make me a very handsome fellow. Haydon pronounces my profile a gem of art – perfectly antique. And, what is worth the praise of ten Haydons, I was told yesterday that Mrs. Littleton, the handsomest woman in London, at least the handsomest woman of forty in London, had paid me exactly the same compliment. She pronounced Mr. Macaulay's profile to be a study for an artist. What say you to that –you who always denied my claims to beauty? Let me tell you that I have bought a new looking glass and razor case on the strength of these compliments, and am meditating on the expediency of having my hair cut in the Burlington Arcade rather than in Lamb's Conduit Street. As Richard says,

> "Since I am crept in favour with myself
> I will maintain it with some little cost."[2]

I begin, like Sir Walter Elliot, to rate all my acquaintance according to their beauty.[3] I hope I shall find my darling in good looks. Have you been using Gowland?[4] But what nonsense I write, – and in times that make many merry men look grave. Kindest love to Margaret and Edward.

Ever yours, my love,

T B M

TO ZACHARY MACAULAY, 29 JULY 1833

Text: From MS in possession of Mr C. S. Menell, who furnished transcript.

London July 29. 1833

My dear Father,

I am heartily glad to find that the course which I have taken is so satisfactory to you. The present week opens under much more cheery

---

[1] TBM means the drawing made by Haydon on 20 July and the engraving published by Reynolds on 24 July. Two of the three paintings are presumably the Reynolds oil from which the engraving was made and Haydon's 'Reform Banquet' for which the sketch was made. No third painting of TBM at this period is known. It is just possible that TBM is referring to a painting made for 'The Reform Bill Receiving the King's Assent'; see 8 July 1831.   [2] *Richard III*, I, ii, 259–60.

[3] Jane Austen, *Persuasion*, ch. 1 and perhaps ch. 15.

[4] A proprietary skin lotion. See *Persuasion*, ch. 16.

circumstances than the last. The government are, I think, safe, and I am on good terms with the government. The abolitionists are softened, and the West Indians are cowed. I really begin to look forward to the close of the session in three weeks or thereabouts.

You charge Stanley with bad faith. He has faults enough. But bad faith is not one of them. He has not been trying to dupe the abolitionists but has himself been duped by the West Indians.[1] This Lord Lansdowne told me in the plainest language.

Edward is in town, and will remain here about a week. I have been so busy that I have not seen Charles for some days. But I hear that he is well again.

Ever yours affectionately,
T B M

TO HANNAH MACAULAY, 29 JULY 1833

MS: Trinity College. *Address:* Miss Macaulay / E Cropper's Esq / Dingle Bank / Liverpool. *Frank:* London July twenty nine 1833 / T B Macaulay. *Partly published:* Trevelyan, I, 317–18.

London July 29. 1833

Dearest Nancy,

As I was shaving my self this morning, I was informed that a gentleman wished to see me. As this announcement is generally followed by the appearance of a beggar – specially of three beggars – old discarded servants of ours who spunge on me without mercy, I put on my dressing-gown and went very sulkily into my sitting-room, fearing that I should not get off under half-a-crown. But behold! there was Edward. So I gave him the newspaper to read while I dressed, and then breakfasted before him, and was so hospitable as to regale him with seeing me devour two eggs and half a loaf, and swallow a bason of tea. We talked about many things – the East Indies, the West Indies, the House of Lords, the Liverpool freemen, and two foolish girls whom nobody else cares a straw about. And, after an hour's chat, he went his way to call on that personage who is designated in the Fifth Commandment as one's father, but in the conversation of the ingenuous youth of this generation as the Governor.[2]

He told me that on Monday morning he expected to find me earlier up. Alas poor, dear, good, young man! How little he knows of us town rakes!

---

[1] In conducting the West India Bill through the House of Commons Stanley offended both sides: the Abolitionists did not like the plan of compensation and apprenticeship; the West Indians were angry that, after defending the original apprenticeship clause, he should then abandon it. Greville concluded that Stanley wanted 'moral and political firmness and courage' (*Memoirs*, II, 402). But he could hardly please either side entirely.

[2] The earliest instance of this use of the word in the *OED* is from 1827.

I dined yesterday at Holland House. There was a very pleasant party. My Lady was very courteous, and my Lord extravagantly entertaining – telling some capital stories about old Bishop Horsley[1] which were set off with some of the drollest mimicry that I ever saw. There was Lord Melbourne, and Lord Essex, and Lord Lilford,[2] and Sir James Graham, and Dr. Holland[3] who is a good scholar as well as a good physician, and Wilkie[4] who is a modest, pleasing, companion as well as an excellent artist, and Allen, and my self for gentlemen. For ladies we had her Grace of Bedford,[5] and her daughter Lady Georgiana,[6] a fine, buxom, sonsy[7] lass, with more colour and firmer flesh than, I am sorry to say, are often seen among fine ladies, and that paragon of old aunts Miss Fox, and that lovely woman Lady Lilford. So our dinner and our soirée were very agreable.

We narrowly escaped a scene at one time. One of the Russells – Lord Edward,[8] – is in the navy and is now on duty in the fleet at the Tagus. We got into a conversation about Portuguese politics. His name was mentioned, and Graham, who is first Lord of the Admiralty, complimented the Duchess on her son's merit, to which he said every dispatch bore witness. The Duchess forthwith began to intreat that he might be recalled. He was very ill – she said. If he staid longer on that station she was sure that he would die; – and then she began to cry. I cannot bear to see women cry, and the matter became serious, for her pretty daughter began to bear her company. That hard-hearted Lord Melbourne seemed to be diverted by the scene. He, by all accounts, has been doing little else than making women cry during the last five and twenty years. However we all were as still as death while the wiping of eyes and the blowing of noses proceeded. At last Lord Holland contrived to restore our spirits. But before the Duchess went away she managed to have a tête à tête with Graham, and, I have no doubt, begged and blubbered to some purpose. I could not help thinking how many honest stout-hearted fellows are left to die on

1 Samuel Horsley (1733–1806: *DNB*), Bishop of St Asaph. It was Horsley who said in the House of Lords that 'he did not know what the mass of the people in any country had to do with the laws but to obey them' (*Parliamentary History*, xxxii, 258).

2 Thomas Powys (1801–61), third Baron Lilford, married Lord Holland's daughter Mary.

3 (Sir) Henry Holland (1788–1873: *DNB*), a fashionable physician, an indefatigable traveller, and a fixture in London society. Physician to the Queen from 1837, he was created Baronet in 1853. Holland's second wife was Sydney Smith's daughter Saba; his son Henry married TBM's niece Margaret in 1858.

4 (Sir) David Wilkie (1785–1841: *DNB*), the painter, an established success since 1807; R.A., 1811; succeeded Lawrence as Painter in Ordinary to the King, 1830; knighted, 1836.

5 Georgiana (1781–1853), second wife to the sixth Duke of Bedford.

6 Lady Georgiana Elizabeth Russell (1810–67), married Charles Romilly in 1842.

7 'Having a thriving, agreeable, or attractive appearance' (*OED*).

8 Lord Edward Russell (1805–87: *Boase*), promoted captain in November 1833; he retired with the rank of admiral in 1870.

the most unhealthy stations for want of being related to some Duchess who has been handsome or to some Lady Georgiana who still is so.[1]

The Duchess said one thing that amused us. We were talking about Lady Morgan. "When she first came to London," said Lord Holland, "I remember that she carried a little Irish harp about with her wherever she went." Others denied this. I mentioned what she says in her Book of the Boudoir.[2] There she relates how she went one evening to Lady Cork's[3] with her little Irish harp, and how strange every body thought it.[4] "I see nothing very strange," said the Duchess, "in her taking her harp to Lady Cork's. If she took it safe away with her, that would have been strange indeed." On this, as a friend of yours says, we la-a-a-a-a-a-ft.

While Edward was sitting with me the letters came – yours among the rest; but none for him. I shewed him his wife's epistle with great ostentation. But he did not seem jealous. As jealousy is a proof of love, I would have a quarrel with him, if I were Margaret.

I am glad to find that you approve of my conduct about the Niggers. I expect, and indeed wish, to be abused by the fools of the Agency Society. My father is quite satisfied, and so are the best part of my Leeds friends.

Had I any thing more to say? Whole volumes. But I have not time to go on gossiping. To day I sent my Indian Speech to the Press.[5] To morrow I am to have the proofs. Perhaps I may send you a proof-sheet. I do not suppose that you know enough about the question to enter into all the reasonings of the speech. It is certainly, I think and those who heard it think, the best that I ever made.

I amuse myself as I walk back from the House at two in the morning with translating Virgil. I am at work on one of the most beautiful episodes, and I think, am succeeding pretty well. You shall hear what I have done when I come to Liverpool, which will be, I hope, in three weeks or thereanent.

I agree with you and Meg in liking the article on Goethe.[6] I do

---

[1] Denis Le Marchant, who was also one of the company at Holland House, reports a very different impression: 'the Dutchess of Bedford passed the day with us – a bold, bad woman – with the remains of beauty. Her elder daughter Lady [blank] a dull dowdy' (A. Aspinall, ed., *Three Early Nineteenth Century Diaries*, p. 366).

[2] 2 vols., 1829.

[3] Mary Monckton (1746–1840: *DNB*), second wife of the seventh Earl of Cork; a prominent literary and political hostess and lion hunter for many years. TBM had met her in 1827 (Selina Macaulay, Diary, 14 June 1827). In her advanced old age, Lady Cork was given to kleptomania.

[4] The story, from 1808, is not quite as TBM tells it. Lady Morgan, then in her first fame as the author of *The Wild Irish Girl*, was asked to bring her harp but did not; Lady Cork sent for the harp and made her guest play (*The Book of the Boudoir*, New York, 1829, I, 74–9).

[5] Published as 'A Speech of T. B. Macaulay, Esq. M.P. on the Second Reading of the East-India Bill,' T. C. Hansard, 1833. There was apparently an earlier printed version: see 9 and 14 August.   [6] In the *ER*: see 24 July.

not yet know who wrote it. But I think it out and out the best in the Number.

A pun! A pun! – The other day Holt Mackenzie – Stewart Mackenzie – and I were talking over Indian politics. I said, "Pray why is our board the most fashionable place in London?" They could not think. "Why," said I, "because we're all Macs." *Almacks*.[1] There is for you. Conceive their raptures of delight and admiration, mixed however with a deep and bitter feeling of envy.

But I must and will stop. Kindest love to Margery.

Ever yours my darling
T B M

TO ZACHARY MACAULAY, 30 JULY 1833

Text: From MS in possession of Mr C. S. Menell, who furnished transcript.

London. July 30, 1833

My dear Father,

You have probably already heard of Mr Wilberforce's death. He expired yesterday morning. I was not aware of the event when I wrote to you.

He preserved his faculties to the very last, and his cheerfulness almost to the very last. On Saturday he was talking politics and relating anecdotes of old times with as much vivacity as ever.

I have not yet seen George who was in attendance on him. All that I know I learned from James Stephen who tells me that he has written to you.

I know how acutely you will feel this event, though it is so far from being unexpected. Even I, who have known so much less of him, cannot but be greatly affected at the loss of so great a man and so affectionate a friend.

I have been talking to several persons of very different parties about the propriety of paying some mark of respect to him. The conjuncture renders this course peculiarly proper. Lushington and Inglis quite agree with me that he ought to be buried in Westminster Abbey with every honour, not at the public expense but by voluntary subscription. I do not, however, know what the wishes of his family or what his own directions may be. / Ever, my dear father,

Yours affectionately,
T B M

[1] Exclusive assembly rooms in King Street, St James's.

TO [EDWARD BAINES], 30 JULY 1833

MS: Duke University.

London July 30. 1833

My dear Sir,

I am truly glad to find that you and the rest of my most valued friends at Leeds approve of the course which I have taken with respect to the Slavery Question. My position has indeed been one of extreme difficulty. To discharge my duty towards the negroes without weakening the hands of the government in the contest with the Lords, and without incurring the suspicion of *ratting* from them at a critical moment in order to gain popularity, was by no means easy. I have done my best to discover what was right. I have acted according to the best judgment which I could form. I expect of course to be maligned by violent people. But I am happy to find that all those whose opinions I most value do me justice.

The ministers have refused to receive my resignation. Lord Althorp in particular has behaved to me, through the whole of this most painful business, with a kindness which I can hardly describe.

The collision with the Lords is, I rejoice to say, postponed. It must come before long. But I think it very desirable that it should come at the beginning and not at the end of a Session. We ought, whenever we really bring the matter to an issue, to have the supplies still at our command, and the Mutiny Act on the point of expiring, so that it may be impossible for the Crown to dissolve us. The ministers are, I think, safe till next year. But it is dangerous to prophecy in times like these.

You will have heard, no doubt, of Mr. Wilberforce's death. He retained his faculties and his cheerfulness to the very last; and exulted in the success which we obtained last week as much as the youngest and most ardent partisan could have done. He was a very kind friend to me, and I loved him much. I hardly know how my father will bear this blow. He is now in Wales; but I shall not fail to communicate to him your kind message.

Remember me kindly to your son and to all your family.

Ever yours
T B Macaulay

TO HANNAH MACAULAY, 31 JULY 1833

MS: Trinity College. *Partly published:* Trevelyan, I, 318–20.

London July 31. 1833

My love,

Political affairs look cheeringly. The Lords passed the Irish Church Bill yesterday, and mean, we understand, to give us little or no trouble about the India Bill. There is still a hitch in the Commons about the West India Bill, – particularly about the twenty millions. But we expect to carry our point by a great majority. By the end of next week we shall be very near the termination of our labours. Heavy labours they have been.

So Wilberforce is gone. We talk of burying him in Westminster Abbey, and many eminent men, both Whigs and Tories, are desirous to join in paying him this honor. There is, however, a story about a promise given to old Stephen that they should both lie in the same grave. That man was resolved to produce every sort of inconvenience even after his death.

Wilberforce kept his faculties, and, except when he was actually in fits, his spirits, to the very last. He was cheerful and full of anecdote only last Saturday. He owned that he enjoyed life much, and that he had a great desire to live longer. – Strange in a man who had, I should have said, so little to attach him to this world, and so firm a belief in another – in a man with a ruined fortune, a weak spine, a worn out stomach, a vixen wife, and a reprobate son. What is this strange fascination which makes us cling to existence in spite of present sufferings and of religious hopes? Yesterday evening I called at the house in Cadogan place[1] where the body is lying. It was deserted. Mrs. Wilberforce had gone into the Country. Henry[2] was out. Samuel[3] was not come. And this great man, so popular, so much worshipped, was left to strangers and servants within thirty six hours after his death. I was truly fond of him – that is "je l'aimais comme l'on aime." And how is that? How very little one human being generally cares for another! How very little the world misses any body! How soon the chasm left by the disappearance of the best and wisest men closes! I thought, as I walked back from Cadogan place, that our own selfishness when others are taken away ought to teach us how little others will suffer at losing us. I thought that, if I were to die to morrow, not one of the fine people whom I dine with every week will take a *cotelette aux petits pois* the less on Saturday at the table to which I was invited to meet them, or will smile less gaily at the ladies over the Champagne. And I am quite even with them. What are those pretty lines of Shelley?

> Oh world – farewell –
> Listen to the passing bell –
> It tells that thou and I must part
> With a light and heavy heart.[4]

---

[1] 19 Cadogan Place, next door to the house where Zachary Macaulay and his family had lived from 1818 to 1823.

[2] Henry Wilberforce (1807–73: *DNB*), youngest son of William Wilberforce; a pupil of Newman at Oxford; clergyman of the Church of England until 1850, when he entered the Roman Catholic Church.

[3] Samuel Wilberforce (1805–73: *DNB*), third son; at this time Rector of Brightstone, Isle of Wight. Appointed Bishop of Oxford, 1845, he was one of the leading Victorian Churchmen.

[4] *The Cenci*, v, iii, 142–5, slightly misquoted.

There are not ten people in the world whose deaths would spoil my dinner. But there are one or two whose deaths would break my heart. The more I see of the world, – the more numerous my acquaintance becomes, the narrower and more exclusive my affection grows, the more I cling to my darling sisters, and to one or two old tried friends of my more quiet days. But why should I go on preaching to you out of Ecclesiastes? And here comes fortunately to break the train of my melancholy reflections the proof of my E[ast] I[ndian] speech from Hansard. So I must put my letter aside, and correct the press.

So the press is corrected, and the sheets sent back, and I sit down with a new pen to finish my letter. I saw Edward under the gallery of the House of Commons yesterday. I called on him to day: but he, like Taffey in the song, w'ant at home. When we shall meet I cannot tell. Charles sees more of him than I do, I believe. For as I get up at friends' dinner hour, and go to bed when friends *is* thinking of rising, we are not likely to take any social meal, unless he will agree to dine at my breakfast.

I will recommend you a book. – Lady Holland recommended it to me. – It is the Dramatic scenes just published by Lady Morgan.[1] Really there is considerable spirit and observation in them, and moreover I should say, a better temper, and a more moral tendency than in most of her performances. Read them at all events and let me know what you think of them.

And now, dearest, good bye. Kindest love to Meg. I shall pass judgment on her housekeeping, I hope, in less than three weeks.

Ever yours, darling,

T B M

P.S. What a wife Meg is! Not one letter for the poor man has passed through my hands since he came to London.

TO MRS THOMAS LISTER, 2 AUGUST 1833

MS: New York Public Library.

East India Board / August 2. 1833

Dear Mrs. Lister,

I shall have the greatest pleasure in dining with you on Saturday. I was truly glad to hear from your brother, a day or two ago, that your health had greatly improved. / Believe me ever, / Dear Mrs. Lister,

Your most faithful Servant

T B Macaulay

[1] *Dramatic Scenes from Real Life*, published in the first week of July.

TO HANNAH MACAULAY, 2 AUGUST 1833

MS: Trinity College. *Partly published:* Trevelyan, I, 320–2.

London August 2. 1833

Dearest Nancy,

I am delighted to hear that you are going on so quietly and pleasantly at the Dingle, and that Margaret does not gad about when her husband is out of the way, as the manner of some is, but stays at home reading, and no doubt sometimes weeping. What a consolation to have a sister with her during so awful a separation! – As to your books I agree with your judgment on them. Grimm's Correspondence[1] is delightful. Light criticism was Diderot's forte. I do not admire him much in any other way. As for Chesterfield[2] his letters are for the most part trash. Their celebrity must be attributed to causes quite distinct from their literary merit, – particularly to the position which the author held in society. We see in our own time that the books written by public men of note are generally rated at more than their real value – Lord Grenville's little compositions[3] for example – Canning's verses[4] – Fox's history[5] – Brougham's treatises.[6] The writings of people of high fashion also have a value set on them far higher than that which intrinsically belongs to them. The little verses of the late Duchess of Devonshire[7] for example, or an occasional prologue by Lord Alvanley[8] attract a most undue share of attention. If the present Duke of Devonshire who is the very " glass of fashion and mould of form "[9] were to publish a book with two good pages it would be extolled as a master piece in half the drawing rooms of London. Now Chesterfield was, what no person in our time has been or can be, a great political leader and at the same time the acknowledged chief of the fashionable world, at the head of the House of Lords and at the head of *ton*, Mr. Canning and the Duke of Devonshire in one. In our time the division of labour is carried so far that such a man could not exist. Politics require the whole energy bodily and mental during half the year, and leave very little time for the bow window at White's in the day or for the crush room

---

[1] Baron Friedrich Melchior Grimm, *Correspondance littéraire, philosophique et critique,* collected in 17 vols., Paris, 1812–14; English translation, 1814. Grimm was assisted by Diderot and others in this work.　　　　[2] *Letters to His Son,* 1774.

[3] Lord Grenville published *Nugae Metricae,* 1824; 'Oxford and Locke,' 1829; 'Dropmore,' 1830, and a few other miscellaneous productions.　　　　[4] *Poetical Works,* 1823.

[5] Charles James Fox, *A History of the Early Part of the Reign of James II,* 1808. TBM discusses it in his essay on Mackintosh.

[6] E.g., 'Discourse of the Objects, Advantages, and Pleasures of Science,' 1827; 'Hydrostatics,' 1827; 'Practical Observations upon the Education of the People,' 1825.

[7] Georgiana (1757–1806), first wife of the fifth Duke, published 'The Passage of the Saint Gothard,' 1802.

[8] Alvanley wrote the epilogue to Lord Glengall's *The Follies of Fashion,* 1829.

[9] *Hamlet,* III, i, 161.

of the Opera at night. A hundred years ago the case was different. Chesterfield was at once the most distinguished orator in the Upper House, and the undisputed Sovereign of wit and fashion. He held this eminence for about forty years. At last it became the regular custom of the higher circles to laugh whenever he opened his mouth without waiting for his bon mot. He used to sit at White's with a circle of young men of rank round him applauding every syllable that he uttered. When the letters of such a man were published, of course they were received more favourably by far than they deserved. They contain some clever passages, I think, and the style is not bad.

If you wish for a proof of the kind of influence which Chesterfield had over his contemporaries, look at the prospectus of Johnson's dictionary.[1] Look even at Johnson's angry letter.[2] It contains the strongest admission of the boundless influence which Chesterfield exercised over society.

So much for criticism. As to politics everything seems tending to repose; and I should think that by this day fortnight we shall probably be prorogued. The Jew Bill was thrown out yesterday night by the Lords. No matter. Our turn will come one of these days.

If you want to see me puffed and abused by somebody who evidently knows nothing about me, look at the New Monthly[3] for this month. Bulwer, I see, has given up editing it.[4] What he is to do for bread and butter I am sure I cannot conceive. For by all accounts he has run himself quite out of cash, and his dress must cost more than that of any five other members of parliament.

To morrow Wilberforce is to be buried. His sons acceded with great eagerness to the application made to them by a considerable number of the members of both houses that the funeral should be public. We meet to morrow at 12 at the House of Commons, and we shall attend the coffin into the Abbey. The Duke of Wellington, Lord Eldon, and Sir R. Peel have put down their names as well as the ministers and the abolitionists.

I was to have dined with Lord John Russell to morrow. But I had an invitation from Mrs. Lister to day; – so I put his Lordship off, as I would have put off the King. Her brother, George Villiers, a very great favourite of mine, is, I am rejoiced to learn, going as minister to Madrid,[5] – an important post particularly at the present conjuncture. Grant and I had wished to secure him as resident in China. But he is better disposed of.

---

[1] 1747: addressed to Chesterfield.

[2] To Chesterfield, 7 February 1755, in Boswell, *Life of Johnson*.

[3] 'On the State of Eloquence in England,' *New Monthly Magazine*, xxxviii (August 1833), 396–7; the article is by Bulwer, who concludes that 'the ineffable *something* is wanting' in TBM's oratory.

[4] Bulwer published his 'Editor's Farewell' in the August number of the *New Monthly*.

[5] Villiers was ambassador to Spain from 1833 to 1839.

Good bye my darling. I cannot tell you with what pleasure I think of meeting you again under our dear Meg's roof, and of visiting Westmoreland and Scotland with you. I think we must change our plan in one respect and go straight from the lakes to Edinburgh. I have not yet made up my mind as to the course which we shall then follow. Much will depend on some official arrangements which are not yet settled. – Edward has my picture; and will, I hope, take care of it. If he does not, and I were his wife, I would give him a fine flyting. Kindest love to dear Margaret.

Ever yours, darling,

T B M

P.S. Pride and Prejudice is out.[1] I bought it yesterday. The pictures are worse than ever.

TO ZACHARY MACAULAY, 3 AUGUST 1833

MS: Huntington Library. *Extracts published:* Trevelyan, I, 310; 322.

London August 3. 1833

My dear Father,

I have this instant returned from Westminster Abbey where Wilberforce has been buried with every honor. Fifteen or sixteen peers, two royal Dukes among them, and more than a hundred members of the House of Commons accompanied the procession. This I think a great number for such a season of the year, when town is very thin, and when it is hard to keep forty members together to make a house. Persons of all parties were there. Lord Grey is out of town. But the Chancellor,[2] Lord Lansdowne, Charles Grant, the Duke of Gloucester,[3] and the Speaker were among the pall-bearers. Lord Althorp, Stanley, Graham, Lord Ripon, the Duke of Wellington, Sir Robert Peel, the Archbishop of Canterbury, the Bishop of London, and indeed almost every conspicuous person, Whig or Tory, who is now in London, was present. We laid him side by side with Canning, at the feet of Pitt, and within two steps of Fox and Grattan. The ceremony was, as it ought to be, quiet and solemn.

---

[1] In the Bentley edition (see 10 June 1833); published on 1 August.

[2] Brougham: writing to Brougham on 6 August Zachary Macaulay says that 'a letter which has reached me from Tom conveys to me the satisfactory result of your efforts to do the merited honours to [Wilberforce's] memory. His account of what passed at Westminster Abbey on Saturday is truly consoling' (MS, University College).

[3] William Frederick (1776–1834: *DNB*), the King's cousin, was the patron of many Evangelical enterprises. Called 'Silly Billy'; but Sir James Stephen states that he 'possessed many virtues, and even considerable talents, which his feeble talk and manners concealed from his occasional associates' ('The Clapham Sect,' *ER*, LXXX, 266–7).

If any debate should take place on the third reading of the West India Bill in which I might take part, I should certainly embrace the opportunity of paying honor to his memory. But I do not expect that such an occasion will arise. The house seems inclined to pass the bill without any more contest: and you must be aware that any thing like theatrical display, any thing like a set funeral oration, not springing naturally out of the discussion of a question, is extremely distasteful to the House of Commons.

I enclose several letters for you. Where is my Uncle Colin? My speech on India will, I believe, be printed in a day or two, and I should like to send him a copy.

Ever yours affectionately

T B M

TO HANNAH MACAULAY, 5 AUGUST 1833

MS: Trinity College.

London August 5. 1833

Dearest Nancy,

I am delighted with what you tell me about Margaret's scheme.[1] The details we can settle when we meet. But it would be in every way most gratifying to me to have her and Edward of the party. The Session has continued so long that it would scarcely have been possible for me to visit Scotland without abridging my stay at the Dingle so much that I should scarcely have seen Margaret. By the plan which you mention I shall be able to have my tour and her society at once. I hope Edward will like the project as much as I do. We will divide the posting expences – and as to other things, eating and drinking and so forth, we will take day and day alternately and see which of us caters best, and treats the ladies most magnificently.

On Saturday I attended Wilberforce's funeral. It was a solemn and gratifying ceremony. There were about twenty peers and more than a hundred members of the House of Commons in the procession. The Chancellor, the Speaker, the Duke of Gloucester, the Marquesses of Lansdowne and Westminster,[2] Lord Bexley,[3] and Charles Grant were among the pall-bearers. The ministers, – the Archbishop of Canterbury, – the Duke of Sussex[4] – the Duke of Wellington and Sir Robert Peel

---

[1] Margaret and Edward hoped to accompany TBM and Hannah on their Scotch tour but gave it up: see 9 August.

[2] Robert Grosvenor (1767–1845: *DNB*), first Marquess of Westminster.

[3] Nicholas Vansittart (1766–1851: *DNB*), first Baron Bexley; Tory politician; Chancellor of the Exchequer, 1812–22. He was associated with some of the Evangelical causes.

[4] Augustus Frederick (1773–1843: *DNB*), sixth son of George III. He supported the abolition movement and patronized several Evangelical societies.

were in the assemblage. We laid him in the North Transept – a corner of the Abbey which you must remember as the place where many eminent statesmen have been interred. Chatham and I believe Lord Mansfield are there. We deposited the coffin next to that of Canning at the foot of Pitt's grave, and within three paces of Fox and Grattan.

In the evening 1 dined at Knightsbridge with the Listers. We had only the Villierses and Lord and Lady Morley.[1] But the party was very agreable – George Villiers, as usual, the most lively and polite of young men, and his sister the most accomplished, intelligent, and graceful of women. Lord Lansdowne asked me to go to Richmond yesterday. But I was so thoroughly tired of bustle that I excused myself, and passed a quiet evening over my books.

To morrow I hope to be able to send you my speech. and by to morrow week, or perhaps earlier, I hope to bring you my self. I have seen very little of Edward. We are brothers of much the same sort with Castor and Pollux, one of whom always set as the other rose. No wonder that we should miss each other. As the song says:

> Ned he is my brother:
> A sober man is Ned:
> He came to my rooms:
> I was asleep in bed.
> I went to Ned's rooms
> He was gone to a Slavery meeting
> Ned came to my rooms
> I was at Lord Holland's, eating.
> I went to Ned's rooms
> And there I left my card:
> Ned came to my rooms
> I was voting in old Palace Yard.

But I must have done with my nonsense. Have you read Village Belles? What do you think of it? Will it be worth my while to read it. Kindest love to Meg.

Ever yours dearest
T B M

---

1 John Parker (1772–1840: *DNB*), first Earl of Morley; a Canningite Tory and a supporter of the Reform Bill. Frances Talbot (1781?–1857) was his second wife.

TO HANNAH MACAULAY, 9 AUGUST 1833

MS: Trinity College. *Extract published:* Trevelyan, I, 322–3.

London August 9. 1833

Dearest Nancy,

I heartily wish that your hopes of seeing me before you receive any more letters from me were well founded. Unhappily this Session seems to lengthen before us: and, if we are up in a fortnight, it will be as much as I expect. I sympathise with the lamentation of the author of the old ballad which you doubtless remember in Percy's reliques,[1]

> "I'm in Lunnun in August –
> Oh woe worth the day!
> The cholera's here
> And Nancy's away."

However the business must end sooner or later. Nothing sublunary is eternal except Mr. William Smith's great coat: and within forty eight hours after the prorogation I mean to be at the Dingle.

I am very sorry indeed to learn that there is no chance of our having the company of Margaret and Edward on our jaunt. This being the case, our best course will be that which you suggest. We must set out for Scotland soon after my arrival at the Dingle, and return to Liverpool instead of going to the Temple. I shall have ample time. I have earned a two months' holiday, and it is not likely that any thing will occur to recall me to London before the middle of October.[2]

As to your plan of visiting Margaret in November,[3] much as I shall miss you, my own darling, you know that I cannot hesitate for a moment. I can imagine what a comfort you must be to her under such circumstances. Indeed, my love, I see your affection for her with scarcely less pleasure than your affection for me. Among all the things which make me fond and proud of my sisters there is none that I love and value more than their friendship for each other – so different from the nauseous, foolish, canting, friendships which are so common among young ladies, and which are so revolting to men of sense. I need not tell you what my feelings are about our dear Margaret. You and she will guess them.

I have been too busy to write for some days. I have been clearing off

---

[1] Thomas Percy, *Reliques of Ancient English Poetry*, 1765.

[2] TBM was in fact back in London by 25 September, since the prospect of his Indian appointment made him wish to be there. Presumably the chance of the appointment was not very definite at the time of this letter.

[3] Margaret expected her child in November (Hannah to Fanny Macaulay [7 August 1833]: MS, Huntington); it was born in December.

a great mass of business which had accumulated at our office while we were conducting our Bill through parliament. I have now got rid of the whole arrear; and to day I had the satisfaction of seeing the green boxes which a week ago were piled up with papers three or four feet high, perfectly empty. Admire my superhuman industry. This I will say for myself that when I do sit down to work, I work harder and faster than any person that I ever knew.

I sent you a copy of my speech – very ill printed. I will in a day or two send you another, much more correct. Kindest love to Margaret and Edward.

Ever yours, dearest,
T B M

TO SELINA MACAULAY, 14 AUGUST 1833

MS: Trinity College.

London August 14 / 1833

Dearest Selina,

I am truly glad that you like my speech. I send you a copy better printed than the former. We are worked to death, and have hardly time to eat and drink.

Give my love to Fanny, and all at the Temple. Tell my Uncle that I will, as he desires, send a copy of the speech to Henry[1] at Madras.

Ever yours affectionately
T B M

TO ZACHARY MACAULAY, 14 AUGUST 1833

MS: Trinity College.

London August 14. 1833

My dear Father,

I send you a letter from Henry. A large packet of papers came with it which I will forward in a day or two. But I wish to make myself master of them that, in case of necessity, I may be able to defend him. He has been very foolish, but pardonably foolish.[2] His errors have proceeded from a high spirit, a love of popularity, and a somewhat Quixotic hatred of oppression. There is an unfavourable impression respecting him at the Colonial Office. What opinion is entertained at the Foreign office I do not know. But I believe that, if he had not been my brother, he would have been recalled. And he must take care how he presumes again on that connection.

---

[1] Henry Babington.   [2] In fighting his duels: see 1 July 1833.

When does the next ship sail? I mean to write very strongly to him: and I do not believe that my franking privileges extend to Sierra Leone.

Ever yours affectionately
T B M

TO HANNAH MACAULAY, 15 AUGUST 1833

MS: Trinity College.

London August 15. 1833

Dearest Nancy,

The Session will, I suppose, end at last like every thing human. But it drags its slow length along very tediously. I still hope that in ten days I shall be at the Dingle. Possibly I may be able to make my escape a day or two earlier. We have been going through all sorts of troubles, – quarreling, blundering, floundering into scrapes and scrambling out of them during the last week. The secret history of the government, and of our department in partciular, would be as strange as a novel. Within the last forty eight hours I have seen turns of fortune, quite unsuspected by the public, but as odd as any that I ever heard or read of. I have my self been an actor in these affairs, – though I have shewn a composure about them which has astonished most of my associates. Yesterday evening at ten I saw two ministers hardly able to speak for vexation, and indeed just shedding tears. At half after eleven I saw them ready to dance for joy. The causes of all these changes were such as I should hardly make you understand in conversation, and certainly not on paper. We will talk about them when we meet.

Robert Wilberforce[1] is writing his father's life – I suppose in order to turn a penny: and that in the process, he may save a penny, he has written to me begging that I will receive and frank all letters, parcels, proof-sheets and so forth relating to this work. I answered him, for his father's sake, with great civility. I mean to send him two old coats and a shocking bad hat when I leave London, though my clerk will grumble, I fear, at losing his perquisites.

On Saturday we – that is to say all the ministers and official men – go to Blackwall in Admiralty Barges to dine on turtle and white-bait, by way

---

[1] Robert Wilberforce (1802–57: *DNB*), second son of William Wilberforce; he had been at Oriel with Newman and was, in 1833, Rector of East Farleigh, Kent. Like his brother Henry, Robert ended his days in the Roman Catholic Church, which he entered in 1854. In collaboration with his brother Samuel he published his father's *Life*, 5 vols., 1838. According to the *Christian Observer's* review, most of the materials for the book, apart from Wilberforce's diary and journals, were furnished by Zachary Macaulay (cited in Ford K. Brown, *Fathers of the Victorians*, Cambridge, 1961, p. 487).

of celebrating the approaching close of our labours. This is an old custom in which I have never yet taken part: and I am curious to see the humours of the festival, though I expect the day to be dull, and though I am quite sure that the bill will be heavy.[1]

On the Saturday after I do hope that I shall be with my own darling. – I wish I could tell her how dearly I love her. But that is impossible; and unnecessary too: for she knows it well. Kindest love to Meg and Ned.

Ever yours, my love
T B M

[1] The ministerial white-bait dinners, dating from the time of Pitt, were traditionally held either at Blackwall or at Greenwich; the custom was maintained until 1883. The dinner on 17 August, held at Lovegrove's Hotel, Blackwall, is described in Littleton's Diary in A. Aspinall, ed., *Three Early Nineteenth Century Diaries*, pp. 357–8. The bill was £3 4s. 6d. Lord Broughton describes another ministerial fish dinner at Blackwall in 1840 at which TBM presided, though disapproving of the undignified style of the affair: 'He mentioned that, when he was last at a fish-dinner, it was in the time of Lord Grey, who presided, and the Cabinet Ministers sat at the upper end of the table; little or nothing was said, either at dinner or afterwards. "Now," added he, "our Saturnalia were too much like a Northern Circuit dinner."...he concluded by saying that he probably should not attend another fish dinner' (*Recollections of a Long Life*, v, 289).

THE PROSPECT OF INDIA,
17 AUGUST – 31 DECEMBER 1833

1833 August
Offered appointment to Supreme Council of India

– August 29–September 20
Tour in Scotland with Hannah

– October 14
Finishes 'Walpole's *Letters to Horace Mann*' (*ER*, October)

– November 7
Speech at Leeds Mechanics' Institute

– December 4
Appointed to Supreme Council of India

– December 26
Resigns Secretaryship of Board of Control

TO HANNAH MACAULAY, 17 AUGUST 1833

MS: Trinity College. *Address:* Miss Macaulay / E Cropper's Esq / Dingle Bank / Liverpool. *Frank:* London August seventeen 1833 / T B Macaulay. *Mostly published:* Trevelyan, I, 323–7.

London August 17. 1833

Dearest Nancy,

I am about to write to you on a subject which to you and Margaret will be one of the most agitating interest; and which, on that account chiefly, is so to me.

By the new India Bill it is provided that one of the members of the Supreme Council which is to govern our Eastern empire is to be chosen from among persons who are not servants of the Company.[1] It is probable, indeed nearly certain, that the situation will be offered to me.[2]

The advantages of the situation are very great. It is a post of the highest dignity and consideration. The salary is ten thousand pounds a year. I am assured by persons who know Calcutta intimately, and who have themselves mixed in the highest circles and held the highest offices at that presidency, that I may live in splendour there for five thousand a year, and may save the rest of the salary with the accruing interest. I may therefore hope to return to England at only thirty nine, in the full vigour of life, with a fortune of thirty thousand pounds. A large fortune I never desired.

I am not fond of money or anxious about it. But though every day makes me less and less eager for wealth, every day shews me more and more strongly how necessary a competence is to a man who desires to be either great or useful. At present the plain fact is that I can continue to be a public man only while I can continue in office. If I left my place in the government, I must leave my seat in parliament too. For I must live. I can live only by my pen. And it is absolutely impossible for any man to write enough to procure him a decent subsistence, and at the same time to take an active part in politics. I have not during this Session been able to send a single line to the Edinburgh Review: and, if I had been out of office, I should have been able to do very little. Edward Bulwer has just

---

[1] The Charter Act, in creating a new Supreme Council for India, specified that a fourth member, not in the Company's service, should sit on the Council to assist it in its legislative (but not executive) capacity; the office of this so-called 'law member' was that to which TBM was appointed.

[2] This is the first reference to the chance of an Indian appointment in TBM's letters, but there is evidence that the prospect had been recognized before. Writing to Hannah, 26 February 1833, Margaret says: 'I have not noticed what you say about India. I must say I do not think it a thing to make yourself uncomfortable about. Tom would not go for anything less than a government, he will not ask for it, and I do not believe they will ever think of such a thing as offering it to him' (MS, Huntington).

given up the New Monthly magazine on the ground that he cannot conduct it and attend to his parliamentary duties. Cobbett has been compelled to neglect his Register so much that its sale has fallen almost to nothing. Now in order to live like a gentleman, it would be necessary for me to write, not as I have done hitherto, but regularly, and even daily. I have never made more than two hundred a year by my pen.[1] I could not support my self in comfort on less than five hundred. And I shall in all probability have many others to support. The prospects of our family are, if possible, darker than ever. My father and my uncle are absolutely at the mercy of William Wilberforce.[2] He will have scarcely any thing but what he can wring out of them. He is, I hear, violently incensed at the state in which he finds himself; and I can hardly blame him. What is to be expected from his forbearance and generosity in a case in which both his avarice and his resentment are excited you may guess: for you know him. I have seen a letter to George from James Stephen, who seems to anticipate the worst. And George tells me plainly that he shall not be surprised if my father should be arrested and my uncle turned out of Rothley Temple.

In the meantime my political prospects are very gloomy. A schism in the ministry is approaching.[3] It requires only that common knowledge of public affairs which any reader of the newspapers may possess to see this. I have more, much more, than common knowledge on the subject. They cannot hold together. I tell you in perfect seriousness that my chance of keeping my present situation for six months is so small that I would willingly sell it for fifty pounds down. If I remain in office I shall, I fear, lose my political character. If I go out and engage in opposition, I shall break most of the private ties which I have formed during the last three years. In England I see nothing before me, for some time to come, but poverty, unpopularity, and the breaking up of old connections.

If there were no way out of these difficulties, I would encounter them with courage. A man can always act honourably and uprightly; and, if I were in the Fleet Prison or the rules of the King's Bench, I believe that I could find in my own mind ressources which would preserve me from being positively unhappy. But if I could escape from these impending disasters I should wish to do so. By accepting the post which is likely to be offered to me, I escape for a short time from the contests of faction here. When I return I find things settled, – parties formed into new

---

[1] TBM's most productive year to this point was 1831, when he contributed six articles to the *ER*; from the evidence available it appears that he was paid at a variable rate (e.g., £60 for a 40-page article on Southey in 1830 but £90 for a 46-page article on Lord Mahon in 1833); there is thus no certain basis for calculating his literary earnings in any year.

[2] Presumably as heir to his father, who no doubt had made loans to Macaulay and Babington.

[3] This occurred in May 1834, over Irish policy.

combinations, – new questions under discussion. I shall then be able, without the scandal of a violent separation, and without exposing myself to the charge of inconsistency, to take my own line. In the meantime I shall save my family from distress. I shall return with a competence honestly earned, – as rich as if I were Duke of Northumberland[1] or Marquess of Westminster,[2] – and able to act on all public questions without even a temptation to deviate from the strict line of duty. While in India, I shall have to discharge duties not painfully laborious, and of the highest and most honorable kind. While there I shall have whatever that country affords of comfort or splendour; nor will my absence be so long that my friends or the public here will be likely to lose sight of me.

The only persons who know what I have written to you are Lord Grey, the Grants, Stewart Mackenzie, and George Babington. Charles Grant and Stewart Mackenzie, who know better than most men the state of the political world, and George, who knows better than any body all the peculiarities of my constitution, think that I should act unwisely in refusing this post: and this though they assure me, and I really believe sincerely, that they shall feel the loss of my society very acutely. But what shall I feel? And with what emotions, loving as I do my country and my family, can I look forward to such a separation, enjoined, as I think it is, by prudence and by duty? Whether the period of my exile shall be one of misery, or of comfort, and, after the first shock, even of happiness, depends on you, my dear, dear Nancy. I can scarcely see the words which I am writing through the tears that force themselves into my eyes. Will you, my own darling, if, as I expect, this offer shall be made to me, will you go with me? Will you entrust to me for a few years the care of your happiness? I call God to witness that it is as dear to me as my own – that I love the very ground that you tread on – that, if I shrink from poverty, it is more for your sake than for my own. I know what a sacrifice I ask of you. I know how many dear and precious ties you must, for a time, sunder. I know that the splendour of the Indian court and the gaieties of that brilliant society of which you would be one of the most conspicuous ornaments have no temptation for you. I can bribe you only by telling you that, if you will go with me, I will love you better than I love you now, if I can.

I have asked George about your health and mine. He says that he has very little apprehension for me and none at all for you. Indeed he seemed to think that the climate would be quite as likely to do you good as harm.

All this, my love, is most strictly secret. You may of course shew the letter to Margaret – dear, dear Margaret – if I could take you both with

---

[1] Hugh Percy (1785–1847: *DNB*), third Duke of Northumberland.
[2] Belgravia was just then being developed on his London property.

me, I should hardly care to return: – and yet I should: for I love my country dearly. Margaret may tell Edward: for I never cabal against the lawful authority of husbands. But further the thing must not go. It would hurt my father, and very justly, to hear of it from any body before he hears it from myself: and if the least hint of it were to get abroad I should be placed in a very awkward position with regard to the people at Leeds. It is possible, though not probable, that difficulties may arise at the India House; and I do not mean to say any thing to any person who is not already in the secret till the Directors have made their choice, and till the King's pleasure has been taken.

And now, my dear, dear love, think calmly over what I have written. I would not have written on the subject even to you, till the matter was quite settled, if I had not thought that you ought to have full time to make up your mind. If you feel an insurmountable aversion to India, I will do all in my power to make your residence in England comfortable during my absence, and to enable you to confer instead of receiving benefits. But if my darling would consent to give me, at this great crisis of my life, that proof, that painful and arduous proof of her affection which I beg of her with tears running down my cheeks, I think that she will not repent of it. She shall not, if the unbounded confidence and the tenderest fondness of one to whom she is dearer than life can compensate her for a few years' absence from much that she justly loves. I do not tell her that my fortune shall be hers. It will be hers, decide as she may. I have only one inducement to offer to her, that she is necessary to my happiness, and that the sacrifice which I intreat of her, painful as I know it will be to her, cannot [be as]¹ painful to her as parting from her would be [to me.]¹

[If my]¹ dearest Nancy consents to what I ask, the [most]¹ acutely painful circumstance attending this matter [will]¹ be the separation from Margaret. Dearest Margaret! She will feel this much. Consult her, my love, and let us both have the advantage of such advice as her excellent understanding and her warm affection for us may furnish. On Monday next, at the latest, I expect to be with you. Our Scotch tour, under these circumstances, must be short. Indeed if I did not feel that my health required a little travelling, I should hardly be inclined to leave the Dingle. By Christmas it will be fit that the new Councillor should leave England. His functions in India commence next April. We shall leave our dear Margaret, I hope, a happy mother.

Farewell, my dear, dear Nancy. You cannot tell how impatiently I shall wait for your answer.

T B M

¹ Paper torn away with seal.

TO FRANCES MACAULAY, 17 AUGUST 1833

MS: Trinity College. *Address:* Miss F Macaulay.

London August 17 / 1833

Dear Fanny,

I am very vain of your praise. I like to be praised by my sisters better than by any body. I send you a copy of the speech.

Let me know whether you succeed in obtaining an escort to the Dingle. I have no hope of being off for another week. Grant has been suddenly summoned to Edinburgh. He will not be back till next Saturday. And till his return I could not stir, even if the House were to finish its work earlier, which is very improbable.

If you cannot obtain a good conveyance without my assistance I will arrange a plan. But – between ourselves – I wish you could manage it without me. For I can hardly pass the Temple without staying a day there: and every day is an object to me. I thought of taking two places in the Manchester mail on Sunday night, and taking you up at the Lodge on Monday morning, – so going on to Manchester, and thence to Liverpool by the rail-road. But I fear that my uncle and aunt would be hurt if I were to take you up within a mile of their house, and were not to stay and see them. However if by next Saturday morning I do not hear from you that you have found some proper person to take charge of you, I will see what can be done. Kindest love to Selina, my Uncle and Aunt, Jane, Lydia, and all the rest of the world.

Ever yours
T B M

TO HANNAH MACAULAY, 21 AUGUST 1833

MS: Trinity College. *Address:* Miss Macaulay / E Cropper's Esq / Dingle Bank / Liverpool. *Frank:* London August twenty one 1833 / T B Macaulay.

London August 21. 1833

My own dear dear Nancy,

I cannot tell you with what feelings I have read your letter[1] and that of our darling Margaret. I fear that I have undertaken what I have not fortitude to go through with. My own distress I could bear while it was only my own: but when I think of the grief of my two dear sisters my heart fails me: and when I look forward to the protracted torture of the approaching four months I lose all my courage.

---

[1] In reply to TBM's request that she accompany him to India, Hannah, who says that she 'abhorred the idea' and thought of India only as a 'region of disease and death,' sent 'an agonised appeal to him entreating him to give it up' (Memoir of TBM, pp. 58–9).

If Charles Grant had been in London this morning, I believe that I should have told him that I had made up my mind not to go. Happily his absence has preserved me from acting hastily in so important a matter. He has been forced to go down to Edinburgh on an important trial, and will not be here again till Friday night. I shall see him on Saturday before I leave town; and I shall then beg him to proceed no further in this matter till he hears from me. We will talk the business over calmly at the Dingle, and decide on our course. I am not yet in the slightest degree committed. Indeed I have every reason to believe that the matter has never been whispered out of the very small circle which I mentioned to you. We shall therefore be at perfect liberty to accept or decline the place as we may think best.

Whatever our determination may be, dearest Nancy, I shall never forget your conduct on this occasion – never – nor the conduct of our beloved Margaret. What a happiness to have two such sisters. I should repay your kindness very ill if I were not to allow to your wishes as much weight as to my own. On Monday I hope to be with you. In the mean time, my dearest love, compose your mind. Consider that the whole question is still open, and that you shall judge both for yourself and for me. It is principally on your account that I feel pained by the precariousness of my present situation. It is that I may have a home for my Nancy, that I may surround her with comforts, and be assured of leaving her safe from poverty, that I am ready to leave a country which I love and a sister who is dearer to me than any thing save one in this world. If, on mature reflection, you really would prefer that we should remain in England, and take the chances of political life here, I will, at once and without a moment's regret, give up the scheme, and forget every thing connected with it, except your generous and confiding affection.

Our other plans will depend on the decision to which we may come as to this great question. Of course, I shall take care of Charles, if we should decide on going. But, for reasons which I will explain when we meet, it would be most unadvisable, and, I rather think, impracticable to take him with us. George thinks and so do I that the greatest service which I could render to the poor lad would be to enable him to complete his professional education with every advantage. This is a subject, however, which, if we resolve on going, we shall have ample opportunity to discuss.

Give my kindest, fondest, love to Margaret. I shall be disposed, and so will you, to be very much guided by her advice. Love to Edward.

Ever, dearest, yours

T B M

TO ZACHARY MACAULAY, 26 AUGUST 1833

MS: Trinity College.

Liverpool August 26. 1833

My dear Father,

Here I am at last. I find a tour absolutely necessary to set me up after my seven month's imprisonment. I mean to take Hannah with me to Edinburgh. We set off on Thursday. On Friday we shall be at York. The Sunday we shall pass at Durham; and we shall not be at Edinburgh till Tuesday. I mention these particulars that you may be able to judge about your letters.

I have written to Henry very strongly indeed. I do not however think the case quite so bad as you do. It is bad enough even in my opinion. The faults of his conduct seem to me to have been occasioned principally by a most absurd desire for the wretched popularity which is to be got among such a set of ragamuffins as the inhabitants of Sierra Leone appear to be. His memorial I thought on the whole well drawn. The part to which you allude is indeed in detestable taste. But tact was never poor Henry's forte. I have spoken of his exploits in terms which will I think make him angry, but which must, I think, do him good.

He will, I believe, keep his place, if he offends no more. But I agree with you that he has for the present at least marred his chance of promotion. At least I should not chuse to ask any thing for him. He has been very leniently treated; and I have done my best to impress this on him.

Ever yours affectionately

T B Macaulay

TO MACVEY NAPIER, 26 AUGUST 1833

MS: British Museum.

Liverpool August 26. 1833

Dear Napier,

I hope to be at Edinburgh the 3d of September – to morrow week, with my sister. I do not expect to be able to stay more than a week. It would therefore, I think, hardly be worth our while to go into lodgings. Which is the most comfortable Hotel?[1] Send me a line to the Post Office at Durham. My sister and I mean to pass next Sunday there.

I will not fail to give you quantity enough – be the quality what it may for the next Number.[2]

Ever yours truly

T B Macaulay

---

[1] They stayed at Oman's Hotel, 6 Charlotte Square: see 29 May 1839.

[2] The article, TBM's first since January 1833, was 'Walpole's *Letters to Sir Horace Mann*,' *ER*, LVIII (October 1833), 227–58.

TO MACVEY NAPIER, 12 SEPTEMBER 1833

MS: British Museum.

Glasgow Septr. 12 / 1833

Dear Napier,

We were detained so long in the course of our journey to the Trosachs that we have but just arrived at this place. Our plan of returning to Edinburgh must therefore be abandoned. We shall always remember with pleasure our short visit and your hospitality.

You need not assure the Lord Advocate how sorry I am to have missed him. – My sister desires to be kindly remembered to Miss Napier.

Ever yours truly
T B Macaulay

P.S. Tell Mr. Thomson[1] that I am strongly inclined to believe that we were all wrong about Dryden and Sir George Mackenzie.[2] I think that it was the other Mackenzie.

TO ZACHARY MACAULAY, 20 SEPTEMBER 1833

Text: From MS in possession of Mr C. S. Menell, who furnished transcript.

Liverpool. Sept. 20. 1833

My dear Father,

I hardly know whether this letter will reach you. However I will run the risk. We have just returned from a tour in which we have gone over much of the same ground that we traversed in 1817. If my recollections do not deceive me, Scotland has made prodigious advances during the last sixteen years. Planting, cultivation, building – all the arts of life – seem to me to have made rapid progress. Large tracts which I remember quite

---

[1] Thomas Thomson (1768–1852: *DNB*), advocate, Deputy Clerk-Register, and Clerk to the Court of Session. Thomson, a friend of Napier, edited many legal and antiquarian works. He contributed a few articles to the *ER* in its early years and occasionally took charge of it in Jeffrey's absence.

[2] In his 'Discourse of Satire' Dryden speaks of that 'noble wit of Scotland, Sir George Mackenzie' (G. R. Noyes, ed., *The Poetical Works of Dryden*, Boston [1950], p. 319). Mackenzie (1636–91: *DNB*), was Lord Advocate and a miscellaneous writer; Thomson had edited his *Memoirs of the Affairs of Scotland*, Edinburgh, 1821. TBM perhaps remembered Dryden's remark in writing of Mackenzie that 'his renown had spread even to the coffeehouses of London and to the cloisters of Oxford' (*History of England*, II [1848], 121). Since Dryden's Mackenzie had been identified at least as early as Scott's edition of Dryden, it is not easy to see how people could be 'wrong' about him. Perhaps the 'other Mackenzie' is Sir George Mackenzie (1630–1714: *DNB*), first Earl of Cromarty.

sterile are covered with wood or with cornfields. The roads are wonderfully improved, the villages look better and smell better than formerly. The towns are enlarging, the gentlemen's houses and policies[1] look like English country seats.

The great features of nature seemed to me more beautiful than ever – probably because I have been so long cooped up in London.

Henry seems to have got through his difficulties wonderfully. I only hope that his escape will not encourage him to fresh acts of imprudence.

I send you a note which I have received from my old school fellow Colquhoun,[2] who is, as you know, now in parliament. I should be glad if it were in your power to direct him to any source of information.

What have you heard about our kind friend Hannah More?[3] I know nothing but what is in the papers. It is impossible to regret an event which, in every point of view, must be considered as a deliverance, and which had been expected for so many years. But I should be glad to hear any particulars with which you may be acquainted and which may not have been given to the public.

Things look well, I think, in the West Indies. It seems not unlikely that the absurd system of apprenticeship will die a natural death.[4]

Ever yours affectionately,

T. B. Macaulay

TO HANNAH MACAULAY, 25 SEPTEMBER 1833

MS: Trinity College. *Address:* Miss H M Macaulay / E Cropper's Esq / Dingle Bank / Liverpool. *Frank:* London September twenty five 1833 / T B Macaulay.

London September 25. 1833

Dearest Nancy,

Here I am quite well and busy. I have only time to thank you for your letter and to congratulate you most heartily on your legacy. Pray do not be angry about mine.[5] I should have valued my poor old friend's library only as a mark of her regard. And I know that I kept her regard as long as she kept her wits.

[1] Scottish, for the park around a country seat.
[2] John Campbell Colquhoun (1803–70: *DNB*) was returned for Dumbarton, 1832. According to Hannah Trevelyan's Memoir of TBM, p. 15, Colquhoun was at Preston's with TBM.
[3] She died on 7 September.
[4] TBM uses the same phrase in his speech of 24 July (*Hansard*, 3rd Series, XIX, 1209). The system was given up in 1838, three years before it was scheduled to come to an end.
[5] Hannah More had left something to her namesake, but it turned out to be only £20: see 8 November. Her bequest of her library to TBM had been revoked in 1832: see 16 July 1830.

I expect my father in London by the end of the week. I shall keep his letters for him as I do not precisely know whither to direct them.

I shall buy Walpole's letters[1] to day, and be up at five every morning till my review is written. One advantage I gained from our expedition which I hope to retain till Christmas. It broke me of the habit of lying in bed till ten, – a habit which I contracted from necessity during the Session of Parliament. It is now disagreable to me to lie later than seven, and I shall find it easy to rise before day.

Grant will not be back for ten days or more. Till he returns every thing is in abeyance. But I must stop, and rummage my green and red boxes, which have been filling fast while I was idling at Edinburgh and Glasgow.

Kindest love to Meg and Fanny. Charles, I suppose, is already in London. George is murmuring at his long absence.

Ever yours, dearest,
T B M

I was much less struck by Chester than I had expected.

TO HANNAH MACAULAY, 28 SEPTEMBER 1833

MS: Trinity College.

London Septr. 28. 1833

Dearest Nancy,

The town is wonderfully thin. I have found only two persons in it whom I know – relations excepted. Those two are Colonel Fox and Leicester Adolphus. But I find my time pass very pleasantly – that is as pleasantly as it can pass at a distance from you, my darling. We are not quite without sights. I passed two hours yesterday very agreably at the Queen's Bazaar in Oxford Street, in looking over Matthews's Gallery of Theatrical portraits.[2] You know – or more likely you do not know – for you have not been much in the way of green-room chit-chat, that Matthews, the actor, has, during several years, been engaged in making a collection of portraits of actors and actresses; and he has at last formed a most complete gallery. There is scarcely an eminent performer from the Restoration down to the present year of whom there is not a likeness

[1] Lord Dover, ed., *Letters of Horace Walpole, Earl of Orford, to Sir Horace Mann*, 3 vols., 1833; they furnished the subject for TBM's essay on Walpole in the October *ER*.

[2] Mathews, in financial difficulties, opened the exhibition of his collection of nearly four hundred theatrical portraits in May. It had for many years been housed in a gallery in Mathews's house in Highgate and was described by Charles Lamb in 'The Old Actors,' 1822. The collection was sold to the Garrick Club.

in his possession; – old Cibber,[1] for example, as Lord Foppington, – Betterton[2] in Hamlet, Quin[3] in Harry the Eighth, – Barry[4] in Othello if I remember right, – Garrick[5] in a great variety of characters – his wonderful face looking just as little like itself as Macbeth to Lord Ogleby,[6] – Cooke[7] in Iago and Shylock, – John Kemble[8] and Mrs. Siddons in a great number of parts. There are Mrs. Clive[9] too and Mrs. Pritchard,[10] and Nell Gwynne,[11] and pretty Mrs. Bracegirdle[12] who turned the heads of all the men of fashion in William the Third's reign, and suffered none of them to turn her head, and Mrs. Robinson[13] who acted Perdita very well on the stage, and too well in real life to the late King's Florizel; and Booth[14] and Dogget,[15] whom you may remember in Cibber's Memoirs, and Lewis[16] and Parsons[17] and King[18] and Palmer,[19] and a crowd of other heroes of whom, I dare say, you never heard. There are two pictures of Peg Woffington who made tea as red as blood for Garrick and Johnson.[20] But the time would fail me to tell of all who are there. I could tell on my fingers those whom I missed. There was not, – at least I did not observe, – any likeness of Sheridan[21] – the father of Richard Brinsley. Nor was there Montford[22] who was the famous actor at the time of the revolution and who was killed in a street brawl about Mrs. Bracegirdle by Lord Mohun.[23] Nor was there Estcourt[24] – the favourite companion of the Whig wits of Anne's reign. One thing which struck me was the extraordinary plainness of the women of former times compared with those of our day. Indeed I seldom

---

[1] Colley Cibber (1671–1757: *DNB*), comedian and playwright.
[2] Thomas Betterton (1635–1710: *DNB*), leading actor of the Restoration stage.
[3] James Quin (1693–1766: *DNB*), rival of Garrick.
[4] Spranger Barry (1719–77: *DNB*), another of Garrick's rivals.
[5] David Garrick (1717–79: *DNB*), the greatest English actor of the eighteenth century.
[6] In *The Clandestine Marriage*, 1766, by Garrick and George Colman the elder.
[7] George Frederick Cooke (1756–1812: *DNB*), noted for his villainous roles.
[8] John Philip Kemble (1757–1823: *DNB*), tragedian, of the famous family of English actors.
[9] Kitty Clive (1711–85: *DNB*), comic actress with Garrick.
[10] Hannah Pritchard (1711–68: *DNB*), another of Garrick's collaborators.
[11] Nell Gwynne (1650–87: *DNB*), actress, and mistress of Charles II.
[12] Anne Bracegirdle (1673?–1748: *DNB*), the leading actress in the era of Congreve.
[13] Mary Robinson (1758–1800: *DNB*), called Perdita after her success in *The Winter's Tale*; briefly the mistress of George IV.
[14] Barton Booth (1681–1733: *DNB*), tragedian.
[15] Thomas Dogget (1670?–1721: *DNB*), comedian.
[16] William Thomas Lewis (1749–1811: *DNB*), comedian.
[17] William Parsons (1736–95: *DNB*), comedian.
[18] Tom King (1730–1804: *DNB*), comedian.
[19] Probably the younger (1742–98: *DNB*) of the two John Palmers famous as actors in the eighteenth century.   [20] Boswell, *Life of Johnson*, 10 April 1778.
[21] Thomas Sheridan (1719–88: *DNB*), actor, author, and teacher.
[22] William Mountfort (1664–92: *DNB*).
[23] William Charles Mohun (1677–1712: *DNB*), fourth Baron; Mohun did not kill Mountfort but held him in conversation when Captain Richard Hill ran him through.
[24] Richard Estcourt (1668–1712: *DNB*), comedian.

see a collection of portraits without making the same remark. But here it is peculiarly observable. For the face and figure have so much to do with the effect produced by an actress that there is every chance that you will find an unusual proportion of beauties among the stage-heroines. In our own time Mrs. Siddons, Miss O'Neill,[1] Miss Foote,[2] Madame Vestris,[3] Miss Chester,[4] have all been famous beauties. And several others might be named. Now there really is scarcely one handsome face among the actresses till you come within the last fifty years. Mrs. Bracegirdle for whom many Lords broke their hearts, and for whom one Lord was on the point of being hanged, Mrs. Robinson, the first love of George the Fourth, Peg Woffington, once a famous beauty, are really as common-place women as you would see. I pass twenty handsomer every day between Charing Cross and my office. And as to Mrs. Clive, Mrs. Cibber,[5] and Mrs. Pritchard, the three most famous actresses eighty years ago, they are all positive frights. Blessings on Lady Mary Montague and Doctor Jenner![6]

But I must have tired you to death with my criticisms. If the exhibition is open when you come to London we will go together to it.

My father is here – very well I think. He has a very wild and impracticable project in his head, about going to Sierra Leone as Henry's colleague. George and I, I have no doubt, shall dissuade him. In fact he would not get the place if he asked for it. Secondly, if he did get it he would not live to the end of the voyage. And thirdly if he did reach Sierra Leone, he would be arrested for debt before he had walked a hundred yards from the beach. It is hardly worth a man's while to sail to a tropical climate only to be put into quod.

Charles is doing very well. You need not plague yourselves about him. I have spoken to George, and there is not the least reason for uneasiness. Do not, however, let him know that I have been pumping George. – Give my love to Meg, Fan, and Ned. What neat monosyllables! I was, to use a phrase of the Leddy of Grippy, beautiful upon the mountains to my father.[7] I told him of his legacy,[8] which will I hope content his desires, and secure you in the peaceable possession of yours. Kindest loves again to all.

Ever yours, dearest,

T B M

[1] Eliza O'Neill (1791–1872: *DNB*), after a few years on the London stage had retired in 1819.
[2] Maria Foote (1797–1867: *DNB*), married the fourth Earl of Harrington in 1831.
[3] Lucia Elizabeth Vestris (1797–1856: *DNB*), actress and theatrical manager, married the younger Charles Mathews in 1838.
[4] Elizabeth Chester (b. 1799); her beauty prompted George IV to appoint her his official 'reader.'
[5] Susannah Maria Cibber (1714–66: *DNB*), wife of Colley Cibber's son.
[6] For inoculation and vaccination against smallpox.
[7] John Galt, *The Entail*, III, ch. 27.   [8] £800 from Hannah More: see 8 November.

TO MACVEY NAPIER, 1 OCTOBER 1833

MS: British Museum. *Published:* Napier, *Correspondence,* p. 138.

London October 1. 1833

Dear Napier,

I am at work for you. But I have other work to do, and I can get on with my article only before breakfast. My hand is a little out. I do not seem to myself to write with as much ease as formerly.

You shall have the article as soon as it is ready. That is all that I can promise: and I will not ask for a proof.

I was sorry not to be able to revisit Edinburgh. But I cannot admit that I justly incurred the Lord Advocate's hospitable resentment. He should blame the Scotch rains, the Scotch inns, the Scotch roads; and the Scotch post-horses.

But here comes a Nabob to bore me. So farewell.

Ever yours truly
T B Macaulay

TO HANNAH MACAULAY, 2 OCTOBER 1833

MS: Trinity College. *Address:* Miss H M Macaulay / E Cropper's Esq / Dingle Bank / Liverpool. *Frank:* London October two 1833 / T B Macaulay.

London October 2. 1833

Dearest Nancy,

I have, as you may well guess, very little to tell you in the present deserted state of London. – I write all the morning for the Edinburgh Review and on Indian business. I then take a long walk and read novels all the evening. More by token, as the Irish say, I have read Elizabeth De Bruce[1] again. I liked the dramatic parts better than ever, and understood the story just as little as ever. Whose daughter the heroine is, I have not the faintest notion. But of whatever family she may come, she is a charming creature – the sweetest female portrait that I remember. I have just got Lawrie Todd,[2] on old Sharp's recommendation, and shall begin it this evening.

Have you seen Galt's autobiography?[3] And did you ever see so foolish a book? In general a fool can write an amusing life of himself, even when his adventures have not been out of the common way. It seems odd therefore that a man of wit, and humour, who has been beaten about the

[1] Mrs Christian Isobel Johnstone, *Elizabeth de Bruce,* 3 vols., 1827.
[2] By John Galt, 1830; TBM mentions it in 3 June 1831.
[3] *The Autobiography of John Galt,* 2 vols., published on 16 September.

world, who has seen many forms of society which few others have seen, should have produced a life of himself as dull as a volume of the Statutes at Large. But Galt was always an odd writer – the most uncertain of writers. He never does any thing well except when he writes dramatically. He can put himself completely into the person of some imaginary character, as in the Annals of the Parish, the Provost, Dr. Pringle's letters,[1] and the conversation of the Leddy of Grippy.[2] But when he writes his own thoughts in his own language, as in his life of Wolsey,[3] his travels,[4] his memoirs of Byron, and in this stupid autobiography, he is an affected twaddler. Poor man! He is very ill and very badly off as to money.[5]

In about a month I shall be forced to run down to Leeds and eat a dinner with my constituents. That will be no time, I imagine, for visiting the Dingle. I may perhaps look in at the Temple or at Sir George Philips's as I return. I have half a dozen invitations to the country. But, on the whole, I prefer my own chambers to other people's palaces.

My father summoned me on Monday to a long conference at George's about pecuniary matters. The result is that you are to go on just as you have gone on. I do not believe that the House in Bernard Street will be given up. I did not know what [your][6] wishes would have been on th[at][6] point, or I would have suppor[ted][6] them. Being ignorant of your sentimen[ts,][6] I spoke my own, and strongly dissuaded a change. My father seemed quite inclined to stay where he is.

I have nothing more to tell you. For you will hardly care I suppose to hear an account of my conferences with George Lamb about the Factory Commission[7] and with Stanley about the Establishment at St Helena. When I write next I will tell you what I think of Lawrie Todd. Love to Meg, Ned, and Fan.

Ever yours, darling

T B M

---

[1] *The Annals of the Parish*, 1821; *The Provost*, 1822; 'Dr. Pringle's letters' is *The Ayrshire Legatees*, 1821.

[2] In *The Entail*.

[3] *The Life and Administration of Cardinal Wolsey*, 1812.

[4] *Voyages and Travels in the Years 1809, 1810, and 1811*, 1812.

[5] Galt (1779–1839: *DNB*), after many vicissitudes, had been in England since 1829, in broken health and attempting to live by his pen.

[6] Paper torn away with seal.

[7] The Royal Commission appointed in 1833 at the instance of the manufacturers to counter the work of Sadler's committee of 1832.

TO HANNAH MACAULAY, 5 OCTOBER 1833

MS: Trinity College. *Address:* Miss H M Macaulay / E Cropper's Esq / Dingle Bank / Liverpool. *Frank:* London October five 1833 / T B Macaulay. *Partly published:* Trevelyan, I, 328–9.

London October 5. 1833

Dearest Nancy,

Life goes on so quietly here, or rather stands so still that I have nothing or next to nothing to say. At the Athenæum I now and then fall in with some person passing through town on his way to the continent or to Brighton. I met the other day with Charles Wynn, and heard him squeak[1] much on his favourite topic, the precedents and rules of the House of Commons. Then I fell in with Sharp, and had a long talk with him about every thing and every body, metaphysics, poetry, politics, scenery, and painting. One thing I have observed in Sharp which is quite peculiar to him among town-wits and diners-out. He never talks scandal. If he can say nothing good of a man he holds his tongue. I do not of course mean that in confidential communication about politics he does not speak freely of public men. But about the foibles of private individuals I do not believe that, much as I have talked with him, I ever heard him utter one word. I passed three or four hours very agreeably in his company at the club.

I have also seen Kenny[2] for an hour or two. I do not know that I ever mentioned Kenny to you. When London is overflowing, I meet such numbers of people that I cannot remember half their names. This is the time at which every acquaintance, however slight, attracts some degree of attention. In the desert island even Poor Poll was something of a companion to Robinson Crusoe. Kenny is a writer of a class which, in our time, is at the very bottom of the literary scale. He is a dramatist. Most of the farces and three-act plays which have succeeded during the last eight or ten years are, I am told, from his pen. Heaven knows that, if they are the farces and plays which I have seen, they do him but little honor. One of them is called *Sweethearts and Wives*.[3] I saw it formerly. It was

---

[1] Wynn's squeaky voice was a by-word. Lord Mahon writes in a note dated 13 December 1849 that 'breakfasting with Macaulay...he told us that once in the House of Commons observing how carefully Mr. Wynn used to muffle up his neck, he had translated or adapted as follows an epigram of Martial:

> Wynn never squeaks a single note
> So much the evening cold he fears
> Without thick cotton round his throat,
> – Would he could spare some for my ears!'

(MS, Stanhope Papers, Chevening).

[2] James Kenney (1780–1849: *DNB*), popular dramatist, had been writing for the London stage since 1803. He was a friend of Samuel Rogers.

[3] 1823: 'one of the most popular dramas ever produced' (*DNB*).

loudly applauded: but I thought that most of the joke lay in Liston's ugly face.[1] However this man is one of our great comic writers. He has the merit, such as it is, of hitting the very bad taste of our modern audiences better than any other person who has stooped to that degrading work. We had a good deal of literary chat; and I thought him a clever shrewd fellow. He has seen a good deal of a kind of society of which I have seen next to nothing, and of which I do not wish to see more – green-room society, – the society of the lower and coarser class of literary men. I am glad to obtain information about those circles at second hand, as I have no wish to mix in them personally. He is very intimate with Charles Lamb and with Cooper,[2] the Yankee Novellist. His account of Cooper agreed with what I had heard from every body else – that he is the most detestable beast that ever infested the face of the earth.

I have read Lawrie Todd, and like it very much. I do not think that any of Galt's longer novels has left so agreable an impression on my mind. There is no single page in it equal to several in the Entail. But I like it better on the whole. The picture of the back-settlement life, the rapid growth of prosperity and civilization – first the desolate and silent forest – then the hut – then the small hamlet, – then the mills, the factories, the Churches, the newspapers, the stage-coaches, – all the transformation wrought in a small part of a single life – it is a very striking subject for thought, and the more striking because it is by no means imaginary.[3] Galt's Lawrie Todd is the favourable view of that state of society of which Mrs. Trollope has given the unfavourable view in her account of Cincinnati and of Rochester.[4]

My father is poorly – not that any thing very serious is the matter with him. But he has a cold and is in low spirits. His affairs are worse than ever. Yet I scarcely know how that is possible. They have been for years as bad as they could be; and no man can well be more than ruined. I only hope that, at any cost to myself, I may be able, during the short life which still remains to him, to avert from him the misery and disgrace of a bank-ruptcy; and I think that it may be averted. Poor Charles tells me that his professional education will be at a stand unless he can procure eighty guineas in a week or two, and I suppose I must pay the money; for I am sure that my father cannot. I am rather impatient for Grant's return, and for the final settlement, one way or other, of my business.

It is some comfort in the midst of our pecuniary difficulties to see the

---

[1] John Liston (1776–1846: *DNB*), comic actor, played Billy Lackaday in *Sweethearts and Wives*.

[2] James Fenimore Cooper (1789–1851), lived in Europe between 1826 and 1833, when he twice visited England. Cooper was a quarrelsome man.

[3] The novel is based on Galt's experiences in Canada, during the years 1826–9.

[4] In her *Domestic Manners of the Americans*.

political horizon clearing. If Lord Spencer lives,[1] and the present temper of the public mind continues we have, I think, a very smooth Session of Parliament before us.

Though I talk about poverty do not imagine that I am too poor to let you have any money that you want. I shall have, after paying Charles's surgical expenses, four hundred and fifty pounds in my desk, and you know that you are welcome to as much of it as you like. Remember that I will never forgive you if I find that you suffer yourself to be distressed for money while I have a[ny.][2]

Kindest love to all at the Dingle.

Ever yours, my love,

T B M

TO HANNAH MACAULAY, 9 [OCTOBER][3] 1833

MS: Trinity College.

London September 9. 1833

Dearest Nancy,

Only a line to shew that I have not forgotten my darling. I must for two or three days to come be busy from morning to night with my article. After all it will, I fear, be a very feeble and bad one. But I am a little consoled by remembering that I have disliked all my most successful articles except that on Southey.

I was so much pleased with Lawrie Tod that I tried Sir Andrew Wylie[4] again: but, as Horace Walpole says of Ranelagh, I did not find the joy of it.[5] In plain words I thought it miserably bad.

Bulwer's last book[6] is sad stuff, I think. But I have not read it through. He has drawn a degrading controversy on himself by drawing a character of Westmacott under the name of Sneak.[7] Why on earth does he foul his fingers with such a filthy blackguard? Above all how could he think that any nickname could be half so opprobrious as Westmacott.

I am pretty well – my father but middling. Cholera has quite disappeared here: but it is raging at Madrid, and I am sorry for it. It could not have gone thither at a more unseasonable moment. For the first time

---

[1] His death would mean that Lord Althorp would succeed him in the earldom and thus be lost to the Whigs in the House of Commons. This happened in November 1834.

[2] Paper torn away with seal.

[3] Internal evidence makes it clear that TBM misdated this letter.

[4] John Galt, *Sir Andrew Wylie of that Ilk*, 3 vols., 1822.

[5] Walpole to Sir Horace Mann, 26 May 1742 (W. S. Lewis, *et al.,* eds., *Horace Walpole's Correspondence*, New Haven, 17 [1954], 434).

[6] *England and the English*, 2 vols., appeared in late July.

[7] *Ibid.* Book 4, ch. 10.

in my life there happens to be a man just on the road to Madrid for whom I have a regard;[1] and the cholera must break out there. Wonder after this that I am a Manichean.[. . .][2]

TO MACVEY NAPIER, 14 OCTOBER 1833

MS: British Museum. *Address:* Macvey Napier Esq / Castle Street / Edinburgh. *Frank:* London October fourteen / 1833 / T B Macaulay. *Mostly published:* Napier, *Correspondence,* p. 138.

London Octr. 14. 1833

Dear Napier,

I send my article to day. I have gone down no further than the beginning of the seven years' war. I have some notion, if you see no objection, of reviewing for the Xtmas number a life of Chatham, by a person of the name of Thackray, in two Quarto Vols.[3] It is dedicated to Peel, and contains some papers furnished from the Secretary of State's office, if I recollect rightly. It has been published some years, – five or six years I think. But I really do not know why that should prevent us from having an article on it, especially as it attracted very little notice at the time of its publication.

Let me know what you think of this plan – and look carefully over the proofs of my article.

Ever yours truly
T B Macaulay

My sister begs that I will present her kind regards to Miss Napier.

TO HANNAH MACAULAY, 14 OCTOBER 1833

MS: Mrs Humphry Trevelyan. *Address:* Miss Macaulay / E Cropper's Esq / Dingle Bank / Liverpool. *Frank:* London October fourteen 1833 / T B Macaulay. *Partly published:* Trevelyan, I, 330.

London October 14. 1833

Dearest Nancy,

I have just finished my article. This is one of the happy moments of my life. A stupid task performed; a weight taken off my mind. I should be

---

[1] George Villiers, just appointed ambassador to Madrid.   [2] The rest is missing.
[3] The Reverend Francis Thackeray, *A History of the Right Honourable William Pitt, Earl of Chatham,* 2 vols., 1827. TBM's article is 'Thackeray's *History of the Earl of Chatham,*' *ER,* LVIII (January 1834), 508–44.

quite joyous if I had only you to read it to. But to Napier it must go forthwith; and, as soon as I have finished this letter, I shall put it into the general post with my own fair hands. I was up at four this morning to put the last hand to it. I often differ with the majority about other people's writings, and still oftener about my own. Therefore I may very likely be mistaken. But I think that this article will be a hit. We shall see. Nothing ever cost me more pains than the first half. I never wrote anything so flowingly as the latter half: and I like the latter half the best. I have laid it on Walpole so unsparingly that I shall not be surprised if Miss Berry should cut me. You know she was Walpole's favourite in her youth. His reminiscences are addressed to her. She edited his correspondence with "the blind woman who was clever,"[1] Mrs. Robert Grant – hum; – and she may resent my freedom with her old friend. Neither am I sure that Lord and Lady Holland will be well pleased. But they ought to be obliged to me. For I refrained for their sake from laying a hand which has been thought to be not a light one on that old rogue the first Lord Holland.[2]

Charles Grant is still at Paris, – ill, he says. I never knew a man who wanted setting to rights so often. He goes as ill as your watch, of which I never think without some CURSORY reflections on Ganthony. – A pun! Very fair!

On the 6th of Novr. I am to dine at Leeds and to make a harangue. I think it a foolish business: but our people will have it so. Before that time I shall probably know something decisive about India.

I was so well pleased with Galt's Lawrie Tod that I tried Sir Andrew Wylie again, and found it more detestable than ever. I could not get through half a volume. What an uncertain writer he is.

I have taken the liberty to send your kind regards to Miss Napier. Knowing your affection for her, I thought that I could not do wrong. But if you wish them to be recalled, I shall be glad to oblige you.

Good bye, my darling. Remember to let me know if you want any money. Kindest love to Edward and dear dear Margaret.

Ever yours, my Nancy

T B Macaulay

[1] *Letters of the Marquise Du Deffand to the Hon. Horace Walpole*, 4 vols., 1810. The phrase quoted is evidently something said by the foolish Mrs Robert Grant: see 26 November 1832.

[2] Henry Fox (1705–74: *DNB*), first Baron Holland; he is only mentioned a couple of times in the essay on Walpole.

TO JAMES STEWART-MACKENZIE, 14 OCTOBER 1833

MS: Scottish Record Office.

London October 14. 1833

Dear Mackenzie,

I have nothing to tell you. Grant is ill at Paris – whether of tooth-ache or head-ache God knows. Gordon is in the country. Even Waterfield[1] is keeping holiday. I have just finished an article on Walpole's letters for the Edinburgh Review, and have now, I suppose, a month of hard work before me. No Chinese superintendent appointed![2] No instructions ready! The Directors sweating, like the bare-headed Captains who ran about "asking every one for Sir John Falstaff";[3] and the President not forthcoming – not engaged, I hope, with any French Doll Tearsheet[4] like Poulett Thompson. There will be much to do within the fortnight after Grant's arrival. I wish that we could have you here and Gordon away. But I expect that my wishing will go by contraries.

About my self of course nothing is settled. The decision cannot, I think, be long delayed.

But I must stop for here comes a Nabob, and, I will be bound for him, a great bore. If you were here I would send him to you. In default of him accept my kindest regards and believe me ever

Yours most truly
T B Macaulay

TO HANNAH MACAULAY, 17 OCTOBER 1833

MS: Trinity College. *Partly published:* Trevelyan, I, 330–2.

London October 17. 1833

Dearest Nancy,

It is the 17th, and no news of Grant. He promised to be here a week ago. The Directors are foaming. The Chairs are sending daily to ask after him. The business is of the most pressing importance. A frigate is ordered to be ready to sail for India on the first of November with dispatches of the highest consequence; and he neither comes, nor writes. This is one of those cases in which we become sensible of the relief derived from swearing. At such seasons I cease to wonder at the maledictory propensities which are thought so vulgar by the ladies. He is at Dieppe, as somebody in London has heard from somebody there: but he himself does

---

[1] Thomas Nelson Waterfield (1799–1862: *Boase*), clerk at the Board of Control, 1818–39, and then assistant secretary to the Board in the Secret and Political Department.
[2] Lord Napier was appointed Chief Superintendent of Trade at Hong Kong in December.
[3] *2 Henry IV*, II, iv, 389.   [4] In *2 Henry IV*.

not take the trouble to send us any intelligence. Of all the Ministers he is most wanted: and he is almost the only one of them who is not in town.

Charles made some strange miscalculation of his wants: for when the expenses for which he required money were drawn out the whole amounted only to sixteen pounds, which I shall pay with a very good will. I have told my father not to trouble himself about the hundred pounds that I lent, or rather gave him: and, in truth, I would as soon give him another hundred as be pestered to provide for Pate Robertson. He is at me on that subject. What on earth have I to do with Pate Robertson? The relationship is one which none but Scotchmen would recognize. The lad is such a fool that he would utterly disgrace my recommendation. And, as if to make the thing more provoking, his sisters say that he must be provided for in England; for that they cannot think of parting with him. This to be sure matters little: for there is at present just as little chance of getting any thing in India as in England.

But what strange folly this is which meets me in every quarter. People wanting posts in the army – the navy – the public offices – and saying that, if they cannot find such posts, they must starve. How do all the rest of mankind live? If I had not happened to be engaged in politics, and if my father had not been connected, by very extraordinary circumstances, with public men, we should never have dreamed of having places. Why cannot Pate be apprenticed to some hatter or tailor? He may do well in such a business. He will do detestably ill as a clerk in my office. He may come to make good coats. He will never, I am sure, write good dispatches. There is nothing truer than poor Richard's saw. We are taxed twice as heavily by our pride as by the state.[1] The curse of England is the obstinate determination of the middle classes to make their sons what they call gentlemen. So we are over-run with clergymen without livings, lawyers without briefs, physicians without patients, authors without readers, clerks soliciting employment, who might have thriven and been above the world as bakers, watch-makers or inn-keepers. The next time my father speaks to me about Pate, I will offer to subscribe twenty guineas towards making a pastry-cook of him. He had a sweet tooth when he was a child; – a child indeed he is and will always be; – and I shall not be surprised if he should succeed as well as Birch[2] in tarts with custard.

So you are reading Burnet. Did you begin from the beginning? What do you think of the old fellow? He was always a great favourite of mine – honest, though careless; a strong party-man on the right side, yet with much kind feeling towards his opponents and even towards his personal

---

[1] *Poor Richard's Almanack, 1758*, Preface: 'We are taxed twice as much by our *Idleness*, three times as much by our *Pride*, and four times as much by our *Folly....*'

[2] Samuel Birch (1757–1841: *DNB*), pastrycook and confectioner at 15 Cornhill; the business dated from the reign of George I.

enemies. He is to me a most entertaining writer; – far superior to Clarendon[1] in the art of amusing – though of course far Clarendon's inferior in discernment, dignity, and correctness of style. Do you know by the bye Clarendon's life of himself.[2] I like it, – the part after the Restoration at least, – better than his great History. I hear that Lister is writing a life of Clarendon.[3] The Villierses could of course furnish him with ample materials: and, if I am not mistaken, Lister would succeed in history. His novels are, to my thinking, the novels of a man who would shine more in working up and arranging a story furnished to him than in constructing one of his own.

I am very quiet, rise at seven or half past, read Spanish till ten, breakfast, walk to my office, stay there till four, take a long walk, dine towards seven, and am in bed before eleven. I am going through Don Quixote again, and admire it more than ever. It is certainly the best novel in the world, beyond all comparison.

In a few days I suppose we shall have the Edinburgh Review. I am impatient to know what you think of my article.

Kindest love to Margaret and Edward. We shall have Fanny soon, I suppose.

Ever yours, my love

T B M

I managed to get a place in the Ordnance at Sierra Leone for a friend of Henry's – a great raff in appearance, but apparently a good sort of fellow of the name of Graham, and I have had a most fervid letter of thanks from him.

TO MACVEY NAPIER, 21 OCTOBER 1833

MS: British Museum. *Address:* Macvey Napier Esq / Castle Street / Edinburgh. *Frank:* London October twenty one / 1833 / T B Macaulay. *Mostly published:* Trevelyan, I, 333–5.

London October 21. 1833

Dear Napier,

I am glad to learn that you like my article. I like it myself, which is not much my habit. Very likely the public which has often been kinder to my performances than I was, may on this, as on other occasions, differ from me in opinion. If the paper has any merit it owes it to the delay of which

---

[1] *The History of the Rebellion,* 1702–4.   [2] *The Life of Edward, Earl of Clarendon,* 1759.
[3] Published as *The Life and Administration of Edward, first Earl of Clarendon,* 3 vols., 1838. Mrs Lister was the sister of the fourth Earl.

you must, I am sure, have complained very bitterly in your heart. I was so thoroughly dissatisfied with the article, as it stood at first, that I completely rewrote it, altered the whole arrangement, left out ten or twelve pages in one part and added twice as many in another. I never wrote any thing so slowly as the first half or so rapidly as the last half.

You are in an error about Akenside which I must clear up for his credit, for mine, and for Dr. Parr's. You are confounding the Ode to Curio and the Epistle to Curio.[1] The latter is generally printed at the end of Akenside's works, and is, I think, the best thing that he ever wrote. The Ode is worthless. It is merely an abridgement of the Epistle executed in the most unskilful way. Johnson says in his life of Akenside that no poet ever so much mistook his powers as Akenside when he took to lyric composition. "Having" – I think the words are – "written with great force and poignancy his Epistle to Curio, he afterwards transformed it into an Ode disgraceful only to its author."[2]

When I said that Chesterfield had lost by the publication of his letters, I of course considered that he had much to lose; – that he has left an immense reputation, founded on the testimony of all his contemporaries of all parties, for wit, taste, and eloquence, – that what remains of his parliamentary oratory is superior to any thing of that time that has come down to us, except a little of Pitt's. The utmost that can be said of the letters is that they are the letters of a cleverish man; and there are not many which are entitled even to that praise. I think he would have stood higher if we had been left to judge of his powers as we judge of those of Chatham, Mansfield,[3] Charles Townshend,[4] and many others, only by tradition and by fragments of speeches preserved in parliamentary reports.

I said nothing about Lord Byron's criticism on Walpole,[5] because I thought it, like most of his Lordship's criticism, below r[efutation.][6] On the drama Lord Byron wr[ote more][6] nonsense than on any subje[ct. He][6] wanted to have restored the unities. His practice proved as unsuccessful as his theory was absurd. His admiration of the mysterious Mother was of a piece with his thinking Gifford and Rogers greater poets than Wordsworth and Coleridge.[7]

But I must have done.

> Ever yours truly
> T B Macaulay

---

[1] TBM says of Akenside's 'Epistle to Curio' that it was 'the best poem that he ever wrote' ('Walpole,' *ER*, LVIII, 252). I do not know what Dr Parr's opinion was.

[2] See the end of 'Akenside,' *Lives of the Poets*. TBM's quotation is almost verbatim.

[3] William Murray (1705–93: *DNB*), first Earl of Mansfield.

[4] Charles Townshend (1725–67: *DNB*), Chancellor of the Exchequer.

[5] Byron praises Walpole's tragedy, *The Mysterious Mother* (1768) in the preface to *Marino Faliero*.

[6] Paper torn away with seal.   [7] In 'English Bards and Scotch Reviewers.'

TO HANNAH MACAULAY, 21 OCTOBER 1833

MS: Trinity College. *Address:* Miss Macaulay / E Cropper's Esq / Dingle Bank / Liverpool. *Frank:* London October twenty one / 1833 / T B Macaulay. *Mostly published:* Trevelyan, I, 332–3.

London October 21. 1833

My love,

Grant is here at last; and we have had a very long talk about matters both public and private. The Government would support my appointment: but he expects violent opposition from the Company. He mentioned my name to the Chairs,[1] and they were furious. They know that I have been against them through the whole course of the negotiations. They put their opposition on the ground of my youth, a very flattering objection to a man who this week completes his thirty third year. They spoke very highly of me in other respects. But they seemed quite obstinate; – as indeed they are on all occasions the most stupid pair of mules that I ever saw.

The question now is whether their opposition will be supported by the other Directors. If it should be so, I have advised Grant most strongly to withdraw my name and to put up some other man, and then to fight the battle to the utmost. We shall be suspected of jobbing if we proceed to extremities on behalf of one of ourselves. But we can do what we like if it is in favour of some person whom we cannot be suspected of supporting from interested motives. From the extreme ill-temper, unreasonableness, and pertinacity, which are discernible in every communication that we receive from the India House at present, I am inclined to think that I have no chance of being chosen by them without a dispute in which I should not wish the government to engage for such a purpose. Lord Grey says that I have a right to their support if I ask for it: but that, for the sake of his administration generally, he is very averse to my going. I do not think that I shall go. However a few days will decide the matter.

I have heard from Napier. He praises my article in terms absolutely extravagant. He says that it is the best that I ever wrote, and, *entre nous*, I am not very far from agreeing with him. I am impatient to have your opinion. No flattery pleases me so much as domestic flattery. You will have the Number within the week. Kindest love to Edward and Margaret.

Ever yours, my darling,

T B M

---

[1] The Chairman of the East India Company was Campbell Marjoribanks (1769–1840). William Wigram (1780–1858: *Boase*) was Deputy Chairman.

P.S. I ought to have told [you that][1] we have carried one point against both the government and the Chairs. Metcalfe[2] is appointed to Agra. Lord Auckland has behaved admirably. He has no intention of going to India in any other situation.

TO HANNAH MACAULAY, 24 OCTOBER 1833

MS: Trinity College. *Address:* Miss Macaulay / E Cropper's Esq / Dingle Bank / Liverpool. *Frank:* London October twenty four / 1833 / T B Macaulay.

London Octr. 24. 1833

Dearest Nancy,

A few lines, and in great haste. Grant has just been closeted for some hours with Wigram, the Deputy Chairman of the Company. Marjoribanks, the Chairman, is ill, and talks of resigning. Grant again pressed my claims. Indeed I have had the undivided support of the Government. Wigram again objected, – disclaimed all unfriendly or disrespectful feelings towards me, – but said that some person who had been long in India ought to be appointed, and suggested one of the puisne Judges of Calcutta. To this proposal Grant objected in his turn, and with great reason. Indeed he argued the matter so strongly that Wigram was silenced.

Here for the present the question rests. If the objection of the Chairs be personal to me, they will persist in their opposition. But if, as they declare, they oppose me only because they think that some person resident in India ought to have the appointment, they will probably give way when they find that the Government will not hear of any person resident in India. Grant means to tell them plainly that, whether they choose me or not, they must choose some person from England. When they know this, they may perhaps think that I shall do as well as another.

Even if they should be refractory, there may be another chance – though a slight one. We may have a majority in the Court though the Chairs may be against us. Grant intends to ascertain, as well as he can, what the general feeling of the Directors is.

---

[1] Paper torn away with seal.

[2] Charles Metcalfe (1785–1846: *DNB*), afterwards first Baron Metcalfe; in the service of the East India Company since 1801. He acted as Governor-General of India in the interval between Bentinck's departure and Auckland's arrival, 1835–6; after leaving India was Governor of Jamaica, 1839–42, and of Canada, 1843–5. In his speech on India of 24 June 1853, TBM calls Metcalfe 'the ablest civil servant I ever knew in India' (*Hansard*, 3rd Series, xxxviii, 751). TBM wrote Metcalfe's epitaph (*The Miscellaneous Writings of Lord Macaulay*, ii, 440).

This day week he is to have another conference with the Chairs; and till that is over we can know nothing more. On my own account, I am perfectly easy. Whatever anxiety I have arises from thinking of your feelings and our dear Margaret's. Pray let me hear from you soon, my love; and tell me that this suspense has not subdued your spirits or broken your rest.

It is impossible to conceive warmer kindness or more perfect confidence than Grant has shown to me. Indeed, between ourselves, I am at least as much President of the Board as he.

You may be curious to know who, if we should go, are likely to be our companions. I suspect that a barrister of the name of Coulson,[1] formerly Editor of the Globe, a very able and intelligent man, though somewhat dry in his manner, will be one of the Law-Commissioners, and will sail in the same vessel that takes out the Councillor. I wish I could hope that we should have Holt Mackenzie too. But he is so much detested by the Company that there is little chance of that, as in his case, the Board has no power to interfere at all.[2]

Remember that all this is still strictly secret. Kindest love to Margaret and Edward.

Ever yours, my darling
T B M

TO HANNAH MACAULAY, 28 OCTOBER 1833

MS: Trinity College. *Address:* Miss Macaulay / E Cropper's Esq / Dingle Bank / Liverpool. *Frank:* London October twenty eight 1833 / T B Macaulay. *Partly published:* Trevelyan, I, 335–6.

London October 28. 1833

Dearest Nancy,

I have nothing more to tell you, – at least nothing of a private nature. Our public arrangements are proceeding fast. Grant was so much and so justly delighted by a very able paper which James Stephen has drawn for the guidance of the new Superintendants who are about to be sent to China that he conceived a wish to send Stephen himself as the Chief of the Commission. I have done my best to dissuade him, and I think I have succeeded. I thought it right to do this both for Stephen's sake and for the sake of the public. I admire his abilities; but I am sure that at

---

[1] Coulson did not go to India.

[2] In a letter to Lord William Bentinck, 25 December 1833, Charles Grant says that he would have appointed Mackenzie to the India Council but could not communicate with him in time, and adds that the Chairs 'had a violent prejudice and hatred against him' (cited in Eric Stokes, *The English Utilitarians and India*, Oxford, 1959, pp. 331–2).

Canton he would be quite out of his sphere, and that he would in all probability injure the interests of the nation and bring discredit on himself. He has great merit in the speculative part of politics, – little or none in the practical. He sees with clearness and expresses with force the arguments for and against a law, when he is sitting quietly at his desk in Downing-Street. But he has none of the presence of mind and readiness of ressource which great emergencies require. He is a nervous, fanciful, scrupulous, man, – a man whom the tremendous load of responsibility which Grant wished to lay on him would have oppressed, and very likely killed. He has drawn us an excellent paper on the general principles which ought to guide our conduct with reference to the government of China. But he would in all probability commit some tremendous blunder, if he had to make up his mind in three minutes as to the course to be pursued when the Viceroy of Canton might be in a rage, the mob bellowing round the doors of the factory, and an English ship of war making preparations to bombard the town. I have advised Grant, if he cannot procure the seat in council for me, to procure it for Stephen.[1] That is just the post which would suit his talents and his temper. If I am made Councillor, Grant will probably try to make Stephen a Law-Commissioner for India. If that plan succeeds, you may perhaps go out under the chaperonage of Mrs. James Stephen.[2] I do not know how you will like it.

Do not breathe a syllable of all this. It is a strict secret on private as well as on public grounds: for, though I can declare before God that I have given my advice with the kindest feelings towards Stephen, and though I believe that I have saved him from a most serious calamity, there is no knowing how he might take it.

I wish to have Malkin at Canton, and Grant seems now to be strongly bent on the same plan. Malkin is a man of singular temper, judgment, and firmness of nerve. Danger and responsibility, instead of agitating and confusing him, always bring out whatever there is in him. This was the reason of his great success at Cambridge. He made a figure there far beyond his learning or his talents – though both his learning and his talents are highly respectable. But the moment that he sate down to be examined, – which is just the situation in which all other people from natural flurry do worse than at other times, – he began to do his very best. His intellect became clearer, and his manner more quiet than usual. He is the very man for this place. Smoke Presto writing politics to M.D.

Apropos of places, my father has been at me again about Pate Robert-

---

[1] James Stephen's son Leslie says that 'Macaulay strongly advised my father to take the post of which he soon became himself the first occupant' (*Life of Sir James Fitzjames Stephen*, p. 235).

[2] Jane Catherine, daughter of Henry Venn, Rector of Clapham, married James Stephen in 1814.

son – unto whom and unto all his generation may the leprosy of Gehazi cleave,[1] as it seems to be cleaving, in return for the plague which I have had with them. Would you think it? This lad Pate has a hundred and twenty pounds a year for life. I could not believe my ears. But so it is. And I who have not a penny and who have half a dozen brothers and sisters as poor as myself am to move heaven and earth to push this boy who, as he is the silliest, is also, I think, the richest relation that I have in the world. I told my father that Pate ought to set up a shop, a hatter's or a grocer's, I rather recommended a pastry-cook's. I shall do nothing for him.

Àpropos of shops and pastry cooks, – see how I wander, – I am to dine on Thursday with the Fishmonger's Company, – the first company for *gourmandise* in the world. Their magnificent Hall near London Bridge is not yet built, but, as respects eating and drinking, I shall be no loser: for we are to be entertained at the Albion Tavern.

This is the first dinner party that I have been to for a long time. There is nobody in town that I know except official men, and they have left their wives and households in the country. I met Poodle Byng, it is true, the day before yesterday in the Street, and he begged me to make haste to Brookes's, for Lord Essex was there, he said, whipping up for a dinner-party, cursing and swearing at all his friends for being out of town, and wishing – what an honor! – that Macaulay was in London. I preserved all the dignity of a young lady in an *affaire du coeur*. "I shall not run after my Lord, I assure you. If he wants me he knows where he may hear of me." This nibble is the nearest approach to a dinner party that I have had.

William Wilberforce has been in London living at free-quarter upon George and Sarah Anne. I would as soon have had a company of dragoons billetted on me. He made Sarah Anne buy him stockings and have them marked: and he paid her for the stockings, but not for the marking. He invited himself to Henry Thornton's house. But Thornton positively told him that it did not suit him to receive guests at present. I am glad to tell you that the money matters are settled with him better than I had expected. At all events they are settled, and my father is out of his power.

William Wilberforce's example seems to be catching. I have heard of ℞ mad dog biting a sheep, and of the sheep then running mad. This is something like what has now happened. Whom of all the creatures on the face of this earth do you think that the disease of Spoonerism[2] has infected? Even William Babington. I cannot think of the affair without

---

[1] II Kings 5: 27.

[2] The elder William Wilberforce married Barbara Spooner of Birmingham. The faults of their children were usually attributed to the mother's side. Marianne Thornton called Mrs Wilberforce 'very deficient in common sense, a woman with narrow views and selfish aims' (E. M. Forster, *Marianne Thornton*, p. 35).

laughing till I am ready to drop. On Saturday last, it being three or four years since I had seen him, (for I have never met him since he was so good as to come to Great Ormond Street in order to treat us with a sight of his sore eye,) he walked into my chambers. I was lolling there on my Sofa in a very smart new dressing gown, finishing my breakfast and reading a volume of Voltaire. It was half after ten. In came my gentleman, took a seat, laid down a large blue bag, and began to ask me for a letter of introduction to Rice about some trumpery job that he has to manage at the Treasury. I told him that he had better go to one of the Lords than to the Secretary, that Rice was overdone with business, and that I would speak to Kennedy.[1] No – he preferred Francis Baring. They had, he said, been friends formerly, when Francis Baring was a pupil of Mr. Venn's. I thought, but I did not say, that this was but a poor dependence. For Francis Baring is one of the driest and most severe official men in the whole government. However I gave him joy of Francis Baring's friendship, and hoped that he would see the fruits of it. "I should like some tea" was the reply. "I beg your pardon;" I exclaimed. "I did not offer you breakfast because I supposed that you had breakfasted. My hours are very late, and you, I know, must be early." "O yes, I have breakfasted: but I should like some tea for all that." Then I had to call my old woman, to have the kettle re-filled, the tea-pot washed, and fresh things put on the table. I drink only black. My self-invited guest could drink only green: so my clerk had to run to the nearest grocer's. My kind friend made himself a cup of tea, fell on the loaf, and proceeded to demand eggs. My good lady, amazed at this second breakfast, asked how many. Two would do: and two were brought and two he ate; as also two pounds of bread and a quart of green tea: and he took up his bag, and went on his way rejoicing,[2] and I saw him no more.

What an enormous letter: and all written in exactly half an hour. I must have done; and not before it is time. Kindest love to Margaret and Edward. Fanny is come at last looking very well.

Ever yours, my darling
T B M

I break open my letter to say that Marjoribanks has resigned the Chair of the Company.[3] Wigram will be Chairman who is as bitter as Marjoribanks. But it is thought that Stanley Clarke,[4] an extremely tractable and friendly person, will be deputy chairman.

---

[1] Thomas Francis Kennedy (1788–1879: *DNB*), Whig M.P. for Ayr, 1818–34; Junior Lord of the Treasury, 1832–4.   [2] Cf. Acts 8: 39.

[3] Marjoribanks resigned on 26 October, giving reasons of health and of hostility to the new charter.

[4] William Stanley Clarke (d. 1844), director of the East India Company since 1815; Deputy Chairman, 1834; Chairman, 1835.

TO HANNAH MACAULAY, 31 OCTOBER 1833

MS: Trinity College. *Extracts published:* Trevelyan, 1, 336–7; 347.

London October 31. 1833

Dearest Nancy,

Nothing is yet settled, nor will be settled for a week to come. But the probability of our going becomes stronger. A complete revolution has taken place in the administration at the India House. I opened my last letter to tell you that Marjoribanks had resigned. Wigram who from being Deputy became Chairman in consequence of Marjoribanks's retirement is inveterately hostile to us, and was resolved to have a deputy whom he could manage, or to resign. The majority of the Directors however were sick of quarrelling with the Board of Controul, and impatient of Wigram's dictation. When he threatened to resign unless a deputy of his party were chosen, a storm broke out. The excitement was so great that the Court adjourned for two hours that the members might cool. When they reassembled they rejected Wigram's man. Wigram instantly resigned: and we have now a new Chairman and Deputy Chairman, both friendly, – one very friendly.[1] They have already given up one of the most important points which was at issue between us and the Company; and this though they were only elected yesterday evening. Grant says that he now fully expects to carry me. He told me with tears in his eyes that he did not know what the Board would do without me. Indeed his kindness has been very great. I attribute it partly to Robert's absence; – not that Robert ever did me ill offices with him; – but Grant's is a mind that cannot stand alone. It is, begging your pardon for my want of gallantry, a feminine mind. It is always turning, like ivy, to some support. When Robert is near him he clings to Robert. Robert being away, he clings to me. This is a great weakness in a public man: but I love him the better for it.

On Monday I go to Leeds.[2] The dinner is on Wednesday. I shall be in London again on Friday. By that time probably all will be settled. There may still be difficulties. But I rather think that I shall have the situation.

My dear, dear, girl, I think of nothing but you and Margaret. But I must not dwell on these things or I shall be caught by my Secretary in a very unofficial situation.

I dine to day with the fishmongers: on Saturday with Lord Essex. My father is gone to Brighton. William Babington has honoured me with another visit, evidently intended to secure another breakfast: but he was

---

[1] John Loch (1781–1868: *Boase*), a director since 1821, was elected Chairman; the Deputy Chairman was Henry St George Tucker (1771–1851: *DNB*).

[2] To attend a political dinner.

too early. He came at a quarter after nine. My old woman had not yet come. The shutters were shut. I let him in with my dressing gown on my back and Don Quixote in my hand, apologized for not being dressed, and bowed him out. What has come over the man?

Though I trifle in this way, I am anxious – not in the least for myself – but for you. Write to me, my darling, and tell me all that you think and feel.

Ever yours dearest
T B M.

If you write on Monday direct to me at Leeds. I do not know whether you should do so on Tuesday. But Edward can tell. I shall be at Leeds till Thursday morning. Kindest love to Margaret and Edward. Remember that all that I tell you about the Directors is secret history.

TO HANNAH MACAULAY, 1 NOVEMBER 1833

MS: Trinity College. *Partly published:* Trevelyan, 1, 336–7.

London November 1. 1833

Dearest Nancy,

I have not much to add to what I told you yesterday. But every thing that I have to add looks one way. Grant tells me that Melville,[1] the most powerful of the officers in the service of the Company, – quite as powerful indeed as any of the Directors, – is strongly in my favour. Sharp by whom I sate yesterday at the Fishmonger's dinner told me that my old enemy James Mill, had spoken to him on the subject. Mill is, as you may have heard, at the head of one of the principal departments of the India House. The late chairman consulted him about me, – hoping, I suppose, to have his support against me. Mill said very handsomely that he would advise the Company to take me: for that, as public men went, I was much above the average, and that, if they rejected me, he thought it very unlikely that they would get any body so fit. This is all the news that I have for you. It is not much. But I wish to keep you as fully informed of what is going on as I am myself.

Old Sharp told me that I was acting quite wisely, but that he should never see me again, – and he cried as he said it. I encouraged him – told him that I hoped to be in England again before the end of 1839, and that there was nothing improbable in our meeting again. He cheered up after

---

[1] (Sir) James Cosmo Melvill (1792–1861: *DNB*), in the service of the East India Company since 1808; Chief Secretary, 1836–58.

a time, – told me that he should correspond with me, and give me all the secret history both of politics and of society, – and promised to select the best books and send them regularly to me.

The Fishmonger's dinner was very good, but not so profusely splendid as I had expected. There has been a change, I find, and not before it was wanted. They had got at one time to dining at ten guineas a head, or some such extravagant sum. They drank my health, and I harangued them with immense applause.[1] Baron Gurney and William Smith were there. But I talked all the evening to Sharp. I told him what a dear sister I had, and how readily she had agreed to go with me. I had told Grant the same in the morning. Both of them extolled my good fortune in having such a companion. In one respect I am not unworthy of that good fortune. For if love deserves love, my sweet friend cannot love me better than I deserve. If she knew all that I feel for her – but I could not write it without being unmanned, and she could not read it without being too much distressed.

Now about Fanny. – I have given no positive answer to her proposal to accompany us: and, as it is possible that within the next ten days things may come to a crisis, I wish to be in full possession of your opinion and Margaret's on that point. I have a sincere affection for Fanny. But I see difficulties. My father requires the attention of at least one daughter. He is likely to require such attention more than ever. The sight of his only eye[2] is failing. George has consulted Travers[3] on the subject; and the opinion of both of them is that the infirmity will go on increasing, and that no remedy can do more than delay its progress. George has not told this to my father. But it becomes more and more obvious daily that something serious is the matter. My father reads with difficulty, and cannot write legibly. I had a note from him to day in which there is a line that I am altogether unable to decypher. Selina's health is not in such a state that he can constantly rely on her care. I am therefore inclined to think that Fanny ought to remain. I should be glad to know what you wish as to this matter.

After all I may not have the appointment. But it is fit that you should fully prepare yourself for what I now think the most probable result. If we go we shall not leave England, I imagine, much before the beginning of February.

Kindest love to dear Margaret and to Edward.

Ever yours, my own darling,

T B M

[1] I have found no report of TBM's speech on this occasion.

[2] Zachary Macaulay was blind in one eye from birth, although, according to family tradition, he did not know it 'until after he had grown to man's estate' (Knutsford, *Zachary Macaulay*, p. 2).

[3] Benjamin Travers (1783–1858: *DNB*), the first to specialize in eye surgery in England.

TO HANNAH MACAULAY, 2 NOVEMBER 1833

MS: Trinity College. *Address:* Miss Macaulay / E Cropper's Esq / Dingle Bank / Liverpool. *Frank:* London November two 1833 / T B Macaulay. *Extract published:* Knutsford, *Zachary Macaulay,* p. 472.

London Novr. 2. 1833

Dearest love,

I have not much to add to what I wrote yesterday. The India House is on excellent terms with us. We receive assurances every day of the willingness of the Court to comply with any proposition of the Board which may not be very unreasonable. But my appointment has not yet been formally discussed. The Chairman is gone into the country; Grant set off to day for Winchester to pass Sunday with Dealtry; and till they return to town nothing can be done.

In the meantime reports are getting abroad. Yesterday at a large party where three directors were present it was asserted that I was going out to India. Some officious person carried the rumour to my father who came to my office this morning in considerable agitation – agitation rather, as I found, of hope than of fear. When I told him exactly how things stood he seemed greatly pleased, – and quite approved of your going with me. The fact is, as I had rather expected, that the pressure of pecuniary distress, the dread of leaving his children quite unprovided for, and the prospect of complete and immediate relief by honorable means and without any obligation to strangers, affected him more strongly than the thought of parting with us. He has of late felt so acutely the constant humiliation and the constant anxieties of poverty, that any mode of relief was welcome. He said, and, I dare say, very correctly, that he had himself been so much tossed about the world, had traversed the ocean so often, and had resided so long in tropical climates, that the separation did not shock him as it would shock other people; and he added that he had fully made up his mind to such a separation; for that he had himself entertained thoughts of soliciting an appointment abroad. You who profess to be a student of human nature – (you remember how we argued that matter on our tour,) may explain, if you can, why the most affectionate of fathers, as he certainly is, shewed less emotion at the thought of parting with me than Sharp or Charles Grant. My own explanation is that people like a fat sorrow better than a lean one, to use the words of the vulgar proverb. I believe that there are very few sentimental sorrows which pinch like the daily and hourly sense of penury. My laundress has a son dying of a consumption. I send him trifling presents now and then. The other day I gave her a dressing gown for him. She complains more of the protraction of his malady than of its certain termination. "It's a hard thing for a poor woman like me to have a poor boy six months a dying." But there is love, I believe, which, as the Bible says, many waters cannot quench nor the floods drown, and for which if a man should give his whole substance it would be utterly contemned.[1] And such love is mine for my Nancy, and, I think, hers for me.

I spoke to Fanny to the same effect with what I wrote to you yesterday. She almost anticipated me. She says that, in my father's present state of health, she should think it wrong to leave him. I fully agree with her. I have another objection to her going which I did not hint to her. My taking out one sister to preside over my establishment is a step which every body must approve. Grant and Sharp were both delighted with it. But to take two unmarried sisters, leaving an infirm father and many other relations in England, is another thing. It looks like a matrimonial venture – a thing from the thought of which you would shrink.

I write, you see, as if all were settled. I believe that all will be settled before long, and settled for our going. I find within myself a firmness and composure of which I did not think myself capable. The anxieties of this week have not cost me three extra beatings of the pulse, not one moment of sleep, not one mouthful of food. It would be thus, I suppose, with a general before a battle. It is thus, I imagine, with those who suffer death on great occasions, – your Russells and Sidneys.[2] I wonder whether I should be as tranquil as they on the scaffold. Very likely I should. I have often thought that in minds not altogether weak and abject the emergency itself produces the qualities which it demands.

I go to Leeds by the mail of Monday night. On Wednesday I dine with my constituents. On Thursday, I am sorry to say, I am forced to attend a meeting for founding a Mechanic's Institute. I shall not be in London till late on Friday night. Your letters of Monday and Tuesday should be directed to me at Leeds. Let me hear from you, my love. It is long since I have had a letter. Kindest love to my dear Margaret and Edward.

Ever yours, darling

T B M

Tom Babington comes to town to day. I shall try to avoid seeing him. The girls are afraid of a scene between him and my father. Sarah Anne predicts a scene between him and George. George cannot speak of him with temper.

---

[1] Song of Solomon 8: 7.
[2] Lord William Russell and Algernon Sidney, among TBM's most-admired Whig martyrs: 'Russell died with the fortitude of a Christian, Sidney with the fortitude of a Stoic' (*History of England*, 1 [1848], 268).

TO [EDWARD BAINES], 2 NOVEMBER 1833

MS: Duke University.

London Novr. 2. 1833

Dear Sir,

The toasts are such as I shall have the greatest pleasure in acknowledging or proposing.[1]

I will attend the meeting on Thursday.[2] I hope that it will be in the morning. But the instant that it breaks up, morning, noon, or night, I must be off for London. We have never been so busy here since I came into office. Kindest remembrances to all your family. / Ever, dear Sir,

Yours most truly

T B Macaulay

TO MACVEY NAPIER, 2 NOVEMBER 1833

MS: British Museum.

London Nov 2. 1833

Dear Napier,

Two persons have applied to me to be their intercessor with you. I forward their letters and an article by one of them. But I leave them absolutely to your disposal without soliciting any favour for them.

One of them is probably known to you at least by reputation. He is a gentleman of the name of Pringle. He was secretary of the Anti-slavery society, which has now completed its mission.[3] He has written for annuals and magazines with some credit, I believe; and he now wishes to contribute a paper about the Cape of Good Hope.[4] He lived there some years, and, I dare say, had his eyes about him. His best poem, as far as I recollect, is a description of a lion-hunt at which he assisted in South Africa.[5]

The other applicant who sends his article as well as his letter is an old college acquaintance of mine. His name is Cookesley.[6] He is son of that

---

[1] TBM responded to the toasts of 'Earl Grey and the Reforming Ministers,' to 'Thomas Babington Macaulay, Esq, and the extension of knowledge, liberty, and commerce in the East,' and to 'The Magna Charta of the Negro, and may the names of W. Wilberforce, Thomas Clarkson, Zachary Macaulay, and Fowell Buxton, be had in everlasting remembrance.' He proposed the toast to 'Corporation reform' (Leeds *Mercury*, 9 November 1833).

[2] Of the Leeds Mechanics' Institute, 7 November; TBM's speech on this occasion appears in the Leeds *Mercury*, 16 November.

[3] Pringle was in consequence out of a job. Zachary Macaulay was urging Pringle's claims to Brougham at this time (letters in Brougham papers, University College, London) and perhaps put some pressure on TBM for a good word to Napier.

[4] 'Kay's *Travels in Caffraria*,' *ER*, LVIII (January 1834), 363–87.

[5] Pringle published a volume of verse, *Ephemerides*, 1828.

[6] William Gifford Cookesley (1802–80: *DNB*), B.A., King's College, 1825; Assistant Master, Eton, 1829–54; from 1854 he held various church livings. He published a number of editions of classical texts.

Cookesley who was Gifford's early patron.[1] Gifford with proper gratitude patronized the family of his benefactor, and, I believe, made my friend his heir. At Cambridge Cookesley was the best mimic that I ever saw in my life, Matthews only excepted: but he shewed no great turn for literature. He picked up however some liberal notions among his friends there; and, when he became one of the Masters of Eton, resolved to attempt a reform in the school. He sent me the article which I enclose[2] and begged me to forward it to you without naming him. I told him that you would publish nothing without knowing the name of the writer; and that, if you could in any case be induced to depart from that rule, it would not be in a case like this, – where the whole argument turned on certain statements of fact, about the truth of which you could know nothing. I told him also that he wrote too much like an Etonian, – that, having passed almost all his life at that school, first as pupil, and then as master, he took it for granted that other people knew its constitution as well as he. He sent me accordingly three or four supplementary sheets, which, he said, you could insert in such a manner as to supply the defect. Whether any thing can be made of his papers I leave you to judge. It seems to me that between a professor of the University of Edinburgh and a Master of Eton – both agreeing in general views – the one furnishing facts and the other reasonings, – a very piquant article on the abuses of the English public schools might be produced. But I leave him to you. Of course you will be secret: for he would draw a fiery persecution on himself if he were to be discovered.

Yours in haste
T B Macaulay

TO HANNAH MACAULAY, 8 NOVEMBER 1833

MS: Trinity College.

London Nov 8. 1833

Dearest love,

I have only time to scrawl a line before post. I arrived in town to day after a most satisfactory visit to Leeds. I have this instant seen Grant. He has spoken to the Chairs; and they have both expressed their assent to my appointment. This is half the battle. They have promised to sound their colleagues, and to let us know what the temper of the Court is.

Many thanks for your letter. I am inclined to agree in all you say.

Hannah More has left you 20 £ only – to my father 800 £ – nothing

---

[1] William Gifford's patron was William Cookesley, who died in 1781; his son, John Gifford, was the father of William Gifford Cookesley and the heir of William Gifford.

[2] Nothing by Cookesley appears in the *ER*.

to the others. If you want more than 20 £ only let me know. I will send you a hundred with pleasure whether we go or stay. Your legacy will be sent to Liverpool to morrow.

But I must positively stop.

Ever yours, darling,

T B M

Kindest love to Margaret and Edward.

TO MACVEY NAPIER, 15 NOVEMBER 1833

MS: British Museum. *Address:* Macvey Napier Esq / Castle Street / Edinburgh. *Frank:* London November fifteen / 1833 / T B Macaulay.

London Novr. 15. 1833

Dear Napier,

I received your letter and the draft[1] this morning. I have sent the article on Eton and your note to Cookesley with a few lines from myself to the effect that, though I did not know the particular reasons which had actuated you in this case, I could guess at their general nature and fully believed them to be cogent. I added that, to my certain knowledge, you sometimes had a hard time of it with your mutinous vassals.

I will try my hand on Thackray if Longman will send me a copy. I had observed the book on a stall. Indeed the glance which I gave to it there suggested to me the thought of reviewing it: but when I called the other day to buy it, it had disappeared.

The last number is, I think, generally good. I agree in what you say of Miss Aikin's performance.[2]

Ever yours faithfully

T B Macaulay

Lady Holland is in a violent rage with me about Walpole – God knows why. I neither know nor care.

---

[1] In payment for the article on Walpole.
[2] Lucy Aikin, 'Life of Mr. Roscoe,' *ER*, LVIII (October 1833), 65–86.

TO [HANNAH MACAULAY, 15? NOVEMBER 1833][1]

MS: Trinity College. *Partly published:* Trevelyan, I, 339–40.

To me George says, I think very justly, that Tom has acted in some respects very dishonestly – dishonestly towards General Macaulay, towards Julia Noel,[2] towards other people in similar situations; – but that, as between Tom and my father, there is much to be said on both sides. Something must be done before I leave England. I think of proposing that my father should appoint me, and that Tom should appoint George, to make an award between them.

I passed all last week in racketting. I dined twice with Rogers, once with Grant, and once with the Hollands. I was to have dined with the Hollands again yesterday, and with Lord Essex on Saturday. But I had so bad a cold that I sent excuses to both. Lady Holland is in a most extraordinary state. She came to Rogers's with Allen in so bad a humour that we were all forced to rally and make common cause against her. There was not a person at table to whom she was not rude: and none of us were much inclined to submit. Rogers sneered. Sydney made merciless sport of her. Tom Moore looked excessively impertinent. Bobus[3] put her down with simple straight-forward rudeness: and I treated her with what I meant to be cold, civil, contempt. Allen flew into a rage with us all and especially with Sydney whose *gaffaws*, as the Scotch say, were indeed tremendous. When she and all the rest were gone, Rogers made Tom Moore and me sit down with him for half an hour, and we coshered[4] over the events of the evening. Rogers said that he thought Allen's firing up in defence of his patroness the best thing that he had seen in him. No sooner had Tom and I got out into the street than he broke forth – " That such an old stager as Rogers should talk such nonsense! – should give Allen any credit for attachment to any thing but his own belly! – Allen was bursting with envy to see us so free, while he was conscious of his own slavery."

Her Ladyship has been the better for this discipline. She has overwhelmed me ever since with civilities and invitations. I have at last found out the cause of her ill-humour – at least of that portion of it of which I was the object. She is in a furious rage at my article on Walpole, at what part of it I cannot tell. I know that they are very intimate with the

1 The beginning of the letter is missing.
2 Juliana Hicks Noel (d. 1855), Babington's sister-in-law.
3 Robert Percy Smith (1770–1845: *DNB*), older brother of Sydney Smith; Advocate-General of Bengal, 1803–7; M.P., 1812–18; 1820–6; a wit and Latin versifier.
4 This is the only instance of the word in the sense of 'to chat in a friendly and familiar fashion' given in the *OED*.

Waldgraves,[1] to whom the manuscripts belong and for whose benefit the letters were published. But my review was surely not calculated to injure the sale of the book. Lord Holland told me, in an aside, that he quite agreed with me, but that we had better not discuss the subject.

I saw her new daughter in law[2] – a pretty little damsel, as red as a cherry and as plump as a partridge, with affectionate, girlish manners, and a sweet low voice. Henry Fox seems still to be fond of her. I hope his love will last.

A note – and, by my life, from my eternal Lady Holland. "Dear Mr. Macaulay – Pray wrap yourself very warm and come to us on Wednesday." No, my good Lady, – I am engaged on Wednesday to dine at the Albion Tavern with the Directors of the East India Company, – now my servants, – next week, I hope, to be my masters. So I shall send your Ladyship an excuse.

I have filled half a dozen sheets of paper or thereabouts, and have not got half through my gossip. I must stop however. Love to dearest Margaret and Edward.

Ever yours my darling
T B M

Have you got your money?

TO HANNAH MACAULAY, 18 NOVEMBER 1833

MS: Trinity College.

London Novr. 18. 1833

Dearest Nancy,

I have much to tell you, and no time to tell it in. I will only say in three words what you will be most interested in hearing. On Wednesday week[3] the Court of Directors will come to a vote upon the question of my appointment. The opinion of Grant – of the Chairs – and, I believe, of all well-informed persons is that the thing is certain. Do your best therefore, my darling, to realize it in your mind.

I will do my best to meet your wishes as to the time of sailing, and as to every thing else. I spoke to Grant to day on the subject. He says that there will be no absolute necessity for our being in India before June. But he will talk to the Chairs about it, and make, if possible, such an

---

[1] The sixth Earl Waldegrave (1785–1835); the second Earl (1715–63: *DNB*) had married Walpole's niece Maria, establishing the connection between the two families.

[2] Mary Augusta (1812–89), daughter of the eighth Earl of Coventry, married Henry Edward Fox in May 1833.

[3] 27 November; but see next letter.

arrangement as may be agreable to us. I have asked Inglis, who knows everything about India,[1] to procure from some of his lady-friends, such information as may be of use to you. Stewart Mackenzie has written to his wife,[2] who was, you know, much in the East with her first husband Sir Samuel Hood, (wicked woman to marry again,) and she will furnish us with some hints which, wicked as she is, may be useful.

But I must stop. Ever yours my dearest Girl. Kindest love to dear Margaret and Edward.

T B M

TO HANNAH MACAULAY, 22 NOVEMBER 1833

MS: Trinity College. *Address:* Miss Macaulay / E Cropper's Esq / Dingle Bank / Liverpool. *Frank:* London November twenty two / 1833 / T B Macaulay. *Partly published:* Trevelyan, I, 340–3; 347.

London Nov 22. 1833

Dearest Love,

You are so much and so naturally pleased to have heard that your suspense is near its close that I am quite sorry to have unpalatable news to communicate. The decision is postponed for a week. The notice will be given next Wednesday. The vote will be taken on Wednesday the 4th of December. But I repeat that there is no chance of an unfavourable result. The Chairs have collected the opinions of their brethren; and the result is that of the twenty four directors only six or seven at the most will vote against me.

I dined with the Directors on Wednesday at the Albion Tavern. The entertainment was given in honor of Sir John Keene,[3] who has just been appointed to the command of the army at Bombay. We had a company of about sixty persons, and many eminent military men amongst them. The very courteous manner in which several of the Directors begged to be introduced to me, and drank my health at dinner, led me to think that the Chairs have not overstated the feeling of the Court. One of them, an old Indian and a great friend of our Uncle the General, told me in plain words that he was glad to hear that I was to be in their service. Another whom I do not even know by sight pressed the Chairman to propose my health.

---

[1] Inglis's father was for many years a director of the East India Company.
[2] Mary Frederica Elizabeth Stewart-Mackenzie (1783–1862: *DNB*), daughter and co-heir of Lord Seaforth, Baron Mackenzie. Her first husband, Vice-Admiral Sir Samuel Hood, died in 1814; in 1817 she married James Alexander Stewart, who took the additional name of Mackenzie. Lord Teignmouth says that she looked like a gypsy and had an 'almost lawless spirit of adventure' (*Reminiscences*, I, 351).
[3] Sir John Keane (1781–1844: *DNB*), later first Baron Keane, appointed Commander-in-Chief at Bombay, 30 October. He held the post until 1839.

The Chairman with great judgment refused. It would have been very awkward to have had to make a speech to them in the present circumstances.

Yesterday I dined with Colonel Fox at Kensington. His wife,[1] the King's favourite daughter, was as agreable as possible. Henry Fox was there, and his pretty little bride. She had a dreadful cold and was as pale as death; but still very attractive. He is, as you know, no favourite of mine. But I cannot deny that his powers of conversation are considerable, and his manner very sweet and courteous. Towards women – both his own wife and other men's wives, – his manner is at once so respectful and so caressing that I do not wonder at the havock which he has made among the ladies. But he is lame and cannot walk without a stick, – a great drawback on his handsome face and figure.

To night I dine with Grant. His kindness through all these negotiations has been such as I really cannot describe. So has that of Ellis[2] and Stewart Mackenzie. By Ellis I mean not my friend, who is out of London as a Corporation Commissioner;[3] but Ellis of our Board, Lord Ripon's brother-in-law.

Of course, my love, all your expenses, from the day of my appointment, are my affair. My present plan, formed after conversation with experienced East Indians is not to burden myself with an extravagant outfit. I shall take only what will be necessary for the voyage. Plate, wine, coaches, furniture, glass, china, can be bought in Calcutta as well as in London. I shall not have money enough to fit myself out handsomely with such things here; and to fit myself out shabbily would be folly. I reckon that we can bring our whole expense for the passage within the twelve hundred pounds allowed by the Company. My calculation is that our cabins and board will cost 250 £ a piece. That is 500 £. The passage of our servants 50 £ a piece. That makes up 600 £. My clothes and etc., as Mrs. Meeke observes, will, I am quite sure, come within £ 200. Yours will of course be more. I will send you £ 300 to lay out as you like, – not meaning to confine you to it by any means. But you would probably prefer having a sum down to sending in all your milliner's bills to me. I reckon my servant's outfit at 50 £ – your maid's at as much more. The whole will be 1200 £.

One word about your maid. You really must chuse with great caution. Hitherto the Company has required that all ladies who take maidservants with them from this country to India should give security to send them back within two years. The reason was that no class of people misconduct

[1] Lady Mary Fitzclarence (d. 1864), second daughter of William IV and Mrs Jordan, married Charles Richard Fox in 1824.
[2] (Sir) Henry Ellis (1777–1855: *DNB*), a Commissioner of the Board of Control, 1830–5.
[3] Ellis was one of the Commissioners of Municipal Corporations, 1833–7.

themselves so much in the East as female servants from this country.
They generally treat the natives with gross insolence – an insolence
natural enough to people accustomed to stand in a servile relation to
others when, for the first time, they find a great population placed in
a servile relation towards them. Then too the state of society is such that
they are very likely to become mistresses of the wealthy Europeans, – and
to flaunt about in magnificent palanquins, bringing discredit on their
country by the immorality of their lives and the vulgarity of their
manners. On these grounds the Company has hitherto insisted upon
their being sent back at the expense of those who take them out. The
late Act will enable your servant to stay in India if she chuses to stay.
I hope therefore that you will be careful in your selection. You see how
much depends upon it. The happiness and concord of our native houshold which will probably consist of sixty or seventy people may be
destroyed by her, if she should be ill-tempered and arrogant. If she
should be weak and vain she will probably form connections that will
ruin her morals and her reputation. I am no preacher, as you very well
know. But I have a strong sense of the responsibility under which we
shall both lie with respect to a poor girl, brought by us into the midst of
temptations of which she cannot be aware and which have turned many
heads that might have been steady enough in a quiet nursery or kitchen
in England. I have, if possible, a still stronger sense of the duty which will
lie upon me of protecting my native dependents against the insolence of
my own countrymen. It is, indeed, for this especial purpose that I am sent
to India. The fourth member of Council is to be, in a peculiar manner,
the guardian of the people of India against the European settlers. I must
not suffer the abuses against which I am to provide in my public capacity
to bring scandal on my own house.

To find a man and wife both of whom would suit us would be very
difficult. And I think it right also to offer to my clerk to keep him in my
service if he likes it. He is honest, intelligent, respectful, and rather
inclined to consumption. The change of climate would probably be
useful to him; and I cannot bear the thought of throwing any person who
has been about me for five years, and with whom I have no fault to find,
out of bread, while it is in my power to retain his services.

If the servant whom you take should be young and attractive, and if
she conducts herself well, I have no doubt that she will very soon marry.
But you need not be uneasy about this. You will be no worse off than
all the English ladies in India. I dare say the Missionaries at Serampore
will furnish you with some good girl from their schools.

This letter is most inordinately long. I had intended to have let you
into my plans for our proceedings when we reach India. I have drawn

out a scale of expence which Mackenzie and Ellis highly approve. Ellis has promised to submit it to the judgment of a friend of his who has resided at Calcutta for years in a very high situation. But I must defer this till next letter.

Ellis who has been long in Bengal assures me that you are quite wrong in being afraid of May. He says that August and September are the awkward months.

We shall hardly sail before the beginning of February. But we may perhaps hasten or retard our voyage a few days for the sake of procuring a very good ship. Love to dearest Margaret and Edward.

Ever yours, dear love

T B M

TO MACVEY NAPIER, 22 NOVEMBER 1833

MS: British Museum. *Address:* Macvey Napier Esq / Castle Street / Edinburgh. *Frank:* London November twenty two / 1833 / T B Macaulay.

London Nov 22 / 1833

Dear Napier,

I send you a letter which I received this morning from Lord Howick.[1] He is a clever man. The subject which he wishes to treat is of high importance. His late situation[2] gave him access to the best information. And, connected as he is, an article from him, even if were not first-rate, would do us credit. But I leave him to you. / Ever, dear Napier,

Yours most truly

T B Macaulay

TO HANNAH MACAULAY, 26 NOVEMBER 1833

MS: Trinity College. *Address:* Miss Macaulay / E Cropper's Esq / Dingle Bank / Liverpool. *Frank:* London November twenty six / 1833 / T B Macaulay. *Extract published:* Trevelyan, I, 347–8.

London Nov 26. 1833

My dearest girl,

Major Carnac[3] has just left me. He was formerly one of the most distinguished servants of the Company of the East. He is now a Director, and very zealous in my favour. He tells me, what I hear from every quarter,

---

[1] Howick proposed to submit an article on the subject of the transportation of criminals (Howick to TBM, 19 November: MS, Napier papers, British Museum). This appeared as 'Secondary Punishments – Transportations,' *ER*, LVIII (January 1834), 336–63.

[2] As Under-Secretary for the Colonies, 1830–3.

[3] Major (Sir) James Carnac (1785–1846: *DNB*), had served in India, 1801–22; Governor of Bombay, 1838–41.

that I am quite certain of the appointment. Some bitter feeling remains, and some hostile votes must be expected. But I have a decided majority. To morrow week, as I told you, is to be the day.

I asked him what was the best time for going out. He said that there were two good times – the best a little before Midsummer, – so as to arrive in India about the beginning of October, – the next best about the beginning of February so as to arrive about the end of May or the beginning of June. I asked him about March. He said that if we went in March and were delayed on the voyage by any accident we might arrive about the beginning of August which is the very worst season in the whole year. He advised me, if I did not go in February, to stay in England till June. But he owned that my staying so long would be much censured by some of his colleagues. Indeed it would deserve censure, and would, I firmly believe, be made matter of parliamentary discussion.

This information quite agrees with what I have heard from all other experienced people, and what I have read in all the medical books which I have consulted. You do not cite Heber correctly. He does not say that the worst months are April, May, September, and October. At least I cannot find any such passage in his journal. He arrived in October himself, and put off his voyage two months in order that he might arrive in October. It is true that the April and May of 1824, – the only April and May which he passed in Bengal, – were unusually hot and unhealthy. But even in that year he says in a letter to Charles Wynne, that during the last week of May the weather became cooler, and that the effect was wonderfully reviving; and early in June he set out on his visitation.[1] But it is unnecessary to discuss the healthiness or unhealthiness of April and May, because we shall not reach Bengal till very near the beginning of June if we sail early in February: and June and July are agreable months.

I hope, my love, that what I have told you will reconcile you to the prospect of setting off early in February. It is the advice of all my friends. The delay of two months which seems to you so short, and which indeed to a disposition so affectionate as yours may well appear short on so trying an occasion, is a long one as things are generally conducted. I can give you an instance at once. On the 30th of last month Sir John Keene was elected Commander of the Forces and member of Council at Bombay. On the 1st of this month the King's pleasure was taken. Yesterday he went to Portsmouth. To morrow he is to sail. Till my departure I shall be a member of parliament. Parliament meets on the 3d of February. Several people, Inglis among the rest, have hinted to me that I shall expose myself to unpleasant remarks if I appear in the house when it will be

[1] Reginald Heber, *Narrative of a Journey through the Upper Provinces of India*, Philadelphia, 1829, I, 99–101; II, 260–1.

thought that I ought to be on my way to discharge my important duties in India. When you consider all these things, my darling, I think you will agree with me that we ought to sail by the first ship that goes to Bengal with good accommodations, in February.

You will not be at all hurried as to your outfit. Every thing can be procured in London at three day's notice. If you would like to come from Liverpool to town in the first place, to give your orders here, and then to go to the Temple, I will with the greatest pleasure escort you backward and forward.

So much for time. As for the money, three hundred pounds will not be a farthing too much for your equipment. If you can save any of it put it by to be the foundation of a private hoard, such as all notable wives and sisters contrive to lay up. But indeed I think that you ought to lay out a hundred pounds or so in ornaments. You may do so now without being accused of dressing above your station.

As to our passage-money, I fear that Edward will turn out to be in the wrong. I doubt whether he has seen much of that class of East India ships which sail from the port of London. I know that the passage of a cadet who has no cabin costs a hundred guineas. George shewed me the other day the bills which he paid for Henry in 1822. Henry was then a young writer of nineteen. The passage-money was 180 £. Henry had a neat little cabin. But we must have the very best accommodations that are to be had. My station will render this necessary. I believe that passage money was unusually high in 1822. But if we get off for 450 £ between us I am told that we shall be fortunate.

I hope that your intended servant will do honour to your choice. But I am much afraid that she will shock your delicacy very soon by the horrible spectacle of a widow marrying again.

I forgot to tell you in my last what I was glad to learn from Selina and Fanny, that my father's talk about sending Charles to Paris was by no means so serious as Charles represented it to George. In fact Charles had no objection, as you may well believe, to such a plan; and therefore spoke of it as a settled thing, when it was by no means mentioned in that way. In my presence my father never alludes to the strange plan which gave us all so much pain. But I am sorry to say that he has been urging George to press me to take Fanny with us. George says that every consideration of delicacy, of œconomy, of Selina's comfort, of my father's health, is against such an arrangement. And really there is nothing for it but a whim.

The question of my appointment came on in the cabinet last week. Many of the ministers certainly knew nothing of the scheme till then. I suspect that Grant had mentioned it to none of them but Lord Grey and the Chancellor. After the council I met Graham at dinner. He took me aside and talked to me on the subject with a warmth of kindness which, though we have always been on good terms, surprised me. But the approach of a long separation, like the approach of death, brings out all friendly feelings with unusual strength. The Government, he said, felt the loss most strongly. It was great at the India Board – much greater in the House of Commons. He used over and over the word – irreparable –. But, he said, they all agreed that a man of honor could not make politics a profession unless he had a competence of his own, without exposing himself to privations of the severest kind. They felt, he said, that they had never had it in their power to do all that they had wished to do for me. They had no means of giving me a provision in England: and they could not refuse me what I asked in India. He said very strongly that they all thought that I judged quite wisely, and added, with tears in his eyes, that if God heard his prayers and spared my health, I should make a far greater figure in public life than if I had remained during the next five or six years in England.

I have had a doleful letter from Lady Holland, filled with lamentations and Alasses. Empson, to whom I yesterday confided the matter, shewed deep and sincere distress. But he quite approves of my decision. Inglis says the same. Indeed I have not yet fallen in with any person, acquainted with the circumstances of our family, who does not think that I have done right.

I dined yesterday at Battersea Rise, and saw Mrs. Henry Thornton. She is a pleasing girl, I think, and he has not been altered in any respect by marriage. Empson was there. He has been in high favour with Sir Robert ever since his review of Signor Pellico's narrative.[1]

I must stop. I have not yet sent you my plan for our establishment at Calcutta. I picked up at a print-shop the other day some superb views of the Esplanade, the suburbs of Chowringhee, and the Villas of the Garden Reach. Selina and Fanny are ready to [die][2] with envy of the fine houses [and][2] verandahs. I heartily wish that [we][2] were back again in a nice plain brick house three windows in front, in Cadogan Place or Russell Square, with twelve or fifteen hundred a year, and a spare bed-room (we, like Mrs. Norris, must always have a spare bed-room,)[3] for Edward and Margaret. Love to them both.

Ever yours, my darling

T B M

---

[1] 'Character of the Austrian Government – Pellico's Narrative of His Imprisonment,' *ER*, LVII (July 1833), 476–85.

[2] Paper torn away with seal.   [3] *Mansfield Park*, ch. 3.

TO THOMAS FLOWER ELLIS, 28 NOVEMBER 1833

MS: Trinity College.

London November 28. 1833

Dear Ellis,

I have for some time been meditating a letter to you. But, hearing a few days ago that you would be in London this morning, I deferred writing. I called to day in Bedford Place, and learned from Mrs. Ellis that your duties are likely to detain you in the country another fortnight. I can therefore no longer postpone a task which is not a little painful to me.

You are one of the very few people who will be really affected by the news which I have to communicate. It is all but absolutely certain that I shall, on Wednesday next, be appointed by the Court of Directors a member of the Supreme Council of India. I see quite clearly the extent of the sacrifices which I must make in accepting this situation. I must leave a country which I love, friends to whom I am strongly attached, and a station in public life higher than any man of my age at present occupies. But on the other hand, by accepting this appointment, I shall have it in my power to retrieve the fortunes of my family, to make the last days of my father comfortable, to support my sisters, to educate my youngest brother, to secure for myself a large fortune, – at least a fortune larger than my desires. At present I have, as you know, nothing. If I were to leave office, – and I was more than once on the point of leaving office during the last Session, – I should have nothing to live by but my pen. I should be a very different person in the estimation of editors and book-sellers, when writing for bread, from what I now am, when writing principally for amusement or for fame. My sisters must be dependent on the charity of relations, – a thing of which I cannot bear to think. The literary drudgery which would be necessary to my subsistence would occupy so much of my time that it would scarcely be possible for me to take a prominent part in politics.

By going to India I secure my independence for life. I have made all the necessary calculations with the aid of the most experienced and judicious advisers: and I am satisfied that it will be in my power to live, as I ought to live, in splendour at Calcutta while I retain my office, to support my family in comfort during my absence, and to return to England before I am forty with a fortune of thirty thousand pounds, honorably gained. In the meantime I may hope to keep myself before the public eye by my writings. My absence will hardly be long enough to blot the remembrance of my parliamentary career from the minds of my countrymen. I shall have, when I return, the paths of literature and politics open before me. I may chuse between them; or I may make

345

excursions in both. I shall be absolutely my own master, and as rich as I ever wished to be.

Though several of those who have been apprised of my intentions have, at first hearing of them, expressed some astonishment, all, I think, agree that I have judged wisely. Few of them, indeed, – perhaps none out of my own family, – will feel so much at parting with me as you will feel. But I think that your judgment cannot but approve of my decision.

I have not time to say more. But I have much to say. We shall have many opportunities of talking together before my departure which will take place, I believe, early in February.

Mrs. Ellis tells me that you expect to be in London on or about the 13th of next month, and that Canterbury will be your last station. I wish to see you. I should also like to see Canterbury; and I have very particular reasons for wishing to be out of London on the 11th of December. Lushington has importuned me to attend at a dinner which the electors of the Tower Hamlets are to give him. As my oratory reconciled an auditory of Leeds manufacturers to the continuance of the corn-laws,[1] I am marvellously in request among members who have to make apologies to their constituents. I could not refuse Lushington directly: but I think that it would be absurd in me to mix myself up with the local politics of the butchers of Whitechapel and the weavers of Spitalfields on the eve of my departure for another hemisphere. I told Lushington that I would attend if I were in London, but that I should probably be in the country. The dinner is to be on the 11th. If I were to run down to Canterbury, would it suit you to return with me? If you can make anything out of this project let me know. / Believe me ever

Yours most affectionately

T B Macaulay

TO THOMAS FLOWER ELLIS, 30 NOVEMBER 1833

MS: Trinity College. *Address:* T F Ellis Esq / etc. etc. etc.

London Novr. 30. 1833

Dear Ellis,

I have very little time to spare this morning. But I cannot let a day pass without thanking you for your very kind letter, and assuring you that there is no person in the world whose friendship I more highly value, or whose society I shall more deeply regret. We shall meet again, I hope

---

[1] 'I hold the Corn Laws to be one of the greatest possible evils. (Cheers.) But I do not think the public mind ripe for putting this question on a sound footing' (speech at Leeds, 6 November: Leeds *Mercury*, 9 November).

and fully believe. In the meantime we will correspond largely. When I come back I shall find Frank, I suppose, vain of his purple gown and writing bad verses for the Chancellors English medal. He will never get it if he writes good ones.

Let me know what your movements are. On the evening of the 10th or the morning of the 11th I will join you, whether you are at Canterbury or Maidstone.[1] Should you have any objection to pass a day at Tunbridge Wells – a beautiful place, and one which I should like to see again before I leave England.

The article on Walpole is mine. It is generally thought one of my best. But it has made Lady Holland and the Miss Berrys very angry. However they have come round.

Ever yours affectionately

T B Macaulay

TO HANNAH MACAULAY, 30 NOVEMBER 1833

MS: Trinity College. *Address:* Miss Macaulay / E Cropper's Esq / Dingle Bank / Liverpool. *Frank:* London November thirty / 1833 / T B Macaulay. *Partly published:* Trevelyan, 1, 338–9.

London November 30 1833

My love,

I enclose you a letter from the Temple. – I have not time to write much to day, nor have I much to tell you if I had time. Things stand as they stood, except that the report of my appointment is every day spreading more widely, and that I am beset by advertising dealers begging leave to make up a hundred cotton shirts for me, and fifty muslin gowns for you, and by clerks out of place begging to be my secretaries.

I am not in very high spirits to day, as I have just received a letter from poor Ellis who is wandering among the corrupt Corporations of Kent, and to whom I had not communicated my intentions till yesterday. He writes so affectionately and so plaintively that he quite cuts me to the heart. Except Margaret, there is no person in England – I say to you in confidence – from whom I shall part with so much pain: and he, poor fellow, says that, except his wife, I am the only person for whom he feels thorough attachment and in whom he places unlimited confidence.

He is to return to London on the 12th or 13th of next month. On the 11th – I forget whether I told you or not, – there is to be a dinner given to Lushington by the electors of the Tower Hamlets. He has persecuted me with importunities to attend and make a speech for him: and my father has joined in the request. It is enough, in these times, Heaven

---

[1] In the event TBM does not seem to have gone: see 10 December.

knows, for a man who represents as I do a town of a hundred and twenty thousand people to keep his own Constituents in good humour: and the Spitalfields weavers and Whitechapel butchers are nothing to me. But, ever since I succeeded in what every body allows to have been the most hazardous attempt of the kind ever made – I mean in persuading an audience of manufacturers, all whigs or radicals, that the immediate alteration of the corn-laws was impossible, I have been considered as a capital physician for desperate cases in politics. Indeed, though I say it who should not say it, I do not think that any public man of our time has shewn so much boldness and dexterity united on any single occasion as I shewed at the Leeds dinner; and such is the general opinion in the political circles here. However – to return from that delightful theme, my own praises, – Lushington, who is very unpopular with the rabble of the Tower Hamlets, thinks that an oration from me would give him a lift. I could not refuse him directly, backed as he was by my father. I only said that I would attend if I were in London on the 11th. But I added that, situated as I was, I thought it very probable that I should be out of town. Now I mean to go down to Ellis on the 10th at Canterbury or Maidstone, I do not know which, – to stay over the 11th with him, – and then to come back with him to London. Do you not admire my Machiavelianism?

I have had a letter full of compliments and regrets from the Philipses at Weston who had written to beg me to pass Xtmas with them. But see the villainy of the world. After saying that the House of Commons would be a blank without me – and that I should be an irreparable loss to London society – they slip in a P S to the effect that a brother-in-law of George Philips is in the service of the Company[1] – resident at Scindia's Court in Malwa – and that, if I could get him promoted to some better embassy – to the Residency at Lucknow or Hydrabad for example, they should be very grateful. I told them that I should, in all probability, have very little to do with the disposing of places, but that I would serve their relation if I could. And I will, not on their account, but on his own. For I know him to be a very valuable public servant.

For to night I had three invitations, from the Parkers, from Lord Essex, and from the Miss Berrys. I have unhappily engaged myself to the least agreable of the three. I dine with the Parkers, and shall go to Miss Berry's soirée at eleven. I do not know whether I told you that she resented my article on Horace Walpole so much that Sir Stratford Canning[2] advised

---

[1] Richard Cavendish (1794–1876), in India since 1813, was Resident at Gwalior, 1831–5; at Nagpore, 1835–9. He was a son of the second Baron Waterpark, whose daughter the younger Philips married.

[2] Sir Stratford Canning (1786–1880: *DNB*), later Viscount Stratford de Redcliffe; in the diplomatic service since 1808, he spent twenty-five years as minister and ambassador at Constantinople between 1808 and 1858.

me not to go near her. She was Walpole's greatest favourite. His Reminiscences are addressed to her in terms of the most gallant eulogy. When
he was dying at past eighty, he asked her to marry him, merely that he
might make her a Countess and leave her his fortune.[1] She edited the
letters which passed between him and "the blind woman who was
clever."[2] [In] that blackguard book Vivian Grey she is called Miss Otranto.[3]
I always expected that my article would put her into a fine passion, and
I was not mistaken. But she has come round again, and sent me a most
pressing and kind invitation the other day. What gossiping! – What a
long letter when I meant to write a very short one. Kindest love to Margaret
and Edward.

Ever yours, dearest

T B M

TO HANNAH MACAULAY, 2 DECEMBER 1833

MS: Trinity College. *Address:* Miss Macaulay / E Cropper's Esq / Dingle Bank / Liverpool. *Frank:* London December two / 1833 / T B Macaulay.

London Decr. 2. / 1833

Dearest love,

I have nothing of importance to say, and little time for saying any
thing. The question will be decided the day after to morrow. But, as the
Directors seldom rise till six or half after six, and as their place of meeting
is in the heart of the city and our Board at the extremity of Westminster,
we shall hardly learn the result in time for the post of that night. On
Thursday I shall write again, – not earlier unless I have something particular to communicate.

You are quite wrong about the wages of European servants in India.
They are enormously high. To be sure it is possible that the free resort
of emigrants from England may so much increase the supply as to lower
the price.

As to Brownrigg's[4] estimate of outfit it is far too low. Indeed I suspect
that, as he had himself been to India before, he was already provided
with a great part of what he wanted. This may have been the case also
with his wife.

---

[1] This was only gossip. When Croker repeated the story in 1843 in the *Quarterly Review*
Miss Berry told Greville that it was 'altogether false' (*Memoirs*, v, 134).
[2] See *to* Hannah Macaulay, 14 October 1833.
[3] Disraeli, *Vivian Grey*, Book 4, ch. 1.
[4] John Studholme Brownrigg (1786?–1853), a member of the East India firm of Cockerell
and Larpent.

I am sorry to tell you bad news of the Wedgwoods[1] – I think you know them. Wedgwood, you must remember, obtained by Lady Holland's interest from Lord Melbourne a place which enabled him to marry Miss Mackintosh. The situation was that of a police magistrate. He has taken it into his head – poor crazy creature – that he cannot retain it without a sin. He says that most of the witnesses whom he examines perjure themselves: and that he is accessory to their guilt by administering to them an oath which, while he administers it, he knows that they will very probably break. From this preposterous scruple, he has resigned his office. The fellow who, in a world bursting with sin and sorrow, pestered Johnson about the ends of packthread was not such a fool.[2] His wife is breaking her heart.

Kindest love to Margaret and Edward.

Ever yours, dearest
T B M

TO HANNAH MACAULAY, 5 DECEMBER 1833

MS: Trinity College.

London Decr. 5. 1833

Dearest love,

I was appointed yesterday. Twenty two directors were present at the Court. Nineteen voted for me; three against me. So complete a victory was beyond our hopes. It is, I hope, an augury of a future good understanding between the two branches of the Indian government.

The news was brought to me at the Admiralty where I dined with Sir James Graham and a party of the ministers.[3] Many kind expressions of regret were employed. But all seemed to think that I had done wisely. Labouchere is most strongly of that opinion.

Labouchere and I mean to go down to Bowood for a few days next week. Lord Lansdowne has sent me a very kind and pressing invitation. After my return I shall be fixed in London till Christmas when I am to resign my secretaryship.

---

[1] Hensleigh Wedgwood (1803–91: *DNB*), B.A., Christ's College, Cambridge, 1824, married in 1832 Sir James Mackintosh's daughter Frances. Appointed police magistrate, Lambeth, 1832, Wedgwood resigned in 1837 on grounds rather different from those given by TBM – *viz.*, the New Testament injunction against oaths. He devoted the rest of his life to philological study.

[2] Mrs Piozzi's *Anecdotes* in G. B. Hill, ed., *Johnsonian Miscellanies*, I, 300–1.

[3] After dining at the Admiralty in 1849 TBM wrote: 'the first time that I dined there I learned at the door by a letter from the India House that I was elected a Member of Council. The first Lord was then Sir James Graham. Of the party were Melbourne and Mrs. Norton – Palmerston then a bachelor. . . . Labouchere was there and poor Auckland' (Journal, I, 530–1: 10 March 1849).

To morrow I shall probably be able to give you some information on the subject of the ships which are about to sail. I shall not fix absolutely without a reference to you. Indeed, indeed, my darling, I never think of your kindness to me and of the sacrifices which you are making for me without feeling the tears well into my eyes. But I will not write thus lest I should infect you with my weakness. My part is to set an example of firmness: and I have never failed in it for a moment except when I have thought of the Dingle.

I had the kindest letter possible from Edward the other day. He insists on being allowed to take some share of the expence of supporting those whom we shall leave behind. Considering the relation in which he stands to us, and still more the real friendship which we have for him, I should think that it would be unjustifiable in me altogether to refuse his assistance. We must take care however that he shall not be allowed to do too much.

I have so much to do, and so many letters to write this morning, as you may imagine, that I must delay what I have further to say till to morrow.

My father has just been with me. He is very calm and did not touch on any unpleasant topic. To morrow he goes into the country.

Kindest love to dear Margaret and Edward.

Ever yours, my darling,

T B M

TO MACVEY NAPIER, 5 DECEMBER 1833

MS: British Museum. *Mostly published*: Trevelyan, I, 348–9.

London Decr. 5. 1833

Dear Napier,

You are probably not unprepared for what I am about to tell you. Yesterday evening the Directors of the East India Company elected me one of the members of the Supreme Council. It will therefore be necessary that in a few weeks, – ten weeks at furthest, I should leave this country for a few years.

I may on some future occasion explain to you all the circumstances which have actuated me on this occasion. You would, I am sure, from friendly feeling to me, take a warm interest in them. But I have much to write and much to do this morning. I will therefore proceed to business.

It would be mere affectation in me to pretend not to know that my support is of some importance to the Edinburgh Review. In the situation in which I shall now be placed, a connection with the Review will be of considerable importance to me. I know well how dangerous it is for a public man wholly to withdraw himself from the public eye. During an absence of six years I run some risk of losing most of the distinction, literary and political, which I have acquired. As a means of keeping myself in the recollection of my countrymen during my sojourn abroad the Review will be invaluable to me. Nor do I foresee that there will be the slightest difficulty in my continuing to write for you at least as much as ever. I have thought over my late articles; and I really can scarcely call to mind a single sentence in any one of them which might not have been written at Calcutta as easily as in London. Perhaps in India I might not have had the means of detecting two or three of the false dates in Croker's Boswell. But that would have been all. Very little, if any, of the effect of my most popular articles is produced by minute research into rare books, or by allusions to the mere topics of the day.

I think therefore that we might easily establish a commerce mutually beneficial. I shall wish to be supplied with all the good books which come out in this part of the world. Indeed many books which in themselves are of little value, and which, if I were in England, I should not think it worth while to read, will be interesting to me in India, just as the commonest daubs and the rudest vessels at Pompeii attract the minute attention of people who would not move their eyes to see a modern signpost or a modern kettle. Distance of place like distance of time makes trifles valuable.

What I propose then is that you should pay me for the articles which I may send to you from India, not in money, but in books. As to the amount I make no stipulations. You know that I have never haggled about such matters. As to the choice of books, the mode of transmission, and other matters, we shall have ample time to discuss them before my departure. Let me know whether you are willing to make an arrangement on this basis.

I heartily wish that I could see you again before I go. But that is out of the question, I fear. My sister is to accompany me and to preside over the seventy or eighty Hindoos and Mahometans who will compose my houshold.

I have not forgotten Chatham in the midst of my avocations. I hope to send you an article on him early next month.

Ever yours sincerely
T B Macaulay

How does Howick's paper turn out?

TO LORD LANSDOWNE, 5 DECEMBER 1833

MS: The Marquess of Lansdowne. *Address:* The Marquess of Lansdowne / Bowood / Calne. *Frank:* London December five / 1833 / T B Macaulay. *Mostly published:* Trevelyan, I, 343–6.

London December 5. 1833

Dear Lord Lansdowne,

I delayed returning an answer to your kind letter till this day, in order that I might be able to send you definitive intelligence. Yesterday evening the Directors appointed me to a seat in the Council of India. The votes were nineteen for me and three against me.

I feel that the sacrifice which I am about to make is great. But the motives which urge me to make it are quite irresistible. Every day that I live I become less and less desirous of great wealth. But every day makes me more sensible of the importance of a competence. Without a competence it is not very easy for a public man to be honest: it is almost impossible for him to be thought so. I am so situated that I can subsist only in two ways, by being in office and by my pen. Hitherto literature has been merely my relaxation, – the amusement of perhaps a month in the year. I have never considered it as the means of support. I have chosen my own topics, taken my own time, and dictated my own terms. The thought of becoming a bookseller's hack, of writing to relieve not the fulness of the mind but the emptiness of the pocket, of spurring a jaded fancy to reluctant exertion, of filling sheets with trash merely that the sheets may be filled, of bearing from publishers and editors what Dryden bore from Tonson[1] and what, to my own knowledge, Mackintosh bore from Lardner, is horrible to me. Yet thus it must be, if I should quit office. Yet to hold office merely for the sake of emolument would be more horrible still. The situation in which I have been placed for some time back would have broken the spirit of many men. It has had no such effect on mine. It has rather tended to make me the most mutinous and unmanageable of the followers of the government. I tendered my resignation twice during the course of the last session. I certainly should not have done so if I had been a man of fortune. You, whom malevolence itself could never accuse of coveting office for the sake of pecuniary gain, and whom your salary very poorly compensates for the sacrifice of ease and of your tastes to the public service, cannot estimate rightly the feelings of a man who knows that his circumstances lay him open to the suspicion of being actuated in his public conduct by the lowest motives. Once or twice, when I have been defending unpopular measures in the house of commons, that thought has disordered my ideas and deprived me of my presence of mind.

---

[1] Jacob Tonson (1656?–1736: *DNB*), publisher.

If this were all, I should feel that, for the sake of my own happiness and of my public utility, a few years would be well spent in obtaining an independence. But this is not all. I am not alone in the world. A family which I love most fondly is dependent on me. Unless I would see my father left in his old age to the charity of less near relations, my youngest brother unable to obtain a good professional education, my sisters, who are more to me than any sisters ever were to a brother, forced to turn governnesses or humble companions, I must do something – I must make some effort. An opportunity has offered itself. It is in my power to make the last days of my father comfortable, to educate my brother, to provide for my sisters, to procure a competence for myself. I may hope by the time that I am thirty nine or forty to return to England with a fortune of thirty thousand pounds. To me that would be affluence. I never wished for more.

As far as English politics are concerned I lose, it is true, a few years. But, if your kindness had not introduced me very early to parliament, if I had been left to climb up the regular path of my profession, and to rise by my own efforts, I should have had very little chance of being in the House of Commons at forty. If I have gained any distinction in the eyes of my countrymen, if I have acquired any knowledge of parliamentary and official business, any habitude for the management of great affairs, I ought to consider these things as pure gain.

Then too the years of my absence, though lost, as far as English politics are concerned, will not, I hope, be wholly lost, as respects either my own mind or the happiness of my fellow-creatures. I can scarcely conceive a nobler field than that which our Indian Empire now presents to a statesman. While some of my partial friends are blaming me for stooping to accept a share in the government of that Empire, I am afraid that I am aspiring to a station too high for my qualifications. I sometimes feel, I most unaffectedly declare, depressed and appalled by the immense responsibility which I have undertaken. You are one of the very few public men of our time who have bestowed on Indian affairs the attention which they deserve; and you will therefore, I am sure, fully enter into my feelings.

I have explained my motives to you at more length than I have yet explained them to any person. You have every right to my confidence: and, fortified as my judgment is by that of most of those for whose opinions I feel the greatest respect, I cannot be quite easy if it differs from yours.

And now, dear Lord Lansdowne, let me thank you most warmly for the kind feeling which has dictated your letter. That letter is indeed but a very small part of what I ought to thank you for. That at an early age

I have gained some credit in public life, that I have done some little service to more than one good cause, that I now have it in my power to repair the ruined fortunes of my family and to save those who are dearest to me from the misery and humiliation of dependence, that I am almost certain, if I live, of obtaining a competence by honorable means before I am past the full vigour of manhood, all this I owe to your kindness. I will say no more. I will only intreat you to believe that neither now nor on any former occasion have I ever said one thousandth part of what I feel.

If it will not be inconvenient to you I propose to go to Bowood on Wednesday next. Labouchere will be my fellow-traveller. On Saturday we must both return to town. Short as my visit must be, I look forward to it with great pleasure. / Believe me ever, / Dear Lord Lansdowne,

Yours most faithfully and affectionately
T B Macaulay

TO HANNAH MACAULAY, 6 DECEMBER 1833

MS: Trinity College. *Extracts published:* Trevelyan, 1, 346–7; 351.

London Decr. 6. 1833

Dearest love,

My letter to day will not be so long as some which I have lately written. I am overwhelmed with business – clearing off my work here, and preparing for my new functions. Plans of ships and letters from Captains pour in without intermission. I really am mobbed by gentlemen begging to have the honor of taking me to India at my own time. The fact is that a member of council is a great catch, not merely on account of the high price which he directly pays for accommodation, but because other people are attracted by him. Every father of a young writer or a young cadet likes to have his son on board the same vessel with the great man, to dine at the same table and to have a chance of attracting his notice. Every thing in India is given by the Governor in Council; and, though I have no direct voice in the disposal of patronage, my indirect influence may be great.

I walked into the city to day and saw Larpent.[1] He has undertaken to manage for us. The doubt seems to be between two ships – the Asia and the Neptune. They will both sail the wind and weather permitting in the middle of February. The precise day they offer to fix as far as it can be fixed at this distance of time with a view to our convenience. I named the 10th, which, Larpent tells me, means in practice the 20th at the earliest.

---

[1] (Sir) George Larpent (1786–1855: *DNB*), of the East India house of Cockerell and Larpent.

The Asia is the finer ship,[1] and has a captain of the highest character.[2] It is a noble vessel of a thousand or eleven hundred tons. But the two best cabins are not quite equal, I should judge from the plan, to the two best cabins in the Neptune which is a ship of 700 tons or thereabouts. Nor is it yet quite certain that we can have the two best cabins of the Asia. One we could have, and another a little inferior. We could undoubtedly have the two best in the Neptune. Larpent thinks however that, in order to secure us as passengers, the Captain and proprietors of the Asia will contrive to give us the two best cabins.

The price demanded exceeds even my calculation which you thought so extravagant. What think you of 300 Guineas for each of us? Happily we can very well afford it, if necessary. But I hope that we may be able to beat them down to 250 or something of that kind. Your maid will sleep, unless you object to it, in your cabin. It will be most comfortable for you and most respectable for her. If you dislike this arrangement let me know, and I will see what other can be made. My servant, whoever he may be, will take his chance with the inferior passengers.

Larpent means to see these ships himself and also any other which he may hear of. He is to make his report to me on my return from Bowood. I shall then go over some of them, probably in company with George Babington, and make my final choice. But I must of course rely principally on other people's judgment. My present leaning is to go in the Asia if we can get the two best cabins. This is strongly the advice of Stewart Mackenzie and the opinion, as far as he yet gives it, of Larpent. I shall spare nothing, my darling, to make a pretty little boudoir for you. You cannot think, dearest, how my friends here praise you. You are quite Sir James Graham's heroine.

I have much more to say, as you may well imagine. But I have no time to say it. We are waiting anxiously for news from the Dingle. Kindest, tenderest, love to our dear Margaret and to Edward.

Ever yours, my darling

T B M

There is another doubt about the Asia. She stops at Madras. If it be only to put passengers on shore so much the better. She will stay in that case only three or four days, and we should both like to see so great a city which we might otherwise return without seeing, particularly as we shall

---

[1] 'For Madras, Bengal, and China, the ASIA, 1020 tons, late a Company's regular ship... equipped in every respect the same as when in the Hon. Company's service' (*The Times*, 10 December 1833).

[2] His name was G. K. Bathie (d. 1834), 'son of the late Rev. Dr. Bathie of Hammersmith' (*Gentleman's Magazine*, 1835, 1, 671). As to his character, Hannah reported that 'he never allows any work but what is absolutely necessary to be done' on Sundays (to Mrs John Cropper, 1 April [1834]: MS, Huntington).

have the strongest recommendations to the highest functionaries there. But if she has a cargo for Madras she may stay there for weeks which would be very unpleasant. We should have all the plagues of India and yet my salary would not begin to run till I reached Bengal. Larpent is to inquire into this matter among other things.

MS: Trinity College.

London Decr. 10. 1833

Dear love,

To day I dine with the Berry's. To morrow at six Labouchere calls for me in his light Britchska, and off we go to Bowood. I escape Lushington's dinner by this manœuvre, and I shall probably have a very pleasant journey and a visit more agreable than most visits, that is to say not much less agreable than staying in my own chambers would be. – We are back on Saturday: but not, I fear, in time to dine with Lord and Lady Grey who have just sent me an invitation for that day.

I have had a very kind letter from Fazakerley.[1] He grumbles bitterly against the ministers for not making some provision for me here. The fact is that they cannot. The late retrenchments have left no mode of obtaining a subsistence by politics, except in the Indian service.

Wits jump – I did recommend Sir John Hobhouse[2] to the electors of Leeds, – that is to the few with whom I have had any correspondence on the subject. But Marshall and his father have conceived, I hardly know why, a strong prejudice against Sir John. They are so important both from their wealth and from their character that no movement can well be made by our party without their full concurrence. This is secret history. It would be very undesirable that it should come round to Sir John Hobhouse's ears. There are other difficulties. Sir John is pretty sure of being returned for North Wiltshire if there should be a vacancy there: and a vacancy is expected. Paul Methuen,[3] one of the present members, is dunning the ministers for a peerage. Now, if Hobhouse were to stand for Leeds, he would be compelled to declare such strong opinions on the

---

[1] John Nicholas Fazakerley (1786–1852), M.P., 1812–20; 1826–41: 'a sensible man and moderate Whig' (Greville, *Memoirs*, IV, 23).

[2] Hobhouse, who had been defeated at Westminster in May, writes in his diary for 2 December that he met TBM, who told Hobhouse that he was going out to India. 'This, he said, would make a vacancy at Leeds, and he hoped I would think of it' (Broughton, *Recollections of a Long Life*, IV, 326).

[3] Paul Methuen (1779–1849), Whig M.P., 1812–19; 1833–7; created Baron Methuen, 1838.

subject of the Corn Laws as would cut him off from all hope of ever representing an agricultural constituent body. And, as he thinks himself more certain of Wiltshire than of Leeds, he will hardly run such a risk. This one of the cabinet ministers told me. Smoke Presto – as I often quote – writing politics to little M D. But you began this time. I could send you politics without beginning or end if I thought that you would care for them.

Grant went to Brighton yesterday. The King had a council for the purpose of proroguing parliament, which is merely a ceremony, and for the purpose of making the order which is to regulate our intercourse with China, – a very serious and substantial matter indeed. The warrant for my appointment has come back from Brighton. His Majesty's splay foot scrawl of William R. figures at the top and Grant's more elegant countersignature at the bottom. Nothing more is necessary. I am now full Councillor.

I admire the skill with which you have conducted your negociation with your servant-maid; and I only regret that so much skill should be thrown away. Fifty pounds is a sum far below the wages of such people in India. She will not stay with you a week unless you raise her wages when you arrive. As to the sending her back, – the East India Company will not let her go at all unless I enter into a bond to send her back: and though, after the 22nd of April next, she will not be liable to be sent back against her will, yet if she requires it, I shall be forced to pay her passage home.

I shall confirm any bargain you may make with her. Of course, as Mrs. Meeke says – (of whose works I am making a collection for India,) the outfit of your servant is quite independent of the money I sent you yesterday.

Pray do not stint yourself in your purchases. I intend to provide changes of linen sufficient for a voyage of five months. I shall order twelve dozen shirts, and other things in the same proportion.

I was in great hopes on Saturday that we should have had James Stephen's company. To day I learn that he has, with great regret, decided on staying. He meant to have taken out his son. He is informed that he cannot safely do so: and he cannot bear the separation. I very much regret this on my own account, on yours, and on that of the public.

As to John it is clear that he ought not to marry till he is quite beforehand with the world.[1] I do not well understand the nature of the transaction on which he has consulted Edward. But what probability is there

---

[1] John Macaulay had been engaged since at least as early as 1831 to Emma Jane Large, whom he married in December 1834. Margaret Macaulay writes on 9 November [1831] that she and TBM 'acted a scene between John and Miss L., which ended in a rupture between the lovers' (*Recollections*, p. 215).

that a person who is borrowing money when single will be able to repay it when burdened with a wife and family. How much does he want? And for what? And what is the nature of the security which he offers? I understand nothing of the matter from your account.

Tom Babington wants to go out to India as my secretary. He has been hinting to George, to Mary, and to Fanny, how advantageous the arrangement would be. "To have a relation near him" – he said to Fanny – "in whom he could confide. What an advantage that would be to a public man!" – I think that his assurance and folly in thinking such a thing possible are pretty nearly on a par. He must see that I entertain a very bad opinion of him: he must know that he deserves it: I should as soon think of taking Frederic Finlay,[1] – nay much sooner, for if Frederic Finlay misbehaved himself I could punish him without scruple: and, for the sake of Tom's relations, I should be forced to treat him with indulgence.

Kindest love to dear Margaret and Edward.

Ever yours, my darling,
T B M

TO HANNAH MACAULAY, 12 DECEMBER 1833

MS: Trinity College. *Address:* Miss Macaulay / E Cropper's Esq / Dingle Bank / Liverpool. *Frank:* Calne December twelve 1833 / T B Macaulay.

Bowood Decr. 12. 1833

Dearest love,

I escaped Lushington's dinner, and came down yesterday with Labouchere as fast as post horses could draw a very light carriage. Here I am surrounded by fine wood, fine water, fine paintings and fine statues. My host and hostess are as kind as possible: the weather is fine: the library good: my room most luxurious: and to day Tom Moore comes to enliven us. On Saturday I return to London. Till Monday I shall not write again unless I have something particular to say. I have considerable arrears of correspondence to clear off; and I must send a farewell epistle to the electors of Leeds. I mean to employ my leisure time to morrow for these purposes.

I am surprised at the negligence of your Liverpool post-office about my letters. I hope that there will be no mistake about that which I sent on Monday. If there is, the deaf shall hear me, as Sancho Panza says.[2]

After a good deal of consideration and after taking the advice of experienced people I spoke to my clerk. I thought it fair to do so, in order

---

[1] Not identified.   [2] *Don Quixote*, Part 2, ch. 3.

that, if he does not chuse to go, he may have time to look out for another situation. He behaved very properly – expressed great respect and gratitude, – but took time, which indeed I insisted on his taking, to consult his friends and to think over the matter. I shall offer him sixty sicca rupees a month (about 70£ a year,) and his passage back if he chuses to go. I have little expectation of his staying with us on those terms long after our arrival in Bengal.

I am waiting anxiously for news from the Dingle. Kindest love to Margaret and Edward.

Ever yours, dearest,

T B M

TO HANNAH MACAULAY, 13 DECEMBER 1833

MS: Morgan Library. *Address:* Miss Macaulay / E Cropper's Esq / Dingle Bank / Liverpool. *Frank:* Calne December thirteen / 1833 / T B Macaulay.

Bowood Decr. 13 / 1833

Dearest Nancy,

A single line to say with what delight I have read your short announcement. How I shall love my little nephew.[1]

Loves on loves and congratulations on congratulations to dearest Margaret and Edward.

Ever yours, darling,

T B Macaulay

TO HANNAH MACAULAY, 16 DECEMBER 1833

MS: Trinity College.

London Decr. 16. 1833

Dearest Nancy,

I came back from Bowood on Saturday night after a very pleasant visit. I have no news for you about our arrangements. It is indeed your own fault. I received by this morning's post letters from you for Fanny and Charles. I wish that you could have found time to write a single line to me in the envelope of either of them, just to say how Margaret was going on. I have been forced to come to Bernard Street before going to the Board, instead of calling on Larpent in Austin Friars' as I had intended. I shall be busy all the rest of the day at my office, and must defer my inquiries in the city till to morrow.

[1] Margaret's son, Charles, born on 10 December.

I need not say how happy I am to find that dear Margaret is going on so well. I doubt whether you have judged wisely in sending so early for Jane Babington. It would have been better to wait a week longer.

Baines is to be put up at Leeds as my successor.[1] I do not think that they have chosen well. He is a highly respectable man, – liberal, moderate, honest, intelligent; – and these qualities have made him very powerful and very useful in his own town. But he has not quite so much polish or literature as the persons among whom he will now be thrown. He is, in fact, John Mills[2] with superior natural powers. His newspaper, which is now decidedly the best and the most widely circulated provincial paper in England, will, I fear, lose its influence, when it is considered, not as containing the sentiments of a disinterested spectator of public affairs, but as the plea of an interested party for his own proceedings. If he persists, however, I shall give him all the support in my power.

To morrow I hope to have some information for you. Bowood stories will keep till we meet.

Kindest love to dear Margaret and Edward. Kiss the baby for me. How are children that are not christened named? Is there any ceremony on the occasion? Had you not better try half a dozen names in succession, each for half a year, and than make your choice on full deliberation.[3]

TO HANNAH MACAULAY, 17 DECEMBER 1833

MS: Trinity College. *Address:* Miss Macaulay / E Cropper's Esq / Dingle Bank / Liverpool. *Frank:* London December seventeen / 1833 / T B Macaulay.

London Decr. 17. 1833

Dearest Nancy,

I have seen Larpent. He has done wonders. George is quite delighted at the skill with which the business has been managed. We may sail by the Asia, a ship of 1020 tons, as soon after the 10th of February as wind and weather will permit, for 500 pounds. The 500 £ include the passage-money of our servants as well as our own. We are to have the two poop-cabins. The ship will only stop forty eight hours at Madras. The Captain is said to be one of the best officers of the Company's old service, and quite a gentleman. A naval officer, a brother of one of Larpent's partners, has gone over the ship, and makes a very favourable report of her.

[1] Baines was elected to succeed TBM and sat in the House of Commons until 1841.
[2] TBM's uncle; John Mills (1775?–1849) had been printer and then owner and editor of the Bristol *Gazette* since 1807.
[3] The MS, which appears to be complete, ends thus.

Larpent's conduct has been very honourable. His house had a ship going – but, though Alderman Thompson, who is one of the owners, pressed him to recommend that ship, he would not, because it was not so convenient a vessel as the Asia.

I am just going to see the Asia at the East India Docks. George is going with me. After looking over the ship, I shall make my final election.

But the carriage is at the door. Sarah Anne who is sitting by me desires her love to you and Margaret. Pray write daily. Though no news is said to be good news we all wish to have a single line by each post to say that every thing is right. Kindest love to Margaret and Edward. To morrow I will give you an account of our expedition eastward.

Ever yours, my love,
T B M

to Hannah Macaulay, 18 December 1833

MS: Trinity College. *Partly published:* Trevelyan, I, 351–2.

London Decr. 18. 1833

Dearest love,

I went with George to the Asia yesterday. We saw her to every disadvantage, – all litter and confusion. But she is a very fine ship; and our two cabins will be very good. Some inconveniences we must of course put up with: but every experienced person says that such inconveniences are inevitable. The worst of them is that every thing that we say in our cabins will be heard by our next neighbours. But so it is in all ships.

The Captain I like much. He is an agreable, intelligent, polished man of forty, – very good looking considering what storms and changes of climate he has gone through. He advised me strongly to put very little furniture into our cabins. A good sofa bed in each – an easy chair, a comfortable table, and a wash-hand-stand, was all that he advised – a carpet of course. I told him to have your cabin made as neat as possible, without regard to expense. He has promised to have it furnished according to his own notions, that is simply, – but prettily; and when you see it, if any addition occurs to you, it shall be made. He assures me that he can make it all that a lady's cabin can be for a small sum.

I find that I shall have more money in hand after paying for our passage than I had reckoned upon. Brownrigg most earnestly advises me to lay out some of it in providing china and glass. I mean to take his counsel. We must have a very large and very fine dinner set and tea set. We must also have less splendid articles for daily use. I intend to defer my purchases till you come to London, as China is peculiarly a lady's article.

I dare say that you will have no objection to go a shopping to Mr. Mortlock's.[1] Who knows, munificent as he is, but that he may insist on supplying us *gratis?*

If I have money enough I may perhaps buy plate in England. I am delighted to learn that it will not be so expensive as I thought. To a person accustomed to Lansdowne house and Holland house the quantity of forks and spoons necessary for a dinner of thirty people would seem to be enormous. But I find that two dinner-forks to a guest is the Calcutta allowance. As every guest brings at least one servant to stand behind his chair, the forks are cleaned in an instant. It is the same with spoons. As for other articles Brownrigg advises me to use plated goods instead of silver, and assures me that I may do so without incurring the charge of shabbiness.

To day I breakfasted with Sharp whose kindness is as warm as possible. Indeed all my friends seem to be in the most amiable mood. I have twice as many invitations as I can accept: and I have been begged to name my own party. Empty as London is I never was so much beset with invitations. Sharp asked me about you. I told him how much I regretted my never having had any opportunity of shewing you the best part of London Society. He said that he would take care that you should see what was best worth seeing before your departure. He promises to give us a few breakfast parties and dinner parties where you will meet as many as he can muster of the best set in town – Rogers, Luttrell, Rice, Tom Moore, Sydney Smith, Grant, and other great wits and politicians. I am quite delighted at this – both because you will, I am sure, be amused and pleased at a time when you ought to have your mind occupied, and because even to have mixed a little in a circle so brilliant will be of advantage to you in India. You have neglected, and very rightly and sensibly, frivolous accomplishments. You have not been at places of fashionable diversion: and it is therefore, I think, the more desirable that you should appear among the dancing, piano-forte playing, opera-going, damsels at Calcutta as one who has seen society better than any that they ever approached. I hope, my love, that you will not disapprove of what I have done. I accepted Sharp's offer for you eagerly, and even with tears, and he was as much affected as I.

I am delighted at your news about Margaret and the baby. And now, my love, I want some advice from you as to my movements. When

---

[1] A Regent Street china and glass dealer (*Post Office London Directory*, 1833). Teignmouth, *Reminiscences*, I, 61, calls Mortlock the 'benevolent but half-crazy porcelain manufacturer'; he was apparently associated with the Evangelicals of Clapham. Maria Edgeworth repeats a story that Mortlock, having bought Wilberforce's house for £10,000, then offered to give the title back to Wilberforce (*Maria Edgeworth: Letters from England 1813–1844*, p. 328).

ought I to go to the Dingle. My stay will be very short. I hate chewing and ruminating on the bitterness of separation – beating out the pain of a moment till it covers weeks. What must be done will be best done quickly. Shall I escort you back from the Dingle – call with you at the Temple – and so bring you home? After Christmas I shall be quite at liberty: and this plan, if you do not object to it, would, I think, be the best. But, if you have any reason against it, – or even if you fancy that you should like to part from Margaret and Jane without my being near, – you shall chuse for yourself. My first wish is, as it ought to be, to consult your tastes in every thing.

Do not let your woman be extravagant in outfit. I shall keep a tight hand in that respect over my clerk.

Kindest love to dear Margaret and Edward. Is Jane with you yet. If she is give her my love.

Ever yours, darling,
T B M.

TO PETER AUBER,[1] 18 DECEMBER 1833

Text: Copy, India Office Library.

India Board / Decr. 18th 1833

Sir,

I have the honor to acknowledge the receipt of the letter which you have addressed to me by command of the Court of Directors of the East India Company.

Let me request that you will have the kindness to inform the Court that I accept the high Office to which they have called me with feelings of the warmest and most respectful gratitude. That gratitude I will attempt to manifest, as they, I am sure, would wish it to be manifested by exerting every faculty which I possess for the benefit of that great empire which the wisdom of parliament has confided to their care.

I have / etc.
Signed T. B. Macaulay

Peter Auber Esqe. / etc. etc. etc.

---

[1] Auber (1760–1836) was Secretary to the Court of Directors of the East India Company, 1829–36.

TO HENRY LABOUCHERE, 18 DECEMBER 1833

MS: Osborn Collection, Yale University.

E[ast] I[ndia] Board / Dec 18. 1833

Dear Labouchere,

I will with the greatest pleasure accept your invitation for Monday. I have looked in Percy's reliques for your favourite ballad. It quite deserves your praise. I have learnt half of it by heart.

Pray remember to let me know what I owe you. These small debts are matter of conscience with me.

Ever yours truly
T B Macaulay

TO HANNAH MACAULAY, 21 DECEMBER 1833

MS: Trinity College. *Address:* Miss Macaulay / E Cropper's Esq / Dingle Bank / Liverpool. *Frank:* London December twenty one / 1833 / T B Macaulay. *Partly published:* Trevelyan, I, 350–1.

London Decr. 21. 1833

Dearest love,

I have nothing or next to nothing to tell you about our arrangements. I have been to a great warehouseman in the Strand whom Grant, George Babington and Larpent agreed in recommending, to order my outfit. He is to prepare a list of necessaries for me and my servant. I shall submit the list to one or two experienced Indians, in order that I may not be taken in and encumbered with more articles than I shall want.

Yesterday I dined at Boddington's. We had a very agreable party – Duncannon, Charles Grant, Sharp, Chantry the sculptor, Bobus Smith, and my old enemy James Mill. Mill and I were extremely friendly, and I found him a very pleasant companion, and a man of more general information than I had imagined.

Bobus was very amusing. He is a great authority on Indian matters. He was during several years Advocate General in Bengal, and made all his large fortune there. I asked him about the climate. Nothing, he said, could be pleasanter except in August and September. He never ate or drank so much in his life. Indeed his looks do credit to Bengal; for a healthier man of his age I never saw. We talked about expenses. "I cannot conceive," he said, "how any body at Calcutta can live on less than 3000 £ a year, or can contrive to spend more than 4000 £ a year." We talked of the insects and snakes: and he said a thing which reminded me of his brother Sydney. "Always, Sir, manage to have at your table some fleshy, blooming, young writer or cadet, just come out, that the musquitoes may stick to him and leave the rest of the company alone."

That fool Tom Babington provokes me out of all patience. He wants a place; and, by active exertion, perhaps some place of small importance, a vice-consulate in Italy for example, might be obtained for him. But he prefers something in China – something in India – the first-commissionership at Sierra Leone. About this last he talked to me this morning till he nearly drove me mad. He must know that I dislike him and despise him. And yet he applies to me, not only to get him a place, – which for the sake of his family I would do if I could, – but to put him over the head of my own brother who, in the regular course of things, would succeed. He sits murmuring and whispering and whining and snuffling with a sort of peevish meekness which makes me ready to give him a kicking. George writhes at the sound of his voice. Sarah Anne thinks him a greater pest than William Wilberforce. Surely – as Lawrie Todd says – the hand of restraining grace was on me; or I had done a murder on the spot.[1]

I am delighted with your account of Margaret. Kindest love to her and Edward. What are your arrangements? How long do you mean to stay at the Temple? I must write an article for Napier before I leave London: and I have not yet done a single line of it.

Ever yours, dearest,

T B M

TO MACVEY NAPIER, 21 DECEMBER 1833

MS: British Museum. *Address:* Macvey Napier Esq / Castle Street / Edinburgh. *Frank:* London December twenty one / 1833 / T B Macaulay.

London Dec 21. 1833

Dear Napier,

I heartily wish that it were in my power to serve your son.[2] But our board has very little to give. Wynne ate up the seed-corn,[3] and Grant has been forced to keep fast in consequence. Wynne gave in one year six writerships and fifty two cadetships. Grant has scarcely had a single appointment at his disposal: and I have reason to believe that all and more than all that he can do is demanded by his constituents who know and are not likely soon to forget the taste of Indian patronage.[4] This

---

[1] Galt, *Lawrie Todd*, Part 5, ch. 2, end.
[2] Also named Macvey Napier (d. 1893); according to Alexander Bain, young Napier was 'an official in the Examiner's Office, in the India House, while [James] Mill was yet alive' – i.e., before 1836 (*James Mill*, p. viii).
[3] As President of the Board of Control, 1822–8.   [4] Grant represented Inverness-shire.

consideration prevented me from applying to him for my own youngest brother who would gladly have gone into the Indian army; and I have pleaded it in answer to many requests from near relations of my own. But I am very unwilling to fail you on such an occasion: and I will therefore overcome a scruple which has hitherto prevented me from employing my influence over Grant for the benefit of my friends. I will speak to him as soon as I find a favourable opportunity. But I tell you plainly that I entertain scarcely any hope of success. I firmly believe that five times the number of cadetships now at his disposal would not enable him to fulfil his existing engagements.

The best way would be, I think, that the Lord Advocate should write to me on the subject. I would then show his letter to Grant and add my own solicitations. You would thus have two godfathers to your request: and, to say the truth, without some such pretext, I should hardly like to begin the subject. Grant has made such exertions to serve me during the last two months that I am very unwilling to ask him to do more. I should therefore much more readily and with a much better grace come forward under cover of the Lord Advocate.

I sent you yesterday a letter from Cookesley. I have not the least guess at its contents: nor do I at all wish you to comply with any request which it may contain.

I have been very busy of late – too busy, to think about Lord Chatham. But to morrow I shall fall to work. When I shall have done I cannot guess: but I fear not before the 12th or 15th of next month.

I shall have occasion to write to you repeatedly before my departure. I need not tell you how strongly sensible I am of the kindness which you have expressed in your letters. I wish we could meet. But I fear there is little chance.

I dined yesterday in company with my old enemy Mill, and found him very friendly and very agreable. / Ever, dear Napier,

Yours most truly,

T B Macaulay

TO HANNAH MACAULAY, 23 DECEMBER 1833

MS: Trinity College.

London Decr. 23. 1833

Dearest love,

My letter must be short. I am engaged in making a round of calls on the twenty-four directors of the East India Company. The day is wet enough for a day in the rainy season in Bengal. I have tired one hackney coachman with paying visits to ten of my masters. There are fourteen to visit still, and while my clerk is looking for another coach, I am writing to you.

I will do as you desire about the Temple and the Dingle. As to your maid's outfit do whatever you think right.

I hardly think that any of my friends except Sharp is likely to make the offer which he made. There are very few people with whom I talk so unreservedly. To be sure it is possible that you may receive invitations from some of the people whom you may meet at his house. With respect to those invitations and with respect to the whole matter you will act exactly as you chuse. It would be not merely unkind but ungrateful in me to urge you to any exertion which would be painful to you. But as to what you say about your family, I cannot allow any weight to that consideration. Selina, Fanny, and George are all acquainted with what passed between Sharp and me. They are all delighted with his proposal, and think, justly in my opinion, that it was too solidly advantageous to be declined. I well know, my darling, what your feelings must be now that you are on the eve of the most painful of all these painful separations, – the separation from our dear Margaret. I went through that misery a year ago. To me the bitterness of that death is past. Whether I am in London or at Calcutta, she is equally lost to me. Instead of wishing to be near her, I rather shrink from it. She is dead to me: and what I see is only her ghost. But her marriage, which has set an impassable gulf between her and me, has united her to you more closely than ever. You have lived with her during the last year and a half more than with any other member of your family. You have been placed close to her under circumstances the most likely to endear you to each other. No wonder that your parting should be a great blow to both. I know how vain consolation is in such cases. Yet remember, my dear dear girl, that you are now committed to the care of the person in all the world who loves you best, of one who has no prospect, no scheme of life, of which your happiness is not the chief part. But I must stop. Only believe this, my love, that in all arrangements here or in India, your advantage and comfort will be my first objects.

Kindest love to dear Margaret and Edward.

Ever yours my darling
T B M

I did not know what you meant by your expressions respecting Sadler in one of your letters last week. I had happened not to see the Morning Chronicle of Tuesday. The story is now in all the London Papers. It is a glorious one. How much of it is true heaven knows. Sadler is such an absurd charlatan that it may all be true. Foster is such a measureless liar

that it may all be false.[1] Dear Margaret's charity will doubtless settle the
question by pronouncing that Sadler has behaved with great perfidy to
Foster and that Foster has grossly calumniated Sadler. She will not,
I believe, be far from the truth.

TO THOMAS FLOWER ELLIS, 23 DECEMBER [1833]

MS: Trinity College.

Gray's Inn Dec 23

Dear Ellis,

My father returns from his circuit to morrow and he and my sisters
have set their hearts on having me at their Christmas dinner. I will make
no apology for breaking my engagement with you under these circumstances.

Shall you be at liberty on Thursday? If the day should be fine I will
take a long walk with you and, as the cockneys say, stand treat-all on the
strength of my 10000 £ a year. I wish to go to some old suburban haunts
of my childhood, and I should be very glad of your company.

I saw Malden yesterday. He leaves London to morrow and will not
return till the 7th of Jany. We will have a grand rouse with him when he
comes back.

Pray have you seen Foster's incomparable letter? What do you think
of Sadler's mode of amusing his children?[2] Do you mean to adopt it?

Ever yours

T B Macaulay

TO HANNAH MACAULAY, 28 DECEMBER 1833

MS: Trinity College.

London December 28. 1833

Dearest love,

This is, I suppose, the last letter which I shall address to you at the
Dingle. In a few days we shall meet. I cannot tell you, my dearest girl,

---

[1] John Foster had edited the Radical–Tory Leeds *Patriot* until the paper failed early in 1833
and Foster went bankrupt. His letter in the *Morning Chronicle*, 17 December, was part of
a quarrel begun some months earlier; it reviewed his grievances against Sadler and others
for failing to perform their promises to him in return for the political support of the *Patriot*.
See Cecil Driver, *Tory Radical: The Life of Richard Oastler*, New York, 1946, pp. 251–5.
[2] In his letter to the *Morning Chronicle*, 17 December, Foster says that Sadler insulted him by
making faces at him, thinking that Foster was not looking. Mrs Sadler reassured Foster,
saying that 'her husband was so constantly doing so, when amusing the children, that it had
become a habit, and he did it unconsciously.'

how impatient I am to see you. It is enough to reconcile me to all the sacrifices which I am about to make that I shall have you so near to me. We have seen very little of each other during the last year. I am not sure that I would not rather, all other things being the same, live at Calcutta with you than live in London while you pass almost all your time at Liverpool.

I have heard again from John who seems very sore. I wish that I could take the same view of the matter which you and Margaret take of it. I would much rather that, in such a case, either he or I should be in the wrong than you. But I must own that I do not understand what the franking has to do with the question. It is scarcely possible to conceive a more anxious time than that which immediately precedes the birth of a young woman's first child. I am sure I felt it so: and I would have given my quarter's salary to have had my solicitude terminated three days earlier. To delay sending John the news for three days in order to save him seven pence was, I think, a strange way of shewing kindness, – particularly as you said in one of your letters that you had to write to fifty people. I do not know which of the fifty had a better claim to early intelligence than John. Fanny was very much to blame if she neglected to write. But she and Selina both maintained, when last I saw them, that you had never said a word to them about John. I have done my best to appease him: and I hope you will find him tractable.

I am laying in books – good, solid, entertaining books, such as I have not, and such as will bear frequent reading. Are there any which you should particularly like. If there are mention them without scruple; and I will try to procure them. There are circulating libraries at Calcutta as well as here. I shall therefore give orders that only the very best novels shall be sent to us.

Kindest love to dear Margaret and Edward. When you leave the Dingle I must begin to write to her.

Ever yours, darling,

T B M

TO MACVEY NAPIER, 28 DECEMBER 1833

MS: British Museum. *Address:* Macvey Napier Esq / Castle Street / Edinburgh. *Frank:* London December twenty eight / 1833 / T B Macaulay.

London Decr. 28. 1833

Dear Napier,

I have spoken to Grant to day. But I find that, as I expected, he has promised more cadetships than are in his gift. He was extremely kind, and recommended an application to Loch, the chairman. Lord Brougham's word would have immense weight with Loch.[1] And you have certainly great claims on Lord Brougham. It seems to me that this would be your best chance.

I do not know whether by means of any of your Scotch Whigs you could get at Cutlar Fergusson.[2] His patronage however is only half of that of Loch.

Grant seems confident that, if Loch's cadetships are not given, Brougham could procure one for you.

I shall be truly glad to learn that you have succeeded. / Ever, dear Napier,

Yours most truly

T B Macaulay

PS I have scarcely begun on Chatham: and I am so fully occupied all day that I can only work on him before breakfast.

Remember me most kindly to the Lord Advocate. I will write to him as soon as I can find time.

TO [THE REVEREND THOMAS SCALES],[3] 30 DECEMBER 1833

MS: Trinity College.

London Dec 30. 1833

Dear Sir,

I will not fail to present your memorial,[4] and to back it – the greater part of it at least – with my own urgent representations.

I am sure that there is no unkind feeling in the Government towards the dissenting body. I dined a day or two ago at Lord Holland's. We talked about Church-Rates and the existing mode of Registration. You will not be surprised to hear that Lord Holland warmly declared it as his opinion that, with respect to these matters, the Dissenters were entitled to all that they asked. The Solicitor General[5] and the Secretary at War[6] who were present were of the same opinion. This is, of course, not intelligence to be made public.

[1] Loch and Brougham were friends from their Edinburgh days.
[2] Fergusson was a director of the East India Company, 1830–5.
[3] Endorsed: 'Addressed to / Rev. T. Scales, Leeds.' Scales (1781?–1860) was the minister of Queen Street Independent Chapel.
[4] The text of the memorial, addressed to Lord Grey, protesting against various disabilities imposed upon Dissenters, is in the Leeds *Mercury*, 28 December.
[5] John Campbell.   [6] Edward Ellice.

Many thanks, my dear Sir, for your kind wishes and prayers. In all situations I shall always gratefully remember your kindness and feel a warm desire to merit your good opinion. / Yours, my dear Sir,

Most sincerely

T B Macaulay

TO HANNAH MACAULAY, 31 DECEMBER 1833

MS: Trinity College. *Address:* Miss Macaulay / E Cropper's Esq / Dingle Bank / Liverpool.
Frank: London December thirty one / 1833 / T B Macaulay.

London Dec. 31. 1833

Dearest love,

I have time only to write a single line. But I cannot help thinking in the midst of other avocations of all that you must have felt to day, – of the cruel separation to which, for my sake, you are submitting, and of the debt which your kindness lays on me. Indeed – indeed, my own darling, I have wept bitterly for the pain which you must be suffering. But time heals every thing, and you know that no tenderness, nothing fond and soothing on my part, will be wanting to aid the operation of time.

Fanny has found your letter desiring her to write to John. This relieves you from much of the blame, but not from all. She has been unpardonably careless. John says that he never felt so much ashamed in his life as when he had to tell Miss Large that his sister had been confined a fortnight. I do not wonder at his feelings. You will think that I see this affair too strongly. But I can hardly tell you how much vexation it has given me.

You will read this early on New Year's morning. A happy New Year to you, dearest; and many new years, each happier than its predecessor. They shall be happy if my love [can][1] make them so.

[Lov][1]e to all at the Temple. [I][1] expect you next week.

Ever yours, my darling,

T B M

[1] Paper torn away with seal.

LETTERS OF UNCERTAIN DATE
1823–1833

TO WILLIAM EMPSON, [1823–31][1]

MS: University of Texas.

Grt. Ormond St Saty.
My dear Empson,
    I will be with you at 1/2 past 4 on Wednesday.

Ever yours
T B Macaulay

TO UNIDENTIFIED RECIPIENT, [1826?–30?][2]

MS: Free Library of Philadelphia.

My dear Sir,
    I could not refrain from calling here, though I meant only to bid you
farewell and return immediately. The indisposition consequent on two
sleepless nights is so powerful that I feel myself unable to enjoy even
your society. I feel great concern at thinking that I may be the cause
of your leaving the company with which you were engaged. But I
hope that you will excuse an involuntary desertion. Either here or in
London it will at all times be most agreable to me to see you, or to
hear that you find yourself comfortable in the country of your adop-
tion, or that you are in hopes of being restored to the country of
your birth.

Ever yours truly
T B Macaulay

---

[1] The only evidence for dating this is the Great Ormond Street address, where the Macaulay
family lived from October 1823 to May 1831. TBM did not live there after 1829 but he
called daily and may well have written from there.

[2] I conjecture, without evidence, that this was written while TBM was on circuit. The MS
is accompanied by a cover addressed by TBM to J. M. Wilson, Advertiser Office, Berwick,
and bearing TBM's frank, London, 7 May 1832. But the remark about 'being restored to
the country of your birth' makes no sense in reference to Wilson (*DNB*), and the letter,
unlike the franked cover, seems not to have been written from London. One might
guess that Panizzi, exiled from Italy, acquainted with TBM in Liverpool, and in London
from 1828, is the recipient, but the evidence is too indistinct to allow even a confident
guess.

TO [RICHARD SHARP, 1830–1?][1]

MS: Mr F. R. Cowell.

My dear Sir,
    Any of the three mornings which you mention will suit me perfectly. –
I am extremely obliged to you for giving me an opportunity of meeting
Mr. Rogers. / Believe me ever

Yours very truly
T B Macaulay

Gray's Inn / Thursday

TO THOMAS CURSON HANSARD,[2] [1831–3][3]

MS: Mr Walter Leuba. *Address:* Mr. Hansard / Paternoster Row.

Gray's Inn Saturday
Sir,
    I enclose the proofs. Be so good as to send me a hundred copies of the
speech. / I am, Sir,

Your most obedient humble Servant
T B Macaulay

---

[1] The letter is endorsed, in a later hand, 'To R. Sharp.' It can be dated only as at some time
after TBM's introduction to Sharp around February 1830, and before 28 May 1831, when
TBM is already on familiar terms with Rogers.

[2] Hansard (1776–1833: *DNB*) was printer to the House of Commons.

[3] According to TBM's own list, he corrected five speeches for Hansard during the time
of his residence at Gray's Inn, between March 1831 and July 1833: see *to* Carey and Hart,
29 November 1844. There is no way to be sure which speech is referred to in this letter,
but it is not later than July 1833.

TO THOMAS FLOWER ELLIS, [1831–3]

MS: State Library of Victoria.

Dear Ellis,

I make you a present of the inclosed letter, as I know no person who will enjoy it more. The only comments with which I accompany it are these – 1st that I never exchanged twenty words with the writer, 2ndly that I know the fact that, s[ince][1] the present ministers came in Lord Grey has not had the gift, even of one single clerkship of 100£ a year in the Treasury, the best paid of all the departments. The writer of this glorious piece of impudence is a Northern Circuit man.

Ever yours
T B Macaulay

[1] Paper torn away with seal.

INDEX

A full index will be published at the end of the work. For the convenience of the reader in the interim this list is given of TBM's contemporaries, with a reference to the place where they are first noted. Persons who clearly need no identification – e.g., Byron, Napoleon, George IV – are not included. Neither are those whom I have been unable to identify.

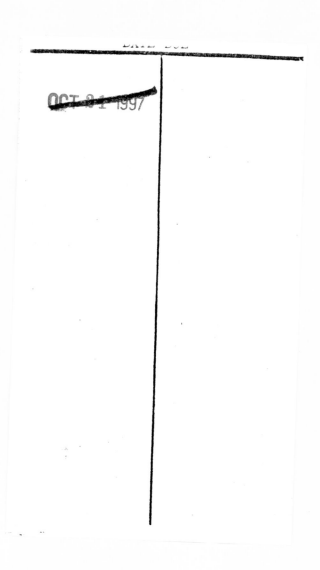